Maverick Genius

ALSO BY PHILLIP F. SCHEWE | *The Grid*

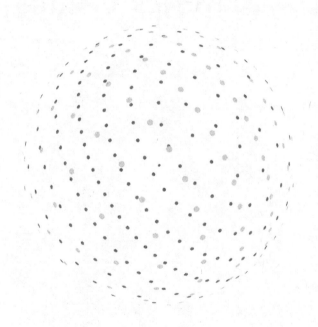

PHILLIP F. SCHEWE

Maverick Genius

The Pioneering Odyssey
of Freeman Dyson

THOMAS DUNNE BOOKS
ST. MARTIN'S PRESS
NEW YORK

THOMAS DUNNE BOOKS.
An imprint of St. Martin's Press.

MAVERICK GENIUS. Copyright © 2013 by Phillip F. Schewe. All rights
reserved. Printed in the United States of America. For information, address
St. Martin's Press, 175 Fifth Avenue, New York, N.Y. 10010.

www.thomasdunnebooks.com
www.stmartins.com

ISBN 978-0-312-64235-8 (hardcover)
ISBN 978-1-250-02101-4 (e-book)

First Edition: February 2013

10 9 8 7 6 5 4 3 2 1

I dedicate this book to my wife, Andrea Schewe, who is lovely in many senses.

Contents

A Many-Colored Glass. *Recent Dyson essays in* New York Review. *The Dalai Lama of physics. Heart condition. Thoughts on death. Dysoniad: 700 years of ancestors.*

Maverick Genius

Introduction

There he is, looking like a war criminal, staring out from the cover of *The New York Times Magazine*. The faint opening of his mouth gives you the impression he is about to speak in his defense. The picture caption relishes the irony: Freeman Dyson is a political liberal, a respected scientist, and yet on the supreme issue of global warming, he's a doubter, even a heretic. He crusades against nuclear weapons but hopes China will burn more coal.

The *Times* article, appearing in March 2009, launched a thousand threads of blog comment. Many people were surprised or dismayed by Dyson's views. Others admired him for his pluck in becoming a lightning rod for controversial views. *Atlantic* magazine named him to a small list of "brave thinkers." In the same magazine a year later a feature article castigated him for promoting dangerous ideas about climate and biotechnology. In *Foreign Affairs* he was declared as one of the world's leading "global thinkers." And yet on the *Charlie Rose* television show, Mr. Rose asked Dyson in mock exasperation, "Why are you driving people crazy?"

Freeman Dyson's notoriety notwithstanding, he is regarded as one of the most important scientists in the world and a notable thinker, speaker, and author. In a 2005 Wikipedia poll of the world's leading living intellectuals, Dyson ranked 25th, just ahead of Steven Pinker and above such other figures as the biologist Edward O. Wilson, the historian Niall Ferguson, the art critic Robert Hughes, and the genome pioneer Craig Venter. Who is Dyson and why does he rank so high?

The physicist Freeman Dyson was born in Britain in 1923 and

immigrated to the United States in 1947. He is still alive and has spent most of his career as a professor at the Institute for Advanced Study in Princeton, New Jersey. Dyson is esteemed for work in a variety of areas—including quantum physics, national defense and arms control, space exploration, the search for extraterrestrial intelligence, nuclear weapons and reactors, biology, astronomy, pure mathematics, and history. He won the million-dollar Templeton Prize for efforts to reconcile science and religion. He is the author of many books. He has six children and sixteen grandchildren.

Dyson comes highly recommended. Nobel physicist Frank Wilczek: "Dyson is the most impressive pure intellect I've ever met. He thinks at the speed of light." Science fiction writer Arthur C. Clarke: "He is one of the few geniuses I have ever met." Nobel physicist Steven Weinberg: "Dyson is as smart as they come." Philosopher Avishai Margalit: "Dyson creates a moral climate for open discussion. He doesn't bullshit. He is never indifferent to the truth. Evidence counts." Physicist and *New Yorker* writer Jeremy Bernstein: "I have always felt Freeman Dyson knows more about everything than I know about anything."

Dyson is a cultural figure. He, or rather his futurist prediction of an energy-absorbing "Dyson sphere," was the centerpiece of an episode of *Star Trek* and several science fiction novels. He is said to be the model for the character Gordon Freeman in the computer game *Half-Life*, as well as being an inspiration for numerous other computer games.

More will be said in the Notes and Acknowledgments sections about who said what during the making of this book. It is pertinent to say here at the outset that although I have had several cordial brief exchanges with Freeman Dyson by phone and by email, he is guarded with his time and declined to be interviewed extensively. He feels that it's too early to tell whether he did anything important.

He did, however, cheerfully acquiesce to this book going forward. I interviewed most members of his family and dozens of his colleagues. But the man himself stayed outside the project, and did not grant access to his correspondence. Fortunately, Dyson is a prolific writer, and many aspects of his life are open to public view.

This book is the first biography of Freeman Dyson. It certainly supplies many facts about his personal, intellectual, and scientific life. But whenever possible the narration will be driven by stories. The book should appeal to many kinds of readers—those interested in science,

science fiction, Cold War history, genetic engineering, space exploration and the search for life outside of Earth, the uses of new technology and its impact on society, and the intersection (and clash) of science and religion.

This is a biography and not science history. Quantum physics is a fascinating subject; it represents an important part of Dyson's career, and merits attention in several early chapters. But this book is not a history of quantum physics. Instead it concentrates on telling the story of Freeman Dyson's life. The same caveat is true for other important topics, such as space exploration, nuclear weapons, biology, and religion. Each of these subjects will be explored, but only insofar as it helps tell the story of Dyson's life. Telling stories has been a central part of Dyson's own writing career, and will be the method used in this book as well.

This book does not have a grand thesis other than to advance the notion that some of the great wide-ranging essayists of the past such as Ralph Waldo Emerson and George Bernard Shaw, if they were alive now, might have been scientists rather like Freeman Dyson—interested in poetry, nuclear weapons, and social justice. Dyson is exactly their sort of modern-day Renaissance man. Both Emerson and Dyson are bold in telling others how things ought to be. Both seek to reconcile the knowledge brought by science with the knowledge rendered by art, history, philosophy, and religion. Dyson does not shun technology, as Henry David Thoreau supposedly did, but he possesses the same abiding scruples and poetic outlook that made Thoreau so interesting a writer about machines and cultural change.

Dyson is a contrarian in the style of Shaw. He holds many politically liberal views and yet also believes, for example, that human space travel should not be scaled down but up (providing we find the right means of transport). Like Shaw, Dyson has had numerous powerful friends, some of whom are also his opponents. These friends include many of the science and technology titans and other notable figures of the past half century, such as Richard Feynman, J. Robert Oppenheimer, George Kennan, and Edward Teller.

Despite being so pragmatic, Dyson is a cosmic optimist. During the Cold War, he argued that we could survive any international crisis as long as we kept our heads, were patient, and took into the account the views of our adversaries. He sees the Internet and biotechnology as the sources of a coming revolution in world standards of living—allowing people in Cairo or New Delhi to be as well off as people in London or Princeton.

The book proceeds generally in chronological order. Chapter 1 is about Dyson's childhood in Winchester, England, and his service with Bomber Command during World War II. Chapter 2 covers the immediate postwar years and his switch from mathematics into physics. Chapters 3, 4, and 5, taking place at Cornell, Princeton, and in Europe, respectively, cover the most illustrious years of his physics research, when he triumphantly helped to reform quantum science. Chapters 6, 7, and 8 carry the story through the 1950s, including a look at Dyson's family (and family problems), his coming to the Institute for Advanced Study, and his work at General Atomic on reactors and rocketships.

Chapter 9 concerns Dyson's role in the effort to find signs of extra-terrestrial intelligence, while Chapter 10 recounts some of the most dramatic moments of the Cold War and Dyson's role in achieving a partial test ban treaty with the Russians. Chapter 11 examines Dyson's part in the Jason program, the organization of elite scientists that advises the government, and his contributions to a report about the use of tactical nuclear weapons in the Vietnam War. Chapters 12 and 13 show Dyson at his busiest—doing research in statistical mechanics, solid state physics, astronomy, and making his decisive swerve from science into writing.

The next few chapters chronicle Dyson's course through the 1980s: his crusade to abolish nuclear weapons, his provocative theory about the origin of life, and his many lectures and essays about science, art, and religion, culminating in his receiving the Templeton Prize. Chapter 17 explores Dyson's role as heretic and sage on such issues as climate, extrasensory perception, biotechnology, and his efforts to promote a visionary, long-term migration from Earth out into the cosmos.

Chapter 18 and the book conclude with a look at Dyson's most recent few years. Officially retired from the Institute, he still goes to work every day, carries out a full schedule of speeches, and is a frequent contributor to *The New York Review of Books*. The reviews he writes, on an astonishing range of topics, sometimes become news events all by themselves. He continues to speak out on genetics, space exploration, nuclear weapons, and, somewhat unwillingly, about the topic that won't go away—climate change, the study of which he helped to pioneer in the 1970s.

"Pioneering." Is the adjective in the subtitle of this book justified?

Well, in physics alone he can be credited with making fundamental contributions to solid-state physics, atomic physics, and statistical mechanics. In the realm of astrophysics he helped to found the search for extraterrestrial intelligence, helped to design the process—adaptive optics—now used on many telescopes to gain sharper imaging, and was the principal early architect of the cosmology of the far-future universe. Engineering: he helped launch the civilian nuclear reactor industry by designing a bestselling reactor used to this day in providing medical isotopes. His plan for a nuclear rocketship was never implemented but is often invoked in discussions of advanced propulsion. Continuing in a nuclear vein: Dyson helped to craft and promote a nuclear test ban, and he might have been influential in the decision to keep tactical nuclear weapons out of Vietnam. Freeman Dyson is exemplary. Even if you disagreed with some of his views, you'd have to admit that the breadth of his interests and experience demonstrates how an individual can influence society in so many ways.

Probably the area where Dyson has had the greatest lasting cultural impact is in pondering the implications of space exploration. His grandest prophecy—thrilling and scary at the same time—is that the inevitable colonization of outer space, accompanied by biotechnology advances, will result in a great increase in liberty. But it could also bring with it increased strife, including the splintering of the human race into rival species. Evidence of this tension might be playing out already in the form of an unfortunate collision between environmentalists and humanists over the formulation of biotechnology and energy policy. Freeman Dyson—not content to be a kindly retired British-American gent—continues to offer important insights on these issues.

1. Killing Time

Dyson Bombs Berlin

(1923–1945)

Increasingly his thoughts turned to death. Freeman Dyson was sure he would die young. The violence had been breaking out in stages—Spain, Czechoslovakia, and China. Now in 1939 Hitler's invasion of Poland made it official. Britain was at war.

Every day on the way to class he passed the monument to the young men of his school who had died in the Great War of 1914–1918. Presently it was his turn, and this time it would be worse. Technology had improved, had become more deadly. The aerial bombardment, experts said, would play a larger role.[1] His Uncle Oliver, a doctor in charge of the ambulance brigade for London, expected 100,000 fatalities.[2]

As they approached manhood in the late 1930s, Dyson and his friends needed to rally around a principle. It was fashionable to proclaim Communist sympathies. But Dyson never liked being with the majority. He became a pacifist and despised the warmonger Winston Churchill the way many American teenagers would later despise Lyndon Johnson and Richard Nixon.[3] Dyson refused to participate in the standby-officers training program. Training for what? Useless killing. Mahatma Gandhi was his hero. Only peaceful methods could save the world. But time was running out.

LOWER SAXONY

Till then Dyson was having a pretty good life. He had grown up in Winchester, an hour's train ride southwest of London. Filled with Roman walls, medieval churches, and blocks of Tudor dwellings, the town was a museum. History dwelt down most streets. When the Danes

7

pressed in upon the Saxons in the ninth century, the capital of England transferred temporarily to Winchester. The Gothic cathedral there, the longest in Britain, contains the bones of several kings and of Jane Austen.

The Dyson household was upper-middle-class. His father, George Dyson, was a composer and conductor. His mother, Mildred Dyson, was a lawyer and ran a birth-control clinic. He ran music schools; she helped run a birth control clinic. They had two children, Alice and Freeman. Four servants smoothed difficulties: a cook, housekeeper, gardener, and nursemaid. A cottage on the southern coast near the Isle of Wight provided relief in warm weather. They made trips to Wales and France. The extended family was perfectly suited for a BBC or PBS docudrama: Aunt Dulcibella was one of the first women to pilot an aeroplane. Aunt Margaret was a nurse. Aunt Ruth won an Olympic silver medal in figure skating.[4]

Freeman's mother was forty-three at the time of his birth in 1923 and he came to view her more as a grandmother; his sister, Alice, seemed to be the mother. Mildred looked formidable but actually was kind. His father, though friendly, was a bit distant. For George Dyson, little Freeman was something to boast about: reading by the age of four and already doing mathematical puzzles. When the father was at a podium conducting an orchestra, the son could follow along in a musical score.

With piercing eyes and aquiline nose, Freeman looked like a little wizard, and so he was, always doing or saying something clever. At the age of seven he was observed reading one of his father's books, Arthur Eddington's *Space, Time and Gravitation*. The son, who himself would later have professional things to say on these subjects, was drawn to a diagram depicting space along the horizontal axis and time along the vertical. Two additional crossed diagonal lines depicted the trajectory of light shooting forward and backward. These lines served to divide the universe into four quadrants: the "absolute future," the "absolute past," and two other parts called merely "elsewhere." One day, as he was absorbing Eddington, the boy's nanny asked the youngster the whereabouts of his sister. "Somewhere in the absolute elsewhere," was his reply. Overhearing this, George sent a description of the encounter to *Punch*, the humor magazine, which later illustrated the affair in the form of a cartoon.[5] The lad was already famous. When shown the cartoon, he didn't think it was funny.

At the age of eight Freeman was sent a few miles south to board at a school called Twyford. It was a common practice for children of his class to be farmed out like this, but he bitterly resented it. These were the worst years of his life, he later said.[6] The headmaster was brutal, and the older boys loved to torture the younger ones. To make matters worse, because of academic overachievement Freeman had been advanced into classes with boys who were much older and bigger. His classmates were severe. The punishment for being smart was sandpaper scraped across skin. His refuge was the school library, where he encountered the adventure stories of Jules Verne and the novels of H. G. Wells.[7] Besides serving as a retreat from the unpleasantness outside, these tales helped Freeman visualize the regions of outer space hinted at in Eddington's diagrams. He began reading the encyclopedia, so his mental inventory extended to the mundane parts of the cosmos also.

Then came Winchester College, one of England's oldest boarding schools, what in the United States are called prep schools. Winchester School is sometimes deemed to be the best academic school in Britain (at least by those at Winchester itself). And since in the year of his entrance Freeman's test scores had been at the top of the list, you might argue that he was something like the best schoolboy in Britain. Twyford School, proud of its star student, declared a holiday.[8] The distinction and burden of being the smartest guy in the room began here.

He spent the years from 1936 to 1941 at Winchester College. Since his father was head of the music staff, Freeman had really grown up there. He knew the hallways and grassy fields beyond. The central quadrangle and many of the buildings date to the fourteenth century when the institution was founded, and so it looks a lot like Harry Potter's fictional Hogwarts School. Freeman had earned a "Scholar" designation, which allowed him to eat in a special dining hall where cutlery was laid out—Hogwarts style—on plain wooden tables dating from the 1600s.

Freeman was helped along by an older boy, Frank Thompson. Frank relished poetry as much as he did. Frank loved medieval history, so Freeman did too. Frank studied Russian, so Freeman studied Russian.[9] He also studied Latin, which was mandatory, and Greek. He dabbled in biology and considered a possible medical career. Because there was no course in physics, Freeman taught himself this subject using a textbook by Georg Joos. As a protest against compulsory Latin and soccer, he helped organize a science club.[10]

Where did Freeman obtain his lifelong love of literature? In his chemistry class. Like the Robin Williams character in the movie *Dead*

Poets Society, Freeman's teacher, Eric James, oddly preferred to recite and passionately discuss poetry with the boys rather than stick to the accepted chemical curriculum.[11] Thus, to Freeman's everlasting delight, Wells's and Verne's adventurism was supplemented with the works of William Blake and T. S. Eliot.

Winchester was particularly strong in mathematics under the direction of Clement Durell, and by the end of his stay Freeman was the regular prize winner. Best of the best. He spent his available prize money on math books, occupied his vacations solving math problems, and worshipped math heroes.

Over one Christmas break, at the age of fifteen, he contented himself each day from morning to night with forging through the difficult textbook on differential calculus by Henry Piaggio, solving all 700 problems supplied by the author. Another book catching his fancy happened to be in Russian, so he (by then taking private tutoring in that language) made his own translation. Instead of going outside and playing like other boys, he practiced Russian verbs in order to learn equations, and to make a little money doing translations.[12] He piled on additional mathematical tutoring from Daniel Pedoe, a teacher at Southampton University who weekly came up to Winchester.[13]

For those that have it, an addiction to mathematics can be as difficult to overcome as an addiction to tobacco or alcohol. The logic of mathematics is different from most habits of mind. Few things in life are as pure and self-consistent. To many teenagers life appears messy and hopeless even without the onset of world war around the corner. The chesslike rigor of mathematics kept chaos at bay, at least temporarily.

Freeman's parents were worried. Mathematics was fine but there are other things in life. The world is a big place. His mother stressed the importance of friendship. Nothing in life is more important, she said, than sympathy for other people. He should keep that in mind.[14] She much admired Goethe and commended Goethe's large outlook on life—he was artist, scientist, diplomat.[15] She told him Goethe's story of Faust, the man who always had his nose in a book. Faust not only became bored with life but was cut off from all human companionship.

She needn't have worried. Freeman was shy but not a loner. Most boys liked him. His best friend was James Lighthill, who later became prominent in mathematics and aeronautics. They shared a love of advanced mathematics and together worked through the pages of a famous textbook, *Cours d'Analyse*, by Camille Jordan. They were less enthusiastic about a rival comprehensive classic, the *Principia Mathematica*, by Alfred North Whitehead and Bertrand Russell, which they felt to be pedantic.[16] Freeman went so far as to write notes into the margin commenting upon or even "correcting" the text here and there. These juvenile scratchings were still there when, seventy years later, Dyson was handed the book off the shelf during a tour of Winchester College.[17]

A tradition at Winchester was the keeping of a logbook, "Chamber Annals," in which boys could write comments about other boys. In these pages are enshrined some of the earliest documentary evidence of Dyson's personality, and it is evident that much of what we see later in the man is present already in the boy. For example, Dyson (then aged fourteen) was said to be a musical genius. He despised authority. Even allowing for sarcasm, the comments about Dyson (aged fifteen) were respectful: "He has never been known to fail at anything." "His life is monotonously regulated." Dyson (aged sixteen) "works standing, sometimes for hours, deep in thought." "He will argue most opinionatedly, but without losing his temper." "He is a vigorous controversialist with a gift for opposing for the sake of opposing."[18]

Dyson played the violin in some school performances. He became prefect of libraries. He was scrawny of build but fast of foot. At one track meet in 1938 he won at several distances and took the steeplechase events. In 1941 he acted in Elmer Rice's play *Judgment Day*. In 1941 he also won an award for a scientific essay. His writing talent began to emerge here alongside his mathematical ability. In English literature he came in third in 1940 and second in 1941.[19]

The Second World War began in 1939, and Dyson's anxiety intensified. What good were mathematics and all the other acquirements if you were going to die? Young Dyson went on passing through the school's war memorial, with its 500 names of Winchester boys lost in the First World War.[20] The graduates of 1914, 1915, and 1916—eighty boys each year—had largely perished in the mud in France or Flanders or at Gallipoli.

Dyson was haunted by the case of the mathematician Evariste Galois (1811–1832). Galois founded group theory and proved that you cannot trisect an angle or square a circle with a compass and ruler alone. He did all this before he died in a duel at the age of twenty. The night before the duel, as if sensing his coming annihilation, Galois crammed a notebook with mathematical insights. The young Dyson, imagining his own early death in the war, saw himself as a new Galois. Would he, Dyson, make a name for himself? Would there be time?

Grappling with the conundrum of human relations—why nations went to war, why the strong tyrannized the weak, why the rich had so much more than the poor—the teenage Dyson suddenly saw the solution. As he approached a notice board to see whether he'd been chosen for a sporting team (he had not) it came to him as a jolt of recognition. He perceived a fundamental kinship among people. We were all related. Indeed we were all one person. When we hurt our neighbor we are hurting ourselves. To inflict violence on others is really to injure oneself. The young man thought about his scheme day after day. He gave it a name: Cosmic Unity. The fundamental truth of his proposition seemed to offer a basis for ethics and much else. It could, to say the least, address the problems blazing forth in Europe and Asia.

He tried to convert his friends to the cause, but his "moral earnestness" was off-putting, a reality many prophets must grapple with.[21] His mother, at least, was sympathetic to his vision, but mostly Dyson remained a party of one. "I always feel uneasy if I have to join a majority," he said later.[22]

But war came. Instead of Cosmic Unity there was widespread killing. Dyson's pacifism waned. He finally joined the officer's training program at Winchester College. He also clung to mathematics.

Night Climbing

In September 1941, a few months shy of eighteen and still not required for military duty, Dyson went up to the University of Cambridge, a powerhouse in mathematics. He quickly reestablished himself there as an academic all-star. It was almost too easy: "After two years in Durell's mathematics class [at Winchester] I found the life of a student at Cambridge University quite relaxing."[23]

At Trinity College Cambridge under wartime conditions his studies were to be compressed into two years. Classroom activity was held to a minimum, which is the way Dyson liked it. He tended to learn best on his own or in the company of one or two friends. With most of the faculty and graduate students off to fight in the war, only the oldest professors remained.

The most notable of these was G. H. Hardy, who is famous for two things. The first is his collaborative series of papers written with two of the other great mathematicians of the twentieth century, John Little-wood and Srinivasa Ramanujan. The second is his expressed dislike for any kind of applied mathematics. In his book *A Mathematician's Apology*, Hardy grumbled about the very fact that he was writing a book rather than practicing his craft. He regarded pure mathematics as something joyful. It was closer to being art than science. "The mathematician's patterns," he said, "like the painter's or the poet's must be beautiful; the ideas, like the colours or the words, must fit together in a harmonious way. Beauty is the first test; there is no permanent place in the world for ugly mathematics."[24]

Hardy, hoping to exemplify pure mathematics, boasted that none of his research had ever been useful. None of his work would contribute to the benefit of the world and certainly not to the cause of warfare. Some would consider this attitude admirable. Others might view it as an expensive or even arrogant form of self-indulgence in a time of war. German armies were filling Europe, and the Japanese navy was fanning out across the West Pacific.

Dyson, while not so dogmatic himself about the glories of mathematics, was in love with the subject and had, since he was a young boy, read Hardy's books with enjoyment. Now at Cambridge Dyson took mathematics classes appropriate for a graduate student and had a chance to sit near Hardy several times a week.

Cambridge was depressing. Dyson had few friends and was afraid of girls. He continued to worry about war. It was evident that his mathematical studies would soon end and he would be thrust into the fighting. He kept feeling that the Cambridge class of 1943 would follow the young men of the class of 1915 into an early grave. There would be no mathematics career, only a long residence in the Absolute Elsewhere. Perhaps he should do what so many other young men he knew were doing: enlist straightaway. This was the proposition that lay before him every day.

One of Dyson's few pleasures was "night climbing," making nocturnal scurries across the towers, roofs, and upright walls of Cambridge buildings. He had done some building climbs during his Winchester years, but here at Cambridge the tradition of ascending drainpipes and spires to the highest places in town was practically a club sport. It was like rock climbing but in the middle of a town. Why couldn't you think of an enclosed quadrangle of medieval buildings, including dining hall, chapel, lecture rooms, and living quarters, as a miniature mountain range? The rock had been quarried, cut into slate tiles, and lapped down the roof of an apse. Was this not a minor Matterhorn? A guidebook written by some former undergraduates offered advice on how to avoid injury and detection, along with assessments of the more challenging climbs. The spire at King's College, for example, was considered to be practically impossible.

Night climbing was illegal, which only increased its allure. Even if you made an inadvertent noise up above you wouldn't attract attention, since after dark it was difficult for pedestrians at street level to see you at rooftop. High up you were anonymous. There, among Gothic gargoyles and arches you could, at least for an hour, take refuge in the Middle Ages, far from the present agony. Dyson loved the evocative sound of chimes at midnight.

The long roll of Dyson's published papers begins with some mathematical efforts sent in 1943 to the university magazine, *Eureka,* and the *Journal of the London Mathematical Society.* Much of his work centered on number theory, which is to numbers what sociology is to people.

Dyson did not speak much to Professor Hardy but he did have thoughtful conversations with the mathematician Abram Besicovitch. Dyson and he took extended walks together. Speaking only in Russian, they would discuss poetry as well as mathematics. They played billiards.[25] Dyson learned from Besicovitch how to write technical papers, how to build a formal argument in such a way that the conclusion would follow clearly from the foregoing groundwork.[26] He also developed a love of Russian literature and a desire to know more about Russian culture.

Dyson attended some lectures by Paul Dirac, one of the founders of quantum mechanics. Dirac was famous for using few words. In class he didn't so much teach as recite, from his own textbook. Dyson found both book and man to be incomprehensible. Dirac did, however, carefully frame replies to Dyson's frequent questions. On one occasion the answer required so much reflection that Dirac was obliged to stop the lecture in order to consider the matter more seriously.[27]

Under ordinary circumstances Dyson would have gone on to obtain an advanced degree and take an academic post. But the war had not gone away. No amount of diplomacy, much less pacifist sentiment, had kept Adolf Hitler at bay. France was defeated and Britain was under dire threat. It was 1943 and Freeman Dyson, now nineteen years old, had to do his bit. He had to go off to war.

Enlistment as a uniformed serviceman was the only option for most men. But one of Hardy's friends was able to offer Dyson another route. C. P. Snow, the physicist and novelist, who would a dozen years later write a testy essay—published as a bestselling book, *The Two Cultures*—about the intellectual divide between the scientific and literary cultures in Britain, was searching for bright young men to do war work of a technical nature.

Dyson was just the sort of chap Snow wanted. So off Dyson went into the war, but not to the places like Malta or Singapore where people were actually dying. Snow's fellows were mostly sent off to do radar work at Maldon, code breaking at Bletchley, or bombing logistics at High Wycombe.[28] Instead of firing a gun Dyson would be practicing his well-cultivated training in logic. He would be performing exactly the kind of applied mathematics Hardy loathed. The work would be purposeful and poignant, involving as it did the saving and taking of lives.

Dyson's last days in Cambridge were pleasant. His best college friend, Oscar Hahn, was confined to a wheelchair owing to polio. Dyson was a guest at Hahn's home, where he was exposed to Jewish customs for the first time, including a Passover Seder.[29] The young men decided to leave Cambridge in style, by walking. Having worked up to the feat, hiking ten miles each day before breakfast, on the final day the two friends departed Cambridge at 3 a.m., Dyson pushing Hahn. Covering fifty miles they reached London at 11 p.m. Part of the fun for Dyson was to refrain from telling his parents quite what he'd done. They thought he'd taken the train.[30]

CROOKED MUSIC

As a prelude to seeing Freeman Dyson in action during the war, we will observe a different Dyson and a different Freeman fighting the previous war, the Great War of 1914–1918.

George Dyson and Freeman Atkey were good friends. Both taught at the Marlborough School, George in music and Freeman in classics. When the war came in 1914 both men went into the army. Freeman became a fine officer and seems to have thrived on army life. He regularly wrote his sister Mildred, known as Muff.[31] So near the presence of death, Freeman never felt so much alive.

Meanwhile, young George, the musician, found himself inadvertently in charge of training men in the making and using of grenades. Good thing he was the son of a blacksmith. To help the men learn the skill he wrote a list of guidelines. This tract was exactly the thing required. It was so successful that the army turned it into the official manual for grenades. The text was sent to America, where (in book form) it became a minor bestseller, earning its author a fair bounty.

In due course both George Dyson and Freeman Atkey found themselves in the front lines. Both had become captains. Both the musician and the classicist had become well versed in bombardment. Both wrote letters home. One letter from Freeman to his father was practically merry: "We are sleeping entirely in the open, last in a field, the night before in a wood, as it has been lovely weather it has been very jolly and we have done our marching at night when it is cool."[32] Two weeks later a telegram arrived announcing the death of Freeman Atkey. He'd been shot by a sniper.

George Dyson was luckier. One fine day the horse he was riding got blown out from under him by an exploding shell. He himself was not harmed, except to suffer thereafter from the mental condition that came to be called shell shock. Out of the war and back in Britain he met up with Muff and they consoled each other.

On November 17, 1917, George Dyson (1883–1964), son of John William Dyson (1859–1923) and Alice Greenwood (1854–1943), married Mildred Lucy Atkey (1880–1975), daughter of Frederick Walter Atkey (1844–1922) and Ellen Louise Haynes (1852–1908). Along came a daughter, Alice. Three years later, on December 15, 1923, their son, Freeman John Dyson, was born, the name Freeman coming from his deceased uncle and the name John coming from his father's father. His place of birth was the town of Crowthorne in the county of Berkshire, thirty miles southwest of London.

Almost twenty years later Freeman John Dyson found himself also in the bombardment business, and he too wrote home frequently. He was fighting in, but not exactly at, a war front. There had been several war fronts so far: the front against the Germans in Western Europe, which collapsed with the fall of France and the evacuation of British forces from Dunkirk in 1940. There was the Battle of Britain, named for the defensive air war over Britain, where RAF fighters grappled with German bombers and stalled a possible invasion. The Battle of the Atlantic consisted of the duel between Allied convoys bringing supplies to Britain and the aggressive German submarine force deployed across the ocean. Largest of all was the Eastern Front, featuring epic infantry and tank battles between colossal German and Russian armies.

Finally there was the Allied strategic bombing front against the Fascist enemy. The generals of this aerial combat viewed the campaign as more than an adjunct to the fighting on land and at sea. They hoped actually to end the war outright through bombing. They figured a land invasion of Europe from the west might not be needed. They wanted to ensure that another Battle of the Somme—the engagement in 1916 that had cost more than a million British, German, and French lives—would not have to be fought. In the new combined air war the Americans bombed during the day, the British after dark.

So night bombing rather than night climbing would now be Freeman Dyson's concern. He was employed as a civilian not directly by the air force but rather by the Ministry of Aircraft Production. He worked at the Bomber Command headquarters in the town of High Wycombe, halfway between London and Oxford. He had a desk job in the Operations Research Section, which examined facts surrounding bombing missions and supposedly rendered independent recommendations to General Sir Arthur Harris.

Dyson's office was located in a heavily wooded area where the layout of buildings presented no apparent target for German planes. This might have been what kept the bombs from falling his way; on the other hand, it was dark all the time. He lived in an underheated house in the town of Hughenden and went to work pedaling a bike five miles uphill. On the way up he was often passed by Sir Arthur's limousine.[33] At the end of the day Dyson coasted back downhill, often thinking about mathematics.

Should he instead enlist and go up in the planes? He'd think more about this and decide again that it was better if he stayed on the ground. That's what his mother had said, and he was inclined to agree. Surely his intelligence and training were making a greater contribution to the war than if he were aloft as a crewman. Even if he wasn't using rigorous higher-level mathematics, his remarkable problem-solving ability would serve the air force well. That's also how it was explained to him by his superiors, and it was easy to concur. Still, staying back left very little for him to say to the other nineteen- or twenty-year-old men, men he saw every day at the airbase, young men who *were* going up on the night flights over Berlin.[34] Many failed to return.

The main activity at Wycombe was the going and coming of bombers. Dyson could easily imagine them flying over their targets. The journey, 600 miles out to Germany and 600 miles back, was filled with peril, chiefly the German antiaircraft batteries firing from below and the Messerschmitts firing from above. Dyson's job did not require him actually to fly in the Lancaster bombers, but it did require him to visualize the experience. To be effective, he had to do some mental night climbing. He had to picture the odyssey into the hostile German airspace and back out. Only then could he effectively quantify risks, weigh alternative crew procedures or aircraft design, and recommend action. He was good at these things.

One of his early assignments was to evaluate MONICA, a radar system for collision avoidance among the bombers flying in formation. Unfortunately, MONICA's warning system, consisting of a squeal coming over the intercom when planes approached each other too closely, had a habit of going off at the wrong time. Crews often disabled the system. Dyson's elaborate mathematical treatment of MONICA— looking at the way it was used by a variety of aircraft for a variety of bombing missions—was an early version of meta-analysis, the process by which epidemiologists ponder the efficacy of drugs by running a variety of clinical trials.[35]

Indeed, this was applied mathematics of the highest order. Dyson's numerical figurings, instead of merely sitting on a page, now related to events unfolding in the sky at speeds of 300 miles per hour and involving hundreds of lives. For example, after tallying the statistical reports, he decided that the collision rate among bombers should be higher than it was. In raids over Germany the Royal Air Force was losing only about one bomber per thousand sorties because of wing-to-wing bang-ups. Dyson thought the number of collisions should be more like five.

Why would more collisions be better than fewer collisions? Where is the logic in that? Well, plane losses from midair collisions stood at one-tenth of a percent per mission, whereas losses from attacking German fighter planes stood at 4 percent. The solution? Convoy the bombers more closely, allowing the bombers' return fire to be more concentrated, thus making defense against the fighters more effective. This bit of provocative advice from a junior analyst, surprisingly, was accepted by Bomber Command. The result? Collisions went up, but losses from fighters went down even more. The crews who had to fly those planes didn't like the anxiety of the close-in flying, but they went along anyway.

Some findings could be sensible but impractical. That is, a particular modification in procedure might save lives and yet be bad for morale. Example: Dyson and his operations colleagues determined that the chances of a bomber surviving would improve by *reducing* the number of guns used to fend off German fighters. Improving aerodynamics and reducing weight resulted in higher speed and maneuverability, more than compensating for the loss of guns. Unlike the proposals addressing bomber bunching, however, this expedient of trading armament for speed was not tried, since middle-level officials felt that the commander-in-chief, or the crewmen themselves, could hardly be expected to accept a plan, even one that might save lives, that removed the chance, however ineffectual, of shooting back at the enemy.

Young as he was, Dyson knew more than most cabinet officials and even many operations officers about the general course of the air campaign.[36] One of the things he knew and others did not was that as the war continued the loss rate for British crewmen was increasing (until very late in the war). Contrary to what the fliers were told, length of experience was not a major factor in enhancing survivability. The reason for this was an innovation called *Schrage Musik*, or "Crooked Music." The Germans had mounted upward-firing guns on some of their fighter planes, allowing them to fly underneath the British bombers without themselves being seen. Crooked Music, Dyson believed, was the German weapon that kept British bomber losses high. He argued later that if the head of operations research, a man named Basil Dickens, had advocated the alternatives (such as removing some gun turrets from Lancasters) pushed by Dyson and his colleagues, thousands of crewmen's lives would have been saved.[37] But Dickens, and many like him, tended to tell commanding generals only what they wanted to hear.[38]

The survival rate for airmen was bad enough for a standard thirty-mission tour. But many pilots signed up for a second tour anyway. The resulting death rate for crewmen was about 40 percent, one of the highest for any major fighting force. Young servicemen think about numbers like this, even if the numbers aren't officially public. Without being told, they knew the odds.

Dyson better than anyone knew the odds. Should he put himself in harm's way by joining up? The question kept presenting itself. How could he go on looking these boys in the eye, boys his own age, who journeyed off after dark toward Berlin? Should he put on a uniform and ride with them? He did not. He would eventually own up to himself that he had been a coward.[39]

Actually, Dyson *had* been up in planes. He had been flown around, at various hours and various altitudes, to measure the brightness of the night sky. His plane was unheated and unpressurized, but he realized that he could breathe unassisted even at altitudes of 20,000 feet.[40] But these were not combat missions. No German bullets were directed at him. Dyson was no Frank Thompson. Dyson had not volunteered, as Thompson had, for work behind enemy lines. Thompson was eventually caught and executed. Dyson's close Cambridge friend, Peter Sankey, also perished in the war.

Were things better because of Dyson's work? Had he saved any lives? Many of his calculations and recommendations had been ignored. With grim precision Dyson reviewed his own slide down a moral slope. First he had been a pacifist. When war came to Britain he joined the military without necessarily condoning the bombing. Then, when it was explained to him that this was total war and that Hitler had been the first to attack London, Dyson acquiesced to the bombing of German cities. He had become part of the killing machine. In effect, Dyson's exercise in applied mathematics had helped to kill women and children. The bombs falling on Berlin were partly *his* bombs. The specter of G. H. Hardy—who feared that mathematics could be used to kill people—haunted Dyson.

LEST YE BE JUDGED

G. H. Hardy believed that the discoveries made by mathematicians actually constitute a reality separate from human minds, a sort of absolute reality. For example, when Pythagoras asserted, in the sixth century B.C.E., that the sum of the squares of the sides of a right-angled triangle equals the square of the third side, this was equivalent to finding a new chemical element or locating a new planet. No wonder Hardy loved mathematics so passionately. Whatever else society did to itself, it was comforting to know that the logic and integrity of mathematics was impervious to doubt or corruption.

Even if you accept this idea, it's not so easy to extend it to the rest of human experience. It can sometimes be difficult to tell right from wrong, especially during wartime. In established cultures it's wrong to take the life of another. During war, however, we encourage killing, at least certain kinds of killing. Moreover, in most circumstances we are careful with our bodies and discourage risky behavior. During war, however, this is turned upside down. Schoolboy things like steeple-chase and Latin orations and differential equations are put aside and replaced by guns and tents. Military maneuvers are plotted by high-ranking authorities but carried out by ordinary folks.

Consider the July 1943 raid over Hamburg, code-named Operation Gomorrah, in which, in addition to the direct destructive effect of the bombs themselves, a firestorm was unleashed, a burning tornado. The devastation has been referred to as Germany's Hiroshima. Here is Dyson's succinct description, written many years after the event: "On the night of July 24 we killed forty thousand people and lost only twelve bombers, by far the best we had ever done." Killing forty thousand, many by asphyxiation, was the "best" we had done. Naturally, he was ambivalent about this. By not actually flying in the planes, by not taking the bombs to Germany, by not sharing the risk, Dyson was afraid he'd not done enough. But in his appointed job at Operations Research, in the act of helping kill all those civilians, he felt perhaps he'd done too much.[41]

Years later, Dyson would repeatedly return, in essays, to examine his wartime exploits and the organization for which he worked. It formed a baseline encounter with technology and the motivation behind it, its costs, its efficiency, and its consequences. Why, Dyson wanted to know, did it take three tons of bombs for the British to kill one German, whereas it took the Germans only one ton to kill a Briton?[42] The goals of strategic bombing were largely not met, Dyson argued. The threat of ruination from the air was supposed to deter Germany from starting a war in the first place. But the Germans were not deterred. Once war began, the goals of strategic bombing became more acute: sap German morale, curtail German war production, and (grandest of all aspirations) win the war. Indeed Bomber Command's motto was "Victory Through Air Power."

But German war production was not curtailed substantially; manufacturing often resumed in bombed factories within days. German morale did not fail, at least not until late in the war. Strategic bombing did not by itself win the war; it did not spare the Allies from having to thrust a million soldiers into France. Dyson estimates that strategic bombing consumed one-fourth of Britain's war budget. The cost of the British offense was far higher (in money and in crew—47,000 killed) than the corresponding cost of the German defense. Germany may have run out of oil but it never ran out of weapons. Spend less on dropping bombs into German cities and spend more for the navy to pursue German submarines, he suggested, and the war might have been shortened considerably, with a great saving of lives.[43] Poor aiming or not, lots of people died because of British bombs. The number over five years of bombing Germans was 400,000, many women and children.

Dyson had learned mathematics from the best teachers at Winchester and Cambridge. Bomber Command was to be his school for morals. His job had been to make bombing more lethal and efficient. This was the applied mathematics that Hardy abhorred. After the war he read about the trials at Nuremberg, where officials who had helped to make the German war machine more efficient and lethal were being judged. Dyson wryly compares his situation with theirs:

> *The main difference was that they were sent to jail or hanged as war criminals, while I went free. I felt a certain sympathy for these men. Probably many of them loathed the SS as much as I loathed Bomber Command, but they, too, had not had the courage to speak out. Probably many of them, like me, lived through the whole six years of war without ever seeing a dead human being.*[44]

Killing 40,000 was the "best" they had ever done? And that was one raid. Dyson again: "In war, there are few real criminals, just a lot of ordinary people who do disgusting things because they're told to."[45]

Kurt Vonnegut wrote *Slaughterhouse-Five*, a novel about the Allied bombing of Dresden. That book, Dyson thought, was so artful and truthful that another book no longer needed to be written. Dyson did, however, create a kind of internal horror story. He began to have a nightmare—repeated at various times over many years—in which he was a bystander to a plane crash. In the dream he was prevented by a paralyzing fear from going to the aid of those inside the burning airplane.

The Allies defeated the Germans without Freeman Dyson flying in a Lancaster. He did not enlist. Mathematics had gotten him through school and now it had gotten him through war. He'd been an analyst instead of a tail gunner. Freed from its commitments against Berlin, Bomber Command steered its aim toward obliterating the remaining Axis power in Tokyo. The British were to be part of an intensified air war in Asia, in preparation for what looked like an invasion of the Japanese home islands. The Royal Air Force, and Dyson along with it, prepared to go to Okinawa. His assignment would continue on the other side of the world.

In the First World War the chemists' most notorious contribution had been poison gas. In the Second World War the end-all technology was supplied by physicists. Things ended in a hurry because of two bombs dropped a few days apart, bombs of stupendous explosive power.

Freeman Dyson did not go to Japan because his services weren't needed. His killing days were over.

2. Life Is a Blur

Dyson as Mathematician
(1945–1947)

He was alive. They wouldn't need to chisel Freeman Dyson's name into that memorial wall at Winchester honoring the war dead. The avoidance of early death was a fact that would powerfully shape his worldview.

After six years the war was over. From Winchester College 2,370 men had served and 269 had perished. Of the 98 admitted to the school with Dyson in 1936, 16 died in service to the king. The Second World War had been terrible but, for Britain at least, not as bad as the First World War.

How had the war risen in the first place? Here is a Dysonian summary based on a conversation with a man who had lived in Germany in the turbulent prewar years. This man implicated the efficiency of the German education system:

> *His argument was this. The very processes of mass education, practiced in the integrated industrial communities of our time, could and did produce the soil in which these monstrous weeds of hysteria and hate could suddenly appear and grow beyond control. We made our people literate without teaching them to think. We gave them technical skills without any controlling judgment. We stimulated their ardor and energy without any commensurate ethical or emotional discipline. We thus made them into the easy victims of any plausible political theory.*[1]

These are the words not of Freeman Dyson but those of his father, George Dyson, in a memoir written years after the war. The father, like the son, was to have a varied career. Besides building grenades, George Dyson was a conductor of orchestras, a teacher at numerous schools, and a composer, mostly of choral music. His thick Yorkshire accent did not prevent him from hosting a radio show about music. In 1937 he became director of the Royal College of Music, one of Britain's leading conservatories. Despite pressure to close up during the Blitz, he kept the college open. In that way he provided badly needed jobs for musicians and helped give London a musical life during its years of greatest trial. In 1941 he was knighted by King George VI, who had been a musical pupil of his many years before.[2] (This is the same king depicted in the movie *The King's Speech*.)

The war was over and life had to begin again. Sir George Dyson's recommendation for keeping such a war from happening again was to inculcate a "controlling judgment" among citizens. "Honest knowledge and creative arts: these should be the goals of education." Three types of people, he believed, helped to keep chaos at bay: saints, who appeal to civic virtue; prophets, including scientists and philosophers, who "fearlessly proclaim truth"; and artists, who can imaginatively offer "an intuition of order and proportion."[3] All three of these idealized human callings would play a part in the life of Sir George's son.

THE GIFT OF MATHEMATICS

The war was over. Reorganizing society and withdrawing armies was the task of politicians and generals. For millions of ordinary people, the survivors, the main thing was to get on with making a living. You were supposed to find a job, reunite with family members, and secure a home. For many this wasn't easy. Rationing continued, jobs were scarce, and for some people nightmares continued to plague their thoughts.

When we see him again Freeman Dyson is in London living with his parents near the Royal College of Music, around the corner from the Royal Albert Hall. His father had many musical duties and his mother was involved with various charitable causes. And what about Freeman? What was his career supposed to be?

Freedom from war meant that you could worry about things other than the close spacing of bombers in the sky. You could worry about the close spacing of electrons inside atoms. During his days at Bomber Command, Dyson had read a book that set his mind on fire. He was impressionable in that way: books, especially those filled with equations, could occupy him and motivate him. In 1938 it had been Piaggio's book on differential calculus. Now it was Walter Heitler's volume on quantum reality. It helped get Dyson through the last months of the war and was now nourishing him in the first months of peace. The material in this book was still largely mathematics, but with a difference. The numbers and symbols on the page stood not for themselves but were instead associated with parcels of energy and particles.

Quantum science was now Dyson's preoccupation even if not yet an occupation. He no longer worked for the air force but he did have another year of national service to perform. Fortunately for him he was assigned to an easy teaching job at Imperial College. His nominal supervisor had nothing for him to teach, so Dyson was free to do as he liked. He often went over to Birbeck College, a short Underground ride away across London. There he befriended a professor, Harold Davenport. Not only did Davenport invite Dyson into the circle of Birbeck mathematicians, but he even served as a sort of unofficial advisor to the young man.

Davenport sustained Dyson's appetite for mathematics by feeding him tough problems to solve. One of these assignments would be a test case. Siegel's conjecture was a tricky algebraic proposition that had resisted many attempts at rigorous proof. Dyson fatefully resolved that if he succeeded in proving the conjecture he would stick with pure mathematics. If he failed he would intensify his pursuit of quantum mathematics—in effect, he would become a physicist.

He labored for three months and was able to tighten the boundaries on the conjecture. But he did not achieve a full proof; that honor fell to another man a decade later.[4] Did this settle the matter? Not exactly. You don't just announce you are going to be a physicist. You have to do research. Where do you work?

Dyson decided to try for a fellowship at Cambridge University. And for this, mathematics would still be his passport to advancement. Davenport supervised Dyson in writing the paper that would serve as his audition piece at Cambridge. The work, in typical Dyson fashion, was an audacious bringing together of elements from several disciplines.

One conjecture had nudged him toward physics and another, Minkowski's conjecture, would now get him into Cambridge. In his cover letter to the university, Dyson wasn't exactly modest in staking his claim:

Hitherto, analysis, geometry, abstract algebra, and almost every branch of mathematics, have been brought into the service of the theory of numbers, but topology has retained its independence. It is therefore the achievement of my paper which I value most highly, to have successfully used in one branch of mathematics ideas belonging to another branch apparently so remote from it.[5]

Cambridge was impressed and Dyson won his fellowship.[6]

A TENSION IN SPACE

He'd been accepted into Cambridge for his mathematical brilliance, but he came to study quantum science. What was this body of thought—part abstruse mathematics, part hard-edged predictions—that he found so irresistible?

In the past, most big turnovers in scientific thinking, such as Copernicus's argument that the planets go around the sun and not the Earth or Charles Darwin's observations about the evolution and heritage of living things, were accompanied by wide skepticism and even hostility. Quantum mechanics, the name for the all-encompassing theory of the microworld, was no exception. It had successfully explained many facts—one mark of good science—but had also prompted troubling philosophical questions. Troubling and wonderful at the same time. Because this subject is going to occupy young Mr. Dyson's attention for years to come, we're going to peek into this strange Alice-in-Wonderland realm to have a look around.

The trouble and wonder began in the year 1900 when scientists were puzzled by the rainbow of light emitted by objects when they were heated. The German scientist Max Planck successfully explained the puzzle by introducing an idea so strange that even he didn't believe it. His hypothesis was that energy was not a continuous thing coming in any and all amounts, but instead was parceled out in bundles, which he called *quanta*. Fortunately, energy quanta were so small that one would ordinarily never notice that the universe was chunky. The world appeared reassuringly continuous at the human level.

But quantum energy wasn't the end of it. Weirder hints of quantum reality started to show themselves. Only twenty-five years after Planck's quantum hypothesis, the young German physicist Werner Heisenberg argued that the very notion of measurement was problematic. The more carefully you measured the position of an object, the less you could know about its velocity, and vice versa. This proposition became known at the Heisenberg uncertainty principle.

Uncertainty as a principle? Not only did energy come in blocks, but also knowledge? Actually, "uncertainty" in this case is not something to do with human psychology or with the fallibility of our instruments. Instead, uncertainty arises from the fact that the particle never had a single velocity or position to begin with.[7] It's as if scientific measurement were a form of photography and the new quantum science was saying that no matter how you fiddled with your camera's shutter speed or focus, all the photos you took will be just slightly blurred. Freeman Dyson was giving up the stately solidity of number theory in order to embrace enforced uncertainty.

Coming out of world war, there were plenty of things for people to be unsure about. And here was a new theory—indeed, its proponents were confident that it was *the* theory of reality—that seemed to say that a sure sense of material existence was problematic. Was it any wonder that many scientists, even some physicists, were doubtful about the theory's rightness?

Freeman Dyson didn't seem to have any doubts. He took to quantum theory with relish. If the quantum books said that a particle such as an electron was usefully described not as a hard object located at a definite place but rather as a kind of spread-out cloud, then that was fine with him. Instead of the firm knowledge of a particle that Isaac Newton's laws provided, the new quantum laws were expressed in terms of probability and uncertainty.

If you like having a sure sense of your reality, if you like your photographs to be sharp, then you're not going to like what came next. The implication of Heisenberg's proposals was that an electron does not actually exist *anywhere* particular until the moment you detect it with some apparatus. Only then does the electron cease being a nebulous, extended cloud of *maybe* and become a definite thing *here*. This bafflement as to the particle's existence is known as the principle of indeterminacy. A thing is nowhere in particular until we make a measurement. Then it's somewhere.

At the human level we're used to some forms of uncertainty. When it comes to choosing a career or a spouse, or remaining in good health, chance seems to play an uncomfortably large role. We expect this. It comes as a surprise, though, that such indeterminacy should also be at the heart of physics, the most exact of sciences.

The blurrings of existence suggested by quantum science—uncertainty and indeterminacy—sound retrograde since they apparently revoke much of the steadfast knowledge of the world seemingly guaranteed by Newton's mighty worldview of two centuries before. Dyson didn't find the blurrings disturbing. For him they were mathematically beautiful. If this was the true nature of the world, then so be it.

Dyson was glad to be out of London. At last in Cambridge he had a physics mentor, an instructor named Nicholas Kemmer. Kemmer had worked on the atomic bomb during the war and was the one who had proposed the names for those two new heavy elements, plutonium and neptunium, that figured so prominently in nuclear weaponry. Now, as if Kemmer were swearing him into some secret society as an apprentice, Dyson received the last of the great inspirational books that would propel him into physics. The author of this book was Gregor Wentzel and the topic was quantum field theory. Kemmer's copy of Wentzel, in German, was one of the few in Britain and was, in Dyson's words, a "treasure without price."[8]

Freeman Dyson has always liked drawing analogies, relating things to other things. That's what quantum field theory does. It is a vast mathematical accounting scheme for describing not one electron but all electrons. Indeed, it says that all electrons are just manifestations of one electron entity, a universal electron field. Recall that as a teenager, amid the fatalistic lead-up to world war, Dyson had dreamed up Cosmic Unity, the idea that all people were aspects of a single human existence.

Well, quantum field theory does for electrons and light what Dyson had hoped to do with people. The big difference, of course, is that humans can't be reduced to equations. The idea of fields is, by contrast, another of those many intellectual efforts to describe reality in terms of numbers, arrows, unseen forces, and evolving states of being. The concept dates back to the middle of the nineteenth century, when the English scientist Michael Faraday tried to explain how magnetic and electric forces projected themselves invisibly through otherwise empty space. Why, for example, should the south end of one magnet attract the north end of a second magnet without the magnets touching each other? Faraday argued that space wasn't empty. It was filled with an unseen but real, forcible agency, a *thing* that was present at every point in the surrounding area, exercising an influence over anything else that was in the vicinity. Even if there were no such object to feel the force, Faraday argued, the force field would still be on duty. It is a sort of tension in space.

The electric, magnetic, and gravitational fields, as understood in the nineteenth century, took on a continuously variable range of strengths and possessed a definite value at each location in space and time. These fields retained the decidedness that characterized nineteenth-century science. Consequently, they are referred to as classical fields. By contrast, quantum fields designate not so much the *presence* of a thing as the *likelihood of the presence* of a thing (an electron, say, or a bit of light) at that point in space.

Freeman Dyson found field theory satisfying. It provided a mathematical framework so consistent that it was practically a kind of philosophy—not just a body of scientific propositions. The main thrust of field theory was to reformulate the nature of existence just as radically as Plato did, two and a half millennia before, when he said that the things we see—a chair, an apple—are not "real." The real chair, Plato argued, was elsewhere, an abstraction, in heaven. All the mundane chairs we see in normal life are but inferior copies, earthly versions, of the ideal chair.

To illustrate his point Plato introduced a famous analogy. Suppose, he said, that you huddle in a dark cave where the only light comes from a fire behind you. By the light of this fire you see shadows of things behind you on the wall in front of you. What you see are the shadows of a chair, not a "real" chair. We are fooled by our experience, by our limited ability to "see," into believing we are encountering real things when in fact we are seeing mere shadows.

Quantum field theory says that there is a universal electron field—a sort of ideal electronness—from which we get, in the act of measurement, a *particular* electron at that place at that time. Before we measure that electron, only the wavelike field exists. In a sense the electron we observe is a kind of coagulation of the electron field at that point in space, and only comes into being by our making a measurement. The same is true for light. A parcel of light, a photon, is no more than the precipitation of the larger electromagnetic field in a particular place during an observation, such as the triggering of a light meter or a twinkling we experience in the retina of our eye.

Modern quantum field theory is more egalitarian than Plato's theory of existence. We don't say that the field is better or more ideal than the particle. Electrons or photons are just as real as the electron field or the electromagnetic field. A raindrop and the cloud of water vapor from which it precipitates are both made of water. They're equally "real."

WITTGENSTEIN IN A BAD MOOD

Dyson's two best friends at Cambridge during his fellowship year were physicists, Hermann Bondi and Thomas Gold. Bondi became famous later as an astronomer and opponent of the big bang theory of cosmology. He was also a longtime scientific advisor to the British government, just as Dyson would later be an advisor to the U.S. government. Gold would become another brilliant scientist who courted controversy. He too dissented from the big bang theory but was more famous for advancing the theory that petroleum is not made from biological material compressed over millions of years. Dyson admired scientists who swam upstream of prevalent thinking.

Cambridge was intellectually rich. We've already met the mathematician G. H. Hardy and the quantum physicist Paul Dirac. Among the many other eminent thinkers and scholars was literary scholar F. R. Leavis, who was just then finishing his book *The Great Tradition*, about the English novel. Another was William L. Bragg, in effect Dyson's boss at the Cavendish Laboratory. Bragg, at the age of twenty-five, had been the youngest person ever to win a Nobel Prize. He and his father had pioneered the use of X-rays to form images of materials. (A few years after Dyson's time at Cambridge X-ray crystallography would reveal the structure of DNA molecules.)

Dyson's interests were wide, but at this moment in his life there was a need to focus on a single topic—his chosen subject of field theory. He loved literature but there wouldn't have been time to see Leavis. Dyson, as an undergraduate, had studied with Hardy and Dirac. Hardy represented pure mathematics, which Dyson was laying aside. Dirac represented field theory, but Dyson had found Dirac hard to understand. The use of X-ray beams to understand biological molecules, an important occupation of Bragg and his lab, would be of intense interest to Dyson—but not for another forty years.

So a lot of Dyson's study, as it would be during much of his life, was solitary. Actually there was a scholar at hand, a man who might have been of interest to Dyson. This man was perhaps the most famous professor at Cambridge, and he lived just down the hall from Dyson in his residence hall at Trinity College.

Like Dyson, philosopher Ludwig Wittgenstein pondered propositions about reality. Both men wondered about how our perceptions of the world are blurred. Wittgenstein wrote about how many arguments in philosophy foundered upon imprecision in our use of language, while Dyson was learning about how quantum fields encapsulated our imperfect knowledge of electrons.

The two men were at different stages of their careers. Wittgenstein was fifty-two and compiling notes for what would be posthumously the second of his two most influential works, *Philosophical Investigations*. Dyson was twenty-three and a student. Although he was angling to be a physicist, he was still submitting papers to mathematical journals.

The two saw each other often on the stairs but had little to say to each other. Neither enjoyed dining at the college's high table, and both usually cooked food alone in their rooms. Dyson could detect the smell of Wittgenstein's fish.

One day Wittgenstein invited Dyson in for a chat. Dyson was offered the one seat in the room, a low-lying canvas deck chair that left him nearly horizontal and close to the floor, while the older man remained standing over him. Trying to break the awkward silence, Dyson asked Wittgenstein if he still believed the ideas in *Tractatus*. This was the earlier of Wittgenstein's major works, a booklet in which he had attempted to build a systematic accounting of logical propositions about the world.

Wittgenstein took offense at Dyson's question. He began sarcastically badgering Dyson, who eventually fled. Dyson's judgment issued many years later—and he seldom speaks so decidedly about people—is that Wittgenstein was a charlatan.[9]

SIXTY SECONDS

Dyson was restless. Where should he go next? London, one of the premier cities of the world, did not suit him. Besides, he wanted to get away from his parents. Cambridge, one of the great universities by any measure, didn't have the right people for him to talk to. He had friends but not enough physics friends. Cavendish Lab, famous for a century of first-rate physics, would soon be famous for other things—molecular biology and radio astronomy.

Dyson felt he was coming into physics at a propitious time. A student friend of his admitted that to avoid controversies growing up around the quantum explanation of reality he was switching from physics to mathematics. Dyson laughed, since he was switching in the opposite direction precisely in order to embrace the controversies. The greater the challenge, the greater the opportunity to do original work. Dyson wanted to be at the frontier.

To do that he needed to leave England. Initially he had hoped to get a job in the Soviet Union working for one of the great scientists there, such as Lev Landau or Pytor Kapitsa.[10] But travel restrictions made this impossible. So he resolved to go to the United States.

He approached Sir Geoffrey Taylor, a man he hardly knew, and asked for advice. Taylor was then a scientist at the Cavendish Laboratory. An expert in blast waves, he had worked at the bomb factory in Los Alamos during the war and therefore knew a lot of American physicists. Considering the kind of work Dyson had in mind, Taylor estimated that Cornell University was the place to be and Hans Bethe was the man to work for. Dyson's encounter with Taylor lasted about sixty seconds but it was to change everything.[11]

Dyson knew little of Cornell or Bethe but he took Taylor's advice anyway and applied for a position at the school and for a fellowship that would support him. Sir Geoffrey did more than render advice. He gave material support. His subsequent letter to Bethe must rank as one of the most succinct and effective, if inflated, graduate school recommendations of all time. After a line or two of formality, the actual encomium is delivered in the space of a single sentence. No more than this was necessary: "Although he is only 23," wrote Taylor, "he is in my view the best mathematician in England."[12]

To clinch the decision, Dyson hopped on a motorcycle and drove in the rain to visit a friend of Bethe's, Rudolf Peierls, a professor at the University of Birmingham.[13] Peierls concurred that Cornell was the place for Dyson to be. Expecting the match to come off, Peierls wrote to Bethe asking him if he would please take good care of Mr. Dyson.[14]

Before going off to America, the wealthiest place on earth, Dyson visited one of the most devastated places on earth, war-torn Germany. Taking part in a program that was supposed to help bring some kind of normalcy back to German citizens, Dyson spent the summer in the city of Münster. What impressed him most that summer were the lack of food (he was hungry all the time), the mountains of rubble left from the bombings (his bombings), and the habit of the residents to make music together.[15] They brought forth battered instruments and coalesced into an impromptu orchestra. Beethoven among the ruins. Dyson was heartened by this.

He was also intrigued by a number of young women in the town, especially Hilde Jacobs. But at the end of the summer she stayed where she was, while he went far away.[16]

3. Ecumenical Councils

Dyson as Seminarian
(1947–1948)

Like Odysseus, Dyson had been entangled in a great war and afterward arrived safely in Ithaca. After side trips by motorcycle from Cambridge to Birmingham and to Germany by train and ship, he proceeded via the *Queen Mary* to America, past the Statue of Liberty. He was shown around New York City by Hermann Bondi and then went by train from New York Bay up to Cayuga Lake. In September 1947 Dyson came to Cornell University in the middle of a heat wave. Oddly it was cold indoors owing to the extravagant laying on of air conditioning, still a novelty. The departmental secretary wore a sweater.[1]

The boots, the muddy boots, were the first thing Dyson noticed in Hans Bethe's office. Muddy boots symbolized something new. Famous professors in Britain did not, in Dyson's experience, hike about with their students and then have lunch with them, sometimes four or six at a time.[2] Dyson, long accustomed to learning alone, would now be part of a community. He was a seminarian at a physics monastery.

Which Dyson?

Most young seminarians are anonymous, but not Dyson. Some people at Cornell, the mathematicians anyway, had heard of a Dyson. Rumor had it that he was one of the best mathematicians in England. The one in front of them was another Dyson, a physics student just starting out. Was *this* Dyson related to *that* Dyson? The mathematician Dyson gave an impressive talk about number theory. The other Dyson, the one coming to study at Cornell, didn't know much physics, or so they said.

This and *that* Dyson were the same man. At first his fellow graduate students didn't know what to make of him. He liked taking his ease, reading the newspaper for hours with his feet up on the table, going for a walk, or just staring dreamily out the window.[3] Maybe that's the way mathematicians were. If so, why was he enrolling in physics?

He was on the frail side. And that aquiline face, with deep-set staring eyes, pointy ears. The bemused smile was a bit odd. Was he concentrating on an idea or was he smirking? He was from London, so maybe he wouldn't like it in Ithaca, which is only a small town perched on the southern fringe of one of New York state's glacier-carved Finger Lakes. "Ithaca is gorges," the tourist office says, but Freeman Dyson had come not for the natural beauty of the place but for the people.

He wanted to talk to people. The most stupendous enterprise in all of physics, maybe all of science, over the past quarter century, had been the creation of an atomic bomb at Los Alamos. And here at Cornell was assembled a considerable cohort of Manhattan Project veterans that had forged the gadget that spawned the nuclear age.

Hans Bethe, the most distinguished, had been head of the bomb design theoretical group. Born in Germany, he had made his name, and much later would win the Nobel Prize, for his explanation of sunshine. Having invented big parts of nuclear physics along the way, Bethe declared that the light we see from the sun and other stars is produced in a series of reactions that fuse hydrogen nuclei into larger nuclei amid the crushing conditions at the heart of our local star.

Philip Morrison had been the baby-sitter of the atomic age. He accompanied the plutonium bomb, the very first nuclear bomb, out to the Trinity test site in New Mexico in July 1945. A month after that he rode out to the West Pacific, shepherding the components destined for the Hiroshima bomb. Weeks later he was one of the first Allied scientists to view the effects of that bomb up close when he strode through what was left of the city. Morrison became a distinguished astrophysicist and popularizer of science. Possessed of a talent for evocative prose, he wrote elegant book reviews in *Scientific American* for decades on a wide spectrum of topics.

Robert R. Wilson, another of the Cornell professors, had been head of the experimental division at Los Alamos. He had grown up on a ranch in Wyoming, was familiar with horses and guns, and had an open disposition. When Dyson arrived, Wilson was then building an electron accelerator at Cornell. Twenty years later Wilson was appointed to construct an immense proton accelerator in Illinois. This was the time of the Vietnam War and Wilson was asked during congressional hearings by a senator what this expensive machine was likely to contribute to the national defense. Nothing, Wilson responded, except that it would help to make America a nation worth defending. The lab was approved. Later called the Fermi National Accelerator Laboratory after Enrico Fermi, it was built within budget, ahead of schedule, and mustered twice the beam energy that was called for in the original design. This machine was for many years the most powerful atom smasher in the world and would be the site for several major physics findings.

These three men were fun to be with and crackled with ideas. A fourth Cornell professor, however, outdid even Wilson and Morrison as a bon vivant. Richard Feynman is now recognized as a brilliant scientist, explainer, and teller of homespun anecdotes. He had been a comparative youngster at the Los Alamos bomb project, where he was in charge of computing. He'd been recruited for the work by Robert Wilson. Even then, in that galaxy of world-class scientists, Feynman was conspicuous for his bright wit, friendliness, and enormous promise. Dyson first talked with Feynman on a car trip to a science meeting in Rochester that fall of 1947.[4] Dyson didn't enroll in any course with Feynman. Instead he got something better—a monthlong conversation with Feynman, conducted mostly at chalkboards.

Dyson was lucky. Not only had he not died during the war, but he was entering into his studies just as the laws of quantum science were about to be rewritten. Indeed, he would be one of the rewriters. But he did not yet have a career. He was mostly self-taught in physics. His knowledge was all top-end: he had a sound grasp of quantum field theory and relativity but knew less about the fundamentals imparted to most beginning students, a deficiency soon to be remedied.

Now he wanted to satisfy others with his work. They were looking over his shoulder. He enjoyed their attention, and he was up to their expectations. Furthermore, his life was, still at this point, rather tidy: no wife, no debts, no debilitating habits. Seminarians must harden their discipline. "For the first time in my life," he said in a letter to his parents, "I can think about physics continually and without effort, and I want to confirm the habit before letting it drop."[5] You can almost hear his mother, remembering her teenage son's obsession with his calculus textbook, admonish Freeman to get out into the sunlight.

Dyson liked life in his adopted country. Growing up, he had listened to the radio broadcasts of Alistair Cooke (much later the genial host of the PBS program *Masterpiece Theatre*), who provided Britons with a regular report on life in America much as Edward R. Murrow's wartime broadcasts from London vividly portrayed British life for Americans. Dyson found America to be pretty much as Cooke described.[6]

Dyson had to register in the fall like any other incoming graduate student. He took a quantum course from Bethe, a course in experimental nuclear physics from Wilson, a course on solid state physics, and one on general laboratory techniques. He wasn't very good at the latter. Performing a routine reenactment of the Millikan oil drop experiment, the famous exercise that established the electrical charge of the electron, Dyson touched the wrong outlet, was zapped by electricity, and left on his back.[7] He wasn't seriously hurt, but this little mishap made him think hard about the reality of electrons.[8] His experimental career ended on that floor. He would stick to theoretical work.

THE COUNCILS OF SOLVAY

We oughtn't to call science a religion. Science accepts assertions on observational grounds not as points of faith. Nevertheless, an air of religiosity lingers among the heirs of Isaac Newton. For example, in their occasionally near-monastic habits and their reverence for laws, their love of classifications, their insistence on consistency, and their rigorous, almost ritual, observance of procedure, scientists at work can resemble a priesthood. For both scientists and clerics the hieratic urge shows itself in a high degree of assurance and a disdain for trivial pursuits. Both desire to encompass the cosmos. All layers of existence, sacred or secular, must be accounted for.

For both the early Christian church and twentieth-century physics, historically significant propositions concerning orthodoxy had to be clarified and a new consensus erected in solemn conclaves of bishops. In the year 325, for instance, several hundred prelates met in Nicaea, located in what is now Turkey, to settle the issue of consubstantiality: God the Father and Christ the Son, it was decided, were of one essence. In 359 another council, this one in Constantinople, pronounced the grand unified theory of the Trinity: Father, Son, and Holy Spirit were all equally aspects of a single underlying godliness.

Like the church in the fourth century, so physics in the twentieth century would sort through some of the most fundamental aspects of existence: space, time, causality, measurement, and the apparent dual nature of matter as particle and field.

Seminarians learn by watching their elders and by studying the great debates of the past. To see what Bethe and Feynman, and then Dyson, were laboring over, it will be useful to recapitulate the quantum age by looking over the deliberations at several important conferences. The first of these meetings—the equivalent of those conclaves in Nicaea or Constantinople—took place in Brussels. It was started by a businessman named Ernest Solvay.

Solvay 1911. This first big gathering of twentieth-century scientific celebrities profiled a series of startling but baffling advances accumulated over the previous fifteen years or so, starting with the observation of several emanations coming from atoms. Atoms were supposed to be *a-tomos,* "uncuttable." They weren't supposed to have moving parts. And yet look at what atoms were spewing forth: Konrad Roentgen found X-rays (1895), Henri Becquerel observed radioactivity (1896), and J. J. Thomson discovered the electron (1897). Ernest Rutherford (1911) found that much of the mass of atoms was actually located at a heavy core called the nucleus. So an atom wasn't so simple after all.

Solvay 1927. Coming right after an intensely revolutionary couple of years of brainwork, this later Solvay meeting showcased the sensational new quantum science. The idea that energy comes only in fixed amounts—the quanta—had at first seemed repellent to many physicists. But a new generation, embracing the quantum energy concept, would soon have success in explaining a variety of phenomena, such as the spectrum of light shining from atoms.

This success, as we have seen, came at a price, since we were asked to surrender several basic notions of reality. In their place came the troubling and wonderful ideas that a particle didn't fully exist until we detected it and that even then there were limits on how much we could know about the particle's location and its motion.

It wasn't much consolation to be told that all these quantum rules, even though valid everywhere, essentially manifested themselves only for happenings at the atomic scale. Were centuries of Western philosophy and scientific probity being thrown out by a coterie of upstarts? Well, yes, but maybe this was good. Like the earlier revolutions begun by Copernicus and Darwin, the quantum upheaval begun by Planck demonstrates that science lurches forward when imaginative people offer disturbing ideas to explain puzzling observations. The bomb throwers making the outrageous quantum assertions—Werner Heisenberg, Wolfgang Pauli, Paul Dirac—were in their twenties. Their audacious efforts were sarcastically referred to as *Knaben Physik,* physics by boys.

At the 1927 Solvay conference the champion of the forces of probability and indeterminacy was a somewhat older man, Niels Bohr of Copenhagen. The reactionary forces objecting to quantum weirdness were led by Albert Einstein, who, ironically, had introduced some of the original quantum ideas. Einstein argued that impressive as it might be in explaining the spectra of atoms, the Copenhagen school (named for Bohr's hometown) of thought, as the consensus quantum outlook came to be known, was surely incomplete. A fuller understanding of quantum phenomena, he insisted, would duly restore the objective and deterministic standards of observations enshrined in science going back to the days of Newton.

Accepting indeterminacy was too much, Einstein argued. Do you mean to say that a radioactive particle inside a nucleus can come flying out whenever it wants, without being kicked, or that an electron can somehow manage to fly through several openings in a screen at the same time? Is the universe really deciding things according to some underlying, unseen spreadsheet of probabilities? "God doesn't play at dice," was Einstein's quip. To which the unflappable Bohr replied, "Albert, stop telling God what to do."

As the 1930s and 1940s wore on the Copenhagen interpretation of quantum reality became catholic doctrine among physicists. Not because some pope said so but because of its own great success in explaining a variety of phenomena at the level of atoms and molecules. Even the much smaller and more powerful realm of the nucleus was apparently ruled by the catechism of quantum mechanics. The making and deployment of a nuclear bomb, felt on the ground in Hiroshima and Nagasaki and splashed across newspapers around the world, was a graphic and lethal demonstration of quantum knowledge at work.

Dyson was too young to have been a participant at the Solvay meetings or the Manhattan Project. But it was still an exciting time to move from pure mathematics into science. Mathematics was, according to G. H. Hardy, closer to art. Art and mathematics can stand alone. A poem and a geometrical theorem can both last forever. Science is different. It is necessarily provisional. It will always have to be replenished, like layers of skin, when new observations become available.

Mathematics and art can be beautiful, said Hardy. They are entertaining. Science, by contrast, is practical. It explains things.

The materials of art, said one of Dyson's favorite poets, T. S. Eliot, keep changing, but the quality of art doesn't improve.[9] How about science? Well, the material conditions of science keep changing (better detectors, faster computers). The "quality" of science, you might say, depends on its ability to explain more phenomena. At its best, art enchants. At its best, science enlightens. It might seem that quantum science, with its themes of uncertainty and indeterminacy, represented something like the opposite of enlightenment. Heisenberg responded by saying that quantum mechanics was only revealing what nature had decreed, namely a blurred reality at the most fundamental level of existence. Knowing what you don't—or can't—know is itself a form of knowledge.

AIRY NOTHING

No scientific accounting of nature can ever be complete. Further measurements uncover new things to explain. So no sooner had quantum mechanics begun to emerge as *the* fundamental description of microscopic reality than it too began to spring leaks. One of the first problems concerned calculations of how electrons interact with themselves.[*] When some calculations were slotted into the quantum equations, the theoretical answers that came back (such as: What was the energy of an electron in some circumstances?) were equal to infinity! What had gone wrong? Here is where Freeman Dyson would make his mark, helping to choreograph the dance of electrons and light.

Dyson had traveled to Ithaca to be where the action was, and he wouldn't be disappointed. Seminarians learn by studying venerable texts. He had been recruited into physics by his reading of those important quantum gospels, Heitler's and Wentzel's textbooks. These books had warned of the deficiencies in quantum science leading to

---

[*] Actually, the 1920s model of quantum mechanics had done an adequate job of describing the relatively slow movements of electrons inside atoms. But scientists quickly realized that quantum descriptions needed to incorporate Einstein's theory of relativity. Einstein had shown that as the velocity of particles came anywhere close to the speed of light, modifications to the equations describing their motion would be needed. The fuller quantum theory not only had to account for high velocities but also had to explain the exciting and disturbing possibility that particles, such as electrons, could be created and destroyed. This was part of Paul Dirac's proposal for the existence of a new class of substance that came to be called antimatter.

the infinities. This was Dyson's hint that something troubling and wonderful was happening.

If we could picture this world what would it look like? It's comparatively easy to think of electrons by the trillion racing through metal wires as electricity. But try visualizing electrons one or two at a time. Each flings out its own electric force, and a magnetic force too, on any charged object passing by. But the electron itself is a charged object, so it ought to feel its own electromagnetic field. And so it does. One way of visualizing this self-interaction is to suppose that an electron is continually shooting out tiny parcels of electromagnetic energy—bundles called virtual photons—which it then promptly reabsorbs.

We don't have spacecraft small enough to journey in toward a single electron to see what happens on this tiny scale. With pencil and paper, however, theorists can go anywhere they like. They can imagine—or with their equations they can predict—what happens when you view the electron (in its guise as a particle) from a distance of a millionth of a meter and then a billionth and then a trillionth, and so on indefinitely, closer and closer.

And the closer you get to the electron, the more crowded this inner space becomes. That is, as you fly along in your minuscule space odyssey in the direction of the electron, as if it were some exotic ball of electric charge, things would get more and more frenzied. First of all, the electron does not have an atmosphere, like our Earth. It doesn't have a surface. There's no reachable center. Instead what you encounter as you go closer is only an ever denser storm of virtual light. These virtual photons could themselves shoot forth particles—such as virtual electrons accompanied by virtual antielectrons—and these virtual particles, in turn, could unleash still more virtual photons, and so forth.

The idea of virtual particles is no stranger than the idea of virtual money. Many people receive their salaries electronically, pay their bills electronically, accrue investment interest electronically, and purchase goods electronically. "Money" in this case is no more than disembodied digits moving about from one place to another, while keeping a proper balance. That's what virtual particles do. They move about, undergo transformation, slip in and out of existence, and keep a balance.

If you took into account all the activity of virtual particles cloaking the electron, and tried to calculate something practical such as the strength of the electron's magnetism, you got an answer that looked like infinity. And that's just for one electron. What about all the rest of them? An inexhaustible supply of electrons in the universe, each with an apparently infinite storehouse of energy: this was infinity squared!

Stop to consider the near fantastical status of this microscopic description of nature, one that calls forth a vapor of virtual particles capering about in the recesses of the atom. It sounds a bit like the story in Shakespeare's *A Midsummer Night's Dream*, which takes place mostly in a forest enchanted by fairies who confound the thinking of all who enter there. Near the end of the play, Theseus, the wise duke, summarizes the delightful power of the events just witnessed:

> *And as imagination bodies forth*
> *The forms of things unknown, the poet's pen*
> *Turns them to shapes, and gives to airy nothing*
> *A local habitation and a name.*

Scientists spin out equations in order to account adroitly for the complexities of nature, such as an electron's local habitation, while playwrights spin out dramas that colorfully account for human complexity. Shakespeare summons fairies to perform magic. Physicists "body forth" electrons and photons out of the airy nothing of empty space. The effectiveness of Shakespeare's play depends on the charm by which he reveals human nature. The effectiveness of quantum science depends on its accuracy in predicting phenomena detected in apparatus, even if we never personally witness quantum fields at work.

CHASING INFINITY

The quantum equations, which looked so clever in the 1920s, now were in danger of being spoiled by nonsensical results. An explanation was needed. Surely, electrons cannot be shrouded in an infinite fog of energy. They are not miniature suns. Infinity, if it is there staring at us from within an atom, from within *every* atom, must somehow be disguised or modified in some way. The quantum catechism needed reforming.

In the late 1930s quantum progress was stymied by this specter of infinity. Then the Second World War arrived and physicists' attention was drawn to radar and nuclear matters, freezing out consideration of nonessential issues. But in the spring of 1947, a great thaw occurred. It was possible to do quantum physics again. A call went out for a new ecumenical council. This time the bishops of physics, at least those concerned with quantum infinity, were summoned to a resort on a hard-to-reach island wedged between the eastern arms of Long Island, a hundred miles from New York City. Not as international as the Solvay conferences had been, the Shelter Island conference brought together mostly American scientists, reflecting the difficulty of postwar travel and also the growing importance of research in the United States.

Indeed, most of the twenty-four participants had been involved with the Manhattan Project or one of the other wartime ventures. The presiding presence on Shelter Island, as he had been at Los Alamos, was J. Robert Oppenheimer. This was the first open physics meeting anyone had attended for many years, and it was a pleasure to talk freely without the encumbrance of security clearances. No barbed wire hemmed them in. They would be pondering not the explosion of uranium nuclei flying apart in the atmosphere but the hypothetical typhoon of virtual photons that swarmed around the electron.

The elite group, which included Bethe and Feynman, started out on the morning of June 2, 1947, by boarding a bus in Manhattan. Led by a police motorcade through Long Island, the bus stopped en route for a festive banquet offered by a patriotic local businessman who wanted to honor the bomb-making and war-ending accomplishments of the nuclear scientists.

The council on Shelter Island consisted chiefly of theorists, but the most important presentation was made by an experimentalist. Willis Lamb, who during the war was absorbed in perfecting a radar scheme in the interest of shooting down German fighters, was now shooting microwaves into a tiny vial of hydrogen at Columbia University. Lamb had the attention of everyone in the room.[10]

What he'd found concerned the light coming out of heated hydrogen. Hydrogen, like all other elements, possesses a unique set of inner energy levels. These quantum levels can be sensitively catalogued by observing the light waves emitted when the atoms are heated. Lamb, using apparatus of unprecedented precision, discovered that at least one of the levels wasn't where it was supposed to be. One type of light ray emitted by hydrogen atoms wasn't at quite the expected frequency. The discrepancy, which became known as the Lamb shift, caused a sensation in physics, and was the prime subject of conversation at Shelter Island.

Here was a vital piece of factual reality. It provided a fixed target to aim at. Many physicists felt that an explanation of this misplaced atomic energy level would offer a clue to the unwanted infinities. Explain the Lamb shift and maybe you would restore, or at least refresh, confidence in the quantum explanation of the cosmos.

THE NOVITIATE ENDS

When Hans Bethe left the Shelter Island meeting, he already had drawn up a rough hypothesis explaining how the electron interacts with itself, and he was able to make a rudimentary calculation of the Lamb shift. Bethe assigned Dyson, a new student in the fall of 1947, a world-class problem: improve Bethe's own explanation of the Lamb shift by attaching the machinery of Einstein's special relativity to the quantum equations. That is, Dyson was to build into the theory the proper relation between the mass and energy of particles moving at high speed.

Dyson threw himself into the work. He had to do a good job, since everyone was watching. Dyson didn't return after four years with the answer and write up a Ph.D. dissertation. Instead he came back after a month, done. He hadn't fully explained why hydrogen atoms were out of tune, but he had nudged Bethe's equations into a more useful form. The professors were delighted, but the other students were appalled. If this guy, who had practically no physics background and who read newspapers half the day, could perform these kinds of calculations so quickly, then what chance was there for them to succeed?[11]

At Bethe's urging, Dyson wrote up his notes for publication in *Physical Review*. This was his first physics paper.[12] Already his days as a novice were coming to an end.

In numerous letters home Dyson kept his parents abreast of his exploits. He never felt so close to them, he said, as when he was away in the United States.[13] More able to gauge his abilities in the world of mathematics than in his adopted field of physics, he understated his new work in comparison to the masterful paper about the Minkowski conjecture he had written to win admittance to Cambridge:

> *I have done nothing in the past two months that you could call very clever or difficult; nothing one-tenth as hard as my fellowship thesis; but because the problems I am now dealing with are public problems*

and all the theoretical physicists have been racking their brains over them for ten years with such negligible results, even the most modest contributions are at once publicized and applauded.[14]

Oh well, he was saying, I might as well be the one to fix things. Note his use of the word "public." Mathematics had been something private, while physics was public. His effort at encompassing the universe, at least the electron part, was modest so far, he insisted, but it had caused at least a small positive disturbance among onlookers.

Indeed, others had started to take notice of Dyson. A follow-up to the Shelter Island meeting was planned. The next invitation-only ecumenical council would take place at a resort in the Pocono Mountains of Pennsylvania. With Oppenheimer again acting as leader, two dozen premier physicists assembled to attack the infinity problem. Bethe requested an invitation for Dyson, who had, after all, cleared some new territory in the study of electrodynamics, the science devoted to the electromagnetic force. Oppie said no. Keeping the attendance elite was necessary if the proper focus was to be maintained. So Dyson was not asked along. He would be a seminarian just a bit longer.

MOUNTAINTOP PHYSICS

At the 1948 Pocono conference the focus would be on the substance of infinity. Specifically, how did the interaction between an electron and the ubiquitous electromagnetic field keep from amplifying itself into an infinite feedback blowup? This was going to be the most important conference of Freeman Dyson's career. Even though he would not be there in person—he would only follow the battle from afar as if it were some distant artillery duel—the ideas to be exchanged over the next few days were to shape his own thinking for years to come.

At Pocono, the showcase matchup would be between Richard Feynman and Julian Schwinger. Both were about thirty years old, so another energetic, youthful battle of ideas was expected, reminiscent of the *Knaben Physik* quantum breakthroughs in the 1920s. Both Feynman and Schwinger had grown up in New York City, had shown brilliance early, and had quickly become professors at Ivy League colleges. Feynman was a professor at Cornell, while Schwinger had beat out Bethe for a job at Harvard. But everything else about them was different.

Feynman was boisterous, while Schwinger was reserved. Feynman drove a grubby Oldsmobile, Schwinger a plush Cadillac. Feynman spent the war years working on the atomic bomb in Los Alamos, while Schwinger had worked on radar at MIT.

Schwinger, in lecture mode, was polished; at the risk of being exhausting he impressed his audiences with comprehensiveness. When he finished speaking you knew you had heard just about everything there was to hear on that subject. The matter had been thought out and presented with the precision of a district attorney.

Feynman, by contrast, was more animated, colloquial. In the sequence of his explanations he cut corners.

Each man had come up the mountain in Pennsylvania to offer his own comprehensive theory of quantum electrodynamics, or QED, the framework that combines the nineteenth-century theory of electromagnetic forces with twentieth-century quantum science. Each took his turn trying to impress a very discriminating audience. Those in attendance included Niels Bohr, who had been so conspicuous at the 1927 Solvay conference and who even now was the very godfather of quantum orthodoxy; Enrico Fermi, who had done pioneering work in nuclear physics and who had built the first working nuclear reactor; Edward Teller, who had been working for many years on plans for a thermonuclear bomb; Paul Dirac, one of the founders of field theory; and even the authors of Dyson's two favorite quantum textbooks, Gregor Wentzel and Walter Heitler.

The topic of discussion was worthy of this august audience. Two rival efforts to chase down the persistent quantum infinities were being offered. Like two politicians rolling up at the party convention to make their cases before the delegates, Julian Schwinger and Richard Feynman arrived amid high expectation. One presentation would be a mesmerizing triumph, the other an embarrassing failure.

Schwinger, speaking first, outlined his attempt to reform quantum science. His scheme, based on a mathematical expression called a Green's function, looked a bit like the sort of field theory already pioneered by Heisenberg and Dirac. Two months before, at the New York meeting of the American Physical Society, Schwinger had presented an early version of the theory. Extra lectures and larger rooms were needed to accommodate the crush of viewers. In the months since, he'd finished his work.

Now came the full Schwinger. Previously physicists had believed the infinities could be fixed by somehow redefining the mass and charge of the electron, and this is what Schwinger had now done.[15] If the electron's mass and charge were infinite it wouldn't matter, since the electron—at least the electron we encounter in actual measurements—would be surrounded by that countervailing blizzard of electromagnetic fields. Schwinger's process of cosmic mitigation at the submicroscopic level, neutralizing the infinities, made electrons—*every* electron—normal again, fit to participate in atomic society. This domestication of the electron was therefore called renormalization.

Schwinger's lecture went on for hours. This masterful expositor, who in a long teaching career at Harvard would supervise the candidacy of eighty physics Ph.D.'s, including future Nobelists, bedazzled and benumbed his audience of experts. Few questions came up during the onslaught of Schwinger's logic. At the end, the auditors, still anesthetized by the extreme density of equations, couldn't be sure, but it looked as if he had done it. Schwinger had tamed the infinities in a consistent way. Oppie was pleased.

Then the second part of the double feature started up. Feynman was different. He became legendary for his wayward habit of assembling ideas from the ground up. He didn't work up his explanations from others' equations. He started fresh, sought a physical view of things, as opposed to being merely mathematical, and frequently made death-defying, mountain-goat leaps from crag to crag, leaving out lots of steps in the proof in order to get to the point sooner. That's the way his mind worked. Those observing the display were worried not because of the math but because here was a man performing high-wire maneuvers without a net beneath.

Feynman didn't deny that Schwinger's field approach to understanding electrons was useful. But he preferred, somewhat quaintly, to imagine electrons as *things* moving about. To calculate how an electron gets from place to place, from *a* to *b*, you should take into account all the possible ways of going, he said, and then add up the possibilities for all those possible paths—each weighted by its relative likelihood—to arrive at a final answer. Driving from New York to Los Angeles, for example, you could take a northern route through Denver or a southern route through Phoenix, or maybe somewhere in between. An electron, going from *here* to *there*, does the same thing. But for the electron there are an infinite number of alternative paths to take.

Feynman offered a gigantic form of bookkeeping that kept track of each path by conjuring an associated picture. Quantum rules, solidified into a secular canon at previous conclaves like Solvay, insisted that we never know precisely which way an electron had gone; in a way, the electron had taken *all* available paths. Feynman seized on this every-which-way reality to describe quantum reality, not for making a cross-country journey but for explaining the perpetual dance of matter with light.

At the Pocono conclave, Feynman's approach didn't go over well. Feynman, who would later be legendary for his sparkling self-assured, animated presentations, was on this occasion unclear and troubling. Questions kept coming. Teller wanted to know if Feynman's theory took into account the exclusion principle, which insists that not more than one electron may occupy a specific quantum state at a time within an electron. Dirac wanted to know if the theory was unitary. Feynman was stumped. He had to be told what unitary meant: it referred to the fact that when you sum over all possible paths that the probability of something happening was somewhere between 0 and 1.

Bohr was particularly bothered. He wanted to know if Feynman's theory was compatible with the uncertainty principle. It didn't seem to be. Didn't Feynman know even elementary quantum mechanics? Here, said Bohr, give me the chalk. And with that the elder statesman of quantum science took over. Feynman's inexplicable ability (some called it magic) to glide over numerous tedious steps in a multistep disquisition—his supernatural power to arrive at the correct answer quicker than anyone else—here tripped him up.

In modern intellectual discourse we use words to convey ideas. In mathematical physics, words are supplemented with symbols, Greek letters, subscripts and superscripts, all packed into equations. Schwinger, difficult as he was to understand, at least used conventional-looking equations to describe electrons. He spoke a language, the equivalent of the church-approved Latin, the other quantum bishops could follow.

Feynman, by contrast, had invented a pictorial language of his own, a new form of hieroglyphs. He showed you how electrons interacted with each other using drawings covered with squiggles going every possible way. Feynman delivered his promotional pitch with the gusto of an auto salesman. But also like the salesman he didn't seem to answer all the questions put to him.

His demanding audience, not to be swept aside, wanted precisely to see all the intermediate levels. If Schwinger could do it, why not Feynman? Schwinger had unpacked his version of reality and had not seen fit to violate any known laws of quantum reality. With Feynman you couldn't be sure what had happened. In the battle of the theories he was clearly the loser.

The Pocono meeting was over. Feynman's Princeton thesis advisor, John Wheeler, compiled and circulated detailed notes. Feynman, put in an awkward position, was asked to summarize the meeting for *Physics Today* magazine. In the modest sentence or two he devoted to his own brand of quantum electrodynamics he had to admit that it wasn't as complete as Schwinger's.[16]

THE THIRD MAN

In hindsight we can say that the prospective reformation of quantum science would have been faster if another man had been present. Two noninvited scientists should have been at the meeting. One, only a hundred miles away at Ithaca, was Freeman Dyson, who, having already formulated a worthy account of the Lamb shift, would soon have much more to say on the subject.

The other missing man was, through accident of birth and by the burden of world war, stranded on the other side of the world. Most Pocono participants had no idea that Japanese physicists were chasing the same quantum infinities bothering those in the West. Infinities know no boundaries. They do not stop for world wars. Electrons are the same whether they plunge out of the ubiquitous electron field in Tokyo or Quito or Helsinki.

Shin'ichiro Tomonaga, working with colleagues at the University of Tokyo, had formulated an infinity-neutralizing explanation very similar to Schwinger's, except that the man in Japan seemed to have arrived at his model several years before the man at Harvard. Neither knew of the other's work, and yet a splendid parallel achievement had come about, testifying to the common genius of human intelligence. Here you had several inquisitive minds pondering the same dilemma of matter at the most basic level, but working in different hemispheres and immersed in very different cultures.

Consider Tomonaga's situation. Even after the U.S. Air Force stopped its bombing attacks at the end of the war, privations continued in Japan. It was hard to obtain food and shelter, much less scientific equipment or journals. It had been hard for Dyson and the rest of the British to restart the rhythms of life in postwar London. And *they* were the victors. In Tokyo rhythms were even harder to regenerate.

For several years after the war, ordinary Japanese were forbidden to travel or even to receive mail from abroad. The piece of news that so electrified the physicists gathered on Shelter Island, namely the Lamb shift, came circuitously to the physicists gathered in Tokyo. In Shelter Island they listened to Lamb himself. In Japan, Lamb arrived in the pages of *Newsweek* magazine, copies of which were placed on the shelves of the public libraries operated by the American Occupation forces.

Bethe in Cornell and Oppenheimer at Princeton had finally received copies of Tomonaga's paper, and Oppie quickly made the Japanese work known to the Pocono attendees. He arranged to have it published in *Physical Review.* Dyson, pondering Tomonaga's plight, considered such an outstanding paper coming from Tokyo to have been a voice from the deep.[17] Thus was forged the beginnings of a true international theory of electrons and light.

ON THE ROAD

In the history of quantum electrodynamics, one of the most important friendships, if not exactly a collaboration, was the one between Richard Feynman and Freeman Dyson. Dyson felt that he stood in relation to Feynman as the playwright Ben Jonson had been to William Shakespeare.

The 1623 collection of Shakespeare's plays features a effusive preface. Written by Jonson, Shakespeare's protégé, friend, and sometime rival, this most famous of literary encomiums gives eyewitness tribute to Shakespeare's good nature, his industry, and his superior talent: "He was not of an age, but for all time!" said Jonson. Not one given to easy charity, the otherwise boastful Jonson admitted that he admired the Swan of Avon (another of Jonson's phrases for Shakespeare) "this side idolatry."

Three and a half centuries later Freeman Dyson would play the same role for Richard Feynman. Writing the Preface to a collection of Feynman essays, Dyson embraced his idolatry.[18] Calling him a sort of American Shakespeare, Dyson commended Feynman for his good cheer and his quicksilver ability to see through to the heart of physical problems.

Since arriving at Cornell months before, Dyson had, in many letters to his parents back in England, provided an apt portrait of his new-found friend. Feynman was not just smart. By his jovial presence he maintained morale. He was the life of every party. He loved to play on bongo drums and perpetually seemed to be in a good mood, but not necessarily in a sweet mood. Dyson, always ready to learn something, would frequently go around to Feynman's office. If Feynman wanted to talk, they talked. If he didn't want to talk, he told Dyson to go away.[19] The first half of Dyson's Cornell year had been spent extending Bethe's work. The second half of the year was devoted to being Feynman's sounding board,[20] and Dyson considered this the best possible education. Feynman was the new Frank Thompson in Dyson's life, an older brother to look up to.[21]

Feynman threw off good physics ideas as a meteor throws sparks. He was, Dyson wrote, part genius and part buffoon.[22] The larger public fame of Feynman-as-Shakespeare did not emerge for some years, until in the 1980s the essence of the man was captured in *Surely You're Joking, Mr. Feynman!* and other books filled with his aphorisms. But among physicists the man's reputation for largeness of soul was already there in the 1940s at Cornell, and before that at Los Alamos.

If you were Ben Jonson and William Shakespeare invited you along on a car trip to Albuquerque you would surely accept. And so it was that starting in Cleveland in June 1948, Dyson found himself in the passenger seat of Feynman's car on a cross-country journey. This would be a great chance for the young man (age thirty) from Queens, New York, and the even younger man (age twenty-four) from Winchester, England, to become better acquainted. They talked about physics, naturally, and many other things.

The war was over but new hostilities were blossoming. Thanks to the weapon that Richard Feynman had helped create in Los Alamos, the world was again quickly becoming a dangerous place, and the overhang of the nuclear threat was preying on their minds. Coming into St. Louis, for instance, Feynman deduced with grim precision, at various mileposts approaching the city, the likely effects of a hypothetical Hiroshima-size bomb detonation. This mordant apocalyptic ritual was played out at several cities, and Dyson came to feel uneasy, as if he were with Lot making his way through Sodom and Gomorrah.[23]

The car glided along at high speed down Route 66, the signature pike of pre-Interstate America. For Dyson, the Englishman from a green isle, it was his first time in a really dry place. Not only did he enjoy the novel geography but also the human panorama. Feynman was fond of picking up hitchhikers, who added a stream of conversational topics. Dyson was amused to see Feynman adapt his speaking style to the successive backseat riders. The farther west they glided the folksier he got.

The automotive part of the trip went well until they hit Oklahoma, where drenching rains flooded the path. Nearby towns were disrupted and drownings were reported. At the town of Supulpa they reached a blockage. So the two scientists were forced to backtrack, and found themselves in the town of Vinita, where they spent the night. Owing to the storm, accommodations were scare, and so they shared the only available room, at fifty cents per man, in a brothel.

With rain beating down outside, a stifling stuffiness inside, and girl-ish noises coming from outside their door, the two men spent the whole night talking in the dark. Feynman spoke of his first wife, Arline, and of her struggle with cancer. He spoke of his loneliness in the years following her death. According to Feynman's biographer James Gleick, "Feynman confided more in Dyson than he had done with any friend in his adult life," at least up to that time.[24]

You can't have Freeman Dyson and Richard Feynman in a room without talk of quantum physics. Feynman, with his pictorial approach, was attempting more than a solution to the infinity problem. He felt that his approach might be applicable to other areas of physics too, such as to the realm of gravity and also to the atomic nucleus. Dyson wasn't sure about this. He mistrusted Feynman's intuition, however valuable it might have been in leading Feynman to physics discoveries. Many all-inclusive physics theories had foundered before, he argued. Conversely, Feynman mistrusted Dyson's reliance on mathematics. Math, to Feynman, was to be used but not to be treasured for its own sake.[25]

In Feynman's account of this night, but not in Dyson's, we learn that the Englishman found himself in need of a toilet. But he was reluctant to open the door, since this would mean having to run a gauntlet of prostitutes on the way to the lavatory at the end of the hall. "Use the sink," said Feynman. "But it's unsanitary," responded Dyson. "Run the water," said Feynman. To this sensible suggestion Dyson had no immediate response. But Feynman reports that later that night he could detect, from the other side of the room, a discreet movement toward the sink.[26]

The rain abated the next day and the men continued on through Texas to New Mexico. They came streaming into Albuquerque, going seventy miles per hour in a twenty-miles-per-hour zone, meriting the highest speeding fine ever issued by the local judge. Feynman, in high spirits, reminisced with the judge about wartime conditions in the town, and cajoled His Honor into reducing the fine. Feynman's main reason for coming all this way had been love. Near the end of the war, Feynman had met a woman in town and was coming back to see how things stood between them. Dyson guessed, incorrectly as it turned out, that the attachment would turn to marriage.

Dyson was himself entangled with a female, at least slightly. He was receiving letters from Hilde Jacobs, one of the German girls he'd met the summer before in Münster. These letters were starting to increase in number.[27] One was especially long and addressed in a roundabout way something on her mind. Her letters to Dyson were usually in German, but at the very end of this letter she quoted in English from "He Wishes for the Cloths of Heaven," a poem by William Butler Yeats:

> Had I the heavens' embroidered cloths,
> Enwrought with golden and silver light,
> The blue and the dim and the dark cloths
> Of night and light and the half-light,
> I would spread the cloths under your feet:
> But I, being poor, have only my dreams;
> I have spread my dreams under your feet;
> Tread softly because you tread on my dreams.

What was Hilde's reason for quoting this passage, he asked himself. What was her dream? He decided he'd better be careful. In matters like this he would have to tread softly.

ON TO PRINCETON

The two buddies now split up. Feynman stayed in Albuquerque while Dyson got on a Greyhound bus. The terms of his fellowship encouraged him to gain wide experience. Dyson had traveled to Germany the previous summer and planned to go to Mexico to do manual labor. But now he decided to spend the summer soaking up still more physics at the Michigan Summer Symposium in Ann Arbor.[28] He loved riding in buses and was eager to survey the geography of his adopted country. His method was to sightsee during the day and ride the bus at night. Not that he slept that much. He came to have a hankering for all-night talk, falling into Feynman-style conversation with the person sitting across the aisle. And so the miles sped by.[29]

Dyson liked Michigan and did some campaign work on behalf of Henry Wallace's 1948 presidential campaign.[30] But his primary purpose was to attend classes where he could hear Julian Schwinger lecture.[31] At first sight Schwinger seemed formidable, but the stiff impression softened a bit when you got to know him privately. Still, his brand of mathematics seemed more difficult, more encumbered with details, than necessary. So thick a forest of equations, surely, could not be the best way of describing nature.[32] When Schwinger came to submit his theory to the pages of *Physical Review* he had to obtain special dispensation from the editors, who for the first time allowed equations to spread out beyond the width of a page and to spill onto a second line.

Dyson did not return to Cornell in the fall term. True to his restless nature and to the expansive spirit of his fellowship, he was moving on to yet another institution. In their turn, London, Cambridge, and Ithaca had been useful but limited. At Cornell, especially under the watchful eye of Hans Bethe, Dyson had learned a lot. But he had officially signed up only as a master's degree student, and Bethe now decided that Princeton would be a better place for Dyson.[33] They agreed a year spent at the Institute for Advanced Study with J. Robert Oppenheimer would be a fine thing.

As usual, Dyson came highly recommended. Oppie could read for himself Dyson's article on the Lamb shift in *Physical Review*, but if that wasn't enough there was Bethe's private letter to Oppenheimer describing Dyson as the best graduate student he'd ever seen.[34]

4. The Secret Signature of Things

Dyson as Artist

(1948–1949)

What is the most important week of your life? Its probably wrapped up with the birth of a child, a vacation in Hawaii, a wedding. It's often hard to say. But for Freeman Dyson—restricting ourselves to his scientific career—his most important week was about to break out.

On top of an exhilarating year at Cornell, Dyson had just had a fulfilling summer. First by bus to Cleveland and by car with Feynman down to New Mexico. Then by bus up to Michigan to hear Schwinger. These were memorable events but they did not, by themselves, afford him his best week.

What his weary mind craved now were mountains and desert scenery. He went by bus out to the Pacific coast. Dyson, his head stuffed with Feynman's diagrams and Schwinger's fields, was on a well-earned holiday. What he now saw from his window passing through Utah gave him particular bliss. The Mormons, having set off on their own with a peculiar vision of the world, had marvelously planted towns up beautiful mountain valleys. Dyson, loving tidy arrangements, appreciated the pattern of their crop cultivation. It struck him as being almost Swiss.[1] But this was not yet the week.

He went to Berkeley and roomed in the International House. The physics building was nearby, but he stayed away.[2] Instead he diverted himself by reading James Joyce's *A Portrait of the Artist as a Young Man*, which tells the story of a spiritual and aesthetic odyssey not unlike what Dyson was undertaking just then.[3]

Dyson's thinking had actually been free of physics for two whole weeks, and still he couldn't relax. Something was turning over in his mind. Restless, he got back on yet another bus and headed east. He had some of his best thoughts on buses. He was not yet twenty-five years old, and precisely now, without him knowing it, *the* week had begun.

NEBRASKA HAILSTORM

Although Dyson had written that article for *Physical Review* about the Lamb shift, he now yearned to provide a fuller explanation. He liked the feeling of adding to knowledge. He enjoyed calculating the behavior of particles at the submicroscopic level. In effect, he was telling electrons what to do. Would they obey? His effort to enunciate new physics rules, or at least to fashion some better version of Feynman's and Schwinger's rules, was to include physics and art: "It is like writing a novel where you as author have complete control over the characters," Dyson said. "It is a self-contained world where you understand everything, the parts and the whole." [4]

This sounds like a formula right out of the book Dyson was reading. Here is Joyce's description, in *A Portrait,* of the literary writer's mission: "The artist, like the God of creation, remains within, or behind or beyond or above his handiwork, invisible, refined out of existence, indifferent, paring his fingernails." [5] Except in the case of Dyson the scientist-creator would be sitting at a desk, with his feet up, reading a newspaper. In Joyce's novel, the artist-hero, Stephen Dedalus, looks for inspiration as he strides through the streets of Dublin. In Dyson's saga, the scientist-hero rumbles across the High Plains in a Greyhound.

"Epiphany" was Joyce's name for the intensest form of artistic apprehension. He borrowed this term from Christian observance where, for example, the nature of Christ is manifested in a sudden realization. In *A Portrait* Joyce uses epiphany as a literary term. It represented a shining forth, an aesthetic revelation by which an artist recognized "the secret signature of things."

Can epiphany also apply to physics? In principle, yes. Dyson did think of himself as "an artist with mathematical tools." [6] His liking for Feynman's geometrically elegant diagrams was practically a form of art appreciation. A semester of heavy discussion with Feynman had primed Dyson's imagination. A summer with Schwinger and his quantum fields had acquainted Dyson with a completely separate but apparently equivalent view of reality. Dyson personally preferred fields over pictures, but it was thrilling to see how Feynman had turned subatomic reality into geometric patterns.

In *A Portrait* epiphany didn't just happen. Stephen Dedalus's subconscious mind had been prepared. Having been schooled by the Jesuits, Stephen went about things logically and methodically. He relied on Thomas Aquinas, whose thirteenth-century theology was even more comprehensive than Schwinger's twentieth-century electrodynamic catechism.

Suppose, said the fictional Stephen, that the artist wants to create something beautiful. Aquinas held that the three necessary ingredients of appreciating beauty were *integritas, consonantia,* and *claritas*.[7] The first of these Stephen translated as *wholeness*. Perceiving beauty must begin by seeing the thing as a separate entity apart from the rest of the universe. The second ingredient Stephen translated as *harmony*, the perception of the parts and the synthesis of those parts into a balanced, consistent whole. The third component in Aquinas's aesthetic triad was harder to translate. *Claritas*: it sounds like clarity, but Stephen believed Aquinas was aiming more at something like the soul of the object, its *quidditas* or *what-ness*.

Words, words, words. Do we really need all these words to describe electrons? Well, we use lots of vocabulary words to describe subtle nuances in basketball, or high cuisine, or religious doctrine, or the anatomy of finches. Therefore it will be useful to stick with the Joyce-Aquinas terms, just for a moment longer, to describe electrons.

Wholeness? An electron isn't a single pinpoint thing. It's there but surrounded by that blizzard of virtual particles. Its wholeness has to take into account this extended nature. It can be a particle in a specific place at a specific time, but only when it is detected.

Harmony? The scientific description of an electron, like an artistic description of a person, can come in many forms. Though they might be quite different in appearance, and though they were social constructs cooked up by scientists standing at chalkboards in places like Tokyo, and Cambridge, and Ithaca, the equations of Schwinger and Tomonaga and the diagrams of Feynman both accounted for the observed properties of the electron. This pointed to an underlying kinship.

What-ness? In quantum science, what an electron *is* consists largely of what an electron is seen *doing* in a laboratory. Consequently an electron is a thing with a dossier of measurable properties: it has mass, electrical charge, and magnetism. Electron existence emerges from observation.

Words like harmony and wholeness are aesthetic terms, words used in literature or philosophy, and not usually applied to science. Physicists don't generally consider that they are making electrons more real—much less bringing them more into existence—through improved-precision measurements. Better experiments are done to gain more knowledge about electrons, and the universe.

But Dyson savored the aesthetic side of things. While James Joyce thought of Aquinas, Dyson thought of Feynman and Schwinger. Dyson's equivalent of Joyce's Jesuit education had been a rigorous grounding in number theory, including infinite series of numbers. Heaving into a fizz of virtual particles in the universal vacuum was for him a delight.

Dyson was on the bus for three days and three nights. The bumps of the road kept him from doing anything but think. He couldn't read and he couldn't write. Jostling along in this way, sleepless and paperless, somewhere in Nebraska a shining forth came to him.[8] In his drowsy trance, on the third day into his journey, he saw the way to bring picture and equation together. They were *consonantia*. In his sleep-deprived mind the exact mathematical bridge between Schwinger and Feynman began to form.

Anxious to record this secret signature of things on paper, the young physicist paused in Chicago for a few days before resuming his trip. Dyson had discovered a sort of Rosetta stone for quantum electrodynamics. He had the mathematical prowess to translate between Feynman and Schwinger. Sensing that he had achieved *claritas* he was eager to consolidate his explanation. Before he could fulfill his mission, however, he would have to make an important convert.

APOSTLES

J. Robert Oppenheimer had been in Europe and no one knew precisely when he'd return. Meanwhile his office had filled with young physicists all waiting to get started. The mood was both anxious and eager. The situation reminded Dyson of another troubled homecoming.

T. S. Eliot was, like Dyson, newly resident at the Institute for Advanced Study that autumn of 1948. Eliot's play *Murder in the Cathedral* was doing well on Broadway. In the opening scene a number of priests have gathered, awaiting their archbishop with a mixture of exhilaration and anxiety. Thomas Beckett, the former friend and now enemy of the king, was returning from the relative safety of Europe to a potentially dangerous environment at home. Beckett was attempting to balance his current position as archbishop of Canterbury with his old position as chancellor under King Henry.

Dyson saw an analogy between the twentieth-century vicar of nuclear weapons and the twelfth-century primate of England. Oppenheimer was struggling just then to reconcile his former job as enthusiastic builder of the atom bomb with his newfound misgivings over the course of postwar nuclear policy. Both Oppenheimer and the archbishop were outgoing yet also deeply introspective.

Oppenheimer was too introspective, some critics felt. He had led the huge wartime effort to build an atom bomb. Now, with the onset of the Cold War, his counsel was more needed than ever. Should a hydrogen bomb be built? Oppenheimer, along with other notable physicists such as Enrico Fermi and Hans Bethe, felt that the hydrogen weapon was too large, too destructive. Others, such as physicists Edward Teller and Stanislaw Ulam, disagreed. They felt that the magnitude of the Soviet threat demanded the utmost in military preparedness. This matter gave Oppie heavy eyebrows.

Oppie did some of his best thinking in a workshop environment. As a young professor in Berkeley he maintained an atelier of brilliant young theoretical physicists, whose desks all sat in a single large room. Now in 1948 it seemed as if Oppenheimer wanted to re-create his Berkeley environment. The main building at the Institute for Advanced Study was undergoing remodeling, so all the physicists' desks were gathered in one room. Oppenheimer, who had been director for about one year, wanted to expand the physics part of the Institute. So he invited a dozen young scientists, ten men and two women, to join him.

Dyson awaited the return of their nuclear archbishop from another of those ecumenical councils scientists keep holding—this time the eighth Solvay conference. In Oppie's absence the Institute newcomers were getting to know each other through daily discussion, a process helped along by numerous parties. Although Dyson was never a big drinker, alcohol's role in lubricating colloquy came as a pleasant surprise to him.[9] The twelve, including Dyson (with no advanced degree), were no longer students but were young professionals, postdoctoral fellows, who with a little guidance would be ready to branch out on their own.

These colleagues included some students of Schwinger's, such as

Kenneth Case and Robert Karplus; a young French woman, Cécile Morette; and Jack Steinberger, who would later win the Nobel Prize. They didn't bother speaking with the mathematicians at the Institute, nor any of the professors. The Young Turks felt that they didn't have anything to learn from these old folks.

For his year at the Institute Dyson considered his best friends to be Steinberger and David Bohm, a former student of Oppenheimer's and now a junior professor at Princeton University. Dyson and Bohm, both bachelors, would eat dinner together many nights, often at a nearby "soul-food" restaurant. Although advised that eating at such an establishment was unwise, they continued to go anyway.[10]

The rivalry between the Schwinger-Tomonaga field theory and the more wayward Feynman picture approach was a prime topic of conversation. Dyson was tempted to blurt out exactly what he had done—namely, that he was about to erect a grand synthesis of the rival views—but to say all that in this way would be unsporting, and so for the moment he held back. He was convinced that with the secret of electrodynamics in his hand he had something that would be of interest to Oppie. He had something that would be able to command his leader's attention.[11]

His task now was to gather his Greyhound insights, sort through his hasty Chicago notes, and turn it all into a masterpiece of fluid explanation. On the seventh day of writing he rested. The effort was, he confided to his parents, the best thing he had ever accomplished. His fifty-page manuscript destined for *Physical Review* might even be great.[12]

He had not merely shown that Schwinger and Feynman were compatible. Exercising his own mathematical talent, Dyson did what they had *not* done: demonstrate that the infinities could be tamed at each successive level of complexity. All those "higher-order" terms, those associated with ever more nested groupings of virtual particles rising up out of the vacuum, adding layer on top of layer of additional frothiness—all were manageable. This achievement would be Dyson's distinctive contribution to the reform of quantum electrodynamics.[13]

Dyson was struck now by another anxiety. In the paper he had blithely summarized the work of Feynman and Schwinger before either of these gentlemen had officially published his own work. Would they be offended by this? Would they charge that Dyson had cribbed their ideas? In the actual paper Dyson gave frequent credit to them as well as to Tomonaga in Japan. But maybe this wasn't enough.

Once again, his friend and mentor Hans Bethe helped to put things right. He and Dyson took a stroll through Riverside Park in New York City. Bethe was spending a semester at Columbia University and this is where Dyson delivered a summary of his theory. They decided the paper should go ahead.[14] If Feynman and Schwinger hadn't published anything yet, whose fault was that? Their reticence was, by this point, holding back the progress of science. By publishing, Dyson was pushing matters along. And, as for credit, hadn't he enshrined the efforts of the three men in the very title of the paper? "The Radiation Theories of Tomonaga, Schwinger, and Feynman" said it all. The paper was sent off. "Of course he had my permission to publish my work in his papers," Feynman later said. "We were good friends."[15]

Dyson sent a copy to Feynman at Cornell and followed up in person. Accompanied by Cécile Morette, Dyson made the ten-hour train journey to Ithaca. Had Feynman read Dyson's article? Well, Feynman had given it to one of his graduate students and then asked whether it was worth reading. The student said no, so Feynman had not read it. And, as if to show why he didn't need to read Dyson's masterpiece, Feynman entertained his visitors from Princeton with a dazzling display, providing solutions on the spot to several difficult physics problems, such as how light can interact with light, dispatching in two hours what had stumped others for years. Dyson took Feynman's gentle rebuff stoically. Nobody disliked Dick Feynman. You could only be amazed by his effervescent personality and quick ability. Here is how Dyson rationalized his fruitful pilgrimage to Cornell in the fall of 1948:

> *I know that he is the one man in the world who has nothing to learn from what I have written; and he doesn't mind telling me so. That afternoon, Feynman produced more brilliant ideas per square minute that I have ever seen anywhere before.*[16]

Back in Princeton, where the archbishop had finally returned, Dyson sought to explain the new quantum ideas. He was invited to give a public talk. On the designated day, things did not go well. Oppenheimer repeatedly interrupted. He bluntly questioned Dyson's methods and located various errors in Dyson's reasoning. It became apparent that Oppenheimer, maker of the atom bomb, the weapon that had vanquished the shogun's heirs, didn't much relish being taught quantum lessons by this not-yet-twenty-five-year-old.

Dyson himself was irritated. Had Oppenheimer become conservative? Had his upper-echelon government consultancy distracted him from seeing ahead in physics? To Dyson, the older man seemed lethargic. He had acquired a defeatist attitude. Oppenheimer's outbursts of rudeness seemed compulsive, as if they were a medical tic. Dyson began to think that he should have stayed with Feynman at Cornell. Ithaca had more snow but it was chillier in Princeton.[17]

Something had to be done. Dyson drafted a manifesto in the form of a memo to his boss. He argued that the new theories had merit. Schwinger's equations and Feynman's pictures, together with Dyson's explanations, would produce sound results. Many of the infinity problems plaguing quantum physics could be explained. Why the resistance?[18]

Dyson wasn't sure he should send such an admonitory note to so august a person. But that night, as Dyson ruminated, the night sky put out an omen. A brilliant display of the aurora borealis erupted briefly. Dyson frequently combed events for historical or literary or philosophical, if not exactly divine, portent. The flashing forth of the northern lights he took as a favorable sign, so he sent the memo. To his surprise, Oppenheimer greeted it in a friendly manner and suggested that Dyson deliver a more thorough series of talks in defense of the quantum pictograms.

Dyson resumed his lectures and Oppenheimer resumed his attacks. Oppie, in his clever repartee, was never to be one-upped. You simply could not get the better of any argument. At one lecture the sarcasm and disruptive interruptions became so bad that the other audience members, genuinely wanting to learn something from the presentation, asked Dyson to repeat the whole two-hour talk the next day when Oppie would not be present.[19] Only in that way could they listen in peace and get to ask some questions of their own.

The hostilities reached a peak in mid-November. At this point Hans Bethe was instrumental once again in pushing forward Dyson's career. Bethe came down to Princeton and, in front of Oppenheimer, gave his own account of Dyson's brand of quantum reality. For the remaining Dyson lectures, Oppenheimer held his tongue. Was he actually listening now, or just simmering? The morning after the last lecture in the sequence, Dyson received one of the most important letters of his life. The text of this missive, coming from the director of the Institute, consisted of only two words. *"Nolo contendere."*[20] Basically: I surrender.

DYSONMANIA

Dyson was not yet through proving his case. He wanted to be clear. He wanted to win supporters. With so many hours at the blackboard now behind him explaining in person, he had more explaining to do on paper. The fifty-page article, already sent off to *Physical Review*, was followed now by an eighty-page paper. All together this represented a 130-page quantum gospel. Dyson had been preaching to his own congregation, the physicists at the Institute, including Oppie. He had made a few more converts at Cornell. It was now time to evangelize further afield. He would be the bringer of Feynman diagrams.

At the January 1949 meeting of the American Physical Society, the APS president, Oppenheimer himself, conspicuously praised Dyson. Another speaker referred glowingly to the value of the "Feynman-Dyson" diagrams. At this point, Feynman, who was sitting in the audience, turned to Dyson and said in a stage whisper, "It looks as if you're in, Doc."[21] The complementary side of Dyson's achievement exists in the naming of certain "Dyson-Schwinger equations," also called "Schwinger-Dyson equations."

Greatness had been thrust upon Freeman Dyson. Like the Beatles in 1964, Dyson in 1949 was young, British, and in demand. Compare and contrast. The Beatles started humbly, as most rock groups do, rehearsing in tiny rooms, playing for their own amusement. They built up stamina and polished their onstage poise by working plenty of mean gigs in Liverpool and Hamburg. The German experience especially paid off, since they got practice performing in front of rowdy, unforgiving audiences.

The Beatles' manager cleaned them up, got them upstanding engagements, signed them to record contracts, and induced them to wear better clothes. Dyson didn't need cleaning up, but Hans Bethe shaped him up in other ways. He gave Dyson a world-class problem to work on—chasing down quantum infinities—introduced him to upper-class physics society, and got him jobs.

The Beatles' first single release, a song called "Love Me Do," was nice but didn't push the charts. Dyson's first physics single, a paper called "The Electromagnetic Shift of Energy Levels," had also been nice, but not nice enough to get him invited to the Pocono physics meeting.

Then the breakout came. The Beatles' January 1963 tune "Please

Please Me" went to number one on the British charts, and the lives of John, Paul, George, and Ringo were never the same. For Dyson, his two hit papers, the ones drafted in October and December of 1948, appeared in February 1949 in *Physical Review*. From then on he and Feynman's diagrams shot to the top. Dyson's talk at Columbia had made an impression. His series of talks in Princeton, culminating in Oppenheimer's surrender, had created a stir. The January 1949 APS meeting was Dyson's national showing. Feynman was now giving more talks himself, but if you wanted to know how the Feynman-Dyson system worked you had to read Dyson. His papers in *Physical Review* constituted the entire must-read literature on the subject. For several years to come Dyson's papers drew more citations than Feynman's.[22] Feynman wasn't entirely pleased.[23]

That spring a follow-up to the Shelter Island and Pocono meetings on quantum science was held at the Oldstone Hotel, fifty miles north of New York City, and it was decidedly "Dyson's show."[24] In March, Dyson gave a talk at the University of Chicago, where he met two great physicists and alumni of the Manhattan Project, Enrico Fermi and Edward Teller, who, Dyson thought, were equivalent to Bethe-Feynman duo in Cornell, the one man acting as a sort of benevolent king (Fermi) while the other man served as the court jester (Teller).[25]

Job offers accumulated. Columbia University wanted him. Bristol University in the U.K. The Observatory in Greenwich intimated that they would make him an assistant Astronomer Royal.[26] A lectureship at Cambridge materialized. Everyone had questions about the new methods. "Soon I shall have to engage a secretary," Dyson said.[27] He missed the old days riding Greyhound buses.

Dyson had been taking his meaningful bus trips around America just about the same time another young man, Jack Kerouac, was covering similar territory by automobile. When he finally rested from his travels, Kerouac taped together many sheets of paper and fed them into a typewriter. This famous scroll of paper, 120 feet long, became the novel *On the Road*. Dyson's equivalent of the scroll, his two articles in *Physical Review*, were nearly as long as Kerouac's, at least in typescript. Kerouac's book, a romantic retelling of his journeys, became a cult favorite and is read by impressionable college students to this day. Dyson's articles, the upright, mathed-up retelling of his Nebraska cerebral hailstorm, had a cult following among physics graduate students, and provided the best explanation of quantum electrodynamics (QED) for several crucial years.

Beatlemania reached frenzy proportion when in 1964 the Fab Four flew from Britain to America. Dyson, at the crest of *his* wave in 1949, was about to abandon America to return to Britain, and he wasn't happy about it. The terms of his foundation grant, the fellowship that allowed him to come to the United States in the first place, discouraged him from taking a regular job in the States for two years. Dyson could have wiggled out of this restriction, but didn't: "It was a matter of honor. I'd given my word as a gentleman."[28] Consequently, he didn't become a professor at Columbia. Instead he chose from among three posts at British institutions.

His newfound friend, Oppenheimer, gave him blunt advice. At the University of Bristol, Dyson would be able to work with the best experimental physicist in the U.K., Cecil Powell. At Birmingham he would get to work with one of the best theoretical physicists in the U.K., Rudolf Peierls. And at Cambridge he would get, well, the best architecture in the U.K.[29]

Oppie, trying to be as cheerful as possible, argued that it would be good to get out and spend time in Europe—seeing what physics was like over there as he himself had done as a younger man—as if Dyson were an American and not a European. And in a sense he was right. Dyson had become American. Oppie hinted, moreover, that Dyson would be welcome back to Princeton on some partial basis, splitting his time among several institutions. For the next five years Dyson could come and go at the Institute as he liked. Only one other foreign scientist had been granted such carte blanche: Niels Bohr.[30]

Dyson would miss being so close to the action. He had thought of taking a job at the University of Toronto. At least there he would be on the same continent as Bethe and Feynman. But that didn't happen. Furthermore, Dyson had another reason to be sad.

DYSON IN LOVE

Freeman Dyson and his pretty Institute colleague Cécile Morette had gone out to social events together. No, they were not dating. At least in Dyson's mind he was sure on this score.[31] On one outing they had gone to Manhattan to shop for some presents Dyson wanted to send his family in Britain. At the end of this long day, Cécile was puzzled and even put out. She had helped Freeman but not gotten even a cup of tea out of it. What kind of gentleman was he?[32]

Dyson had little experience with females, certainly not at the all-boy schools where he'd spent so many years. "Winchester has a homosexual culture and is famous for producing homosexuals," said Dyson. "In Winchester you formed these intense emotional ties which are not quite homosexual, but platonic homosexual. . . . I was not sure at that point whether I was a homosexual." He was relieved, later at Cambridge while hanging out with his popular friend Oscar Hahn, to find himself smitten by a girl. He was greatly relieved by this feeling, which he regarded as a kind of discovery.[33]

His year at Cornell seemed to have been all physics, all the time. But his thoughts about the opposite sex had not vanished. In fact, he envied his married friends. He looked forward to marriage.[34]

A year later, as he was ready to leave again, this time from Princeton to Birmingham, Cécile invited him to a picnic. There he met another Institute scholar. He'd seen her before, knew that she was smart, and now he had a chance to speak to her. A week later he chivalrously accompanied her to traffic court—a matter relating to her having run a stop sign—since he felt she shouldn't have to go alone.

Verena Huber had traveled more widely even than Dyson. She was born on May 6, 1923, in Naples, Italy, where her father worked as a businessman. She grew up in Athens, Greece, where her father had taken up a post at the International Red Cross. In 1942, at the age of nineteen, she married mathematician Hans Haefeli, four years her senior. Three years later she was the mother of a daughter. The little girl was named Katarina for Catherine the Great, whose biography Verena had been reading.

The young mother earned a Ph.D. in mathematics from the University of Zurich, and then she, Hans, and Katarina embarked for America in January 1948. Verena felt that the marriage was not working out, and by an amicable arrangement, the couple divorced; Hans went to Harvard for a fellowship, while Verena moved temporarily to Urbana, Illinois, taking Katarina with her.

Verena soon secured a new research spot, at the Institute for Advanced Study, but arrived too late in the fall of 1948 to receive much financial support. Freeman Dyson's first impression of her was that she was glamorous and brilliant. Her first impression of him? She was intrigued that he possessed enough detachment to be able to fall asleep on the leather couches of the Institute's common room and to remain asleep even amid the dozens of people around him having their afternoon tea.

This was an exhilarating moment for Dyson. The rigors of Winchester College and the coming of world war meant that he'd never really been a teenager. Now he had the chance. A hectic ride in Verena's car was for him living on the wild side.[35]

Shortly thereafter, while Verena was preparing dinner one evening and with Katarina playing out front on the lawn, the little girl came inside. "Look who I am bringing you for tea," she said, pulling Freeman into the room. And since the dinner then under preparation wasn't fancy enough for guests, that's all he got—tea. He was offered something stronger to drink but declined.

A few nights later, Freeman was over again and an awkward conversation took place. Freeman's mother was getting on in age, he said, and desired to have grandchildren while she could still enjoy them. "Well," asked Verena, "do you have any suitable girl in mind?" His one-word reply, "You," took her by surprise. She suspected that he might have been relieved when she quickly declined his preposterous offer. Her actual words were more tactful. They hardly knew each other. They'd just met. Besides, she was already having a pleasant romance with another Institute physicist, Abraham Pais.[36]

The academic year was running to a close. Verena secured a job at nearby Goucher College outside Baltimore and would be spending the summer in California. Freeman, with a job waiting in Britain, sailed for Europe in July. While he crossed the ocean east, she drove her Dodge west in the company of Cécile and Katrina. In several cities they passed along the way, in the main post office, under the address of general delivery, was a letter from the persistent and punctilious Englishman.[37]

5. Recessional

Dyson as Professor

(1949–1953)

Freeman Dyson was arguably the most in demand physicist in the world. Not the most famous: Albert Einstein and Niels Bohr were still alive. Nor had he outdone Richard Feynman in creativity, pulling new physics ideas out of airy nothingness. But if you wanted to know the new quantum rules of the road, if you wanted to manipulate the new diagrams, then Dyson was the guy you invited to give the departmental seminar. His papers in *Physical Review* were the ones you had to read. Hans Bethe, commending Dyson for yet another fellowship, called Dyson the best English theoretical physicist since Paul Dirac.[1]

BIRMINGHAM

Dyson had returned to Europe for a victory lap. His mission, as he referred to it in self-mocking terms in a letter to his parents, was "to teach these backward Europeans some physics."[2] In September 1949 he attended meetings in Basle and at Lake Como, where he was an object of curiosity, even among the now middle-aged wunderkinder of quantum mechanics. Wolfgang Pauli, a little gruff at first, showed friendly interest. Werner Heisenberg solicited Dyson's opinion on several topics.

Just as the British Empire in Victorian times had spread across the globe, so Dyson's handiwork was making landfall everywhere. Dyson had talked up his QED methods to his Princeton colleagues, who, as they accepted permanent jobs elsewhere, transmitted Dyson's approach. During the five-year period 1949–1954, 80 percent of the *Physical Review* papers devoted to the diagrams originated with people who had been at the Institute for Advanced Study.[3] The QED diagrams were spreading like an epidemic.[4] Even Gregor Wentzel, the man whose textbook had taught Dyson about field theory in the first place, was now at the University of Chicago and was using Dyson's articles from *Physical Review*.

In Britain, Dyson's new boss, Rudolf Peierls at the University of Birmingham, wanted to learn more about QED and how to wield those doodley diagrams. The man who had coached Dyson through Wentzel's book, Nicholas Kemmer at Cambridge, also employed using Dyson's papers. Physicists in Japan, home to Shin'ichiro Tomonaga, were avidly pursuing the papers.[5] The same was true for scientists in the Soviet Union.[6]

Like Feynman, Dyson allowed himself to believe or at least to hope that quantum electrodynamics was just the starting point for a more comprehensive theoretical description of nature. Here is maximum Dyson, at the high-water mark of his ambition: "We have the key to the universe. Quantum electrodynamics works and does everything you wanted it to do. We understand how to calculate everything concerned with electrons and photons. Now all that remains is merely to apply the same methods to understand weak interactions, to understand gravitation and to understand nuclear forces."[7]

This was Dyson trying to encompass the universe within a single theory. Things were of course going to be more complicated than that. There would be no "merely" about applying the methods of QED to explain the rest of physics.

Dyson the bachelor moved into Peierls's home and took many of his meals there. Peierls's children remember Dyson as being fastidious. He seemingly examined every single pea before eating it.[8] Peierls was another of those friendly father figures who helped Dyson through the early phases of his career. Like Hans Bethe, Peierls was an expert in a number of physics areas, especially nuclear physics, and had been a notable contributor to the development of the atomic bomb. He accurately calculated the critical mass of uranium needed for detonation. Niels Bohr's earlier, larger, and incorrect estimate of the critical mass had made it seem unlikely that a bomb could be built at all. Peierls's estimate of a much lower amount, by contrast, reassured researchers—if reassurance is the right word for such a thing—that making a bomb was feasible after all.

Peierls and Bethe had both obtained Ph.D.'s at the University of Munich in the late 1920s and were friends and correspondents for over sixty years. Not only did letters travel between the two men and their respective universities, Cornell and Birmingham, but also people. Dyson was one of a parade of students or postdoctoral fellows who went in one direction or the other. Some of the other prominent physicists included James Langer, Richard Dalitz, Elliott Lieb, Edwin Salpeter, Nina Byers, and Gerry Brown.

Peierls's wife, Genia, was also kindly toward their scientist boarders. A few years before, another young physicist, Klaus Fuchs, had roomed at the Peierls home and had taken dinner at this same table. Fuchs still came by for a visit now and then. He was a German by birth but had gone off to do wartime nuclear bomb work for the Allies. With Peierls's recommendation, Fuchs had been invited to do sensitive research at Los Alamos, the very epicenter of secret nuclear research. On these postwar visits to the Peierls home, Fuchs liked to play with the children. Dyson met him and thought him a fine fellow.

It came as a great shock when in February 1950 Fuchs was arrested and later convicted of espionage for having passed Los Alamos secrets to the Soviets.[9] Rudolf Peierls felt betrayed. It was he who had brought Fuchs into the bomb's inner circle. Fuchs was not only a spy but *the* atomic spy. Genia Peierls, so trusting, was even more devastated than her husband.[10]

Being back in Britain meant that Dyson saw more of his parents. And while he missed them when he was away in the United States, he found that he quarreled with them when he was in England. Verena was a point of contention. Couldn't he choose another girl?[11]

ANN ARBOR

Dyson liked Peierls and liked bringing the gospel of electrodynamics to Europe. But he longed to return to the western side of the Atlantic. That's where the interesting physics was taking place, and that's where Verena was. He and she had been keeping up a correspondence for the year Freeman was away. Under the terms of his fellowship at Birmingham he would be allowed to come back to the United States for the summer of 1950.

He would circle back to the same summer school in Ann Arbor where he himself had been a student only two years before. But now he'd be there as a teacher. Couldn't Verena find a way also of coming to Michigan?

Freeman was inwardly following a policy of never allowing himself to be attracted to a woman if he wasn't prepared to marry her.[12]

Let's consider the consequences of this extraordinary injunction. A young man who fills most of his hours with differential equations, who gets the highest scores and wins the best prizes at the top schools, who has carefully cultivated a regimen in which all thoughts are bent toward science—what does he see when he looks up from the page in the presence of a pretty woman? He sees nothing. Or rather he has disciplined himself against this particular force of attraction.

Or maybe now when he gazed at Verena things were different. Having won a deserved breathing space after this quantum labors and triumphant publications in *Physical Review,* he allowed himself an extra helping of human feeling. Under these circumstances the pursuit of the lady became as ardent as the pursuit of the Lamb shift had been. In his letters to Verena, however, Freeman had tactfully not renewed his proposal of marriage. Instead he merely pined.

Actually, Freeman's gaze had settled on other women, at least a little bit, during the previous year. Freeman wanted Verena to know about Hilde Jacob, the girl he'd met in Germany the summer of 1947. It's true she didn't mean that much to him, he said, but he had sort of promised Hilde that he and she would take a hiking tour of Switzerland together. This was confusing enough for Verena—did he love her or this German girl?—but now Freeman was asking Verena's help in arranging this hike. Freeman was hoping that Verena's sister, Heidy, who lived in Geneva, could suggest an itinerary. Freeman made clear that he and Hilde would always room separately.[13]

Now in 1950, Freeman returned to New York by ship and rushed down to Verena in Baltimore. Together with Katarina they drove up to Michigan. Freeman would teach QED at the summer school and Verena would audit a course taught by a former Zurich colleague. Freeman lived in a dormitory, Verena and Katarina in a small apartment. Although they would see each other many evenings, letters back and forth continued even though now there was no ocean between them.

Or maybe there was. Verena wanted Freeman to know something important. A few years earlier she had met a man in Europe who proved to be, so she said, the great love of her life. She loved this other man with such deep feeling that she felt that he would always be at the core of her life. He was much older than she, and there was no question of marrying him. He, not her former husband, Hans Haefeli, was Katarina's father. Hans, informed of all this, had been very understanding; he was willing to go on living with Verena and Katarina. It was Verena who thought that things would be better for Hans if he and she divorced, and he had accepted this judgment.

Now it was Freeman's turn to be unreasonably understanding. How could he accept such an arrangement? He accommodated the notion that Verena would forever keep an emotional corner of herself in reserve for this other man. Freeman wondered why his colleague at the Institute, Abraham Pais, had not proposed marriage to Verena. It turns out that Pais was not so accepting of Verena's previous love. *"Der alter Mann muss vergessen werden,"* Pais had said using the German phrase, meaning that the old man must be forgotten when the new man arrived.[14] This Verena could not do, so Pais and she had parted.

Freeman was attracted to Verena and so, by his particular rules of engagement, marriage was his official aim. His suit was renewed. The mating dance moved to its next level.

Sexual attraction is naturally a vital force in the lives of women and men. The interaction between two people is more complicated than the interaction between two electrons. Instead of a swarm of virtual photons being exchanged at the microscopic level, the attraction (or its opposite, revulsion) between humans is expressed in waves of emotions sent flying through the nervous system. Surges of hormones launch themselves into the body's biochemical environment. General attraction begins in adolescence as a ticklish curiosity and then proceeds to an active abiding interest in the other person. But be careful. The first foray into actual sexual practice, when it finally comes, can be a confusing mixture of exhilaration and dismay.

So it was for Freeman. After several tentative sessions with Verena, success, of a sort, was finally achieved. When he showed his face again the next day at Verena's apartment, he voiced his ambivalence. According to Verena, Freeman admitted to feeling cheap. On another day he went so far as to say that she, the more experienced one, had made him feel cheap.[15] Maybe they shouldn't have rushed into doing this thing. How was she supposed to feel at the sound of this, especially when Freeman's formal proposal of marriage remained in force?

Freeman had accepted Verena's extenuation—the existence of the older man in Europe. Would he also accommodate himself to her need for privacy and her need to continue mathematical research? And for her part, could she accept him as he was, the cerebral scientist absorbed in his work? She wasn't sure she loved him. He was not so much shy as he was socially awkward. He was too stiff and trapped in his own ways, she thought, too legalistic, too economical. Should she marry Freeman? Katarina deserved a more stable home and badly needed a father.

Freeman pressed his case. His mind was made up. They simply must get married. And on August 11, 1950, they were. On this day Freeman Dyson, aged twenty-six, son of Sir George and Lady Dyson of 40 Albert Hall Mansions, London SW7, England, and Verena Haefeli-Huber, aged twenty-seven, daughter of the late Charles and Berthy Huber of Zurich, Switzerland, were married in Ann Arbor.[16] The ceremony was conducted by a justice of the peace before only a few witnesses. Freeman had bought two bottles of wine and then didn't bring them out.[17] Leaving Katarina with some friends, groom and bride went on a two-day honeymoon in northern Michigan.

Taking advantage of Robert Oppenheimer's open invitation to stop over at the Institute whenever he wanted and Rudolf Peierls's liberal leave policy at Birmingham, Freeman and his family spent the fall of 1950 in Princeton, with Verena continuing to teach at Goucher College near Baltimore.

Freeman, eager to get married, was no less eager to become a father. So after only five weeks of marriage and with no palpable signs of pregnancy, Verena was dispatched to an obstetrician, not one in Princeton but in New York City. Nothing was happening, the doctor said, and sent her home. Verena spent a few hours in the Museum of Modern Art before getting in her car and driving back across New Jersey to Princeton. A month after that she was pregnant.[18]

Shortly after Christmas they went to Britain by ship. In London Verena met Sir George and Lady Dyson, who previously had not been particularly keen on their son marrying this woman. Then the new Dyson family took up residence in Birmingham. That winter Verena came down with pneumonia. Katarina was also ill a lot, and in general England's dreariness drained their morale. The newlyweds concluded that this could not be their final home.

Dyson liked his Birmingham mentor. Like Dyson himself, Peierls was interested in a wide spectrum of physics problems. Paraphrasing a common sentiment, Peierls said that a specialist is a "person who learns more and more about less and less until he knows everything about nothing," while a generalist "learns less and less about more and more until he knows nothing about everything."[19] Both men tended toward being generalists, although no one would say that Dyson and Peierls knew nothing about everything.

Despite his affection for Peierls, Dyson decided to leave Britain. He wanted to return to where the physics action was, in the United States. The chance for doing this had already arisen months before. When Richard Feynman announced that he would be leaving Cornell for a new post at the California Institute of Technology, Hans Bethe obtained permission to extend a faculty offer to Dyson. Only Dyson, Bethe argued, could fill the vacuum left by Feynman. With the understanding that Dyson had to wait out the two-year period before he could occupy a permanent post outside Britain, he accepted Cornell's offer. Starting in the fall of 1951 he would return to Cornell as a professor.

Meanwhile, what was Dyson's status at the University of Birmingham? He wasn't quite a professor, although he was teaching classes. He certainly was not a student, although he was eligible for a doctorate, which he still lacked. But you can't give such a famous person a mere Ph.D. His accomplishments far outweighed any dissertation he could have written. His several papers in *Physical Review* already exceeded in impact the lifetime work of most physicists.

They had a degree for people like that: doctor of science. But here too he was to be thwarted by having fallen afoul of residency rules. You had to have been physically at the university for a period of two years. And what with his summer in Ann Arbor and his semester at Princeton, Dyson had been *of*, but not entirely *at*, the University of Birmingham. Consequently, no degree. Sorry, no exceptions allowed. A year later he was a made a fellow of the Royal Society, at the age of twenty-eight. He was destined to receive two dozen honorary doctorates but never one of the ordinary kind. He was to remain Mr.

ZURICH

Dyson was uncommonly creative in choosing his summer retreats, especially when closing one chapter in his life and opening another. His farewell to Birmingham and his return to Cornell would in this case be marked by a three-month side trip to Zurich in 1951.

Here he worked with the pugnacious Wolfgang Pauli. One of the original boy physicists, Pauli had helped found quantum science in the 1920s. Among other ideas, he had contributed the notion that particles such as electrons and protons possessed a quality called "spin." A particle with spin might not be literally twirling around, but you could imagine that they were twirling and this made them act as if they were little magnets. Through his self-appointed role as inspirer of good ideas or tormentor of scientists with bad ideas, Pauli helped cultivate fresh thinking. He enjoyed sitting in the front row of many a seminar, where he could skewer a speaker who, in Pauli's opinion, was delivering half-baked opinions. His most notable insult: "That idea is so bad it's not even wrong."

That summer Pauli was alone, except for Dyson. The two of them took long walks into the hills and valleys and around town, stopping at coffee shops, eating ice cream.[20] Pauli was in a cheerful mood, Dyson a somewhat dreary mood. Why? Because his momentum was stalling.

Dyson and the other scientists who had developed QED to tame the infinity lurking inside atoms had done what scientists often do—broken the problem down into smaller parts and then reassembled them into a compact solution. The "parts," in this case, correspond to the various levels of complexity (each illustrated by its own Feynman picture) in that blizzard of virtual particles near each electron. It had been Dyson's distinction to show that each part, by itself, added a sensible (non-infinite) amount to the electron's properties. But was the whole sum sensible or infinitely large?

It sounds strange to say that quantum scientists were no longer particularly bothered by the idea of possible infinities. Now that they knew how infinity arose they could neutralize it by redefining the mass and charge of the electron.

For Dyson this wasn't enough. As you reassembled more and more parts of the interaction he wanted the sum to converge to a finite number, not diverge to infinity. Dyson was pretty sure that the sum converged, but he had to prove it. We might call this hunch "Dyson's conjecture," perhaps the most important of many mathematical conjectures in his career, and he now gave it his fullest attention.

He wanted the theory not merely to be useful but to be elegant, to be consistent, and this meant convergence. Aesthetics was an issue here. In this, he was more mathematician than physicist, maybe even an artist. He was the true student of G. H. Hardy, who had said that mathematics was a kind of art.

Pauli felt that the convergence effort would fail. But Dyson kept on. What if he fell short of proof as he had done during his brief career as a mathematician? Would he leave physics? More work and more mountain walks with Pauli failed to deliver perfection. His recent efforts, published in a series of papers, had won few allies to the cause. This wasn't at all like the *Physical Review* papers of 1949, the publications that had won him acclaim and an armful of job offers. Feynman and Schwinger, Dyson ruefully noted, had not attempted a convergence proof. They had gotten out of the QED business when they were ahead.[21]

Even Dyson could see it now. Pauli had been right; convergence could not be proved. Indeed, he recognized that the grand sum actually diverged. This finding itself had to be declared in the form of a scientific paper.[22] Dyson's un-epiphany came to him on one of those walks into the hills outside Zurich, this time without Pauli. It was time to change course. Dyson had indeed fallen short, but he would not go so far as to leave physics. His frustration at not bringing closure to the subject of quantum electrodynamics did make him resolve, however, never again to commit himself with such intellectual force to a single research topic. His dogged pursuit of infinity had led him, this time anyway, into a wilderness. He had explored with great energy and courage and persistence, only to see the trail go cold or, as he put it, "see the river dwindle and disappear into the sand."[23] It was over, and in a way it was a relief. He didn't have to go further.[24]

He had spent four years, from the start of his student studies with Bethe (1947) up to this summer with Pauli (1951), on this issue of QED. According to Dyson's friend Silvan Schweber, a physicist who would later write a comprehensive history of QED, Dyson arrived at a decision: "Thereafter he never invested the same amount of energy and commitment into any fundamental physics program."[25]

It's as if Dyson were an imperial power that finding itself overextended in distant colonies, began a sad, slow withdrawal from its unsustainable position. The chief promoter, if not originator, of QED, Dyson would now intellectually draw back his unachievable ambition of making QED converge. His retreat was a like a miniature version of the rollback of the British Empire depicted in Rudyard Kipling's poem "Recessional," a word usually referring to the trim ceremony marking the end of a church service as the congregants exit from the space:

Far-called, our navies melt away—
  On dune and headland sinks the fire—
Lo, all our pomp of yesterday
  Is one with Nineveh and Tyre!

That is not to say that Dyson's work was a failure. Far from it. Let's break chronological order and leap forward fifty years and see how well QED is performing. During this span of time experimental and theoretical techniques both have improved dramatically. By the year 2006 the measured and predicted values of the electron's magnetic moment agreed at the level of better than one part per trillion. What does that mean? Well, it means that theorists at their blackboards, or now at their computers, can compute the strength of the electron's magnetism with terrific specificity. Then an experimenter, with no less finesse, actually measures the electron's magnetism. Then the two numbers are compared. They differ only after many decimal places.

This is the current state of the art—or we should say state of the science—of human ingenuity in explaining nature, at least in terms of preponderance of numerical expressiveness. The agreement of these two numbers out to so many decimals doesn't necessarily signify perfect wisdom, much less "truth," but it does signify high knowledge. And it doesn't matter whether the predictions or measurements are performed in Tokyo or Cambridge or Jakarta. In a letter from Dyson congratulating the experimenters on those QED measurements in 2006, Dyson expressed his pleased surprise:

> *We thought of QED in 1949 as a jerry-built structure. We didn't expect it to last more than 10 years before a more solidly built theory replaced it. But the ramshackle structure still stands. The revealing discrepancies we hoped for have not yet appeared. I'm amazed at how precisely Nature dances to the tune we scribbled so carelessly 57 years ago, and at how the experimenters and theorists can measure and calculate her dance to a part in a trillion.*[26]

HIEROGLYPHICS

A perfection of sorts *was* achieved on July 14, 1951, when Mrs. and Mr. Dyson became the parents of a baby daughter, Esther. Freeman's parents—his mother now, finally, a grandmother—came over from London for the christening ceremony. Owing to legal complications in the jurisdiction of Zurich, the newborn Swiss miss did not immediately qualify for citizenship. Verena, born in Italy and raised in Greece, did have a Swiss passport because of her parents' nationality. But Verena's citizenship was now trumped by her marriage to Freeman, a British citizen just then about to relocate back to the United States. To make matters worse, Verena's divorce from Hans Haefeli was not being recognized. Officially lovely little Esther was a bastard.

This became a problem two months later. Freeman had left for America in order to obtain accommodations for the family in Ithaca. Meanwhile, Verena, Katarina, baby Esther, and a nurse boarded a train from Zurich for Genoa, intending to catch a ship there to the United States. At the Swiss-Italian border, however, Esther's lack of papers snagged their movement. The train, with Katarina and the nurse aboard, continued into Italy, while Verena and the infant remained at the border guard station.

Several phone calls and levied fees later, mother and daughter were allowed to proceed. With only a few hours to spare Verena arrived in Genoa for the sailing. They crossed the ocean and arrived safely in Ithaca. The Dyson family goods were not so lucky. A strike by dockworkers in New York meant that the luggage on the ship was sent back to Italy. For the first months of their life at Cornell, the Dysons ate from borrowed plates.[27]

Eventually the dishes caught up with them, and their home was complete. In the fall of 1951 Freeman was a professor, Verena a math instructor, Katarina (now six) enrolled in school, and Esther was getting teeth.

Continuing the habit established long before by Hans Bethe, students and professors lunched together, crossing the street from the Nuclear Institute to the Home Economics cafeteria. The Journal Club, meeting every Friday at 3:30, would examine the contents of recent physics articles or scrutinize an article written by some nervous student who would then have to account for his work. Bethe, Robert Wilson, and Philip Morrison gave parties to which professors and students were invited. The Dysons would often appear.

Freeman was not just back in Ithaca, but welcomed and needed. He inherited a franchise at Cornell University. The academic course on quantum science, formerly in the hands of Hans Bethe and Richard

Feynman, would now be taught by Freeman Dyson. The lucky Cornell students now received the freshest tutelage from the most in demand expositor of quantum reality. Two precocious undergraduates showed up for this course meant for graduate students. Steven Weinberg and Sheldon Glashow would both win the Nobel Prize decades later for helping link QED with a description of the weak nuclear force. But Dyson's course was a bit too advanced for them and so they stopped coming.[28]

Dyson was a good teacher. He really wanted his students to understand. Notes from his lectures were gathered into the form of a rudimentary textbook on quantum science, which quickly circulated around to other physics departments. The notes, along with the twin 1949 papers in *Physical Review,* constituted a QED Bible.[29] One book company, Wiley, offered to publish it as a textbook, but Dyson didn't follow through until decades later.[30]

Accounts of Dyson as a scholar and as a man often stress his generosity, his good manners, his desire to explain. Despite his correct clothing, nearly always including a necktie, he did not conform to the stereotype of the reserved Englishman. He did not stand on ceremony. One graduate student, emigrating from India and arriving at the Ithaca train station, was stunned to find Professor Dyson, the famous physicist, waiting for him.[31] The student must have been thinking of the classic German model of the imposing *Herr Professor.* Dyson wasn't this.

He was not a typical scientist either in being content to write up his results and sending them off to the technical journal for fellow experts to appreciate. His first chance to reach a wider audience came with an article about QED in the pages of *Physics Today* magazine. He began with an inscription drawn from a letter written in 1857 by the non-mathematical Michael Faraday to the very mathematical James Clerk Maxwell:

> *There is one thing I would be glad to ask you. When a mathematician engaged in investigating physical actions and results has arrived at his conclusions, may they not be expressed in common language as fully, clearly, and definitely as in mathematical formulae? If so, would it not be a great boon to such as I to express them so?— translating them out of their hieroglyphics, that we might also work upon them by experiment.[32]*

In his own article Dyson took Faraday's advice. He converted hiero-glyphics into prose. He proudly declared QED to be "the only part of our science which has been completely reduced to a set of precise equations. It is the only field in which we could choose a hypothetical experiment and predict the result to five places of decimals." That didn't mean science was done. Physics is not the whole of science. QED isn't the whole of physics. It describes only things governed by the electromagnetic force. Other precincts of the universe came under the influence of other forces, such as the nuclear force and gravity.

We have seen how Dyson, striving to crystallize his ideas about electrons and light, compared his work as a scientist to a novelist creating stories and characters. Others have felt this way too. The mathematician and writer Jacob Bronowski argued that science and art were equally creative. Both required imagination. Playful activity was a large part of being an artist or a scientist.

As for the appreciation of art and science, things were not as equal. Reading a poem, Bronowski said, involved the reader in an active process of appraisal. Beauty, manifested in art, is in the eye of the beholder. You have partially to create, or at least re-create, the poem for yourself in the act of reading, in order to derive the greatest pleasure. This isn't as easy to do with physics. Physics is not as readily in the eye of the unprepared beholder. Bronowski felt that if people find science dull, it's because they find it difficult to participate in the creative side of science.[33]

Dyson began to do his part to mitigate the apparently nonparticipatory veneer of science. He sought to expand the circumference of appreciation for science. He wrote a succession of articles for *Scientific American*, a magazine with a large popular readership.[34] The articles reported the latest findings from the shifting forefront of physics research in the 1950s and early 1960s. All that training in Latin rhetoric at Winchester, all those schoolboy essays demanded at a weekly clip, all the poems he encountered in chemistry class (of all places) now paid off. His writing was quotable: "A physicist builds theories with mathematical materials because the mathematics enables him to imagine more than he can clearly think."[35] His *Scientific American* pieces sparkled with analogies and historical comparisons. They showed how scientists, like explorers of coasts and forests, were bringing more territory onto their maps.

NUCLEAR INFINITY

The territory he himself explored now was the atomic nucleus. Nucleus: the name proclaims centeredness. Even though the nucleus is 100,000 times smaller than the atom in which it sits, it accounts for a vast majority of the atom's mass. More importantly, the forces operating at the nucleus are a million times stronger than those governing the rest of the atom.

At this time, in the early 1950s, physicists thought that just as photons carried the electromagnetic force among electrons flying around the atom, so the strong nuclear force would be carried among the inhabitants of the nucleus, protons and neutrons, by particles called mesons. Experiments were then beginning to measure how protons and mesons interacted. These nuclear tests weren't as precise as the earlier atomic tests (like the Lamb shift) that probed the interaction between electrons and photons, but they were giving theorists like Dyson some "truth" to aim at.

Was it possible to contrive an explanation for the nuclear force analogous to QED, one that portrayed the nuclear force as the sum of a series of terms, representing ever more complicated scenarios of particle interactions? This time the process of dividing up a complicated process into smaller parts wasn't going to be easy. At least with QED the successive terms were smaller and smaller since the electromagnetic force was relatively weak. By comparison, the main nuclear force is more potent, and the successive terms did not shrink down to nothing; instead they remained sizable.

Here was another potential infinity. If Dyson wasn't careful, his equations would yield nonsense predictions for nuclear activities just as, twenty years before, quantum science had yielded nonsense predictions for atomic activities.

Dyson's new conjecture was that he could accurately calculate nuclear properties by segregating the parts of the problem corresponding to the high-energy interactions and low-energy interactions among the nucleons and mesons, and deal with them separately. Then he would tame these collections of terms, or at least sweep them under a carpet somehow. Moreover, Dyson suspected that gravity might play a role in making this theory work.

As a new graduate student in the fall of 1947 Dyson had cleverly worked out a form of the electromagnetic force that could predict a value for the Lamb shift that matched the value actually measured in experiments. Now he wanted to do the same sort of thing with the strong force. Dyson and his students compared their calculated numbers with the early nucleon-meson scattering experiments being conducted by Enrico Fermi at the University of Chicago, and found an intriguing similarity. Had Dyson succeeded in creating a model for the nucleus?

In trying to settle the QED business two years before, he had consulted with Wolfgang Pauli. Now he would take his nuclear conjecture to another master. He decided to go to Chicago and confer with Fermi in person. Fermi, one of the few scientists renowned for both experimental and theoretical work, would be in a good position to judge Dyson's progress.

In April 1953 Dyson made another of his lengthy travels on a Greyhound bus, this time from Ithaca to Chicago. A month before, Dyson's son, George, had been born. So the first thing Fermi did when Dyson arrived was to ask him to sit. How was the baby?

Then they got to the point. Dyson made his case and Fermi rendered his verdict. A good theory, Fermi said, had to be built either on a clear physical picture of what was going on at the microscopic level or on a structure of rigorous mathematics. Dyson's theory, Fermi declared, had neither clarity nor rigor. The tentative agreement between Fermi's data and Dyson's theory was only accidental, he argued.[36]

Dyson, who prided himself on his rigorous mathematics, was crestfallen. He had defended his explanation of the electron-photon interaction against a skeptical Oppenheimer and had prevailed. This time things were different. Dyson knew not to dispute Fermi's dismissal of the proton-meson explanation. Fermi was right. Dyson's model was feeble.

His personal recessional continued. Dyson retreated to Ithaca. This defeat, coming on top of his earlier problems with proving the consistency of QED, was a heavy blow. When he failed to finish QED, his folly (if it can be called that) affected only himself, since he had been doing the work by himself. But now he was a professor, with graduate students to guide. He had persisted with theoretical nuclear research that was leading nowhere, and he had led others with him into this blind alley. Trying to find consolation in his dreary sojourn in Chicago, Dyson could say that at least Fermi had saved him and his students even more years of wasted effort. What this new round of fruitless work had shown him, however, was that he was not really a particle physicist at all.[37]

BERKELEY

For some time Dyson had been frustrated by academic life. He enjoyed teaching, but the graduate study framework, in which a senior scientist oversees the years-long research of a student working toward a doctorate, was for Dyson too constraining. It committed him to a particular research direction, whereas by nature he wanted to try new ideas as the fancy struck him, and he had been around long enough to see that his fancy changed often. Richard Feynman, who disliked ceremony and pedigrees, agreed. He envied Dyson his lack of a Ph.D.[38]

Even before the sobering trip to Chicago, Dyson had resolved to alter his circumstances. In December 1952 he discreetly contacted Robert Oppenheimer and asked if the liberal visiting arrangement with the Institute for Advanced Study could be turned into something more lasting. Since his days in Bomber Command, Dyson hadn't worked in one place for more than a year or so. He wanted to establish himself and not have to move around so much. Oppie readily responded with the offer of a permanent faculty position. In his position as Institute director he had sent many such offers, he said, but none had given him such so much pleasure as this one.[39] The starting salary would be $12,500, a pretty good salary by university standards.

Before moving to Princeton, Dyson and his family crossed the continent to Berkeley. For three months they lived on the edge of the West Coast in a rented house in the Berkeley Hills on Buena Vista Way, a street name that encapsulated the gorgeous view of San Francisco Bay. Dyson appreciated lovely views. From this perch he could think about what he wanted to do with the rest of his life.

Previously he had studied the inner workings of atoms and then the inner workings of nuclei. He had turned his hand to writing popular articles. Now he would try to encompass another part of the world, namely the interactions among atoms, trillions and trillions of atoms at a time locked within a solid material. The branch of science devoted to this inquiry is called condensed matter physics. Collaborating with University of California professor Charles Kittel, Dyson reveled in the work of drawing up explanations of how the atoms tangle with each other. This work wasn't as fundamental as QED had been, but it was just as satisfying. Why? Because it was another occasion for bringing elegant mathematics to bear on a practical problem.[40]

There was no guilt here, no frustration, since no one was expecting him to change the world. He was studying something as commonplace as the jiggling of atoms in a glasslike solid. But even this motion was difficult to understand. Dyson had not moved into the study of condensed matter because the problems were easier. Once again he resorted to the trick of transforming a complicated problem into something simpler. He pretended that the solid consisted of a one-dimensional string of interacting atoms, like birds sitting on a telephone line. Working in one dimension instead of three made the mathematics much simpler. True, a one-dimensional solution can't fully explain a three-dimensional problem. But a retreat in dimensionality just might provide some clues about how to address the fuller reality.

As so often happens, one scientist will have a brilliant idea that is later carried to fruition by someone else. In this case Dyson's mathematical work from that summer of 1953 was streamlined and generalized by a physicist named Helmut Schmidt.[41] There is to this day an equation, the Dyson-Schmidt equation, which describes one-dimensional "solids."

Dyson's summer in Berkeley was therapeutic. Years later, at the height of the hallucinogenic 1960s, when Dyson was reviewing a book about one-dimensional physics, he extolled the virtues of making strategic simplifications:

> *A man grows stale if he works all the time on insoluble problems, and a trip to the beautiful world of one dimension will refresh his imagination better than a dose of LSD.*[42]

6. Nuclear Opera

Dyson and the Cold War

(1954–1956)

The detonation proceeds. Seeing the manicured lawn and the ivy-covered halls, you wouldn't have guessed that an unprecedented device, bristling with wires and vacuum tubes, is shuttling through a phased escalation of violence. Right there at the Institute for Advanced Study, in a building off by itself through the woods, a bomb explodes. Not just any bomb, but a hydrogen bomb. Over microsecond increments internal conditions ratchet toward catastrophe.

Outside the room few know. Above, the sky is not being riven by X-rays. Inside the wood-paneled central hall, looking like a posh gentleman's club, the members are taking their afternoon tea. At the Institute, which even the director, J. Robert Oppenheimer, refers to as an intellectual hotel, the only obligation you incur is to undertake advanced study. Actually you aren't even required to do that. You can stare out the window for nine months if you like. Of course, most that come do more than stare, but they don't have to account for themselves in any way. This is exactly what Freeman Dyson wants.

All are brilliant and arrive highly recommended. Nearly all are thinkers rather than doers. Few did experiments. In fact, the permanent faculty frowns upon the construction of apparatus. This would go against the spirit of the place, which is intellectual efflorescence. And yet here is John von Neumann doing an experiment. Worse, he is exploding a bomb by unleashing a runaway chain reaction. But von Neumann is a senior man, and he has permission to proceed from Oppenheimer himself.

Bombs at Princeton? There was a time when Oppenheimer opposed the development of a hydrogen bomb, but now he was coming around. He had originally felt that the atom bomb, the one he invented in that desert lab during the war, was enough, more than enough, to deter future wars. Now he was seeing things differently. From a physics viewpoint and from a political viewpoint it had started to make sense. He allowed the explosion to proceed.

The bomb at Princeton would implode no building and ultraviolate no bystanders. No mushroom cloud would appear over southwestern New Jersey. Instead, the bomb would explode entirely within von Neumann's computer. Von Neumann, like his friend and compatriot Hungarian Edward Teller, was now an American and ardent anti-Communist. Having promoted the importance of the more destructive hydrogen bomb even as the "smaller" atom bomb was being developed during World War II, Teller had helped finally to contrive a workable design, and von Neumann was carrying out a trial run in the form of a computer simulation.

Von Neumann was brilliant. He made important contributions to quantum physics, mathematics, economics, and game theory. But his two most important achievements were in the development of thermonuclear weaponry that has dominated strategic defense planning for the past sixty years and in the development of one of the first stored-program digital computers.

The Institute's Electronic Computer Project would later go on to perform some of the first ever simulations of weather fronts and of biological evolution. But now on its maiden voyage, for a period of sixty days and nights, executing the largest arithmetical calculation ever performed at the time, von Neumann's room-sized machine was serving as a proxy for an H-bomb blast.[1] The actual test detonation of the bomb would occur a few years later on a remote Pacific island. The sponsors who helped put up money for the computer included RCA (maker of all those vacuum tubes), the army, the navy, and the still young Atomic Energy Commission (AEC).

A potential misnomer is at work here. In both the atomic bomb and the hydrogen bomb the energy of the explosion comes out of the nucleus at the core of atoms, zillions of atoms. In an A-bomb or H-bomb what explodes is not atoms but the nuclei at the hearts of atoms. But Berkeley physicist Richard Muller has pointed out that it is not entirely inappropriate to refer to the bombs developed at Los Alamos and dropped on Hiroshima and Nagasaki as *atom* bombs. All previous bombs in history, Muller argues, were *molecular* bombs. They depended on the unleashing of chemical energy locked up in the bonds of molecules, which are groupings of atoms. Only in the 1945 bombs did this kind of chemical energy *not* play a role. Molecules weren't involved, only atoms—uranium and plutonium atoms. True, only the energy at the center of those atoms, in the nuclei, mattered. But it was energy flying out of atoms and not molecules.[2] In general, for the same weight of fuel, an atomic bomb is a million times more powerful than any molecular bomb.

So what's the difference between an A-bomb and an H-bomb? Both involve the release of pent nuclear energy but are otherwise very different in their methods. The A-bomb explosion occurs when the nuclei of special heavy atoms like uranium break in half. By contrast, the H-bomb explosion occurs when the nuclei of light atoms, specifically the variant forms of hydrogen known as deuterium and tritium, weld together. These two processes are called, respectively, fission and fusion.

The fusion bomb was much more powerful than the fission bomb, but was harder to design. Also, the politics surrounding the two bombs was different. The A-bomb was a child of World War II and was built originally to be dropped on Germany, although the targeting later shifted to Japan. The H-bomb was a child of the Cold War and was thought of as a response to the Communist menace.

Freeman Dyson hadn't been present at the creation of either the H- or A-bombs. In the 1940s he'd been a junior partner in the dropping of conventional molecular bombs on Germany. Now in the early 1950s he was a theoretical physicist. But he too would be drawn into nuclear matters in a big way, first as an observer, later as a participant, and finally as a critic.

NUCLEAR FRISSON

To account for Dyson in the 1940s, the biographer needs to supply a quantum context. Quantum science is what Dyson loved; it's what he did well; it's how he came to distinction. To explain Dyson in the 1950s, the surrounding context is one of nuclearism. This means not only performing theoretical nuclear physics at a chalkboard, but also designing and implementing nuclear things—bombs, reactors, spaceships, and treaties.

In Michael Frayn's play *Copenhagen*, Niels Bohr and Werner Heisenberg meet for a posthumous argument over their wartime behavior and the development of atomic bombs. The most chilling line in the play comes when Bohr, who at this moment in the drama believes, mistakenly, that a nuclear explosion is impossible, says, "I don't think anyone has yet discovered a way you can use theoretical physics to kill people." Interestingly, the same nuclear reactions that kill people when wielded as a weapon can, when deployed in diluted form in a reactor, usefully light up a city with electricity.

Manifestly, the nuclear age, in which we still live, is operatic in scope. It's practically Wagnerian. In the first of Richard Wagner's cycle of operas devoted to the Nordic myths, the evil troll Alberich forges a powerful ring from a critical mass of gold pulled out of the River Rhine. Thereafter this ring is the focus of contention—a sort of strategic weapon—between warring superpowers. Alberich, leader of the underground Niebelung nation, went to war with Wotan, leader of the sky-dwelling gods.

Like the development of the ring by Alberich, the development of nuclear weaponry seemed at first to have conferred absolute power. But this illusion was short lived. Two powerful dynasties, the Soviet and the American, struggled to amass the deeper stockpile of megaton explosiveness. In this feverish competition, perceived internal enemies were just as loathsome as external enemies. In Russia show trials were common; even more common would be quiet arrests and liquidations without any public hearings. In America, the number of executions (such as those of Julius and Ethel Rosenberg) was much smaller but the public investigations were conspicuous. Senator Joseph McCarthy led a crusade of press conference denunciation and floodlit hearings to root out apparent Communist influence wherever it existed, whether in government, at universities, or in the film industry.

Robert Oppenheimer was a tempting target of suspicion, partly because of his prewar leftist leanings and partly because his stewardship of the nation's nuclear program seemed to be less than enthusiastic. The AEC General Advisory Committee, which Oppenheimer chaired, had initially been against the development of an H-bomb, chiefly on the grounds of its over-powerfulness. Oppenheimer was joined in this opinion by a majority of the influential physicists involved, including Enrico Fermi, Isidor Rabi, and Hans Bethe. They felt the much more destructive H-bomb could only be an instrument of genocide and not an effective defensive weapon. One could easily imagine that the use of such an ultimate weapon would ignite the sort of global conflagration portrayed in the concluding opera of Wagner's *Ring* cycle, the aptly named *Götterdämmerung*.

Actually an opera has since been constructed around this nuclear theme. John Adams's 2005 work *Doctor Atomic* is about the 1945 test shot in the New Mexico desert, but it captures the nuclear paranoia that typified the following decades, a tempestuous time when Oppenheimer jousted with powerful rivals over the political use being made of nuclear force.

When in 1949 the Soviet Union tested an A-bomb of its own, H-bomb skeptics on the American side, including Oppenheimer, began to view the H-bomb more favorably, partly because they could see that the Cold War was heading toward a more dangerous phase.[3] Partly Oppenheimer's view of the H-bomb changed because as a scientist, as a bomb designer himself, he could be seduced: "When you see something that is technically sweet you go ahead and do it . . . and you argue about what to do about it only after you had your technical success."[4]

Freeman Dyson had not worked at Los Alamos on the A-bomb, but he came to know many who had, especially those at the top of the organizational pyramid—Oppie, Bethe, and Teller. Moreover, Dyson himself would in coming years be associated with the design and potential use of nuclear devices. He was a frequent commentator in *The Day After Trinity,* a 1981 television documentary about the early nuclear age. He had by then become an opponent of nuclear weaponry, but even he marveled over the lure of bomb research:

> *I have felt it myself. The glitter of nuclear weapons. It is irresistible if you come to them as a scientist. To feel it's there in your hands, to release this energy that fuels the stars, to let it do your bidding. To perform these miracles, to lift a million tons of rock into the sky. It is something that gives people an illusion of illimitable power, and it is, in some ways, responsible for all our troubles.*[5]

Oppenheimer was the prime example of how this Faustian bargain worked. His picture had been on the cover of *Time* magazine. His was the face of big science. He had engineered the explosions that, many believed, led to the Japanese surrender. Following the war, his responsibilities were still great. He continued to help shape America's nuclear policy.

But fortunes can change suddenly. The spirit of the time can swerve. Old resentments can produce fault lines. New personalities come to power. Oppenheimer, long an influencer of events, was himself about to be buffeted.

In the fall of 1953 a portfolio of accusations against him, or at least queries pertaining to his past views and activities, was being prepared by men with grudges. Two Oppenheimer antagonists merit attention. One was Edward Teller, who, even while the A-bomb was being built in Los Alamos, directed his energies toward designing the more powerful H-bomb. He resented Oppenheimer's apparent attempts, during and after the war, to rein in H-bomb development. Teller's tireless advocacy of the thermonuclear weapon won him powerful friends in Congress and elsewhere. By 1953 he had built up a new weapons lab, at Livermore, California, which thereafter competed with the lab in Los Alamos for the design of nuclear devices.

The other opponent was Lewis Strauss. A businessman by profession, Strauss had risen during World War II to a prominent advisory position in government, and had acquired the honorary rank of rear admiral in the Naval Reserve. After the war he became an AEC official, and at an otherwise innocuous hearing in 1949, Oppenheimer had made sarcastic remarks at Strauss's expense. Strauss, a man easily offended, would thereafter look for a chance to revenge himself. As an AEC commissioner and as a close advisor to presidents Harry Truman and Dwight Eisenhower, he had wide latitude to oversee nuclear matters. To Strauss the continued presence and influence of Oppenheimer in shaping policy was offensive.

Strauss's chance came in December 1953. The renewal of Oppenheimer's security clearance should have been a routine matter, but Strauss transformed the process into a tribunal resembling a criminal prosecution. In the spring of 1954 the shrill hunt for Communist influences in American government was reaching its peak intensity. Televised hearings conducted by Senator McCarthy sought red infiltration of the army. In these same weeks, the matter of J. Robert Oppenheimer also came to a crescendo.

Strauss had not discovered any major new revelations against Oppenheimer. Oppie's 1930s leftist affiliations, his admission years before of lying during an interview in order to protect his friend Haakon Chevalier, and his brother Frank's membership in the Communist Party were brought up again. Oppenheimer's wartime boss, General

Leslie Groves, had known all these things and had, for the sake of the war effort, condoned these aspects of Oppenheimer's résumé.

Political climate change had occurred. The Soviet Union was seen as the paramount threat and any leftist sympathies, even if they had long since been modified or rejected, were taken as possibly incriminating. Should America's ultimate defense depend so prominently on the views of a man of leftist sympathies?

Weeks of draining testimony brought into public view Oppenheimer's deeds, his adulteries, his political opinions, and his private thoughts. He admitted to mistakes. Why had he lied during that interview a dozen years before? Because, he admitted, he was an idiot.

Dyson and other scientists were of course watching the proceedings, and like many others they were worried about the implications. Not only could the holding of certain political views lead to being fired from your job—and not just government jobs, but also as teachers, artists, and other occupations—but even holding certain views pertaining to the application of physics to military technology, in this case to doubt the efficacy of H-bombs, could bring accusations of disloyalty.

Robert Oppenheimer, facing the principal crisis of his professional life, was practically incommunicado. One day, Freeman Dyson, down from Princeton to Washington, D.C., delivered Oppenheimer's laundry to a hotel. In the lobby Dyson ran into his friend Hans Bethe, who was fresh from what Bethe would later refer to as the most unpleasant conversation of his life. Bethe had failed to talk Teller out of testifying against Oppenheimer.[6]

In determining this vital question of Oppenheimer's security clearance, nothing would be as decisive as the words of Edward Teller. While not exactly calling Oppenheimer disloyal, Teller made it clear at the hearing that America's nuclear arsenal could be better served:

> *I thoroughly disagreed with him in numerous issues, and his actions, frankly, appeared to me confused and complicated. To this extent, I feel that I would like to see the vital interests of this country in hands which I understood better and therefore trust more.*[7]

Leaving the room, Teller reached out his hand to Oppenheimer and said, "I'm sorry." Oppenheimer took the hand but responded, "After what you've just said I don't know what you mean."

The investigation ruled against Oppenheimer. His security clearance was not renewed. His classified papers, held at the Institute for Advanced Study in a safe protected by guards, were withdrawn. His days as a high-level government advisor were over. This whole episode has entered the political history of science and society, almost on a par with Galileo's seventeenth-century interrogation by the Catholic Church over the holding of heretical views.

Freeman Dyson was not yet a government advisor himself. He had played a peripheral role in the Oppenheimer drama. But he wasn't entirely free from the fallout of the security frenzy. By a cruel stroke of irony, Oppenheimer's arch-nemesis, Lewis Strauss, was also chairman of the Institute's board of directors. In this capacity he now tried to have Oppenheimer fired.

Dyson, who had lived through the melancholy atmosphere of the late 1930s as Europe veered toward war, felt now in 1950s America that something bad might be happening too. He resolved that if Oppenheimer could be fired from his Princeton job for holding certain views, then he, Dyson, would consider returning to Europe. He wasn't sure how far the McCarthyite inquisition would proceed. In his mind at least he kept a suitcase packed and was ready to depart. He made discreet inquiries about a job, and talked to people at Birmingham and at Imperial College in London.[8]

Some physicists lost jobs. David Bohm, Dyson's Princeton friend during his 1947–48 year at the Institute, was suspended by Princeton University when he would not cooperate with the House Committee on Un-American Activities. He left the country. Robert Oppenheimer's brother, Frank, also a physicist, had belonged to the Communist Party in the 1930s, and as a consequence was unable to find a job. Years later he founded the Exploratorium science museum in San Francisco.

Writing about these events later, Freeman Dyson saw tragedy all around. The Bethe-Teller friendship expired. Oppenheimer was in disgrace—McCarthyism's "most prominent victim," said two historians.[9] And Teller was regarded thereafter as a great betrayer. Like the villain in Wagner's opera who treacherously stabs the noble hero Siegfried in the back, Teller was perceived by many scientists as envious and even evil. At a scientific meeting a few months after the hearing, several physicists, including the usually statesmanlike Rabi, refused to shake Teller's hand. This hard attitude persisted for many years.

Fear of nuclear conflict also persisted for as long as the Cold War held sway, but it was particularly intense in the 1950s. What would a nuclear explosion look like? Survivors of the Nagasaki and Hiroshima blasts provide many gripping eyewitness accounts. Works of art, like *Doctor Atomic*, also vividly portrayed the general sense of nuclear dread. In the opera's production on the grand stage of the Metropolitan Opera House, the climax of the story, the nighttime detonation of the "gadget" in the New Mexico desert, comes in the very last moment of the opera. In slow motion, with all the characters leaning in toward the distant explosion, as if to listen in on the revelation of an awful secret, the blast seems to shiver space itself apart and turn darkness into a ball of fire.

A CRACK IN THE MIRROR

The war was over. Not the Cold War; that would go on for decades. But the war over Oppenheimer. His security clearance was revoked and his involvement with government matters ceased. But at least he had not been fired from his post at the Institute. Dyson felt that Oppie, back in Princeton with fewer distractions, was a better director than ever.[10] He met each Tuesday afternoon with senior Institute scientists, and continued with his sharp questioning of seminar speakers.

Freeman Dyson had one of the most prestigious jobs a scientist could have. He was a professor at the Institute for Advanced Study. The most famous residents at the Institute were physicist Albert Einstein and mathematician Kurt Gödel. Dyson never got to know either man. When Dyson came for the 1948–49 academic year, he didn't know enough physics and had been too shy to talk to Einstein.[11] Now, coming to the Institute as a professor, Dyson still generally avoided seeing the man because of Einstein's outmoded views about quantum mechanics.[12]

Dyson also spoke little with Gödel. It was said that Gödel and Einstein only talked with each other. The ideas Gödel introduced were no less important for mathematics than Heisenberg's uncertainty principle had been for physics. Gödel demonstrated that within a formal mathematical system with a finite number of rules some logical propositions existed that could not be proved or disproved by the logical rules of that system. In other words, no finite system of mathematics, no matter how extensive, would ever be satisfactorily complete. This demonstration is now generally called Gödel's incompleteness theorem. And then, like his friend Einstein, Gödel effectively retired from active participation in forefront research. In later years, however, Gödel became interested in cosmology and would occasionally ask Dyson to update him on the latest astronomical observations.[13]

A few years after the H-bomb tests, von Neumann moved over to the AEC, and his computer project became endangered. It was seen by many as an engineering endeavor intruding amid a grove of intellectuals. Dyson was one of those who fought (unsuccessfully) for its survival. Years later he observed that the Institute had thrown away its chance to have been a leader in the birth of two new sciences, weather forecasting and computer science.[14]

Coming to the Institute gave Dyson the intellectual freedom he wanted. Sometimes that meant something in "pure mathematics."[15] Mostly, though, Dyson's mathematical thinking was used in the service of physics.

In the summer of 1955 Freeman flew west while Verena, the children, and Freeman's sister, Alice, drove out, dropping Katarina at a summer camp in Ohio on the way. In Berkeley, Dyson again worked in condensed matter physics. This time he studied how the atoms in a magnet interact with each other. These atoms can themselves be considered as little magnets oriented at various angles. Sometimes the atoms can interact with each other in a collective way, not just with their immediate neighbors, in the form of a traveling magnetic disturbance. Dyson showed how these disturbances, called spin waves, could be described using the mathematical tricks of field theory.

Indeed, Dyson was one of the first to introduce quantum fields, and some of the other techniques he'd used in formulating the equations of quantum electrodynamics, into condensed matter physics.[16] This work was just as much fun to do as QED. Dyson felt that it might just be the most important physics work he ever did.[17]

He'd never entirely given up on QED. In fact in 1954 he spent the whole summer teaching QED at a school, launched by his friend Cécile Morette, perched on a mountain in Les Houches, France. It rained for six weeks. During this time Enrico Fermi and some of the teachers took a hazardous trip to a nearby mountaintop to visit a cosmic ray experiment.[18]

Besides adding to his catalog of physics interests, Dyson continued to cultivate his desire to explain science to the public. For example, his interest in atoms and magnetism grew into a general article about heat, energy, and disorder in Scientific American.[19]

In the mid-1950s the next thing that captured Dyson's attention was the idea of symmetry. Artists love symmetry as an element of design, and so does nature. The balance of bilateral symmetry in architecture—the same number of windows to the left of the door as to the right—tends to be satisfying. In choosing mates, psychologists tell us, we take reassurance from facial symmetry, the left side looking just like the right, as if this outward beauty were a sign of healthfulness within. Plenty of things in nature, such as pinecones, have symmetry. Snowflakes are hexagonally symmetric. Turn them one-sixth of the way around and they look the same. Another sixth, and they are still the same.

Scientists think of symmetry in a more general way to refer to the properties of an object that remain the same even when a certain transformation takes place. For example, when two billiard balls collide, we expect the process to be mirror symmetric: we shouldn't be able to tell whether we're seeing the movie straight on or in a mirror. The collision should also be symmetric with respect to time: watching the movie of the balls knocking about momentarily we shouldn't be able to tell whether we're seeing the movie in forward or reverse. Of course for complicated objects symmetry might be hard to sustain; watching a movie of an egg falling to the ground and breaking we would know whether it's forward or reverse.

Scientists' belief in symmetries like these, and for simple things like billiard balls or interactions between two atoms, wasn't exactly a law. There is no way to prove that mirror or time symmetry should be true, but the evidence of experiments up until then seemed to suggest that they were. That's equivalent to saying that swans must be white, an assertion based on the experience of seeing only white swans. The jarring discovery of a black swan, however unexpected, would of course end the swans-must-be-white rule.

Then two of Dyson's colleagues at the Institute, Chen Ning Yang and Tsung-Dao Lee, predicted that nature might not be mirror symmetric after all at the level of subatomic particles. Some rare decays of nuclear particles, they said, might exhibit a left-right imbalance. Extended to all three spatial dimensions (left-right, up-down, back and forth), the idea of mirror symmetry is referred to as parity. Like all swans seeming to be white, subatomic transactions seemed to be parity symmetric.

Maybe not, said Lee and Yang. Parity might not be conserved in some circumstances. How could such a blemish in nature—if indeed it was a fault to be nonsymmetric—reveal itself? Physicists had previously discovered that the nuclear force is not one but two forces. The stronger of the two is responsible mainly for holding the nucleus together most of the time and, in the case of some unstable nuclei, for fission. The weaker of the two nuclear forces presides over radioactive nuclear decays, such as the transformation of neutrons into protons. The weak nuclear force, Yang and Lee figured, could make a distinction between left and right.

Dyson read the Yang-Lee paper. He read it twice, was intrigued, and talked with the authors. But even then, he claims, he did not have the imagination to see the implications of what Lee and Yang were saying.

And then it happened. A black swan turned up. An experiment displayed a small hint as to the secret signature of things. Experiments at the National Bureau of Standards involving the radioactivity of cobalt nuclei showed that parity was not sacred. Suddenly the study of the symmetries that scientists thought were sacred was a hot topic. Dyson excitedly incorporated his thoughts into another *Scientific American* article, one devoted to the way theoretical physicists like himself absorb new observed facts into an updated framework.[20]

The discovery that the universe isn't so supremely symmetric—nature seems to differentiate between left and right or back and forth or up and down—shows once again that science is provisional. "Rules" have to be removed from the roll of knowledge when they are shown to be incorrect. Like a compost heap, science needs to be turned over. The more turning it gets the more nourishing it becomes.

His Own Cold War

Freeman Dyson was a professor at a premier institution of higher learning, an author of several important technical articles and numerous science popularizations in magazines. He was a much invited lecturer, and a candidate for the Nobel Prize.

He was also a husband, a brother, a son, and a father. A biography must be part bio and part graph. We've looked at the intellectual interests, the letters of recommendations, the research papers, and the nuclear politics that have shaped Dyson's career so far. Now we must look at the home front.

We saw Dyson, in the spring of 1949, at the end of a long period of almost continuous intellectual exertion, his QED frenzy, suddenly letting his guard down and being smitten by Verena Huber. Like King Henry at the end of Shakespeare's *Henry V* climbing out of the saddle after the Battle of Agincourt and, out of his element for the first time, awkwardly wooing the beautiful French princess, so Dyson, fresh from his single-minded battle with electrons and photons, now turned from chalkboards and departmental colloquia to court, in his fashion, the beautiful Dr. Huber. Freeman sent Verena letters filled with poetic quotation and with details from his daily life. He missed her terribly, he said, while they were apart. But he seldom seemed to respond to the things she said in her letters back to him. He didn't tender the personalized endearments a lady wants to hear. It's as if he were responding to a generic sweetheart.[21]

Verena, pondering many years later, finds that she didn't particularly love Freeman at the time of their wedding. She never felt entirely comfortable with him. He was deep as a thinker, he was valuable as a scientist, but he wasn't fully socially formed, she thought. Her plaintive solution to this quandary sounded like a line from a play by Samuel Beckett: "I did not want to marry him. I did marry him."[22]

Her hope was that she could help make him come alive. She would help him become more of a human being. Besides, Katarina needed a father. For Verena, the summer of 1951 in Zurich, when Esther was born, was a high point. Verena had also been happy at Cornell, where the couple had many friends and where she could teach math.

The thing with Hilde Jacob, the German girl whom Freeman had met in the summer of 1947, had not fully gone away. In one letter Hilde sent to Ithaca she reminded Freeman that he had mentioned the possibility of marriage with her. Freeman had to remind the confused woman that he was married to Verena.[23]

The summer of 1955 was another happy time. The view of the Golden Gate in San Francisco Bay was splendid from the Dysons' rented home in the Berkeley Hills. And because Freeman's sister, Alice, was with them, Freeman and Verena were able to go off on their own, hiking in the Sierras for a week. Verena would soon be pregnant again. This kept them on track for Freeman's plan—to which Verena had consented—of having six children together. Even taking into account the fact that American families were larger in the 1950s than they are now, this was an ambitious plan.

One day the Dysons had been out walking in the eucalyptus-scented Berkeley Hills and returned to hear music coming from their living room. Someone was playing Bach on the piano, and playing it well. Dyson's first thought was that it was his father, who used to play this particular prelude of Bach's. Had he come on a surprise visit all the way from Britain?

But no, it wasn't his father. It was Edward Teller, who apologized for the intrusion. Learning that Dyson was in town for the summer, Teller had come to invite him to a party he was giving. In that instant Dyson was won over to liking the man, no matter what his role in the Oppenheimer hearing might have been.[24] Teller was to be an important element in Dyson's professional life for years to come. He took the Dyson family on a sightseeing drive up nearby Mount Diablo.

When the summer ended, it was back to regular life in Princeton. That fall another figure who would figure prominently in Dyson's life turned up. Georg Kreisel was not a stranger. An Austrian by birth, Kreisel had been at Trinity College during Dyson's time there and was now building an illustrious career in mathematics, specializing in logic. At Trinity, Dyson might not have gotten on well with Wittgenstein, but Kreisel had. Kreisel would become known chiefly for his brilliant research articles, his devastating wit, and for the many intrigues and scandals surrounding his personal life, especially when it came to women.[25] Nevertheless, Dyson had recommended Kreisel to Kurt Gödel, who invited Kreisel to join the Institute for Advanced Study as a temporary member.

Kreisel had stomach problems, and found eating difficult. Food at the Dyson household prepared by Verena was much more to his liking. There he participated in many intense discussions that resonated with Verena, especially the issue of reviving her mathematics research. In order to raise a family, Mrs. Dyson had suspended her career, but was coming to view her domestic situation as a stifling cage. She had arrived at the Institute in 1948 as a respected mathematician. Now her status had become that of a faculty wife. She was expected to cook, host parties, and look good. Kreisel's dazzling conversation was starting to awaken intellectual longings in her.

Verena had three children and a fourth was on the way. The baby inside her kicked frequently. Katarina and little Esther had given him a name, Fishli, for the little fish that was swimming around inside

Mummy. In late December, however, well into the fifth month of the pregnancy, the kicking inside ceased. The doctors conducted tests.

On January 19, after having lunch at the Institute with her husband and with Wolfgang Pauli, Verena entered the hospital. Labor was induced, and a stillborn baby was delivered. Verena understandably was devastated. Kisses from George and roses from Katarina helped, but Freeman's suggestions—"We have to be strong" and "We can try again"—did not. Verena remembers weeping a lot and Freeman being annoyed at this.[26]

Winter and spring were miserable. Katarina (now eleven) came down with sinusitis. George (three years old) had chickenpox in February; a few days later Esther (not yet five) had it, and a few days later Katarina as well. Freeman was away at meetings in Pittsburgh and Rochester. He was gone for almost the whole month of May—to Britain, Finland, and then Russia.

Then bigger trips. Freeman was going to La Jolla, California, for the entire summer of 1956, to work on a nuclear project, while the rest of the family was due to travel in the opposite direction, across the ocean to Europe.

Verena and the kids stopped first in London to visit Freeman's parents. They saw an Old Vic production of *Romeo and Juliet* with Claire Bloom and John Neville. The Romeo reminded Verena of Freeman, "all bony awkwardness and a grasshopper's jumpiness."[27] Romeo's mooning letters to his girlfriend, the one he had before Juliet, reminded her of the forlorn letters she had received from Freeman.

Her feelings for Freeman had always been ambivalent and were becoming more so. Irritation, that great abrasive force in daily life, was becoming more common. A brilliant mathematical physicist he might be but he was not, she felt, equipped to deal with ordinary human events. He had no sense for food, like or dislike, and would eat anything put in front of him. When Verena told other wives of his indifference, they were envious.[28] When Verena and Freeman went out together, he would often walk right behind her, as if she were his mother and not his wife.

A wife knows her husband better than others do. But Verena's is just one view of Freeman Dyson. Outsiders have opinions too. And there are worse things than practicality. Philip Morrison, physics professor at

Cornell and later at MIT, was impressed but puzzled by Dyson. Dyson was, Morrison thought, very private, enigmatic, and extremely learned.[29] Another baffled but admiring opinion comes from one of Dyson's colleagues at the Institute, Abraham Pais, who first took note of the young Englishman while Dyson was still a student of Bethe's. Himself a graceful writer and future scientific biographer, Pais quickly formed a lasting estimation of Dyson:

> The kid is smart. . . . He looked a bit unusual: stiff white collar and light blue eyes that would stare piercingly at you. I recall my first impression: that fellow must be an eccentric, an opinion which I have never changed.
>
> It is not so simple, however, to define what one means by eccentricity. In my view eccentrics are people with a strong sense of personal liberty, strong individuals whose actions never include acting, who have strong inclinations of their own that they are not afraid to express and on which they refuse to compromise.[30]

In the wake of the miscarriage, Verena was depressed. She wanted to see a psychiatrist, but Freeman felt this was unnecessary. His mother, Lady Dyson, hinted that perhaps at her age and condition, Verena was no longer up to the rigors of having six babies. Actually Verena felt fit enough. Perhaps Freeman was the one lacking sufficient energy. According to Verena, Freeman was "satisfied with simply sitting and watching me and the kids live." He seemed to have retreated to a world of concepts and not one of direct experience.[31]

Verena was annoyed by Freeman's incessant quoting of poetry, both in his letters and in his conversation; it was another way that Freeman insulated himself from ordinary reality. She fantasized that he was an alien robot who had blended into human society, including marriage, by memorizing all possible literature, a task easier for robots than for humans, allowing him to interject selected passages into his discourse when appropriate.[32]

One more member of the Dyson household, Katarina, had another view. She liked her stepfather. They climbed buildings together in Princeton, a daytime version of Freeman's old night climbing habits in Cambridge and Winchester. They went on walks together. It was on one of these expeditions that she first became aware of a hearing problem (not being able to detect high-frequency sounds) that was to remain with her for the rest of her life. "Oh Daddy," she said, "I can't hear you with the sun in my eyes."[33]

Katarina liked Freeman's poetic habit. She remembered and even memorized some of the poems they recited together, and could still recall them fifty years later. One of these was T. S. Eliot's "Ash Wednesday," which had a mournful but philosophical air:

> *Because I know that time is always time*
> *And place is always and only place*
> *And what is actual is actual only for one time*
> *And only for one place*

Another poem they shared was "Fern Hill" by Dylan Thomas. It too portrays the inexorable, melancholy, irreversible but lovely passage of time:

> *Oh as I was young and easy in the mercy of his measure,*
> *Time held me in green and dying*
> *Though I sang in my chains like the sea.*

Verena felt that Freeman didn't want to grow up. He wanted to remain Peter Pan. Katarina agrees with that assessment but sees it as a positive attribute. If Freeman had some childlike qualities—his curiosity, his willingness to consider strange possibilities—then this would surely be a useful part of his being a scientist.[34]

In June 1956, Freeman saw his family off on their ship to Europe. Verena would be staying near the Austrian city of Salzburg. A few weeks after arriving Verena had picked up one of Freeman's letters from the local post office. She and her children were riding through town on a bus, and Katarina asked her to read Daddy's letter out loud. Verena began but suddenly gasped and stopped.

An entry in Verena's diary for June 21, 1956, caught the flash of this sensation, as if it were a bomb going off in the bus. Freeman calmly declared in this letter that on his last night in Princeton, before heading off for California, he had slept with another woman, whom he named, a woman Verena knew. The tone of his letter was not angry, but neither was it apologetic. He didn't pretend to be self-righteous anymore, he asserted. Then came the obligatory poetic outtake, that helped illuminate the intended meaning. His text came from the work of William Blake.[35] It was his short poem "Eternity":

> *He who binds to himself a joy*
> *Does the wined life destroy;*
> *But he who kisses the joy as it flies*
> *Lives in eternity's sunrise.*

7. Intrinsically Safe

Dyson as Engineer
(1956–1957)

What would happen, Verena asked herself, if she were to remain in Europe at the end of the summer and not go back to Princeton? Not as a permanent settlement of things—the idea was not to break completely from Freeman—but to do some mathematics research and perhaps to teach. Excellent schools were available for the children. Women were increasingly getting academic jobs. Maybe a year's separation from Freeman would give them a chance to see things in a new light.[1] Surprisingly, Freeman was not averse to the idea. Also, with Freeman's encouragement, Verena had met with her former love, the older gentleman who had kindled such a passion in her years before.

Not yet decided about whether to return to Princeton or stay in Salzburg, Verena planned for both possibilities. In July she interviewed a young German girl, Imme Jung, who had been recommended by a friend of Verena's. The girl, brought to Salzburg by her father, mother, and oldest brother, made a good impression.[2] The tentative plan was that she would come to America at the end of the year, after the Dysons had moved into their new home in the fall of 1956. Her job would be to help with the children and do some of the housework.

In July Freeman's parents, wanting to see their grandchildren, visited Verena. Lady Dyson, normally reserved, had some candid words for her daughter-in-law. Thoughtfully, she spoke of the role of women in men's lives. Being a mistress and a wife were very different, with the role of the wife being much more difficult. If Verena and Freeman were having troubles, Mama Dyson hinted, it might be because Verena was trying too hard to play both roles.[3]

On August 11, their wedding anniversary, Verena in Salzburg received roses from Freeman in San Diego. He implored her to return home, and she did.

NUCLEAR AFFAIRS

Ted Taylor is so cool that he once used a nuclear explosion to light a cigarette. He had designed the bomb, knew its likely yield, helped rig the test shot, and had set up a parabolic reflecting mirror at a distance of twelve miles from ground zero. At the appointed moment, and with him gingerly leaning in from the side of the mirror, the brilliant light rays streaming out of the detonation hit the reflector and converged at the focal point, where they set the tobacco aflame. Taylor saved the cigarette, what was left of it, as a souvenir.[4]

Taylor had become a legend. While some bomb designers, coveting nuclear explosions in the multi-megatonnage range, proceeded to make bombs bigger and bigger, Ted Taylor was making an interesting career for himself by building downward. His specialty was crafting the smallest possible thing that would constitute a fission bomb. For example, the *Davy Crockett*, a warhead only twelve inches across and weighing sixty pounds, was supposed to produce a yield of only 1 kiloton. But this was all the army wanted from a short-run, gun-fired tactical nuclear weapon, perhaps enough, launched in salvos, to keep the Russian army from spilling across Western Europe.

Taylor's artistry with the tight packing of nuclear explosives came at a price, however, since he worried a lot about the rightness of what he was doing. Like the wartime letters the young Freeman Dyson wrote about Bomber Command to his parents, Taylor wrote soul-searching letters to *his* parents, who were missionaries, about why he was mixed up with such a dreadful business:

> *If A bombs in their present form will make another war something which mankind cannot bear then, I say, there is only one thing to do: develop a bomb which will leave no doubt in anyone's mind. This idea, is repulsive to most people I know, and yet I feel, as strongly as I have ever felt anything, that it is the only way out. The basic principles of a superbomb are all there. If a war with conventional weapons did not effectively wipe out civilization (as I think it would), I am certain that a superbomb would be developed during*

the war, as it was during the last, and would be used until civiliza-
tion really was wiped out. So, again, I think that the thing to do is
to find that horrible thing now, *before a shooting war starts and*
people completely lose their ability to reason.[5]

Eventually Taylor had had enough. He vowed to find some other way to use nuclear energy, one that didn't kill people. In later years he would become a crusader for greater controls on nuclear bombs and more stringent rules about the handling of nuclear materials. His career was featured in a series of sensational articles by John McPhee in *The New Yorker* that later grew into a book, *The Curve of Binding Energy.*

In 1956 Ted Taylor left Los Alamos in order to join General Dynamics Corporation, one of the largest defense contractors in the country. There he wanted to turn his sword into a plowshare. A plowshare is a sharp metal edge that divides difficult soil in order to furnish future food. The nuclear plowshare is a nuclear reactor, which would divide uranium nuclei in order to furnish useful electricity.

Along with Taylor, Freeman Dyson had been invited to attend a summer-long study session in San Diego devoted to reactor design. Dyson of course had intimate knowledge of the nuclear force at the microscopic level, but was not otherwise qualified in the job of extracting macroscopic energy from a large machine. He was by then well known for his versatile use of mathematics and physics, and would probably be a welcome addition to any research team. But the real reason for Dyson's invitation, he supposed, was his acquaintance with Edward Teller.[6] Teller, with the triumph of developing the H-bomb behind him, would be putting aside his work at the new weapons lab in Livermore and coming for the summer study in San Diego too, and this in turn was a prime attraction for Dyson.

The mastermind behind the San Diego venture was Frederic de Hoffmann. The year before, de Hoffmann had been one of the two American delegates at a meeting in Geneva about the peaceful uses of nuclear power, one of the first times Western and Russian scientists had met. De Hoffman had been instrumental in making the event a success. A protégé of Teller's and a Ph.D. student under Julian Schwinger, de Hoffman, at the age of thirty-one, was now a senior official at General Dynamics, where he was in charge of creating a new department, called General Atomic, devoted to designing reactors for the civilian marketplace. He would later help to found the San Diego branch of the University of California and the Salk Institute, where he was its longtime president.

De Hoffmann wanted to build reactors. Ever since Enrico Fermi's prototype reactor, tested beneath the football stands at the University of Chicago in 1942, nuclear reactors had been a military concern, either to spawn plutonium for use in bombs or to propel submarines. The 1955 Geneva meeting had helped break the aura of secrecy covering the whole subject of nuclear research. Many hoped that once reactor design was freed from the layers of military encumbrance it could quickly assume a central role in providing electrical power for homes and factories.

De Hoffmann knew lots of high-ranking people in business, the military, and government. Yet he was always friendly, always had time to listen to your ideas. De Hoffmann was not only in charge of General Atomic, but he seemed to be personally trying to jump-start the entire civilian reactor endeavor.

The headquarters for General Atomic and for the summer study was a rented schoolhouse in La Jolla, near San Diego. Like the wartime bomb effort at Los Alamos, the reactor routine in La Jolla would be a mixture of morning lectures and afternoon design work. The lectures would inform the forty or so participants, including physicists, chemists, and engineers, on all aspects of the enterprise.

Dyson was grateful for the daily lectures, which exposed him to chemistry and engineering issues he hadn't encountered before, and he was thrilled to work with Edward Teller. Whatever Teller had done during the Oppenheimer affair, here in San Diego he provided immediate intellectual gratification. Teller had the ability to listen to the details of a scientific or engineering problem and almost instantly summon intelligent, perhaps even decisive, things to say on the matter.

He shared this ability with several personalities described in this book, such as Richard Feynman, Robert Oppenheimer, Hans Bethe, and Freeman Dyson himself. That's one of the reasons the paths of these men kept crossing. Making frequent jokes, Teller had a brilliant idea every sixty seconds or so. They worked well together as a team—Teller triggering a train of thoughts and Dyson embodying the ideas in equations. Teller, like Richard Feynman, possessed a strong intuitive grasp of physical phenomena, while Dyson possessed the complementary rigorous mathematics needed to crystallize a concept quantitatively.

That summer Dyson and Teller were part of a ten-person group designing a safe reactor. Safe in this case meant not merely "engineered safety"—providing a number of redundant shut-down mechanisms under a variety of emergency scenarios. True safety, or inherent safety, holds to a higher standard. Reactors would be *inherently* safe only if there were no conceivable sequences of events in which the control system for the reactor, or a stupid or even malicious human operator, could unleash a catastrophic chemical explosion or meltdown of critical components.

An inherently safe reactor would be safe even in the hands of schoolkids. No matter how you spun the dials or what you did to the control panel with a crowbar, the reactor would still shut down. Teller was insistent on inherent safety. Only if this were achieved, he argued, could reactors become a large, efficient, and trustworthy part of society's energy infrastructure.

CHILDPROOF REACTORS

Freeman Dyson's career is manifestly linked to the instability of fissionable nuclei. Uranium is number 92 in the periodic table, the heaviest naturally occurring element. But an element can exist in several forms, or isotopes, depending on how the nucleus is stocked. Both uranium-235 and its slightly heavier and much commoner cousin, uranium-238, contain a complement of ninety-two protons, the positively charged subnuclear particle. But U-238 has three more neutrons (the neutral subnuclear particle) than U-235; the number to the right of the U is just the sum of the protons and neutrons.

All these protons and neutrons are packed into a wiggly little ball, the nucleus, which has a volume only a fraction that of the atom as a whole. One of the reasons the uranium nucleus wiggles is that it can't quite properly accommodate its cargo of protons and neutrons. Like a restless sleeper tossing and turning, U tries to find a comfortable position. Both uranium isotopes are fitfully active. In fact, they are radioactive; that is, they vibrate until small fragments come flying out, leaving behind a more stable consignment of protons and neutrons. In this process the parent atom changes its identity. It is now a different, lighter chemical element. It's not uranium anymore.

U-235 has another means of expressing its agitation. It can indulge in the process called fission. A passing solitary neutron of just the right energy, if it intrudes upon the nucleus, can unleash a miniature cataclysm. The U–235 nucleus sunders in half, creating such daughter nuclei as iodine, strontium, and cesium. Among the debris will be two or three energetic neutrons that can seed further fission of more U–235 nuclei. These fissions, in turn, release still more neutrons that can pry apart further nuclei, and so on. The result is a sequential breakdown.

Such a chain reaction is what makes both nuclear bombs and nuclear reactors work. In reactors the fission is controlled and the liberated energy used to make electricity. In bombs the chain reaction is uncontrolled and the surplus energy is used to make destructive pressure, fire, and radiation. In a bomb the energy stored in U–235 nuclei is extracted in a fraction of a second. At a reactor the U–235 in a fuel rod can be used over several years. The goal is to moderate the chain reaction so that it releases as much energy as you need to make electricity right then. In a bomb the goal is to encourage the chain reaction to double and redouble its propagation as quickly as possible before the bomb blows itself apart.

If Dyson had worked at Los Alamos the summer of 1945 his concern would have been for nuclear bombs. But at La Jolla in the summer of 1956 his concern was for nuclear electricity. Why do we want to handle radioactive and fissile materials at all? Nuclear materials are nasty. The spent fuel rods, in which many of the U–235 atoms have, in the course of nuclear reactions, been replaced by even more radioactive daughter atoms, are so hot when pulled from the reactor that they would melt if they weren't quickly placed back in a pool of cooling water. The absence of that water is what worsened the accident at the Japanese reactors in the wake of the huge earthquake and tsunami in 2011.

So for making electricity, why not stick to the old reliable fuels, like coal? Why invest the billions of dollars needed to start up a uranium furnace? Putting aside for the moment the virtue of uranium's not emitting clouds of climate-changing carbon dioxide or pollutants, the development of the nuclear industry got down to this: a kilogram of nuclear fuel surrenders a million times more energy than a kilogram of coal.

Therefore with the prospect of plentiful electricity, derived from relatively cheap fuel, producing very little pollution, many scientists were eager to push ahead. That's why Dyson, the quantum theorist, and bomb makers such as Teller, Taylor, and de Hoffmann, were cheer-

fully on hand in the schoolhouse. What they accomplished that summer was to rethink the way in which the subtle control mechanisms
work together inside a reactor.★

It was fitting that Dyson and his friends were working in a schoolhouse, because here they were, grown men all, but schoolkids again,
trying to learn by doing. Some of their time had been spent at picnic
tables out back. Their school project was to design an inherently safe
reactor. If they were kids they surely would have gotten stars put next
to their names.

Edward Teller was the dominant personality. He fought fiercely,
even angrily, for his ideas. But then he would calm down, and come
up with another scheme. Few of the participants liked Teller's political
views—the Oppenheimer security hearings were only two years in
the past—but everyone liked Teller anyway.[7]

At summer's end Dyson made a day trip to Tijuana, where he was
bitten by a dog. Not wanting to take any chances catching rabies, Dyson
underwent the painful treatment. Teller stayed with him for this period. Dyson was grateful.[8]

These three-month volunteers at what was essentially a nuclear summer camp did something rare in the world of high technology. They
and their full-time General Atomic collaborators would design, blueprint, build, and sell a new type of reactor, all in the space of three

---

★Left to itself, the uranium hydride fuel, encased in skinny tubes made of zirconium metal, would
continue to fission, producing more and more heat. The fission rate can be controlled by thrusting
sticks of neutron-absorbing material in among the fuel rods. These control rods rob the chain reaction of the itinerant neutrons needed for fissioning of uranium. Pull the control rods back out and
fission starts back up.

In the most popular reactor design, called a light water reactor, the heat generated by all those
falling-apart uranium nuclei is carried away by the circulation of water through the core. This
water can be turned directly into steam, or used to heat steam in a separate set of pipes. The steam
then rotates the turbines used to generate electricity. The water in the reactor also bathes the fuel
tubes, ensuring that they don't get too hot.

The water plays another important role insofar as the hydrogen atoms in the water continuously
intercept some of the neutrons flying around the core. These little encounters can sap some of the
neutrons' energy. This is not a detriment but exactly what you want, since for triggering a fission
event it can often be the case that the neutron has too much energy. They have to be slowed a bit,
or cooled, by interactions with the lightweight hydrogen atoms. The hydrogen doesn't absorb the
neutrons, but merely "moderates" their speed, making them suitable for fission.

What if some saboteur disabled the mechanism for engaging the control rods? Or what if he just
removed them entirely? How could the fission be turned off in this case? Teller, Dyson, and their
colleagues arrived at a clever solution: fold some of the neutron-moderating hydrogen into the fuel
elements themselves. Even in the absence of control rods, as the fuel grew hotter the extra hydrogen
would speed up the neutrons, making them useless for enabling fission. This whole negative-
feedback process, happening in a thousandth of a second, would always be ready to act like a circuit
breaker to keep the reactor operation from speeding too far ahead.

years. The reactor Teller and Dyson had helped design that summer was called TRIGA, for Training, Research, Isotope production, General Atomic. It was destined to be one of the bestselling reactor models in history, with seventy units later installed in two dozen countries spread across five continents.[9] The prototype unit operated for forty years and was given a historical designation. Another early unit became the first working reactor in Africa.

The ceremony marking the debut of TRIGA as a commercial product and the dedication of the new headquarters building for General Atomic occurred with great fanfare a few years later. The guest of honor was Niels Bohr, who, in the 1940s, had tried to persuade President Franklin Roosevelt and Prime Minister Winston Churchill to share bomb secrets with the Russians as a way of mitigating mistrust. Now he was arguing that the West and East should share reactor secrets, partly as a practical effort to speed up reactor development and, perhaps more importantly, as a gesture of trust and peaceful intentions.

At this time the phrase "peaceful use of atomic power" could mean many things, including the use of nuclear bombs to excavate canals or to mine minerals. In practice atomic power meant the generation of electricity. Many hoped, at least in the late 1950s, that nuclear-derived electricity would be "too cheap to meter." This cornucopia would transform cities and raise up poor nations. Arthur Eddington, whose book on space and time had so inspired Dyson as a boy, prophesized in another book that subatomic power would one day transform society. It could offer a great supply of cheap energy, but it also posed a danger, since it might enable destructive forces on a large scale.[10] Dyson always kept this duality in mind.

On the day of the General Atomic dedication, Dyson was granted a great privilege: a stroll along the nearby beach with Bohr, just the two of them. Bohr was famous both for his philosophical discourse and for the fact that he often spoke very softly and in a mumble, making it hard for others to hear him. And so it was this day when Dyson leaned in to hear the great man's words. Dyson, almost as if he knew already about the issues that would occupy so much of his time over the coming decades, issues like curbing nuclear weaponry, understanding the Russian point of view in international diplomacy, and harnessing technology, suspected that the Danish sage had a storehouse of useful insights. Dyson strained to catch Bohr's words, but most of them were blown away by the wind.[11]

A blacksmith and his wife: FJD's paternal grandparents, Alice and John Dyson, c. 1900. Coming from humble origins in Yorkshire, they saw to it that their son George received a first-rate musical education. George attended and later was director of the Royal College of Music in London.

TOP LEFT FJD in a pram. His earliest memory, from the age of about three, was of adding and arranging numbers while lying in a crib. Young Freeman was often in the care of a nanny. His parents led busy lives, his father as a music teacher and conductor, his mother with a busy schedule of social work.

ABOVE The Dyson family, c. 1930. FJD and sister, Alice, in front, and parents Mildred and George in back. George Dyson's participation in the First World War ended when the horse he rode was blown out from beneath him by a bomb.

LOWER LEFT Serious even then: Slight of build and academically advanced several years past boys his own age, FJD was often bullied. He took refuge in the library, where he liked reading adventure books by H. G. Wells and Jules Verne. At age nine he wrote a story involving a visit to the Moon.

TOP Looking like a miniature adult, FJD's sweater or vest, necktie, and the cut of his hair looked pretty much the same eighty years later. His boyhood passion was mathematics.

ABOVE FJD on stilts with an unidentified young woman. As a change from the family home in built-up Winchester, the Dysons owned a holiday cottage on the south coast of England, where George Dyson spent much time on drainage projects. The family employed four servants.

TOP The Dysons, c. 1935. As a choirmaster and composer, George Dyson was frequently associated with churches. FJD, living in Winchester and then Cambridge, was often around gothic structures, some of which he climbed in the dark as a kind of sport.

ABOVE FJD at Winchester College, late 1930s. For the year 1936, he had the highest entrance scores for Winchester, considered then (and still) by some to be the top school in the land academically, so arguably he was the best schoolboy in Britain.

About to go to war: FJD, far right, as prefect of libraries at
Winchester College, c. 1941. Many Winchester boys entered
the war and some of them did not return. The First World
War had been even worse; several Winchester graduating
classes were virtually annihilated.

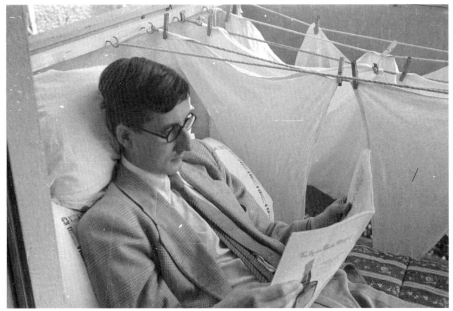

ABOVE FJD among the diapers, mid 1950s. When FJD first arrived at Cornell to study in 1947, his fellow students noticed that he loved to read newspapers and magazines for hours with his feet up on the desk. They could also see, however, that he possessed great powers of concentration and could work very rapidly.

LEFT Freeman proposed to Verena Huber a week after they met formally in Princeton at a picnic in 1949. A year later they married in Ann Arbor, Michigan. A year after that—here in Switzerland—they were parents. Freeman wanted them to have six children and Verena agreed. This summer of 1951, FJD worked alongside Wolfgang Pauli.

ABOVE A grandmother at last, Lady Dyson (third from left) journeyed with her husband, Sir George (second from left), to Zurich for Esther's Christening ceremony in July 1951. FJD's stepdaughter, Katarina, is the shorter of the two girls in front.

BELOW Picnic outing, c. 1952. FJD, second from right, holds Esther. After the mid 1960s many summer family vacations were tied to his participation in study sessions of the JASON organization, a select group of scientists who advised the federal government. These meetings were held mostly in southern California.

PHOTO COURTESY OF VERENA HUBER DYSON

LEFT Esther, new to walking, and Freeman, new to teaching. In the fall of 1951 FJD, not yet twenty-eight years old, became a full professor at Cornell, taking responsibility for the quantum course previously taught by Richard Feynman and Hans Bethe.

BELOW Freeman holding Esther, with George off to the side, 1955. This was to be the second of three summers FJD spent in Berkeley, California. The family had a rental house on Buena Vista Way in the Berkeley Hills. The university campanile tower can be seen down the hill.

PHOTO COURTESY OF VERENA HUBER DYSON

NOT FUN ANYMORE

Dyson had been exhilarated by his brief foray into engineering. He considered his schoolhouse summer as one of the turning points in his life. He had learned, to his surprise, that he could apply science to practical ends.[12]

Nevertheless, years later, after he had time to gain some perspective on the multibillion-dollar industry he had helped launch, he came to see the history of nuclear power as a tragedy. His reservations about what happened can be sorted into categories of concerns over specific critical issues, issues that haunt energy policy to this day.

Safety. Avoiding catastrophe should be at the heart of all engineering efforts, Dyson felt. TRIGA had been designed with inherent safety as the main goal. General Atomic sold plenty of their little training reactors, but they also wanted to sell billion-watt power plant behemoths as well. General Atomic's contender at the heavyweight level was called the High Temperature Graphite Reactor (HTGR). Its chief opponent was the Light Water Reactor (LWR). Dyson asserted that HTGR, with its much larger core, was a thousand times safer than LWR, at least against the possibility of a meltdown of the fuel assembly.[13] The hitch was that the HTGR cost more and took up more space. Teller and Dyson argued, long before the disaster at Chernobyl, that safety, and along with it public trust, should override other factors in sustaining a healthy nuclear power industry.

Bandwagon Effect. What the navy wants the navy gets, and what they wanted in the 1950s was nuclear propulsion, allowing submarines to run further, longer, quieter, and deeper than with diesel power. In submarines space is at a premium, so a compact reactor core is desired. Admiral Hyman Rickover's zealous pursuit of a nuclear navy provided the construction incentive the reactor industry needed. But it also favored the small-core LWR layout over the larger-core HTGR layout in the competition for reactor design.[14] Compactness was allowed to trump safety.

Economy of Scale. In embracing high technology, companies seemed to favor a larger-is-better attitude, especially in the electricity business. This tendency toward gigantism was reaching its peak just as the reactor business was taking off in the 1960s. For many years it was indeed true that larger power plants produced more electricity per fuel input than small plants. But largeness has its drawbacks. Larger machines can be disproportionately down for repairs; this was often the case for reactors in the 1970s and 1980s. In this way, Dyson asserted, a false economy of scale developed.

Flexibility. Not only does a large reactor needing repairs throw off the daily operation of a utility, but the construction of such an immense machine can take a decade or longer to complete, tying up financial resources, making it even harder for the power company to respond quickly to new increases (and sometimes decreases) in demand. "If a plant takes ten years to build," said Dyson, "it is almost certainly too big."[15]

Marketplace. In a free market, competition for customers by rival products should, in principle, optimize design and price. But what market is totally free from qualifications such as regulations, insider information, collusion, false advertising, and hidden costs? The environmental burden of nuclear power—the social cost of pulling uranium out of the ground, or enriching uranium, or storing the spent fuel rods—was for a long time not fully factored into the cost of nuclear power.[16]

Accountants shouldered aside the young inventors and scientists that might have come up with better solutions. Existing designs became rigid. New engineering concepts, the kind of thing that came out of the General Atomic schoolhouse, no longer emerged. For scientists and engineers working on reactors, Dyson laments, "Sometime between 1960 and 1970, the fun went out of the business."[17]

In the summer of 1956, at least, the design of reactors had still been fun. Ted Taylor, having made his mark in building bombs, left Los Alamos to work with Freddie de Hoffmann full-time at General Atomic. Freeman Dyson headed back east for Princeton.

Something interesting happened to him on the way home. He had spent the whole summer studying controlled fission inside reactors. Now, stopping off at Los Alamos by invitation, he would study for two days how nuclear fusion unfolds inside bombs. Apparently Los Alamos wanted some advice about how tritium, a heavy form of hydrogen, was produced at reactors. Tritium is a vital material needed to create the fusion reactions that power a hydrogen bomb. So great was the lab's need to talk to someone of Dyson's ability that his lack of American citizenship did not stand in the way of his dropping in and being given, as part of his visit, a quick but thorough education in the physics of bombs.[18] This crash course did not have any immediate consequence, but two years later his new knowledge would be valuable when he came to work on a nuclear device much larger than any reactor.

HEDDA GABLER

In Henrik Ibsen's play *Hedda Gabler*, a headstrong, beautiful, and dangerously bored young woman, Hedda Gabler, marries George Tesman, a maladroit scholar preoccupied with his studies. The wife, forever pacing about her new home, is recharged when she makes contact again with Eilert Lövborg, a former lover and now an academic rival of her husband's. To make matters still more complicated, Hedda and her husband are frequently visited by George's mischievous friend, Judge Brack, who, we quickly notice, is there more to flirt with Hedda than to see George. This and a lot of other things escape George's notice.

Freeman Dyson is not George Tesman. The scientific achievements of Dyson's public career give us to understand that not a lot escapes his notice. What about the private Dyson?

While the Dysons lived in Ithaca, they were visited by Abraham Pais, formerly linked romantically to Verena. They were visited several times, at Freeman's invitation, by Hans Haefeli, Verena's former husband.[19] Moreover, during the past summer, at Freeman's suggestion, Verena in Europe visited her very own Eilert Lövborg, her "older man," the man to whom she had pledged her heart. Freeman knew all this. What was going on? Was there a pattern at work here? This was not an inherently safe arrangement.

In the fall of 1956, back from La Jolla and reunited with his family in Princeton, Freeman settled into his new house. Purchase price: $30,000.[20] Georg Kreisel, whose appointment at the Institute the year before had been made at Freeman's urging, now became an ever more frequent visitor. What kind of man was Kreisel? Was he a potential Judge Brack?

Kreisel was a friend of biologist Francis Crick. In the Prologue to Crick's autobiography, Crick said this: "When I met Kreisel I was a sloppy thinker. His powerful, rigorous mind gently but steadily made my thinking more incisive and occasionally more precise. Quite a number of my mental mannerisms spring from him."[21]

Kreisel had a reputation as a ladies' man and was an intimate friend of the British novelist Iris Murdoch. Supposedly he is the model for characters in several of Murdoch's books. According to Verena, Kreisel had an affair with Brigitte Bardot. Even little Esther Dyson was captivated by the man. At one dull moment during the Salzburg summer, Esther (then five years old) had said, "I'm bored. I wish Kreisel was here."[22]

Kreisel came to the Dyson home for the food and for the conversation. Verena had over the summer given much thought to resuming a mathematical career, and was prodded in this direction by Kreisel. She wanted to be a good mother, but she felt hemmed in by domesticity.[23] She was cultivating an interest in photography, but this wasn't enough.[24]

In Ibsen's play, Hedda accidentally comes into possession of the only manuscript copy of Lövborg's sensational new book, a book that might give him an academic edge over George Tesman. Thinking partly to cut herself off from her own past, partly to help her husband, and partly for the sheer drama of it, Hedda burns Lövborg's manuscript.

Now in the new home on Princeton's Battle Road Circle, Verena gathered up all copies of her Ph.D. dissertation. Going to the backyard, and with her husband looking on, she set fire to the collection. Her mathematical work went up in smoke and flame. She was symbolically declaring her allegiance to husband and children.

Things seemed to be stabilizing between Freeman and Verena. The family returned to normal life in Princeton. The kids went to school. At the annual ball given at the Institute, Freeman spontaneously got up on a sturdy table and did a Russian dance, which he'd learned on his visit to the Soviet Union the previous spring. He became a U.S. citizen, taking the oath in nearby Trenton, New Jersey. The first Christmas in the new home was celebrated with a beautiful tree, covered with real candles. Buckets of water stood by in case of fire.

Kreisel's stomach complaints were being ignored by his doctors, he said. Only at the Dyson's could he get the nourishment he needed. Besides, he and Verena could speak in German. She was starved for German language and literature.

Right after Christmas Freeman left for a meeting at Los Alamos. A few weeks later, Imme Jung, twenty years of age, arrived in America to take up her post of mother's helper. Verena met her in New York harbor and brought her back to Princeton, where she quickly got to know the children and familiarized herself with the household.

Freeman left Los Alamos and, along with a few of his colleagues, flew to Aspen, Colorado. There he would be joined by Verena for some skiing. Imme, establishing herself in the Dyson home, would take care of Katarina, Esther, and George.

Georg Kreisel drove Verena to the airport in Newark. On the way they spent a night together in a hotel.

Years later, in a volume of reminiscences by colleagues published in honor of Kreisel, Verena openly spoke of the affair that was now unfolding. With Dyson she was trapped in an "iron cage of Princeton domesticity," she said, whereas Kreisel represented freedom, or at least a return to intellectual rigor. Furthermore, one reason Kreisel had been attracted to her, Verena suspected, was that he might be exacting some kind of revenge on Freeman Dyson, who was seen by Kreisel as a great rival from their time together at Cambridge when they vied for preeminence in the mathematical tripos competition.[25]

Verena went ahead to Aspen. A few days later, and after an exhilarating day of fine outdoor activity, Verena told Freeman of her night spent with Kreisel. His first reaction was to laugh. Then he was angry, then ruthlessly practical. He insisted that she repeat her confession in the form of a written statement—"My wife informed me, Freeman J. Dyson, that on January 21, 1957 she committed adultery. I in no way condone this, and will have no further conjugal . . ."—which she should sign before a notary public. At that hour, with no notary available, they went to dinner. There, in the presence of his colleagues, Freeman amusedly announced that soon he would have some news for them. In the meantime, he and Verena would be leaving early.

The next day they followed through with the notary public. At Verena's insistence, Kreisel's name was left out.[26] They left for Denver the following morning, got a plane for New York City, then the last train to Princeton, and took a cab to their home. On the threshold Freeman turned to Verena: "Of course you understand," he said, "this is no longer your home any more, but you can spend the night here. In the morning you will leave."[27]

The standards of the 1950s being what they were, it was not incongruous that the husband should enjoy a fling and justify this as a heroic action out of a poem by Blake, whereas when the wife does the same thing it results in a notarized statement and her being ejected from the home.

Kicked out, Verena found a run-down house to rent in the nearby town of Hightstown. She borrowed some bedding and kitchen utensils. In March she moved to Philadelphia and began a job at Remington Rand UNIVAC. This was close to Princeton so that she could easily see the children on the weekends.

Kicked out: this was Verena's side of the story. Imme insists that Verena, frequently moody, left of her own accord. Freeman was devastated by Verena's departure, Imme insists.[28]

On one of Verena's weekend visits in late spring, Freeman led Verena over to the Oppenheimers' home for brunch. This was something of an honor; many Institute members came to the director's residence for parties, but few came for breakfast in the kitchen. On the way in Verena saw a four-leaf clover. She stooped to pluck the thing and has kept it to this day. Inside, Freeman, with a laugh, declared that he and his wife did not live like other people, and that their marriage was ending (paraphrasing from the poetry of T. S. Eliot) "with a bang, not a whimper."[29]

That summer Verena Huber-Dyson, as she would call herself from then on, and Georg Kreisel traveled to a mathematics conference at Cornell University, where their appearance as a couple created a stir.[30] After that they left for Britain, where Kreisel had an appointment at the University of Reading. This was, Verena thought, a new start for her, as a woman and as a mathematician. Some of this was her doing and some of it she credits to Kreisel. He was a difficult personality, but conversations with him were helping her to think analytically again. "Being with Kreisel was not fun," she had to admit, "but it was meaningful."[31]

In June, Freeman drove with Esther, George, and Imme west to California, where again he would be working with Charles Kittel in Berkeley. But once there Freeman found that he couldn't concentrate. "While I was supposed to be thinking about ferromagnets, my head was full of conservation laws and high energy experiments. Kittel and I agreed that I should not come back until I had a summer free of competing distractions. This never happened."[32]

8. Space Traveler's Manifesto

Dyson as Rocketeer

(1957–1959)

As a boy of nine Freeman Dyson visited the Moon. He wrote a story, "Sir Phillip Roberts's Erolunar Collision," about a wandering celestial object called Eros on a collision course with Earth's Moon. The hero of the story is an explorer and scientist in the manner of Indiana Jones who wants to put himself in the path of danger. He journeys to the Moon to see the collision close-up. The rest of Dyson's juvenile sketch described the vehicle for shooting Sir Phillip from a huge barrel in Jules Verne fashion. Dyson, who just then was being bullied by bigger boys, had retreated to the school library and escaped into fiction. He gave loving attention to calculating the necessary dimensions for the lunar projectile-craft.[1]

The nine-year-old Dyson didn't have enough fortitude, and the story petered out before the Erolunar plans were complete. Now, a quarter century later, the adult Dyson was about to get a second chance. He would attempt to finish what Sir Phillip had started.

THE RIGHT STUFF

The year is 1957 and there isn't any Moon-impacting comet in sight. But there is something nearly as bad. The menace isn't out there beyond Neptune but right here on Earth, at the horizon, stretching itself across half a dozen time zones. The Soviet Union, and not some inert celestial object, was coming in our direction, threatening Western civilization. Actually, part of the threat *was* in space. The Russians had just done what American engineers were not yet able to do: place a small radio transmitter into orbit around the Earth. The Soviets referred to Sputnik as a scientific experiment, but many in the West viewed the tiny satellite as a menacing portent. Its mere radio ping, given off as it looped overhead, could be taken as an affront to American know-how.

Suddenly space was hot. Space, the gigantic empty ocean above us, wasn't just a void stretching between Earth and Moon or the planets and stars. It could be viewed as a potential theater of war where weapons might be deployed. Worse; the Soviets wanted to make it their private lake. Dyson was not among those caught off guard. He had long been interested in Russia, and he knew people who knew what the Soviets were up to. But for most of the American public, in and out of government, Sputnik had come as a shock. Naturally there had to be an American response.

The U.S. Army was aiming to send a craft to the Moon. The first step was getting something, anything, into orbit. After a humiliating failure or two, orbital altitude and velocity were finally accomplished using vehicles designed by Wernher von Braun, formerly Hitler's master of rocketry and now a resident of Alabama. Indeed, the army rockets were a modified version of the V-2 missiles that had rained down on Freeman Dyson and his countrymen during the Blitz.

Generally the progression here was from propeller to jet to rocket. All three produce propulsion by the combustion of fuel in an engine. The propeller moves the craft by twirling about and pushing masses of air to the rear. The jet scoops up air as the craft flies, burns the air with fuel, and then develops thrust by forceful backward ejection of the combustion products. Jet vehicles are much faster than propeller vehicles. Faster still is a rocket, which like the jet produces thrust by chemical combustion. The key difference: rockets carry all their own oxygen; they don't need to scoop up air as they go. Recognizing no boundary, they can zoom into space, where air-breathing jets may not go.

Were other forms of propulsion possible, better and faster than jets? Ted Taylor had the answer. The very night of the Sputnik launch, an idea had come to him, and he shared it with his General Atomic colleague Freddie de Hoffmann.[2] In due course Dyson would be informed.

Other branches of the U.S. government were also interested in attaining high velocity in space. The air force was looking for orbital opportunities. The Advanced Research Projects Agency—ARPA, the predecessor of the modern DARPA, the Defense Department program for developing high-tech equipment—showed definite interest and had seed money available. Things were moving quickly. Just as the Atomic Energy Commission had taken over civilian control of nuclear research and custodianship of nuclear weapons, so too a new civilian government entity in charge of operations in space would make its debut the following year. Its name was the National Aeronautics and Space Administration—NASA.

Somewhere among these mighty conglomerates an upstart alternative space venture would struggle for survival, and Dyson would be at the heart of it. Chemical rockets, von Braun–style rockets, were getting all the attention, but no final decision had yet been made about the kind of missile to be used to carry America into space. Maybe chemical wasn't the best way to go. Taylor and a few others wanted to build a new kind of ship, something much grander than what von Braun had in mind.

General Atomic would again provide the institutional home. "Give me a roomful of theoretical physicists," Freddie de Hoffmann said, "and I will conquer the world."[3] The odds of defeating chemical rockets were slim, but de Hoffmann felt there was a period of opportunity, maybe only one or two years, for demonstrating a better plan for getting into space and out there among the planets. Like a movie producer who had just hired himself a hotshot director (Taylor), de Hoffmann now wanted to procure a hotshot actor for the lead role. He hinted at the creation of an immense project and was offering Dyson the chance to get in at the beginning.

Because of the radical nature of the propulsion being contemplated, national security was going to be an issue. A full clearance would be needed, and de Hoffmann therefore wasn't able to tell Dyson more than a few of the details. What seemed to be in prospect, however, was the engineering equivalent of the Manhattan Project, a project potentially just as big and just as important, but without the killing. Take the TRIGA reactor project, multiply by a thousand or a million, and that's what the new thing might turn out to be. It was that big.

Dyson was just then on another one of his tours into mathematical physics, the kind of work that concerned the representation of quantum fields and, like number theory, involved detailed and rigorous proofs. Having submitted his conclusions to *Physical Review*, he discovered to his horror that he'd made a mistake. Perhaps still somewhat distracted by general events in this life, he'd slipped up and now had to do what every scientist hates to do—submit a retraction. Dyson told a friend of his humiliation at having presented a nonrigorous proof. The friend's reply: "What do you mean non-rigorous proof? There is no such thing as a non-rigorous proof. Either it is a proof, or it is not a proof."[4]

Dyson accepted de Hoffmann's offer and in January 1958 began occasional consulting visits to General Atomic. He asked his boss at the Institute, J. Robert Oppenheimer, for a leave of absence. Oppie, who himself had once taken leave from an important position at the University of California to take up a gamesome nuclear design project in the desert, could hardly say no. Besides, Hans Bethe had endorsed the project, which was to be called Orion.[5]

Freeman left the children behind in Princeton in the care of Imme Jung. Katarina had spent the 1957–58 school year boarding in the home of her ballet teacher nearby. Verena would now be returning from Europe and would live in the home on Battle Road Circle while Freeman was away. She had spent the fall months with Georg Kreisel in Britain and several more months alone in Zurich, where she'd been doing mathematics research again.

On the day before Freeman's departure for San Diego, Verena arrived in the United States and asked Freeman if she could live again as his wife. According to her, his answer was no.[6]

DARWIN ON MARS

Much is made of the mountain-and-plateau New Mexico setting for the Manhattan Project. You could think of its location on that isolated mesa as if it were a giant anvil on which the first nuclear bomb was forged. It was off by itself. By contrast, the seacoast-and-palm-tree setting and jaunty shirtsleeve insouciance of Project Orion would be typical of the whole aerospace industry that was sprouting up around suburban Southern California. Before long Dyson himself would own a 1957 Chevrolet Bel Air, which with its pastel shading and signature tail fins would become associated with the iconic look of the 1950s, especially emblematic of California surfer culture. He joined a glider club.

If anything it was a bit too sunny there. Dyson was having eye problems and had to wear dark glasses to keep out the glare. But he was there to work and not to sunbathe. He was determined to get it right this time. In 1943, freshly out of college at the age of nineteen,

Dyson had joined Bomber Command, whose mission was to defeat Fascism. In practice, however, this meant maximizing the number of killed Germans. Now, in 1958, as an eminent scientist, he was joining a new sort of Bomber Command, only this time the goal was not to kill civilians but to reach planets. The new work required the explosion of nuclear bombs, lots of them.

Basically Orion was a nuclear-powered spaceship, and it worked like this: An atom bomb is shoved out the back of the craft. At a certain distance, a hundred feet or so, it explodes. Part of the blast slams into the back of the ship. The explosion pushes a gigantic disk coated with a thin layer of sacrificial material. The layer is vaporized into fiery plasma, a cloud of hot atoms from which electrons have been stripped off. This plasma, in turn, pushes violently on the disk, propelling it away from the blast. The disk is attached to a manned spacecraft through an elaborate system of shock absorbers that cushion the riders from the immense forward jerk.

Let's stop right there. Having heard scarcely the merest description of Orion, many will have been quickly brought to incredulity. Cinematically it might be easy to visualize a series of nuclear explosions but not so easy to believe that anything nearby could survive intact. A dozen urgent questions scream out: Where do the bombs come from? How big is the craft and how does it get off the ground? Why doesn't it melt from the effect of the bomb? Where are the astronauts? Why aren't they incinerated or at least irradiated into a state of blue glow?

First, the disk does not melt if it has a proper coating sprayed on just before detonation. This coating, thin as it is, makes all the difference. Tests of actual nuclear bomb blasts showed that certain nearby metal objects, properly sheathed, could survive. The highest heat during the explosion lasts a mere fraction of a second. The sacrificial layer not only takes the brunt of the blast but provides the actual propulsive force. The rest of the ship, starting with the disk, is pushed away from the explosion by the plasma cloud. The craft does not so much gain thrust by sending exhaust out the back, the way rockets do, as it is pushed ahead by the plasma action of the cloud. Much of the blast and radiation is left behind and does not penetrate the disk and other parts of the craft situated further along.

The ship, in effect, would be surfing through space on a hot plasma plume triggered by and flung outward from a nuclear detonation. The process is repeated many times. A new sacrificial layer is deposited across the back of the pusher plate, another bomb is brought out of the storehouse at the center of the ship and ejected out the back, another explosion occurs, another plasma cloud envelops and pushes the craft, and still more speed is achieved.

Isn't this going to be a bumpy ride? Yes, the blast-created plasma impinging on the craft does impart a violent kick, but this is smoothed out by the stacked shock absorbers. The timing of the blasts, every few seconds or so, at least at first, and the coordinated working of the springs would average out to something like an acceleration equivalent to about 3 or 4 g's, no more than what the Apollo astronauts later put up with on their journey into space.[7]

Still incredible? They've got the bombs loaded on the ship from the beginning? Yes, thousands of them, lined up on an inside rack. They descend a chute one at a time like cans in a soda machine. In fact, the Coca-Cola Company was consulted on this issue.[8] The astronauts on board aren't affected by the bombs going off only a hundred feet away? No, because the thick pusher plate sits in between. Furthermore, the expanding plasma shoves the ship away from the bomb blast. How would you ever get used to an acceleration of several times that of Earth's gravity? This acceleration wouldn't be there all the time, but only when you were in a boost phase.

Boost phase? How does the whole thing get off the ground at all? Well, it blasts off from a tall tower. As you might imagine, a takeoff on top of an exploding atom bomb would make an Apollo launch, even with its roar and billowing smoke, look sedate. The early blasts would be small at first, enough to get Orion up off the ground and into space. Later explosions, the ones needed to gain really high speed, would be larger and come less often. For much of the time during a long mission there would be no explosions at all. The craft would be coasting.

Does the mind still reel at the audacity and the improbability of the whole scheme? Suspend for a moment your disbelief, along with arguments about the political, environmental, and budgeting impracticalities, and consider the plan's virtues. Consider Orion from Freeman Dyson's point of view. The energy density in U-235 is so large that even when you take into account the fact that much of the effect of any nuclear explosion would wastefully shoot off in a direction away from the ship, the conversion ratio for the nuclear rocket scenario used in

Orion is still far superior to that for the chemical rocket scenario contemplated for the Apollo mission.★

Payloads and destinations are what motivated the people who had dreamed up Orion. This mad scheme of using bomb blasts to propel a ship first came to Stanislaw Ulam, the scientist who along with Edward Teller had been the chief creator of the first hydrogen bomb. Now Ted Taylor had commandeered the idea. Freddie de Hoffmann, with the organization of General Atomic behind him, provided the infrastructure. An ARPA grant allowed the project to grow quickly. With such an ambitious goal in mind, a proliferation of problems needed solving. That was where Dyson came in. If de Hoffmann was to be Orion's equivalent of General Leslie Groves, and if Taylor was to be the Oppenheimer for the project, then Dyson would be its Hans Bethe, the chief theoretician.

The Orion team was bursting with ideas. Eager, dedicated engineers and scientists converged on the rapidly enlarging, fenced-off, high-security campus of buildings at the new General Atomic headquarters in La Jolla, north of San Diego. The schoolhouse used for TRIGA two years before was no longer needed.

It struck several participants that this new effort to harness nuclear power could and should be compared with the famous work done not so many years before in Los Alamos. The Manhattan Project had been completed very quickly, in a matter of a few years, under conditions of wartime necessity. Could Orion be completed as quickly? If Oppenheimer and his colleagues could hasten nuclear science from the level of tiny tabletop experiments to the level of a city-destroying weapon carried in the belly of a bomber, then why couldn't Ted Taylor, Dyson, and their comrades take proven nuclear technology to the next level—providing planetary propulsion—over a comparable span of years?

Dyson was there to deliver numbers and to use his fertile imagination to spur discussion in startling ways. When the planning would

---

★The very process by which thrust comes about in a chemical rocket is limited by the temperature of exhaust gases, and this limits the amount of acceleration. That limitation does not apply to the nuclear propulsion plan just described. For the same mass of fuel a nuclear ship can attain higher speeds, can visit remoter destinations, and carry larger payloads than any chemically powered ship.

With Saturn-style rockets, Dyson argued, the weight of the fuel severely limited the payload. The ship would require multiple stages, which would wastefully have to be discarded along the way. Dyson estimated that for chemical rockets, the ratio of the ship's takeoff weight to its return weight for low Earth orbit would be 16; for high-earth orbit it would be 64; for a Moon landing mission it would be 1,024. By comparison, Orion's return trip Moon mission weight ratio would be only 10. (FJD in *PT*, October 1968.)

bump up against the laws of physics, Dyson would be the chief problem solver; he would determine whether the obstacle could be surmounted. Dyson's mind, Taylor suggested, was like Mozart's in that Dyson could see the entire composition in one vision. He "saw more interconnections between more things than almost anybody. He sees the interrelationships, whether it is in some microscopic physical process or in a big complicated machine like Orion. He has been, from the time he was in his teens, capable of understanding essentially anything that he's interested in. He is the most intelligent person I know," said Taylor.[9] Brian Dunne, an Orion engineer who knew of Dyson's standing as a theoretical physicist, was impressed by how much engineering Dyson knew, electrical or mechanical. He went so far as to say that Dyson's grasp of things was unnerving. His immense common sense was a valuable resource.[10]

Many of the Orion documents Dyson produced remain classified to this day owing to the nature of the fuel at the heart of the whole enterprise—nuclear bombs. However, an unclassified list of the report titles tells an interesting story about the problems Dyson was addressing: the stability and control of the craft, the shaping of the bomb blast so as to maximize thrust, Orion's prospective itinerary to the outer planets and their moons, the shape of the plasma plume as it enveloped the tail end of the ship, the radioactive fallout from Orion as it plowed through the atmosphere, and the critical incineration, layer by layer, of the pusher plate coating in successive bomb blasts.

Freeman Dyson, the theoretical physicist, the former mathematician and student of G. H. Hardy ("I don't believe in indulging in practical problems"), loved the practical problems he was allowed and encouraged to pursue. The designers' ambitions and expectations flew along as rapidly as Orion itself: why couldn't we reach Mars in years rather than decades? In overall ability, Orion outmatched chemical rockets, even if chemical rockets like Saturn V temporarily were receiving favored treatment by space planners.

And once you're at Mars, don't merely scoop up some soil and leave. Stay awhile. Enjoy the scenery. Dyson thought a four-year exploration of the Red Planet's surface would be about right. Charles Darwin's comparable sojourn on board the HMS *Beagle* had had an enormous impact on our knowledge of the living part of the cosmos. The theory of evolution sprang from Darwin's fruitful voyage around the tip of South America. What might come of a landing on Mars and a pole-to-pole survey of the topography? Maybe we'd find in the orange sand something as revealing as the varieties of finch beaks on the Galápagos Islands, suggesting to Darwin the whole mechanism of evolution through adaptation to local conditions in the islands. On Mars fossilized life forms might be lying there in the ground. Even the discovery of micron-sized organisms would give us a new perspective on the universe. Imagine adding a whole new Martian limb to the diagrammed tree of life. And if we struck out on Mars, there would be other worlds to visit such as Jupiter's moons Europa or Calisto, or Saturn's moon Titan.

First you had to get from here to there. The most important part of this billion-mile trip would be the first quarter inch. The great test would be the liftoff from blueprint to construction.

Freeman Dyson loved Orion. As soon as he returned to La Jolla for the summer he could see that this was going to be much more all-encompassing work than TRIGA had been. He needed more time. He asked Robert Oppenheimer for the whole of the coming academic year off in order to concentrate on his rocket ship.

In laying out his case to Oppie, Dyson enunciated some of the themes that were to enter into his writings decades later. Since his childhood he had wanted to be involved in launching planetary expeditions; it is important, he said, for society that certain hardy individuals break free of existing rules by journeying past all frontiers; new things would be discovered by science but only if we actually took the trouble to venture out there. Dyson assured his boss that he still enjoyed the Institute connection but hinted that if Orion, as he hoped, took on the importance and size of the Manhattan Project, then he might have to shift his affiliation permanently.[11] He'd been asked to become a vice president of General Atomic.[12] The impact of nuclear explosives on national security and international diplomacy had been great. Wouldn't the nuclearization of propulsion be just as great if it led to an era of planetary exploration?

SECOND MORTGAGE

The children were glad to have their mother back with them that summer of 1958. Verena had been away for a year. Esther, now seven years old, had come to suspect that the miscarriage had been behind the difficulties between her parents. She expected that when her mother returned from Europe she might be bringing a new baby.[13] There was no baby this time.

Then in July, unannounced, Freeman turned up in Princeton, just when Imme was off on vacation in New England. When the children woke that morning they discovered both Freeman and Verena in the same house for the first time in a year and a half. She had to explain to them that, no, he wouldn't be staying long. He had to get back to his new job in California.

Only a month before Verena had asked to be taken back. Freeman had said no. Here he was, reversing himself, asking Verena to rejoin the marriage. Now it was her turn to hesitate. She didn't say no, but she did need time to think over the offer.[14]

A major complication now appeared, once again in the person of Georg Kreisel, who was returning to the United States to take up a post at Stanford University. Even though he and Verena had been apart for eight months, he gentlemanly proposed—as if it were the eminently practical thing to do—that Verena could make up her mind about her future by coming to live with him at Stanford, where she too could have a part-time mathematics job.

By early September, the issue had been settled. Writing from California, Freeman informed Oppenheimer that he had failed to persuade Verena to return to the family and expected a divorce within months.[15]

Without asking Verena, Kreisel consulted a lawyer on her behalf. Freeman himself now hired a lawyer, but then fired him. A plan began to emerge: Verena would spend a residency period in Reno, Nevada, which would facilitate the granting of a divorce request.

Freeman was committed to spending at least the coming academic year in La Jolla, and so the Princeton home would have to be rented out. Freeman asked Imme to fly out to California with George, while Verena would drive west in the car with Esther and Katarina. Imme thought this plan was unfair to Verena, so the two women and the three children all drove.[16]

What was the arrangement between Imme and Freeman? Back in the fall of 1957, Verena had thought it was proper to inform Imme's father that she, Verena, was no longer in the Dyson household since this might make it awkward for Imme. The father's response was that Imme was an adult and could handle herself. About this time too, Freeman had indicated in a letter to Verena that he was considering marrying Imme if circumstances permitted.[17] In a letter to Oppenheimer he said that he expected Verena to become Mrs. Kreisel.[18]

Now in the fall of 1958, with the divorce of Verena and Freeman in the works, the engagement of Imme and Freeman became a reality. Esther was unhappy when she spotted an engagement ring on Imme's finger and understood the implications. Imme tactfully removed the ring.[19] Moreover, to make things more seemly, Imme returned to Germany to visit her family.[20] A new German au pair arrived to shoulder household duties.[21]

The terms of divorce were drawn up. Freeman was to have custody of Esther and George during the bulk of the year. Verena would have them during the summer and holidays. Katarina would of course remain with Verena.[22]

And the money. Freeman's view: Verena's lawyer was holding out for a ruinous payout from Freeman, an amount so large that he would probably have to sell the Princeton house.[23] Verena's view: all she wanted was to get back the money she'd contributed as a down payment on the home.[24]

Freeman wasn't sure where he would come up with the money for the cash payment, but was rescued by Oppenheimer, who, on behalf of the Institute, offered Freeman a second mortgage for his house in the amount of $7,500.[25] In response Freeman thanked Oppie and informed him of the secret news that he and Imme were to be married.[26]

The morning of the divorce hearing, Verena was in tears. She couldn't go through with it. Of course you can, said Freeman. You're strong.[27] On November 12, 1958, the divorce was official. Verena moved to Stanford to live and work with Georg Kreisel. At a party one night, he introduced her to his friends as "my wife, Mrs. Dyson."[28]

Freeman Dyson and Imme Jung were married on November 21, 1958. He was nearly thirty-five, she nearly twenty-two. The children had a good time at the event. The newlyweds hoped for a honeymoon in Mexico but Imme, at the last moment, noticed that her passport was expiring the next day. So they settled for a two-day swing up to San Francisco. For Freeman, life was about to start all over again.[29]

MAYFLOWER COMPACT

Freeman Dyson lived with his new wife and two children (and another one on the way) in La Jolla, one of the most beautiful places in

America. He had a terrific job at the Institute for Advanced Study to return to, if he wanted it back.

Meanwhile, he was enjoying himself in California. Two years before he had, in his modest way, helped to fire up the early nuclear power industry. Now he was at work on Orion, a project just as important, or more so—developing a radical new technology for launching humans into space.

He and Ted Taylor saw this task in terms of a great competition between the Orion approach, which used nuclear power in the form of exploding bombs, and the Apollo approach, which used chemical power in the form of rockets, like Saturn V, achieved when oxygen and hydrogen were combined to create conventional explosive thrust.

NASA, born just the previous summer, was to be the civilian agency overseeing the trek into space. The competition between propulsion modes, Dyson and Taylor felt, would be settled soon, perhaps this very year, in 1959.[30] They had this year to demonstrate that nuclear was the way to go.

Juggling numerous engineering parameters, the Orion team arrived at a standard-issue design. The total weight of the vehicle would be about 4,000 tons, or 8 million pounds, not much different from a fully loaded Apollo craft sitting on the pad. Of this about one-fourth would be for the pusher plate, one-fourth for payload (including the human occupants), one-fourth for the nuclear inventory of 400 nuclear bombs, and one-fourth for the rest of the craft. The thing would look like a rather blunt artillery shell, 135 feet wide at the bottom and about twice as tall. A typical launch would require a succession of shots of the 5-kiloton Hiroshima class, with larger blasts to follow once the craft cleared the atmosphere.

Who would be strapped in when this behemoth heaved off? We now have a dedicated corps of astronauts, mostly daring test pilots who, along with a few payload specialists, are the ones who go up into space. But the Orion designers had no intention of staying behind. Freeman Dyson anticipated going. Longingly viewing the sky as a marvelous-but-fictional realm wasn't enough for him. No, he would actually go there. Ted Taylor not only planned to go but wanted to take his young son with him. This was part of the fun. Who else in history—certainly not fictionalists like Jules Verne or H. G. Wells—had been in a position to dream about space *and* do something about it? Dyson and Taylor would personally venture forth. The two of them had sat together in

Taylor's backyard, sipping cognac while gazing at Jupiter through a telescope.[31] They just might be in a position to do what backyard astronomers had always dreamed of doing—going in person to those distant spots in space.

Dyson would outdo his 1933 childhood Erolunar fantasy. He would *become* Sir Phillip Roberts. He would not bother to stop at the Moon. With Orion's propulsion you could think much more grandly. "Saturn by 1970" became the motto. Dyson would be on board when Orion swung past the glorious system of rings; they had made sure to include expansive windows for viewing.

The voyage of Orion would be many things: exploration, adventure, science, and redemption. Dyson prepared himself mentally for the trip by drafting a Space Traveler's Manifesto. In this little document we see that the Orion project would not only match the excitement and achievement of the Manhattan Project. La Jolla would also be atonement for Los Alamos. "Our purpose, and our belief, is that the bombs which killed and maimed at Hiroshima and Nagasaki shall one day open the skies to men," said the document. From the time he was a lad Dyson had been convinced "that men would reach the planets in my lifetime, and that I would help in the enterprise." It was essential for humans "to escape from their neighbors and from their governments, to go live as they pleased in the wilderness."[32]

This was the language of the Pilgrims, who, before leaving the *Mayflower*, swore a pact concerning the government for the forlorn outcrop of North America now known as Massachusetts. This was the aim of the seventeenth-century Puritans who left England to escape the problems of their ancestral home. They and their twentieth-century counterparts wanted to set things right.

With the voyage of Orion the new land was going to be not the sandy beaches of New England but the moons of Jupiter or Saturn. It's interesting to ponder the pioneer sentiment of Dyson's manifesto, considering that he was an Englishman born, a graduate of Cambridge, a son of the director of the Royal Academy of Music, and a man who for much of his career had studied nature only theoretically from an office perch in Princeton. Here he was propounding an updated sailing of the *Beagle*. More than this, future Orion missions would carry forth colonists to establish new civilizations. Orion would be another *Mayflower*. Gliding up beneath the rings of Saturn, the spacecraft of 1970 would, like the Pilgrim vessel hoving up offshore Plymouth in 1620, offer the chance, at least in Dyson's estimation, of restarting civilization. Only a small portion of this attitude made its way into official Orion documents. The rest was in the minds of the Orion fraternity.

Could it happen? A proposed nuclear trip to Saturn and back lasting three years was all in accord with the known laws of physics. The wildest plans drew upon aerodynamic or nuclear technology that was either available then or was expected to materialize after not too many years.

In the case of Orion, what was the grandest scenario? First, there was standard Orion. This would transport humans to Saturn by 1970. Much less likely, but delightful to contemplate, was Super-Orion. This was a craft some 400 meters in diameter, a fourth of a mile wide, and weighing 8 million tons. Assembled in Earth orbit and set in motion, it might eventually reach speeds of hundreds of km/sec by firing megaton-class hydrogen bombs out the back. At full performance, it would be able to traverse the solar system in about a month. With a dedicated crew, resigned to leaving Earth forever, along with their children and grandchildren, and confronting the sort of posterity faced by Polynesian explorers long ago heading out into the open Pacific, Super-Orion would be able to reach the nearest star, Alpha Centauri, in about 150 years.[33] Wilderness indeed.

Outside La Jolla, talk like this was understandably viewed with some skepticism. Aside from the cost of realizing these schemes, two large impediments to nuclear propulsion loomed: bureaucratic inertia and nuclear squeamishness. First, bureaucracy. Although associated with several government agencies, Orion had been the undertaking of a private company, General Atomic, a subsidiary of General Dynamics, under contract to ARPA, a subsidiary of the Department of Defense. Orion needed a permanent home and official status.

It was unlikely that NASA, AEC, or the Pentagon would welcome the orphan. Even though Wernher von Braun had come to see some virtue in the nuclear propulsion concept—a round-trip to Saturn in three years he found impressive—NASA didn't like the bomb detonation aspect, and so it declined to take possession of Orion. NASA would stick with its chemical rockets. The AEC was already in the bomb design and detonation business, so Orion's bomb load didn't worry them. But Orion's chief function, providing Greyhound bus service to the planets, stood pretty far from AEC's own mission. Besides, the AEC already had three nuclear installations of its own: the labs at Los Alamos, Livermore, and Sandia (just outside Albuquerque).

Then there was the Pentagon. Would the U.S. Air Force take possession? Those air force officials who had themselves been scientists liked the project. Dyson, Dunne, and Taylor went to New Mexico to brief them. The air force researchers were impressed, but their superiors, mostly combat veterans, had difficulty justifying support for a ship with few military attributes. In summary, Orion was a promising but unloved foster child.

Just as worrisome was Orion's nuclear debris. Even if the bomb blasts did no lasting harm to ship or crew, where exactly did the radioactive spewings *go*, as Orion struggled against gravity on its way through the atmosphere? This problem had not eluded Freeman Dyson. In fact it was one of the issues uppermost in his thinking. First, as Dyson was to remind people for years to come whenever the subject of actually deploying Orion came up, in these years of the 1950s open-air testing of nuclear weapons by the U.S. and the USSR was common. An estimated 1,000 people a year died from illnesses related to the extra radiation from these tests.[34]

Such a large radiation death rate seems outrageous to us now. But *then*, in the core years of the nuclear-tipped Cold War, an annual casualty rate of 1,000 people was the statistical background. This was an era when the deaths of hundreds of millions from a nuclear exchange could easily be imagined. A level of 1,000 nuclear fallout–related deaths worldwide was absorbed into conventional thinking as were the 50,000 U.S. highway fatalities per year. Many more died from cigarettes.

Nuclear deaths were not exactly taken for granted. Protests eventually led to a ban on open-air nuclear testing. But that would be years later. Orion and its exhaust, set against the then known yearly radioactivity budget, seemed feasible. Still, the likely sting of Orion's plume, even if statistically it were no more than one person killed per mission, ate away at Dyson's conscience. The Bomber Command ethos—killing innocent people in the interest of victory—had kicked in. His enthusiasm cooled.[35]

Von Braun's rockets were winning the race. They were already scheduled for hurling astronauts into near-Earth orbit. In an effort to address the problem of Orion's radioactive exhaust, Dyson went to the weapons lab at Livermore, California, where he worked on the problem with Edward Teller. Dyson, in the role of a bomb designer for the one time in his life, struggled for a brilliant, frenzied couple of weeks on trying to devise a nuclear device that minimized the ill effects of bombs exploded in a good cause. He enjoyed working with Teller and with his young colleagues, who all toiled in anonymity. But they ran out of time. The kind of bomb Teller and Dyson were seeking, now called a neutron bomb, wouldn't be possible for many years.[36]

Away from Princeton now for months, Dyson had to decide. Should he stay out west with Orion or return east? He enjoyed the Orion camaraderie, especially his friendship with Ted Taylor. He had surprised himself at the depth of his commitment to doing practical research:

> *The fifteen months I spent on Orion were the most exciting and in many ways the happiest of my scientific life. I particularly enjoyed being immersed in the ethos of engineering, which is very different from the ethos of science. A good scientist is a person with original ideas. A good engineer is a person who makes a design that works with as few original ideas as possible.*[37]

Dyson could tell, however, that the project's momentum was slipping away. Had the recessional begun? Should he convert his Orion consultant's position into something permanent at General Atomic or return to the Institute for Advanced Study?

Freeman Dyson, thinking now of a test firing of the rocket, went with Ted Taylor to a remote site in the Nevada desert, a place called Jackass Flats. Here he had another one of those moments when his inner universe got disturbed. Standing there in the middle of nowhere, what impressed him was not so much the natural beauty of the place but the utter silence. The silence was so profound that he referred to it later as "soul shattering." What he and his fellow Orion-eers were preparing to do was to invade this sound-less, wind-less preserve with the high-decibel screech of powered machinery, the bustle of construction crews, and, finally and grandly, the blast-and-flash takeoff of a nuclear rocket. Dyson was uncomfortably tickled by a sensation he recognized as shame. "The first shadow of doubt about the rightness of Orion came into my mind with that silence."[38]

9. Civilized Behavior

Dyson Searches for Extraterrestrial Intelligence
(EARLY 1960S)

Was invasion the right word? The opposing forces met but were oblivious to each other—the Martians too small to be seen by the Earthlings and the Earthlings too slow to be perceived by the Martians. The invaders from Mars consisted of a cloud of microorganisms; they possessed radio telepathy and distributed consciousness but did not otherwise have a solid body. The Earthlings had bodies but had to resort to spoken words or machines to transmit messages among themselves. Insubstantial as they were, the Martians had a sophisticated culture. They had come to Earth looking for resources, especially diamonds. They found diamonds but looked right past the human inhabitants of the planet.

This story about first contact comes from *Last and First Men*, the 1931 novel by Olaf Stapledon.[1] If we encountered an intelligent alien species, would we even recognize it? Maybe not. Stapledon's books contain much discussion of sociology, the relations between the sexes, and how organisms sense their environment and survive in hostile conditions. The novels have little in the way of plot or complex characters. Some science fiction readers have never heard of Stapledon. Others believe he might be, along with H. G. Wells, the greatest writer in the genre.[2] Stanislaw Lem and C. S. Lewis were influenced by him. Arthur C. Clarke, author of *2001: A Space Odyssey*, was infatuated by Stapledon's book; "It transformed my life," he said.[3]

You are partly what you read. The things found in books can be absorbed into your thinking, where they resonate for years. Such was the case with Freeman Dyson, who in wartime London stumbled upon Stapledon's writings. Years later they were to provide Dyson with rich ideas about the diversity of life in the universe, a theme that would be at the heart of his own writing career.

In Stapledon's 1937 novel, *Star Maker*, the reader encounters an even wider spectrum of intelligent beings, including the Nautiloids, an ocean-going race of galleon-like creatures with rudders, sails, and hulls. In another story, we meet the Flames, a species living entirely within stars. Stapledon's 1944 novel *Sirius* is about a dog with the mental abilities of a man. The creature has a human lover and he struggles to reconcile human and canine worlds. Are such things possible? Can the boundaries among species be transgressed? Can life survive in vacuum or at low temperatures? Can things like stars be alive? Stapledon pondered these topics through fiction, Dyson through science.

Multiple human species do not currently exist (the Neanderthals died out 30,000 years ago), Martian organisms have not come into our midst (as far as we know), and Orion-class ships aren't yet capable of ferrying astronauts to Mars, much less to the stars. Dyson found this unsatisfactory. He continued to argue for Orion's approval. But in the meantime, his dreams of interplanetary or interstellar travel would have to take a different form. Reconciling himself to an earthbound existence, he sought other creative outlets for putting his Space Traveler's Manifesto into practice.

Lebensraum

Dyson's fifteen months in La Jolla were up. Back on Earth, things had changed a lot. At the beginning of those fifteen months his family had consisted of Verena, Esther, George, and Katarina. Now his family was Imme, Esther, George, and Dorothy, a new daughter born in September 1959, just two weeks before the Dysons were due to leave La Jolla. One branch of the family split off: Katarina remained in California with Verena, who had a job at San Jose State College. (Georg Kreisel returned to a job in Britain.) The main Dyson branch returned to Princeton. Imme was not a mother's helper anymore. She was the mother.

Dyson was not done with Orion. He went back to San Diego in November 1959 for a test firing of a nonnuclear Orion mock-up. A refrigerator-sized craft, powered by a succession of conventional chemical blasts, was lofted up past a tower. Dyson collected some shards from this experiment and for many years kept them in his desk drawer. In 1960, Project Orion passed over into the custody of the U.S. Air Force.

Instead of immigrating to another star system aboard Orion, Dyson remained on his home planet, safely in his office at the Institute for Advanced Study, and did what scientists have long done—allowed stars to come to them in the form of light waves. For the last few centuries lenses mounted in telescopes helped to gather the feeble light cast by distant suns. Later, photography extended astronomical prospects by performing two important services. First, it fixed the images of the sky in a permanent record on a coated glass plate and later in an electronic array of pixels. Second, it accumulated light for seconds or minutes—something the human retina could not do—greatly strengthening the image. For instance, when you see a picture of the pinwheel-shaped Andromeda galaxy you see an image accumulated over many seconds. A human eye, even using a powerful telescope, would not be able to form such a sharp image.

Additional technology allowed astronomers to see the universe in a new way using light that was previously invisible. The frequency of this light was not matched to our eyes, which are sensitive only to a small portion of a wide spectrum of electromagnetic radiation. Practice with radio and television broadcasts and wartime development of radar meant we could "look" at the sky at those frequencies. It's as if we could suddenly perceive new colors. Then still more colors became available; after the first rockets could loft objects into orbit above the absorbent blanket of our atmosphere, astronomers could image the heavens at very high frequencies, encompassing the ultraviolet and X ray portions of the spectrum.

Through these new windows scientists uncovered unexpected phenomena, such as X-rays from the sun, showing that the temperature of the solar corona was far higher than that of the sun's surface. Radio waves from Jupiter suggested the presence of a powerful magnetic field welling up from inside the planet. Could the new light provide signs of living things at remote planets or stars? Better still, could we discern hints of an intelligent civilization in the form of radio broadcasts?

In a pioneering 1959 paper two Cornell physicists, Philip Morrison and Giuseppe Cocconi, calculated optimal radio frequencies for locating distant civilizations.[4] Another Cornell scientist, Frank Drake, was just then preparing antennas in order to search for exactly such signals. Listening in to the universe with radio waves became the primary approach to the search for extraterrestrial intelligence, an endeavor called SETI for short.

Dyson took a contrarian view. He believed that the radio method of searching the sky would result in a frustrating game of hide-and-seek. First, he said, the hypothetical aliens might not be talkative. They might be shy or devious and want to hide their existence rather than proclaim it. Second, whether or not they were in a talkative mood they would not be able to hide their heat. All physical objects at temperatures above absolute zero emit heat waves. Especially in our world, typified by a temperature of about 300 degrees kelvin, what we commonly refer to as room temperature, things cast off a lot of waste heat in the form of infrared radiation. As with radio waves and X-rays, infrared (IR) waves can be detected.

IR sensors show, for example, where heat is leaking out of a home on a cold winter's night (usually around un-insulated windows and doors) or show where heat is suffusing from a human body just after vigorous exercise (around the heart, muscles, and any place where warm blood copiously flows). The same principle applies to cities and whole civilizations. They all leak heat on a large scale. Dyson was inspired to thinking about how intelligent bustle could be apparent to outsiders by looking at early satellite pictures showing nocturnal evidence of human activity: oil flares, city lights, and forest-clearing fires.[5] What this suggested to him was that while we might not directly observe hints of intelligence, such as episodes of *I Love Lucy*, we would probably see the warmth of technology at work.

Dyson explored extrasolar civilizations with thought experiments. He tinkered with the outer limits of what was physically possible and squeezed a lot of ideas into a one-page article in *Science*. Before addressing hypothetical evidence for alien heat, Dyson first assessed the technological civilization we have ourselves already produced in the past few thousand years and how much more complex it could become if we kept going for thousands of years more. Barring catastrophic wars or epidemics, he figured, we could build a society larger and more technically advanced by a huge factor. Assuming a modest growth of 1 percent per year in the population and in industrial complexity, society would enlarge by a factor of one billion after only 3,000 years.[6] A civilization that large would have outgrown its home planet.

In his paper Dyson therefore had reason to refer to a Malthusian scramble for the material means of survival. He referred to the need for more living space, or *Lebensraum*—the German term associated with Adolf Hitler's territorial aspirations in Eastern Europe—when characterizing the expansion of society over eons. To reach an advanced state, Dyson argued, a civilization would need to command amounts of energy and material far above current earthly levels. Right now the Earth's surface intercepts only a tiny amount of the energy the sun sends into space. And of that amount only a tiny fraction is exploited by living things, mostly in the form of photosynthesis.

For human culture to go on expanding it would need much more of the precious solar radiation, eventually *all* of it. Moreover, available habitable real estate would have to keep pace, far outrunning the portion of the planet's surface that we currently occupy. As for raw materials, the minerals and metal of all our planet's mountains would not be enough to equip a future billion-fold-larger population.

The demographic struggles of future societies are an important part of the books of Olaf Stapledon. And so are the solutions to those struggles. In addressing the *Lebensraum* issue, Dyson specifically borrowed from Stapledon's novel *Star Maker* in suggesting that an advanced society, whether for Earthlings or for hypothetical aliens, could procure the extra energy it needed by disassembling an asteroid or even a planet.[7] With this scrounged material you could fashion a large array of light-harvesting panels surrounding the star. These panels would serve as both solar energy absorbers and as additional homes for people, the off-Earth continuation of suburbanization.[8]

What would this array look like? In his thought experiment, Dyson suggested that an advanced society could build a fleet of platforms only a few meters thick or even less, all orbiting the sun at the same distance as Earth. In practice this archipelago would not entirely surround the sun. Owing to mechanical instabilities, the array could not rotate or orbit the sun as a single rigid ball. Nevertheless, this hypothetical energy collector scheme has come to be known as a "Dyson sphere." Viewed from afar, these arrays, drinking in solar energy and then glowing at a wavelength of 10 microns, would be the tip-off that something intelligent was happening in space in that region.[9]

While writing up his article for *Science*, Dyson became afraid that some people might consider it undignified for a professor at the Institute for Advanced Study to be making conjectures like this. So as a courtesy he sheepishly sought Oppenheimer's permission to venture onto such speculation.[10] Oppie gave his consent, and the paper was published. Dyson never again felt inhibited from letting his imagination roam widely.

The leviathan space habitat construction Dyson had in mind is obviously beyond our current technical means. Mustering a Jupiter-sized load of building materials would make even Project Orion look puny. Dyson course recognized the magnitude and impracticality of his plan. His self-appointed task was not to say what *will* happen but what *could* happen. Furthermore, he wasn't even necessarily talking about what future Earthlings could do but about what might have happened already in some far-away planetary culture.

How common are such societies? Frank Drake devised a formula for computing the likelihood of intelligent life existing in our galaxy. The probability for this would be roughly proportional to a number of factors, such as the fraction of stars with planets, the fraction of planets supporting living things, and the fraction of intelligent societies that possess the means of interstellar communication.

VIKING TECHNOLOGY

Dyson did not trust such formulas. It's hard enough to predict the advent of life and intelligence on our own planet. The chemical circumstances surrounding the appearance of primitive living cells are so murky as to preclude saying anything meaningful about how things are alive on remote planets, much less saying anything about flourishing civilizations.[11] Perhaps we should look at the hallmarks of civilization here on Earth.

"What is civilisation?" asked Kenneth Clark. "I don't know. I can't define it in abstract terms—yet. But I think I can recognize it when I see it; and I am looking at it now." Clark, an art historian, opened his 1968 television series *Civilisation* with a cinematic view of the Pont des Arts in Paris, a pedestrian bridge across the Seine linking the Louvre museum and the Institut du France, two great fixtures in the cultural life of the French nation. Visible in other directions are Notre Dame cathedral, quaint bookstalls along the river embankment, charming bistros, art studios, government ministries, and still more museums, all constructed in a variety of architectural styles over centuries. Is this the most civilized place on Earth? Clark was too polite to say so exactly.[12]

What is the most civilized place in the galaxy? There is no answer to this absurd question. For Dyson, in his *Science* article, civilization is defined, or at least revealed, by high technology. For Clark it usually means high art. Dyson asks to see solar energy collection, while Clark asks to see Rembrandts. Actually Clark lists things like art and good manners as being but the outward signs of civilization. The actual causes of civilization have more to do with outlook. This Clark illustrates with a shot of the 2,000-year-old Roman aqueduct, the Pont du Gard, in southern France:

> *Of course civilisation requires a modicum of material prosperity—enough to provide a little leisure. But, far more, it requires confidence—confidence in the society in which one lives, belief in its philosophy, belief in its laws, and confidence in one's own mental powers. The way in which the stones of the Pont du Gard are laid is not only a triumph of technical skill, but shows a vigorous belief in law and discipline. Vigour, energy, vitality: all the great civilizations—or civilizing epochs—have had a weight of energy behind them.*[13]

As Clark reminds us, civilization doesn't need to be kind. The Vikings, who in the eighth century had terrorized the earlier inhabitants of the place that is now Paris, were very cruel and yet capable of producing art objects of great beauty.

Cultural historians divide up the years into periods: classic Mayan, late Mayan, Renaissance, Baroque, Song Dynasty, Ming Dynasty, and so forth. Can we do the same for civilizations residing on a nether arm of the Milky Way? Novelists do this. Olaf Stapledon writes of the succession of civilizations, even assigning them numbers.

Dyson does this too. Taking his cue from Stapledon and from Russian scientist Nikolai Kardashev, Dyson recognizes three advanced civilization types: those that command respectively the entire resources of a planet, a star, and a galaxy.[14] Our current terrestrial civilization wouldn't rate even as Type I. It certainly has a global reach and seems to be altering worldwide climate by vigorously unleashing various gases and minerals. On the other hand, nature still strikes back easily in the form of hurricane and earthquake. Human efforts at engineering, such as cities and agriculture, are easily upended.

Dyson believes that we can achieve Type I status in a few centuries. To be Type II, commandeering an entire star, the civilization will have to be capable of making a Dyson sphere for itself. That involves doing something like disassembling Jupiter for its raw material. Since we've just started sending robot scouts there in the past few decades it would seem that Type II technology lies at least several thousand years in our future.

Type III civilizations, those that use the resources of whole galaxies, are so advanced as to be almost unimaginable. Even here, though, conceivable arrangements can be pondered. The Milky Way is a big place, but traveling at 1 percent of light speed, a craft could cross the galaxy in 10 million years.[15] It would take much longer actually to command the resources of the galaxy, but at least one can set a rough scale for a Type III accomplishment. How can one achieve such high-energy feats? At a birthday party for Hans Bethe in 1965, Dyson gave a talk that expanded on his earlier Dyson sphere ideas. One way we could tap really large amounts of energy would be to reposition stars or, more grandly still, smash stars together in order to extract their contents.[16]

In the scientific and engineering realms, Dyson's ideas for advanced civilizations were no more than speculation, as he cheerfully conceded. But in the realm of art, Dyson's speculations have already had fair play. The Dyson sphere concept helped inspire numerous novels, including Larry Nivens's popular *Ringworld*. The sphere was featured on an episode of *Star Trek: The Next Generation*.[17] Dyson was pleased that *Star Trek* had made him "part of popular culture," but recognized that the episode was otherwise filled with physics errors.[18]

The Dyson sphere proposal might have struck a chord, but the favored mode for searching out meaningful extraterrestrial light has remained radio waves or microwaves, and not infrared radiation. Project Cyclops was an early proposed array of more than a thousand radio telescopes, each in the shape of a large dish, dedicated to the effort. A Cyclops design study reaffirmed radio waves as the preferred searchable wavelength and specifically questioned the viability of Dyson's idea that advanced civilization could profitably harvest energy with an orbiting armada of Dyson spheres, which the study snidely referred to as "mobile homes." "Dyson appears haunted by Malthusian principles," the report said, "and apparently considers astro-engineering a simpler solution than birth control."[19]

One can't declare from reading the 1960 *Science* article alone that Dyson was haunted by the prognostications of Thomas Malthus—that burgeoning populations tended to overrun their territory and outrun available food—but Dyson's subsequent writings would reveal a growing interest in exactly this subject. He would indeed write frequently about voyages into space and how to marshal scarce resources in a cold vacuum environment. But in so doing Dyson would prove to be not a Malthusian but an anti-Malthusian. He would consistently argue that many demographic threats could be counteracted with technological innovations. He wasn't sure what those innovations would be. No one could predict these things. "In the long run, qualitative changes outweigh quantitative ones."[20] But he was pretty sure that the solution to the problem of overcrowding on Earth was to venture out among the stars. This was the destiny of the race, he heartfully felt.

The Morrison-Cocconi and the Dyson papers are two of the founding documents of SETI. For decades now astronomers have scrutinized the skies at both radio and infrared wavelengths and found no purposeful broadcasts from the abyss. In 1966, the young Carl Sagan wrote an article about why finding such "Dyson civilizations" would be difficult.[21] What subsequent observers have found is plenty of heat, but not meaningful heat signifying technological busyness. Alien creatures, if they're out there, aren't talking. As far as we can tell, they're not even perspiring.

DEATH OF ORION

Not long after Dyson left La Jolla in the fall of 1959 Orion had passed quietly into the custodianship of the air force, and new compromises and new levels of bureaucracy were imposed. The purpose of exploring planets was not forgotten, but by law an air force project must contribute to the national defense. A militarized version of Orion was cooked up, a thing called Deep Space Bombardment Force.[22] Essentially a battleship floating in the ocean of space, this craft would be a doomsday weapon of the kind described in Stanley Kubrick's movie *Dr. Strangelove.* Deep Space Force would consist of a fleet of Orion ships parked in distant orbits, out next to Neptune. Each ship would bristle with nuclear missiles to be hurled in a retaliatory strike if ever the United States were attacked. When the Orion project was brought to the attention of John Kennedy, the new president was intrigued by the planet-visiting version of Orion but appalled by the doomsday version.[23]

Ted Taylor, like a traveling salesman, boosted the idea of Orion wherever he could. Seeking to surmount the blatant problem of fouling Earth's atmosphere with nuclear fallout, Orion engineers reconfigured the whole thing so that the craft could be ferried by Saturn V rockets, the same that were due to carry Apollo into space, at least as far as the jumping-off point of Earth orbit.

But even this didn't solve the problem of Orion's mission. In January 1965 the project was canceled. Shortly thereafter Dyson wrote an extension of his Space Traveler's Manifesto. It appeared later that year in the pages of *Science*, in the form of a funeral oration. Like Marc Antony in Shakespeare's *Julius Caesar*, Dyson assumed the pose of dispassionate historian: "The purpose of this article is neither to bury Orion nor to praise it. It is only to tell the public for the first time the facts of Orion's life and death, and to explain as fairly as possible the political and philosophical issues which are involved in its fate."[24]

"Who killed Orion, and why?" he asked. The Defense Department (Orion wasn't militaristic enough), NASA (Orion was too nuclear and encumbered with security issues), the test ban treaty (prohibiting nuclear tests), and scientists in general (who found the topic of propulsion uninteresting). Like Antony declaring throughout his funeral speech for Caesar that the regicide Brutus was an honorable man, Dyson commended Orion's killers: "each group of men who killed Orion acted from high and responsible motives. And yet their motives were strangely irrelevant to the real issues at stake in this highly individual case."

The chief function of the article was to argue that Orion represented a "major expansion of human technology," insofar as it provided a radically new way of achieving high velocity, the kind of velocity you need to travel to other stars within a few human generations, and that this magnificent enterprise had been suppressed for political reasons. Then, like Antony working his audience into a final froth of indignation, Dyson concluded with a thundering expression of solidarity with his comrades from the days in La Jolla:

> They must continue to hope that they may see their work bear fruit in their own lifetimes. They cannot lose sight of the dream that fired their imaginations in 1958 and sustained them through the years of struggle afterward—the dream that the bombs which killed and maimed at Hiroshima and Nagasaki may one day open the skies to mankind.[25]

Ted Taylor, had called Dyson the most intelligent man he'd ever met. What did Dyson think of Taylor?

> *There is something tragic about his life. He was the Columbus who never got to go and discover America. I just felt that he—much more than von Braun or anyone else—was the real Columbus of our days. I think he is probably the greatest man I ever knew well. And he is completely unknown.*[26]

1966: A SPACE ODYSSEY

The brash director of *Lolita* and *Dr. Strangelove* wanted to meet Freeman Dyson. Stanley Kubrick was making a movie about space travel and liked Dyson's idea of nuclear propulsion. The look and function of Kubrick's fictional rocketship, *Discovery*, was borrowed from Orion. More than that, Kubrick wanted Dyson to speak on camera about life in space.

That's why in 1966 Dyson had come to the MGM Studios outside London, where *2001: A Space Odyssey* was being shot. Orion wouldn't be getting to Saturn by 1970, but *Discovery* would be getting to Jupiter by 2001, at least fictionally, and Dyson was going to be part of it. On film he talked about humans colonizing comets. Others interviewed included science writer Isaac Asimov and anthropologist Margaret Mead.

When Dyson arrived, a scene inside the ship was being filmed. The actor Keir Dullea, playing astronaut Dave Bowman, was called upon to look undemonstrably at some monitors and walk about the annular-shaped flight deck. An Orion crew compartment might have looked something like this. Instead of Dave Bowman and Frank Poole, the protagonists in the movie, it might have been Freeman Dyson and Ted Taylor striding about taking readings.

The trouble in the movie version, as Mr. Dullea confided to Dyson when they fell into conversation, was that the director wasn't allowing him to act. He wasn't being called upon to exhibit emotion or to react heroically. He felt as if he were sleepwalking through the part of Bowman, a man asked to undertake a mission vital to the inhabitants back on Earth—or so the earlier part of the script would have us believe.[27]

Space Odyssey is about the evolution of the human race on Earth and its encounter with alien intelligence. In Philip Morrison's search for extraterrestrial thinking creatures the expected signature would have been radio signals. In Dyson's search it would have been heat waves. In Kubrick's film the signature consists of an upright black slab and the magnetic forces that pour forth from it now and then.

The humans who see the slab or who measure its magnetism are impressed but don't otherwise behave in the melodramatic way characteristic of many science fiction movies. Even Kubrick's soundtrack was understated. When music does play, the humans on screen are mute; we hear the incomparable Blue Danube Waltz while the pilots toil wordlessly. When humans speak there is no music. On the ship the only sounds are those of Dave, Frank, and HAL (the master onboard computer) talking, or of the incessant, mechanical, reassuring hum of the ventilation system.

Along with Dullea, Dyson was baffled by this straitened approach to space travel. Couldn't or shouldn't a journey to Jupiter be more exciting? Dyson had enjoyed Kubrick's previous film, *Dr. Strangelove*, which was also about saving the human race, not from aliens but from human folly in the form of a stupidly triggered catastrophic exchange of nuclear weapons. *Dr. Strangelove* was filled with colorful characters and mordant wit. The sequence of events could easily be followed. *Space Odyssey* had none of this. What was Kubrick up to?

It was time for Dyson himself to act or, to be more exact, to come across on camera as a serious scientist, which he was, and to speak in interview style about space. It was Dyson's impression that Kubrick wanted him and a few other select scientists appearing at the beginning of the film to lend credibility to the fictional events that followed. To further this impression of scientific reliability and seriousness, the scientists were asked to appear in front of a computer. The only computer on the lot, not counting the infamous HAL, was a business machine churning out paychecks for MGM personnel. Since its clatter interfered with the movie's own acoustics, the computer had to be turned off in order to provide a clear sound level.[28]

While Dyson had the attention of the director, he asked about the seeming chilliness of the story. Even taking into account that *Strangelove* was a smirking parody of war pictures while *Space Odyssey* was a more or less serious presentation of explorers going into the vacuum of space, the latter seemed overly somber. Why was this? Kubrick's clipped reply: see the film.

When it finally came, the picture was a surprise. *Discovery* no longer had overt nuclear propulsion. Dyson's and the other interviews had been cut. And the unfolding action was even slower than it seemed on the day of the shooting. But gradually, as he watched the film, Dyson was won over. Kubrick's inexplicable, impersonal approach to the story now seemed appropriate.

Space Odyssey was not like *Strangelove*. It was not even like the Arthur C. Clarke novel written in tandem with the screenplay. In the film human motivations are not explored. Alien intentions remain unexplained. Indeed except for the black slab we don't encounter symptoms of any extraterrestrial intelligence at all, only their technology. So ultimately Kubrick's movie and Dyson's writings about space aren't about *them*, the aliens, but about *us*, about the human journey into the solar system and beyond.

10. Nuclear Manifesto

Dyson as Diplomat

(EARLY 1960S)

Freeman Dyson wanted to fly to Saturn, but no seats were available on Orion. Instead of using nuclear bombs to whisk people into deep space, defense planners wanted to keep them all in reserve for blowing up Russian cities in the event of a war.

In the early 1960s open-air testing of nuclear weapons was on the increase. This testing amounted to dropping bombs on your own country—Nevada in the case of the United States and Central Asia in the case of the USSR. Many objected to the radioactive debris from the tests and wanted them stopped. The two superpowers began talking about a treaty to this effect.

Dyson decided to be against a ban on nuclear testing, even if this put him into opposition with good friends such as Hans Bethe. Dyson felt a debt of loyalty to his friend Ted Taylor, who was trying to get Orion, not yet canceled, into space. Without proper testing of its nuclear propulsion, Orion would never happen. Dyson also thought of Edward Teller and his associates, who labored away behind the barbed wire at Livermore designing new weapons.

Dyson was one of the few who knew what went on behind that fence. With Teller he had tried to create a bomb that would produce more neutrons, one that could penetrate oncoming Soviet tanks and kill their drivers, but with less radioactive debris. Creating such a neutron bomb suited Dyson since it would make it easier for Orion to chug through the atmosphere, boosting itself upward on a series of detonations as it went, without leaving such a dirty trail.

Caltech chemist Linus Pauling, risking the displeasure of some of *his* friends, wrote, testified, marched, and spoke out as often as he could to halt the testing and spread of nuclear weapons. On one occasion he walked a picket line outside the White House fence the day before he found himself inside the fence, where he and forty other Nobel laureates sat down to dinner with President John Kennedy.[1]

Dyson was anything but a Cold War hardhead. But the Soviet threat was formidable and the United States had to be prepared. That meant having up-to-date weapons. As he so often did, Dyson put his thoughts into the form of a prominent manifesto. He liked explaining things, clarifying complicated problems, summing up. His thoughtful prose in *Physical Review* had helped lift the veil from the mysteries of quantum electrodynamics. His imaginative schemes for artificial habitats, set forth in the pages of *Science*, helped launch the search for extraterrestrial civilizations. He had penned eloquent arguments in favor of nuclear reactors and nuclear rockets. Now he wrote about the proposed treaty.

In the April 1960 issue of *Foreign Affairs,* he told readers why a test ban was a mistake. We couldn't stop testing, he argued, because the United States couldn't stop designing. Versatile new weapons, like the compact neutron bomb, were waiting to be carried through. By halting testing we would be fostering a false sense of security. Leaving aside the USSR for the moment, other adversaries such as the Chinese and even friends like France, neither one of which was party to the current round of test ban negotiations, might be tempted to design a new generation of bombs that would leave the U.S. behind. Dyson didn't like nuclear bombs any more than did Linus Pauling. But we had to have them, the right kind, and the right number. What if an opponent were to undertake tests in secret, leaving us outfoxed?

On Thermonuclear War

Dyson often said that the key to smoothing out the relations between East and West was to understand the Russian point of view. If it was true that the Russians had enough bombs and missiles to destroy many of American's cities in the space of thirty minutes, then it was important to know how the Russians thought.[2]

As a boy Dyson had taught himself Russian in order to study certain textbooks. Later he used his Russian language skills to appreciate the work of Russian astronomers and physicists. He tried to visit Russia as a private citizen and scientist in 1955, when he and Richard Feynman were invited to lecture about electrodynamics. But U.S. authorities would not allow them to go. Just one year later conditions had changed sufficiently—a post-Stalin, post-McCarthy interglacial period had ensued—and Dyson was permitted to attend a physics meeting in Moscow. On a side trip to Leningrad he and a few of his colleagues wandered by accident into a forbidden zone, a coast guard compound near the shore. When a guard coming up to them to investigate discovered that they were the same scientists mentioned in the newspaper, he brought them into a nearby building to meet the other sailors. There they all had a friendly conversation. "Why do you not come to our country more often?" the guard asked. "Be sure to tell the people in your countries, and your wives and children, that we would like to see more of them."[3]

To lessen the chances of hostilities reaching the nuclear level, a series of meetings between Eastern and Western negotiators had taken place in Geneva since 1955. Disarmament of conventional forces was a general aim, but most felt that a more practical immediate goal would be to halt the testing of nuclear explosives, mainly to reduce the annual dose of radioactive fallout deposited in the atmosphere and to slow the spread of nuclear capability to new nations. This is why Linus Pauling had been out there in front of the White House.

Dyson's liking for things Russian came in handy in 1962 when he was a summer employee of the Arms Control and Disarmament Agency, with an office in the old State Department Building in Washington, D.C. Here his facility with Russian allowed him to scan Soviet military journals, which in turn allowed him gain fresh insights about Cold War military mentality.

The ACDA was formed in September 1961 to help guide the American approach to the test ban treaty negotiations. The Geneva meetings were often testy, and matters were made worse just about this time by the resumption of open nuclear testing, including a fresh run of American weapons tests. One of Dyson's jobs in the summer of 1962 was to tally the tests. In the march of years since Hiroshima in 1945, the number of nuclear bombs exploded in tests had doubled about every two or three years. Even if the bombs since 1945 had not been deliberately dropped on people, the fallout that came along with the explosions *was* killing people in the form of increased cancers. Dyson's earlier prick of conscience over the expected fallout from Orion missions was magnified now into something alarming. The tests could not continue to grow at this rate. The day Dyson graphed the explosions was the day he began to change his mind about the treaty.[4]

This advance in thinking was aided by his growing understanding of Russian military and political doctrine. For example, Dyson drew up an assessment of the Soviet "defense-by-bluff style." The USSR defended itself, Dyson argued, by boasting of its lead over the United States in nuclear missiles. The United States countered this by meticulously demonstrating the falsity of the Russian claims. This served only to oblige the Russians to make good on their bluff by building many more missiles. We should have allowed the Soviets their bluff, Dyson reasoned, allowing them to maintain a smaller inventory of missiles, rather than goading them into actually building the missiles they said they had.

The same American blunder might now be repeated with antimissile technology. The Russians would overstate their capabilities, the Americans would refute the claim, and the Russians would consequently accelerate their actual antimissile deployment. Wouldn't it be better, Dyson insisted in an ACDA memo, to allow the Soviets to keep up the fiction of high technology rather than to have them quicken toward a truly sophisticated defense?

Dyson knew that his ACDA memo, like many of his Bomber Command memos in the 1940s calling for abrupt changes in reasoning, had little chance of acceptance in high government circles. After all, how could a responsible American official publicly acquiesce to a proclaimed Russian technical superiority—even if the superiority was a sham? An escalating arms race was the result. Such was the military-political-technological climate of the early 1960s.

This was a fatalistic time, perhaps not unlike the era in which the young Freeman Dyson came of age—the late 1930s, when it seemed as if war was inevitable, a war that would be more terrible than the previous Great War. Now in the 1960s Dyson would return home some days feeling grim. It was also exciting. To be at the office was to see telegrams arriving from around the world bringing sensitive intelligence from trouble spots. Dyson's office was at ground level, with windows looking directly out onto the sidewalk. He was concerned that passersby would look in and read the secret communications.[5]

The government had to prepare for the worst. Within solemn meetings called to discuss the most dire nuclear war scenarios, certain bureaucrats could dispassionately produce estimates of startling vividness, enumerating buildings knocked down and bodies left in the streets. The most apocalyptic of these nuclear assessors was Herman Kahn, who, working from his consultant's office at the RAND Corporation, produced the fullest nonclassified accounting of how a hydrogen bomb conflict would unroll. Kahn's 1960 book, *On Thermonuclear War*, took upon itself the grim job of depicting exactly what would happen if the bombs started to fall for real. Yes, he said, nuclear war between two powers would be an unprecedented catastrophe for at least one but not necessarily both participants, depending on the preparations made previous to hostilities and the manner in which the nuclear salvos were begun and continued.

Kahn accumulated gruesomely fascinating details about the expected course of nuclear holocaust. For example, one table in the book, labeled "tragic but distinguishable postwar states," attempted to correlate possible American casualty figures with the expected economic recuperation time: 40 million dead would entail a twenty-year recovery period, while 80 million fatalities would require a fifty-year comeback.[6] Under these circumstances, would the living envy the dead? Not particularly, he answered confidently. A majority of the survivors would, after a number of adjustment years, lead nearly normal, happy lives.

One of Kahn's appendices, "War Damage Equalization Corporation," outlined a government-supported insurance scheme for getting things going again once the mushroom clouds had dissipated.[7] While certainly not advocating nuclear war or minimizing the blighting effects of even a "small" war, Kahn demonstrated on page after page that such a war could, at least in a numerical sense, be "won."

The most famous part of Kahn's book was his description of a Doomsday Machine. This ultimate deterrent worked as follows: a central computer is buried far underground and is invulnerable to any attack from above. The computer, through a vast system of sensors, monitors activities on the surface. If the sensors should pick up evidence of multiple nuclear detonations on U.S. targets, the computer would automatically and irrevocably trigger a retaliatory nuclear attack in other parts of the world. The nation that possessed such a doomsday device might itself be consumed in the process, but at least there would be no surviving victor.[8] Of course the point of having such a menacing mechanism is that it would scare an adversary into not launching an attack in the first place.

Offered by Kahn as a hypothetical über-weapon and bargaining chip, the Doomsday Machine turned up in Stanley Kubrick's movie *Dr. Strangelove* where, with tragicomic effect, it destroyed the world. Kubrick studied *On Thermonuclear War* while preparing his film, and some have argued that Kahn was a model for the character of Dr. Strangelove.

Dr. Strangelove ends amid farcical destruction, courtesy of the doomsday device, but much of the rest of the movie is devoted to a plausible story about the accidental launch of a nuclear war. Some flamboyant actorly performances notwithstanding, the drama is mostly not a farce. Sequences showing the arming of bombs, the scrambling of jet aircraft, the revealing of secret flight paths, and the breaking down of the fail-safe chain of command structure all give the viewer the impression that the cataclysmic end of world civilization could happen exactly like this.

Surely some kind of controlling judgment was needed here. To help prevent this kind of nightmare, Soviet and Western scientists, including Dyson, met in England in the fall of 1962. The point of this Pugwash conference (so named from the first such meeting in 1957, in Pugwash, Nova Scotia) was to diffuse mistrust between the two sides and to propose peaceful alternatives. The first of the two meetings was held at Cambridge University. Although there was much vigorous debate, the discussion revealed that the gulf between East and West was bridgeable. Here, perhaps helped along by sherry and by the sheltered environment of English gardens and being away from official government posturing, the scientists found a zone of hopefulness.

Dyson's impression: "I lived for four days mentally in a disarmed world, with all its difficulties, and the longer I was there the better I liked it."[9]

Nevertheless, only weeks after this Pugwash meeting, a Strangelove-like sequence began unfolding in the real world. Aerial photographs of Cuba revealed a dreadful reality, what looked like Russian nuclear missile sites. Quickly more disturbing photos arrived: the missiles themselves were visible. The United States government demanded publicly that the missiles be removed. The Soviet government, after first denying that the missiles were there at all, refused.

The nuclear-armed chess game continued. The United States threatened an air strike against the sites. The USSR threatened a missile strike against the U.S. The U.S. planned a naval blockade against additional Russian vessels delivering in new missiles. The USSR sent new missiles anyway. At the United Nations the United States displayed photographic evidence of the offending missiles. Then the USSR shot down an American surveillance plane flying over Cuba. Every day, almost by the hour, tension grew. Some American generals were for attacking Cuba right then, regardless of larger consequences. The potential toll of a nuclear war—the hundreds of millions of fatalities and the flattened cities depicted in Kahn's appendices—would dwarf all past wars and the worst of contemporary terrorist strikes.

The danger escalated. Russian ships approached, while the American naval ships were poised to intercept them. Salvos of messages—not yet missiles—flew secretly back and forth. Conflicting Russian cables offered to withdraw the missile sites in exchange for a promise that there would be no U.S. attack on Cuba. A second Russian gambit was to withdraw Soviet missiles from Cuba on the American doorstep, in return for a withdrawal of U.S. missiles from Turkey on the Soviet doorstep. Meanwhile the Russian and American ships were closing upon each other at sea. American planes were prepared for an imminent action. The pages of *On Thermonuclear War* seemed to be coming alive.

ON THE BEACH

No one knows how the exchange of nuclear explosions began. The only apparent survivors of the holocaust were a few pockets of civilization in Australia and a lone U.S. submarine emerging from the protective depths of the Pacific Ocean. Cautiously creeping into San Francisco Bay, officers in the sub squint through a periscope at Fisherman's Wharf and see . . . nothing. The buildings are intact but the streets are empty. The sub's instruments detect dangerously high radiation levels. The nuclear blasts, wherever they were, apparently didn't kill through their blast effects but only through the aggregate burden of fallout. But where did all the people go?

Stanley Kubrick's *Dr. Strangelove* shows how the catastrophe might have begun. Another movie, Stanley Kramer's *On the Beach*, shows how it might end. In the story, based on the novel by Nevil Shute, the Australians, spared temporarily by their remoteness, are eventually engulfed by the same radioactive cloud that has snuffed out life everywhere else on the planet. In a real war, Dyson pointed out, such a fatal cloud could not have persisted. The intense radioactivity in the aftermath of a nuclear explosion washes out of the sky relatively quickly. The science was wrong, but Dyson felt the movie had been truthful nevertheless, especially in depicting the blunt facts of a nuclear war.[10] The dropping of thermonuclear weapons would create havoc.

The scenario depicted in *On the Beach* did not actually take place. The Americans did not launch their planes, and the Russians did not try to run the naval blockade. Shortly after the events of October 1962, Russian missiles were withdrawn from Cuba and the following year American missiles from Turkey. The two sides had drawn back from their state of hair-trigger alert. "The greatest crisis the world has known," as American secretary of state Dean Rusk called the affair, was over.[11]

To say the least, an event like the Cuban Missile Crisis made people think. One way Dyson responded to this actual event was to become even more engaged in the public scientific discussion over nuclear issues. "We are human beings first and scientists second. Knowledge implies responsibility," Dyson said.[12]

He had first been involved with the Federation of American Scientists (FAS) in the 1940s, not long after it was formed by veterans of the Manhattan Project. Later he was on the FAS council. They were glad to have him, since his early opposition to the test ban treaty helped to counteract the FAS's perceived liberal tilt.[13] Moreover, as a consultant for the Livermore and Los Alamos weapons labs, Dyson had excellent nuclear credentials.[14] Then, during the period of greatest peril—parts of 1962 and 1963—Dyson was FAS chairman.

He was also a contributor to the *Bulletin of the Atomic Scientists*, another offspring of the nuclear age. This is the publication whose cover featured a clock face. From month to month, year to year, the hands of the clock were positioned closer or further from midnight depending on the degree of world danger, as judged by the editors. The hands were, at this time, very close to the zero hour.

The March 1962 issue carried an article by Dyson about bomb shelters. The subject of civil defense was a matter of grave concern, especially the concerted construction of temporary habitats for protecting the citizenry from the blast and fallout residues of detonations. Some commentators felt that nothing less than an extensive shelter program was vital.

Dyson, the contrarian, suggested that shelters could become *too* effective. He argued that a nation too self-assured of its survivability against nuclear attack might tend to be reckless in its international dealings, or at least less cautious than it ought to be. A nation that felt it could prevail in a nuclear exchange, in the way Herman Kahn had suggested, and that felt emboldened by the comparative safety of its underground redoubts, might be a nation preparing to trespass the ultimate boundary. It might be a nation contemplating thermonuclear war. Consequently there could be, in addition to a race to build more bombs or more missiles, a spiraling race to build deeper and more bombproof shelters.

Dyson, always looking for commonplace illustrations, told the story of his living in Münster, Germany, in the summer of 1947. There the inhabitants, including his onetime admirer Hilde Jacob, lived immersed in the rubble created, as Dyson likes to admit, by his own Bomber Command. That the residents of Münster, the hardy survivors, could emerge from their own shelters, clear a path, and put on rudimentary opera performances amid the debris, was a fine testimony to human tenacity and resourcefulness. But what if, Dyson asked, this same tenacity allowed them to believe that they could survive a nuclear equivalent of Bomber Command?[15]

Science magazine, impressed with Dyson's assessment, devoted an editorial to his quantification of the radioactive burden shelters must contend with. The partially tongue-in-cheek essay looked at Dyson's units of fission energy needed to produce various outcomes. A "Beach" (the term coming from *On the Beach*) was the explosive yield that would render a global fallout dose fatal to half the world's population. A "Kahn" (the term coming from the name of the author of *On Thermonuclear War*) was the explosive yield, said *Science*, needed to thoroughly kill the population of the target nation, presumably the United States attacking the USSR or vice versa. A third unit was the "Stockpile," the effective explosive yield that would actually be available for use in bombs in the coming decade.

A Kahn was smaller than a Beach; without effective shelters, the U.S. or USSR, aiming only at each other, just might kill off the other and spare the rest of the human race. But a Stockpile was bigger than a Beach. *With* effective shelters, the U.S. or USSR would be harder to defeat, and the attacker would have to pound harder, possibly creating thereby the human extinction scenario dramatized in *On the Beach*.

Having summarized Dyson's doomsday deliberations, *Science* magazine went on to define a fourth term, the "Dyson," as the "measure of the speculation you must introduce into an argument in order to go from the premise to the conclusion." The editorial concluded that Dyson's own argument ranked high on the Dyson scale, and that some kind of shelter-building preparation, if not exactly of the provocatively deep construction that Dyson feared, would be in order.[16]

Thus the Dyson name, which already had been attached to a particle physics protocol (Feynman-Dyson diagrams), to a description of how ferromagnets behave (the Dyson-Schmidt equation), and to a hypothetical solar energy collector (Dyson spheres), was now associated with the weighing of extremely unlikely but dire nuclear contingencies.

RADIOACTIVE MILK

Ideological differences and intense mistrust had so far kept East and West from concluding a test ban treaty. The negotiations had particularly foundered on the issue of on-site inspections. The Americans, who wanted the inspections, feared Soviet cheating. The Soviets, who didn't want inspections, feared American spying. Years of bickering in Geneva had accomplished little.

The Cuban Missile Crisis changed things. Both Chairman Nikita Khrushchev and President John Kennedy indicated that the near-disaster had underscored the need for a treaty. On June 10, 1963, Kennedy gave a speech making prominent reference to the loss of 20 million Russians during World War II and how such a calamity must be avoided. He announced that the United States was suspending further bomb tests in the interest of getting the treaty process rolling again.[17]

The Russians responded positively, and new talks were scheduled. This time the stepped-up effort would take place not in neutral Geneva but in the capital of the USSR. Instead of consuming further years of argument, the settlement would wrap up in a mere dozen days in July. Both sides agreed that a complete ban on nuclear tests was impractical. A limited ban on tests in space, the atmosphere, and the sea was the new goal.

The last major impediment to a treaty, ironically enough, concerned limitations on bomb explosions for peaceful uses—things like digging canals and propelling rockets toward Saturn. The Russians were against exempting tests for this kind of activity. The Americans, particularly senators enamored with peaceful nuclear projects (which, within the Atomic Energy Commission, went under the name of Project Plowshare), were ardently in favor. When Averell Harriman, the chief U.S. negotiator in Moscow, had extracted as many concessions as he could from the Soviets, and still found the them adamant against peaceful tests, he cabled the president to see if Plowshare could be sacrificed in the interest of obtaining a treaty.

The president sought the advice of ACDA director William Foster, who in turn consulted Al Wadman, leader of the ACDA science and technology bureau. Wadman turned to Freeman Dyson. Should we cling to Plowshare or aim for a treaty? Dyson weighed his loyalties to Edward Teller at Livermore (where much of the Plowshare work was undertaken) and to Ted Taylor at General Atomic (where Orion was still struggling to survive) against his loyalty to friends like Bethe and, of course, to the prospects for greater comity with the Soviets. Dyson's considered opinion, which percolated its way back up the chain of command and thence to Moscow, was that the Soviets should have their way. "Peaceful" tests of nuclear explosions in the air, space, and ocean were abandoned, and a treaty was achieved.

Dyson diminishes his own role in this saga. No doubt the president and ACDA officials consulted numerous experts along the way, Dyson said, leading to the concession on peaceful testing.[18] Furthermore, even though Plowshare had many advocates in and out of government, its implementation seemed to be, at best, many years in the future. Maybe trading in Plowshare for a test ban wasn't such a hardship.[19]

Next came the necessary Senate approval for the treaty. Most high-ranking government officials, such as the secretaries of state and defense, the AEC chairman, and the Joint Chiefs of the military branches, testified in favor of the treaty. Dyson, on behalf of the Federation of American Scientists, not in his capacity as a part-time employee of ACDA, testified positively. Testifying negatively were, among others, Robert Oppenheimer's twin antagonists, Lewis Strauss and Edward Teller.

One day after Dyson's Senate testimony in August 1963, another historic event occurred on the streets of Washington, D.C. A quarter million people marched in opposition to racial injustice. Freeman Dyson joined the procession only a few blocks from his office. He flowed with the crowd to the culminating event, the series of speeches delivered from the steps of the Lincoln Memorial. Dyson stood nearby and was moved to tears, like thousands of others, by Martin Luther King's

"I have a dream" speech, perhaps the greatest American oration since Lincoln's Gettysburg Address. "I would be ready to go to jail for him anytime," Dyson wrote in a letter that night.[20]

The Senate, voting 80 to 19, approved the limited test ban treaty. And not too soon. The government reported that the amount of radio-active strontium-90 in milk had doubled over the past year. Little wonder: the fallout from tests during 1962, the year of the Cuban crisis, was comparable to the sum of the fallout from all earlier nuclear testing back to 1945.[21] One report calculated that in Nevada and Utah, in a zone downwind of the Nevada test site not far from where Freeman Dyson had encountered his profound quietude at Jackass Flats, an estimated 3,000 children had received "excessive radiation that would possibly lead to 10 to 12 cases of thyroid cancer."[22] So, nursing infants and schoolkids were now incorporating artifacts of Cold War preparedness into the marrow of their bones.

11. On the Oregon Trail

Dyson as Pentagon Consultant
(1960s–1970s)

At a reception, in ordinary conversation about the worsening military situation in Vietnam, General Maxwell Taylor had actually said "I think it might be a good idea to throw in a nuke now and then just to keep the other side guessing." Freeman Dyson, who was insider enough to have been invited to the reception, had seen and heard many notable things in his professional life, but at this instant he was too startled by the general's remark to say anything back or to be certain he'd even heard the words correctly. So he consulted with his three scientist colleagues who had been within earshot to confirm that the quip had not been made in jest. They all agreed that the general had said what they thought he'd said, and it was no joke.[1]

For General Taylor and some other high government officials, deploying tactical nuclear bombs was not an abstract concept, a doomsday last-resort measure, but something to be employed *now* in the fight against Communist aggression. The year was 1966 and the United States was becoming ever more entangled in the jungles of Vietnam. General Taylor was no longer chairman of the Joint Chiefs of Staff but was still an important military advisor to President Lyndon Johnson. For dealing with a pesky enemy it must have been tempting to use a weapon that could wipe combatants off the board in a millionth of a second.

Still, the general was talking, almost casually, about using the nuclear option in Vietnam. He couldn't just say that, could he? Dyson and his colleagues decided to do something.

THE VIETNAMIZATION OF PHYSICS

Among scientists, physicists have had a disproportionate influence on matters of technology policy and national security in the United States. A majority of presidential science advisors have been physicists. Asked about this, the physicists themselves say that this is because of their broad training in the principles behind the big-ticket topics that command critical attention and large budgets—armaments, transport, energy, sensors, telecommunications, computers, space. The single biggest factor in the need for solemn science advice was the critical centrality of nuclear weaponry in defense planning.

After World War II, Manhattan Project scientists and their heirs established several earnest institutions, such as the *Bulletin of the Atomic Scientists*, which published articles about the implications of nuclear research and other social issues. Another institution, the Federation of American Scientists, also carefully scrutinized and commented upon—sometimes loudly—U.S. government policies and actions. The scientist organization with the biggest impact on postwar government research, at least for classified research, was called Jason. Taking its name from the ancient story of the hero and his mates on the ship *Argo* seeking treasure and adventure, Jason was formed in 1960 by some notable physicists such as John Wheeler of Princeton and Charles Townes of Bell Labs.[2]

The name Jason denotes the group or any particular member. It was—and *is,* since it still functions to this day—funded by federal money but is largely independent of federal interference. It generally has between thirty and sixty active members. Newcomers are chosen by existing members and have to possess a top secret clearance qualifying them to handle classified documents. At first the members were mostly physicists and all male, but this changed in later years. The Jasons meet for six or seven weeks each summer and for briefer times in other months.

Dyson was one of the first to be invited to join. Summer work, such as his stint with the Arms Control and Disarmament Agency, kept him from participating at first. But from 1965 onward, he has been one of the most active members. His first Jason project was to assess the Nike missile defense system.

Jasons were stellar in their fields of study or, like Dyson, pretty good at everything. Put them in a room, give them a month and a half to solve a technical problem or assess a weapon proposal, and they'd come back with an answer or sometimes a devastating dismissal. Jason members were discouraged from rendering moral views of the political or military issue at stake. That's not what the consumers of the reports wanted to see. Instead, it was Jason's job to ensure that the known laws of physics were being obeyed. As Freeman Dyson had learned from his days at Bomber Command, the crazier the scheme being considered by generals, the more valuable it was to have independent, objective, civilian, informed comment.

Problems would be brought to Jason from a "sponsor," typically one of the military services or the Pentagon's ARPA, the Advanced Research Projects Agency, the same outfit that oversaw Orion. The problem might involve some new detector technology or the basing of missiles or the effectiveness of a new airplane design. Jason usually spun off a committee of their members to look at each problem. This team would proceed to read documents, interview officials—often military personnel or civilian contractors—occasionally make site visits, perform calculations, get together for discussions, and then write up a report.

What Jason produced was "deliverables," consisting of shrewd scientific analyses of single topics. Thereafter the sponsor owned that report. The navy might make the findings public or lock them up for thirty years. You could never be sure the Pentagon would use Jason's assessment, but at least the requests for Jason input kept coming.

What made it enticing for Dyson to join, and for the others too, was the idea that you were helping your country, that you got to work on challenging projects with potentially important consequences, and that you would be in the company of some of the brightest scientists in the world. Early members included Murray Gell-Mann, who received the Nobel Prize for his theory that led to the idea of quarks; Steven Weinberg, who also got a Nobel Prize for particle physics theory; and Richard Garwin, one of the developers of the H-bomb. Like the Masons, the Jasons tended to be earnest, upstanding gentlemen (no lady members yet) who could keep a secret. There was no special handshake.

What about that glib utterance by General Taylor at the reception? The four scientists in attendance—all of them Jasons—set to work. Although no sponsor had officially asked for a study on the subject of tactical nuclear weapons in Vietnam, they were going to get one anyway. Jason funding allowed for this kind of discretionary inquiry.

The four—Dyson, Weinberg, University of Chicago chemist Robert Gomer, and Chicago physicist Courtenay Wright—began to pore over documents. One of these was entitled "Oregon Trail." The Oregon Trail, besides being the nineteenth-century wagon road used by white settlers heading outward from Missouri to various Northwest destinations, was the name given by American officials to the corridor used by insurgents bringing supplies from North to South Vietnam in the 1960s.

The name also applied to a massive survey prepared by the U.S. Army around 1965 concerning recent conflicts in Indochina. Dyson was fascinated by the part of the report devoted to assessing the general legacy of colonial involvement in Southeast Asia. The professional historians who prepared this material concluded that in uprisings for which the European overlords devoted most of their attention and resources to military rather than social problems, such as the French in Indochina, the war was "lost." Things went better if the European powers emphasized social over military solutions, as with the British in Malaya. These lessons were to serve presently as lessons for American behavior in Vietnam.

"Oregon Trail" remained classified and mostly unused, as far as Dyson could tell. Why, he wanted to know, weren't the lessons taken to heart? If "the Army had read their own documents they would never have gotten us into Vietnam. It was clear that what happened in Vietnam went exactly contrary to what "Oregon Trail" was saying should happen."[3] The more immediate value of "Oregon," however, was not the historical lessons but its sections devoted to the possibility of using small, 1-kiloton-level nuclear bombs in Vietnam. The Jason effort would be the assessment of this part of "Oregon."

Dyson was not the main organizer of this work. Indeed, he never sought a leadership role in Jason. He didn't want to become a heavyweight in advisory circles, like some Jasons. He didn't like formulating policy. All of these things he left to others. He enjoyed being told what to do. What he did do he did well. Given something practical to calculate, an engineering problem to solve—that's what he wanted. His work on TRIGA and Orion had whetted his appetite for these things. With his flair for writing he was often the one designated to prepare the report.

The four-man Jason team decided early that their summary would avoid all political or ethical considerations and concentrate entirely on the military utility of tactical nukes in Vietnam. Only in this way, they figured, could their unsolicited, independent view have any chance of influencing deliberations higher up the Pentagon chain of command.

Tactical bombs, in contrast to city-destroying strategic bombs, were intended to halt massed troops or armored formations, or to block mountain passes. Jason concluded that the 1-kT devices would do all those things, but that you'd need a lot of them, perhaps a thousand a year. Even then, felled forests could be cleared by the enemy relatively quickly. Furthermore, soil would be fouled by radioactivity, presenting a continuing health hazard. You'd be hurting civilians while not much holding back soldiers.

There was another argument against the use of nukes. This was the fact that U.S. forces, concentrated in fixed and conspicuously built-up fortifications, represented a much larger and more visible target than the one posed by insurgent forces. The introduction of U.S. nukes in Vietnam would encourage Russia or China to sneak nukes of their own into the action. Instead of dropped from planes or missiles, the bombs would be trucked toward or tunneled beneath fat American targets.

Prepared in the fall of 1966, the Jason report, "Tactical Nuclear Weapons in South-East Asia," was presented to the Pentagon. As usual, no response came back, so no one can be sure of how instrumental it might have been in keeping nuclear weapons out of the war in Indochina. Even if the Jason work did no more than buttress the arguments used by those senior Pentagon officials who were themselves against tactical nukes, then Dyson considered his work on this subject worthwhile.[4] Even the title of the Jason report was classified until 1970. The Jason report in full was declassified only in December 2002.[5]

Freeman Dyson disliked everything about the Vietnam War. He continued to confer with the other Jasons, and to respect their work, but he felt that Jason Vietnam-related projects were being undercut. Dyson's crashing airplane nightmares continued. In 1968 he decided to quit Jason, but was talked out of this decision by Jason's leader Hal Lewis.[6] Dyson was of course not the only one disgusted by the Vietnam War. A vast protest movement grew up in the United States and in other countries. In 1971, this protest touched upon Jason directly.

Since its inception Jason's existence was practically unknown to the public, until it was dragged into prominence by the publication of the

"Pentagon Papers." This name refers to a series of classified reports—internal army documents assessing America's conduct of the war—that were leaked and then published in the pages of *The New York Times* and other newspapers. There for all to see was reference to Jason and to specific scientists doing secret work on behalf of the military establishment. Some Jason members, such as Gell-Mann, Garwin, Leon Lederman, and Stanford physicist Sidney Drell, were castigated for contributing their talents to conducting a dirty war.[7]

Dyson and his fellow authors on the Vietnam nukes report were criticized. Only the title of their report but not its arguments against the deployment of nukes had been revealed. So it might have been supposed from the title, if that's all you saw, that the Jason authors were in favor of tactical nukes rather than opposed. One of those authors, Steven Weinberg, returning on a visit to Berkeley, California, where he had been a professor years before, drove past his old home. There on the sidewalk someone had scrawled the message, "Steve Weinberg, War Criminal."[8]

Dyson was criticized for belonging to Jason at all, despite his professed loathing of the Vietnam War, on the grounds that the honorable thing would have been to resign. Dyson was specifically criticized for his involvement with the "Tactical Nuclear Weapons in South-East Asia" report. Even while forbearing to disclose the conclusions of the report, which was still classified, to his high-minded critics, Dyson ably defended himself:

> It is true that I helped write this paper under Jason auspices, and it is possible it may have had some slight influence upon US policy in Vietnam. The question is whether I am ashamed or proud of what I have done. I am glad to state publicly that I am proud of it. If my work had no effect on government policy, I can have done no great harm. If my work had some effect, I can be proud to have helped to avert a human tragedy far greater even than the one we have witnessed.[9]

Some of the war protests were violent. In 1969 Dyson came to Santa Barbara to give a talk at the University of California. Staying at the faculty club, he was wrenched from sleep by an explosion. He was frozen with fear, as he had been in his recurring plane crash dream. After what must have been only a minute or two, he finally moved into action. He came downstairs to find the hotel caretaker, badly burned, being taken away by some students. The victim, a man named Dover Sharp, had picked up a bomb-rigged package. No perpetrators were found, but the bombing of the faculty club was suspected of being an act of protest against the Vietnam War, one of many such deadly protests.

Dover Sharp died of his injuries and Dyson, writing about the episode years later, blamed himself. If only he hadn't been frozen, as in past enactments of his dream, he might have been able to offer assistance more quickly. He might have saved Sharp's life.

After that night Dyson never again had the burning-plane nightmare.[10]

Out of the Black

Much of Jason's work was narrowly focused on military projects, things like tactical nuclear weapons and antipersonnel devices. But other problems were interesting also for their potential civilian applications. An important example was the detection or imaging of luminous objects in the sky with ground-based telescopes. The air force wanted to track enemy ballistic missiles, whereas astronomers wanted to look at distant stars. Both these activities were frustrated by the light-distorting effects of the Earth's atmosphere. You can get a sense of this optical smearing when you look out to the horizon along an asphalt highway on a hot day. The rising heat wafts the air around just above the road, blurring the view and making mirages.

In 1972 the Pentagon sought Jason's opinion of a proposal by a military contractor to undo the distortion with an optical system that, moment by moment, assessed the degree of overhead turbulence and quickly compensated by a selective steering or flexing of segmented reflective surfaces. This clever idea had been around since the early 1950s but had languished for want of agile enough instruments.[11]

By the 1970s this "active optics" scheme had become a possibility. Freeman Dyson and Steven Weinberg were grappling with the problem when into their office came a new Jason, Berkeley physicist Richard Muller, who had come up with an independent approach to the challenge of undoing the effects of turbulence. Feeling a bit intimidated by his exposure to so many senior and illustrious colleagues all at once, Muller, who later became an illustrious cosmologist himself, cautiously shared his mathematical insight with Weinberg and Dyson.

Weinberg's first reaction was that the new idea wouldn't work. Dyson gently disagreed, and then explained how. The men grappled with the problem at the blackboard.[12] It was tractable after all.

At first Jason's labors on this topic were not under the heaviest of classification restrictions, and Dyson presented a summary in the open scientific literature.[13] An active optical system, he said, would consist of the following parts:

1. A primary light-collecting mirror (the main part of every telescope), the fixed surface that captures light from the celestial object;

2. A secondary mirror with segmented parts that could be steered independently so as to subtly alter the incoming light waves in order to undo atmospheric distortions;

3. A set of little motors that could quickly reposition the segmented mirrors with great precision;

4. A digital camera recording the light signals from the object;

5. A computer able to make use of the video signal, turning it into feedback commands that actuate the adjustment motors; and

6. Software that turns the video input into the proper feedback output.

In other words, the flexible mirrors were adroitly reconfigured to counteract the bad effects of the atmosphere. The whole process struck a balance between making the sampling time too long, in which case the overhead turbulence would blur the image, or too short, in which case the intermittant arrival of straggling photons from the distant object would render a dim image.[14]

Dyson, designer of nuclear spaceships and nuclear reactors, knew a promising technology when he saw it and urged astronomers to embrace the new "adaptive optics" method, as it would come to be called. This they failed to do, feeling, as Dyson supposed, that the military was going to be doing the hard work of perfecting the image-sharpening process. Indeed, they were right. Developmental work was just beginning.

The air force had produced prototype corrective systems that worked only for objects that were bright to start with. For fainter stars something else was needed. Another Jason, Princeton physicist William Happer, suggested shining a laser up into the sky in the direction of the target object and observe the light reflected from a thin layer of sodium atoms that hung at an altitude of 90–100 km.[15] The sodium, debris from the breakup of past meteorites, resided above most of the atmosphere, and so laser light traveling up to the sodium layer and back would traverse the region of turbulent air twice, providing just what we needed to know about the turbulence above—a weather report for the next fraction of a second—in order to undo the distortion.

The government sponsors were now so keen for this kind of image sharpening that Jason devoted three separate reports to the subject over the period 1982–1984. The U.S. Air Force was so pleased with the results that the "laser guide star" concept and tests were placed under an especially tight security blanket. When President Ronald Reagan declared the start of his Strategic Defense Initiative, the system of space-based detectors and antimissile lasers commonly known as Star Wars, any hope of quickly transferring adaptive optics to the service of astronomers studying the cosmos was quashed. Only in 1992, through the efforts of astronomer (and first woman Jason) Claire Max, was the laser guide star concept made public.

Dyson considered his work on this turbulence-correcting technology to be his most valuable scientific contribution to Jason. Withholding knowledge from scientists, in Dyson's opinion, delayed the use of adaptive optics in astronomy for a decade. He was appalled: "As often happens when secrecy is imposed on a government program, secrecy hides failure and exaggerates success."[16]

MODELING CLIMATE

Jason was good at analyzing hypothetical threats, such as Soviet missiles hurtling across the Arctic Ocean. A fuzzier threat, at least as viewed in the 1970s, was the one posed by possible climate changes arising from the emission of sunlight-trapping carbon dioxide spewed by automobiles burning gasoline and power plants burning coal. Such combustion combines hydrocarbons with oxygen to make harmless water plus CO_2, a molecule made of two oxygen atoms and one carbon atom. A blanket of atmospheric carbon dioxide mimics a greenhouse in that it lets sunlight in but reduces the amount of reflected sunlight returning to space. The result is a slow buildup of warmth.

CO_2 has resided in the atmosphere for millions of years and has helped to keep the surface of Earth warmer than it would have been without it. That's good; many species owe their existence to this greenhouse warming. Since the onset of industrial civilization, however, the levels of CO_2 have risen greatly. After studying the matter in great earnestness, geoscientists, at least a large majority of those who publish their work in peer-reviewed journals, have concluded that on top of whatever natural climate fluctuations may occur, additional and deleterious climate changes owing to human activity are now under way. These changes include an accelerated rise in global temperature (many places are getting warmer, although a few places will be getting cooler), a rising of the sea level from the gradual melting of icecaps, and a strengthening of droughts in some places. The exact magnitude and timing of these changes is difficult to predict accurately, but a preponderance of climate scientists now believe the trends are ominous, and that society should act decisively in lowering the emission of greenhouse gases, especially CO_2.[17]

One of the largest challenges in monitoring climate has been to separate human from natural effects. Even less was known about these issues in 1972 when Freeman Dyson began his work on climate change—another inspired summer project—working with Alvin Weinberg at Oak Ridge National Laboratory in Tennessee. Rising oceans, drought, wilder swings in weather: there were plenty of bad things that might result from too much CO_2. Dyson tried to look for the good things.

He pointed to three examples of past or future environmental modification: a greener England, a wetter Sahara, and a warmer Siberia. First, England. This demi-paradise, Dyson's homeland, with its gardens, farms, and pastures, was, he argued, utterly unnatural. The forests and swamps of primordial England had been made over into an artificial ecology to suit the needs of its human inhabitants.[18] Dyson didn't deny the possible dangers in fooling around with Mother Nature, but felt that we shouldn't ignore the possible benefits of climate or habitat modification. We should weigh the good with the bad. The advantage of a wetter Sahara and a warmer Siberia, for example, would be a possible doubling of the arable land on Earth.

Genetic engineering and weather modification are two phrases likely nowadays to make us pause, and rightly so. But tinkering with nature is exactly what the human species has been doing since the advent of agriculture 12,000 years ago. Animal husbandry, the culling of grain species, in vitro fertilization, the damming of rivers, the burning of forests, are just a few of the large-scale human interventions in nature. First came Green England. Then, with the help of artificial fertilizer, came Green India. Fertilizer in excess can do harm, but in moderation it can and does feed millions. That's why, when the subject of global climate change arose, Dyson could at least ponder welcoming it as a potentially good thing.

Oak Ridge's Institute for Energy Analysis was hospitable. Dyson spent at least a few weeks there each summer over several years during the 1970s. In these years he participated in some of the first extensive computer simulations of climate change. Even then he began to have reservations about other people's reservations about CO_2. For one thing, the assumptions about climate and the data inserted into the computer simulations were poorly understood, circa 1975. The amount of carbon stored in the oceans and atmosphere were pretty well known, but the amounts stored in other reservoirs, such as topsoil or forests, were less well understood.★

Dyson was dissatisfied with this. The computer models, he thought, put too much emphasis on the atmosphere, not enough on soil. The scientists at Oak Ridge produced an official report on climate model-

---

★ Climate modeling is sort of like writing a vast play about Mother Nature. The principal actors are Ocean, Atmosphere, Soil, Plants, Forest, Fossil Fuels, Wind, and Humanity. The drama unrolls according to the known laws of geology and physics—those that pertain to fluid dynamics and thermodynamics. Compare the measurement of stars with the measurement of greenhouse warming: adaptive optics looks at local weather over periods of a fraction of a second. The study of climate change, by great contrast, looks at local and global weather trends over periods of decades, centuries, and millennia. For doing the latter, many assumptions have to be made and approximations used.

For the sake of computation, you can't simulate the progress of weather from moment to moment for every tiny volume of air, much less for individual air molecules. No supercomputer would be up to the job. Even if it could, what would you do with all the data? Instead, you have to divide up the sky and ocean and land into imaginary blocks. The smaller these volumes are the better, in order to get a more accurate simulation. But the smaller the sample volumes, the more expensive and time-consuming will be the computer's task of crunching numbers. There must be a compromise between computer time spent and accuracy obtained. The *granularity* of the simulation—how much detail you expect—becomes a major issue. This was true in the 1970s and is still true decades later when computers are much more powerful.

Typically simulations seek to show what will happen if, over a stretch of years, we increase the amount of CO_2 by 20 percent or 50 percent, and so forth. Will the mean world temperature rise by 1 degree or 3? Or will the extra CO_2 be taken up and absorbed into rocks or soil or ocean? Can you be confident enough in your computer models that you could make a cogent policy decision on what to do about CO_2? This policy would necessarily have a costly impact on the driving of automobiles and the generation of electricity.

ing. Dyson did not play a role in this report. And when shortly thereafter (1979) Jason prepared a climate report, Dyson was not a part of that either. He worked with colleagues, took part in the discussion, but did not sign as a coauthor.

Instead he prepared a report of his own, concentrating on what he felt the other reports had left out. He cited the fact, as an example of dramatic carbon uptake, that a field of corn will consume, in the course of ordinary photosynthesis, all of the CO_2 within a few feet of the ground in about five minutes.[19] Of course the circulation of air brings in fresh CO_2, so photosynthesis never stops. But the uptake is impressive. Feed a plant more CO_2 and it will grow bigger, he said. If the extra plant substance were in the form of stem and leaf, then indeed this form of CO_2 storage would find its way back into the atmosphere since in the fall the plant would die or surrender its leaves. If, however, the CO_2-enhanced growth (whether naturally or through genetic modification) can produce thicker roots, then the extra CO_2 would effectively be locked up in subsurface storage.[20]

Dyson did not deny that a heightened CO_2 fraction in the atmosphere could pose a threat through global warming. He only wished in his rebuttal—which he again referred to as a "manifesto"—to the Oak Ridge report to draw attention to the possible countervailing effect going on in the botanic world.[21] He never fully concluded that enhanced CO_2 led to a greater roots-to-shoots ratio. He couldn't; the data wasn't there. That was one of his main points: we needed more direct measurements; we needed to know more about what happens in the hidden realm of soil. Maybe that's where the carbon was going. We needed a fuller exploration of dirt.

Dyson held what could be called politely by his scientific colleagues a minority opinion. This wasn't unusual for him. He had held minority views before: he had promoted nuclear spaceships; he had opposed (at least at first) the test ban treaty. Dyson rather liked having a minority view, and this didn't seem to lessen his friends' regard for him. Henry Abarbanel, a physicist at the University of California, San Diego, joined Jason in the 1970s and was a member of the Jason climate group. He disagreed with Dyson's climate views but was thrilled to argue with him. Being at the Jason summer study meeting allowed one to exchange ideas with many of the world's top scientists; it was like attending the famous 1927 Solvay conference. "Inside there is an equality at play among the best thinkers," Abarbanel said, "and the reward of arguing with a Dyson or a Garwin is a supreme scientific experience. And they feel the same way."[22]

Dyson's interest in the climate debate would come and go over the years. As we shall see, the research devoted to the subject, the worldwide average surface temperature, and the notoriety of Dyson's views were all going to rise over the coming decades. His continued questionings of climate modeling assumptions, his critiques of research funding patterns, and his dismissal of apocalyptic projections for future climate were to become ever more grating on a lot of scientists. To this Dyson could only respond: that can't be helped.

12. Success in Life

Dyson as Astronomer
(MID 1960S TO MID 1970S)

Did he win the Nobel? When measuring a scientist's success, this is what they ask. When weighing the relative importance of things, a scientist will say that the work itself is its own reward, not the early-morning October call from Stockholm.

In practice, though, getting or not getting that prize does matter, both to you and to the people you pass in the hall. They know whether you have it. In the faculty roster or on those long lists of notable signatories on petitions sent to newspapers you get an asterisk next to your name. True, you never have peace again. Everyone wants your opinion or recommendation. They want to borrow that asterisk. It becomes hard to do research at the old pace. Noblesse oblige comes with the asterisk. Committees, statements, good causes, moral weight.

In October 1965 at last the Swedish call went out to three men for their work on quantum electrodynamics. Nobody disputed the importance of QED. It provided the full quantum explanation of how atoms and light interact, how particles can be created or annihilated, how lasers work. It made possible advances in a variety of practical fields like optics, chemistry, and electronics. The awkwardness lay in the fact that the Nobel Prize can be given to a maximum of three people. As the fourth man, Dyson had to be left out.

Shin'ichiro Tomonaga, Julian Schwinger, and Richard Feynman won the physics Nobel that year, and it fell to Freeman Dyson to write about it in *Science* rather than to receive it. Graciously leaving his own efforts out of the account, Dyson said that QED was still essential in explaining high-precision atomic experiments. For example, Dyson pointed to a recent measurement of the inherent magnetism of the electron. The experimental and calculated values agreed to better than 1 part in 10 million.[1]

When asked whether he felt bad about not getting the prize Dyson invariably relegated his historical role in forging QED to that of a mediator among the approaches taken by the three others. Decades later, as he was asked about this repeatedly, Dyson developed an even more sophisticated riposte: it was better to be asked why you *didn't* win the Nobel than to be asked why you *did* win.

Over the years, others have taken up Dyson's cause. Here are the opinions of some Nobelists: Steven Weinberg, who received the prize for uniting the weak nuclear force and the electromagnetic force into a single theory, thought that Dyson should have the prize. If the three-person rule kept him out that year, he should have gotten it another year. Chen Ning Yang, who won for his theory about why nature is not mirror symmetric, felt that Dyson should have gotten a Nobel because he had done something that the other three hadn't: proven that each of the many component terms in the calculations were finite.[2] Frank Wilczek, whose Nobel came for his work developing a quantum theory of the strong nuclear force, holds that Dyson deserves the prize, and since he couldn't receive it at the same time as the other three, then it was appropriate to have given it to him in 1999 along with Martinus Veltman and Gerardus 't Hooft for their work on field theories.[3] And dissenting opinions? Murray Gell-Mann argued that Dyson contributed to the formal look of QED by harmonizing the work of Tomonaga, Schwinger, and Feynman, but that this wasn't enough to win him the Nobel.[4]

FAMILY FIRST

When pressed further about the Nobel Prize, Dyson's answer, polite but with an edge of exasperation, was to say, Look, I've had a great life. As a young man on the eve of the Second World War I fully expected to die. But I came out of it alive. I've got a great job. Do whatever I like. Study fascinating problems. Keep up ties with learned colleagues around the world.

And family. He hadn't won the Nobel but he had plenty else to be happy about. In the hierarchy of important things, Dyson's ranking of things that made for a good life was as follows: (1) family, (2) friends, (3) work.[5] His family life in the home on Battle Road Circle was indeed full. In addition to Esther (born 1951) and George (1953) by his first wife, he and Imme Jung were to have four daughters: Dorothy (1959), Emily (1961), Miriam (1963, often called Mia), and Rebecca (1967). Although the parents spoke mainly English to each other, the young mother spoke mainly German to her babies.[6]

Dyson's parents had also lived full lives. His father, Sir George Dyson, had a prolific musical career as a conductor, administrator, and popular composer of oratorios. He died in 1964. Freeman's mother, Mildred Dyson, a lawyer and prominent crusader for women's issues, would die at the age of ninety-four. Alice, Freeman's sister, still lived in Winchester, England. She remained unmarried. She did social work, taught French, and converted to Catholicism. In 2011 she turned ninety.

Esther and George lived with their father for much of the year and with their mother during summers and at Christmas. Their half-sister, Katarina, remained with Verena Huber-Dyson. Katarina was serious about ballet. Esther and George both went off to college at the age of sixteen, Esther to Harvard (Radcliffe, to be exact) and George to the University of California (San Diego and then Berkeley). Esther was a good girl and George a bad boy. Before going to college, Esther spent the academic year in London with friends of Freeman's, establishing for her what would become a lifelong habit of travel. At Harvard she was an economics major, worked on the school newspaper, and then went to work for *Forbes* magazine.

George Dyson, by contrast with well-behaved Esther, was a handful. He was given to brooding and was not a good student. He was brilliant but didn't want to do the assigned work. He frequently cut class and would read books at the nearby library at Princeton University. Starting at the age of twelve he built a kayak in his bedroom and then in the garage.

In 1968, at the age of fourteen, he was arrested for possessing drug paraphernalia, for which he spent a week in jail. His father at first declined to bail George out since he wanted to teach him a lesson. Several days along and still in jail, George called his mother, who was then teaching in Chicago. George was soon released. Divorced now for ten years, Verena and Freeman found one more thing to argue about. Verena was outraged by Freeman having left George in jail, while Freeman blamed George's familiarity with drugs on Verena's Berkeley friends.[7]

George did well in his college classes but he was restless and didn't remain long at the university. In 1971 he attended Katarina's wedding in Vancouver and decided to stay on there. For three years he lived in a treehouse, ninety-five feet off the ground. There he read about exploration, such as the journals of Captain James Cook and histories of the Pacific Northwest, especially those about the native peoples and Russian hunters of sea otters.[8]

As the 1960s and 1970s wore on George and Esther became less of a presence at the home in Princeton. Instead things revolved around the four little girls—Dorothy, Emily, Mia, and Becca. What was life like in the Dyson household? The family culture was mostly in the European style, tending toward strictness. If you acted up at the dinner table you were sent to eat in the kitchen. There was little TV or candy. An au pair, usually a young woman from Europe, was always around, and one of these brought television into the home. All the kids went to public school in Princeton. Freeman insisted on this.[9]

Freeman had no particular hobbies, played no sports. He and his family seldom went to church. Freeman had played violin as a child, and all his children took some kind of lessons, but otherwise music was not a big part of the life at Battle Road Circle. Freeman would attend concerts if invited.[10] The children would practice their instruments on an old wooden music stand once owned by Einstein. Sometimes Freeman and Imme would play recorder duets.[11]

Freeman liked to read books to his kids, sometimes poetry. The Laura Ingalls Wilder *Little House on the Prairie* books were the favorite. They'd play the occasional board game such as Scrabble. Family vacations often consisted of summertime trips to Jason meetings, usually in California. Imme would take the kids (sometimes without Freeman) to visit her mother in Germany. Freeman's days during the week were pretty regular: breakfast at seven, off to the Institute at eight, and back for dinner at six or seven. Freeman didn't cook but would regularly help with the cleanup.[12] Dinner would sometimes go on a bit if Freeman was holding forth on some topic. The children were expected to stay and listen.[13] On snowy days Freeman might use the kids' sled to get to work going downhill. Esther, if she wanted the sled, would have to fetch it back from the Institute.

Overall, domestic life was pretty comfortable. At the time of Freeman's divorce from Verena he admitted to her that perhaps he hadn't been prepared for marriage.[14] With Imme, things were different. He was happy to be married to a German wife, he said, since he appreciated the warmth of a German family.[15] Esther remembers as a child reading *The Diary of Anne Frank* and being charmed by the fact that Peter and Anne, who fell in love, should be living in the same attic (hiding from the Nazis). Freeman told her that sometimes you love the one you're with. Esther felt at the time that this was an unromantic view, but later she saw wisdom in the remark.[16]

FRIENDS SECOND

In a professional life crowded with research, attendance at international meetings, and contributions to journals and books, Dyson had many opportunities for friendship. Start with those who had stood as mentor figures: Dyson and Feynman were still friendly in the 1960s but didn't see much of each other. In 1965 Dyson spoke at a special birthday celebration for Hans Bethe. In the summer of 1969 he worked with Rudolf Peierls at the University of Washington. He saw a fair amount of Ted Taylor, especially since the two were both becoming more interested in arresting the spread of nuclear weapons.

And Robert Oppenheimer? Was he a friend? When Dyson first came to the Institute for Advanced Study in the fall of 1948, aflame with his ideas for making QED work, Oppenheimer had been an enemy, or at least a severe critic. Even after Oppie had come around to accepting QED (*"Nolo Contendere"*), and indeed becoming one of Dyson's biggest boosters, he never was much of a mentor to Dyson in the way that Bethe or Peierls had been.

Following the debacle of Oppenheimer's security clearance hearings in 1954, and with more time to devote to his duties as Institute director, he and Dyson saw a lot more of each other. The Dysons and Oppenheimers grew closer socially as the years went by. Dyson, along with several Institute colleagues, nominated Oppenheimer for the Enrico Fermi Award of the Atomic Energy Commission, the highest award (now bestowed by the Department of Energy) by the U.S. government for nuclear work.*

---

*Oppenheimer won the award but in a roundabout way. The Fermi Award winner was then decided by the AEC General Advisory Committee, the same committee chaired by Oppenheimer that passed negative judgment on the H-bomb back in 1949. The name of the designated winner is then passed along to the president for his approval. Along the way it is routed through the President's Science Advisory Committee. Richard Garwin, one of the most illustrious physicists of the second half of the twentieth century, a notable expert on defense matters, and a participant in Jason studies, sat on that committee and had this to say about what happened in 1962 when the nomination of Edward Teller was considered:

Dyson also helped to arrange a grand party for Oppie's sixtieth birthday in 1964, including a commemorative series of essays published in the *Review of Modern Physics*.[17]

Oppie died in 1967, and Dyson helped with the funeral arrangements.[18] He also participated in a sort of annual memorial for the man in the form of a small by-invitation gathering of scientists at the home of Oppenheimer's widow, Kitty, for a number of years on the anniversary of Oppie's death. At one of these Steven Weinberg presented an early description of his theory unifying the weak nuclear force and the electromagnetic forces into a single mathematical framework. At the end of his talk Weinberg was a bit nervous when he saw Dyson begin to make a remark. Years before, when Weinberg was a graduate student at Princeton, he had come over to Dyson's office to ask the professor some questions. Dyson, usually polite, was on this occasion cold to Weinberg and dismissive of his work. The student left very disappointed. Now, years later, Dyson was about to comment again on Weinberg—this time not to criticize but instead to ask the moderator that Weinberg, who had made such a brilliant presentation, be allowed to speak beyond his allotted time.[19]

Oppenheimer's death marked a new phase in the life of the Institute for Advanced Study. A new jurisdiction within the Institute, the School of Natural Sciences, was created in 1966. For most of the years covered in this chapter (mid-1960s to mid-1970s) the faculty of this school consisted of Dyson, Tullio Regge, Roger Dashen, Stephen Adler (all particle theorists), John Bahcall (astrophysics), and Marshall Rosenbluth (nuclear and plasma physics). This permanent faculty was supplemented by a perpetually changing succession of young scientists, "members," who would visit for a year or two, often collaborating or just consulting with the faculty. This suited Dyson. He could provide important advice to a novice theorist, but was not tied down for years of overseeing dissertation research. At the Institute, seminars were frequent, and

---

While there was no dissent that Teller's accomplishments warranted the award, the preponderance of feeling was that the award should not be made, because of Teller's role in the Oppenheimer trial. In one of the few political acts of my life, I commented that I abhorred what I judged to be Teller's attack on Oppenheimer, but that I thought that Oppenheimer certainly himself merited the Fermi Award and that it could only happen if Teller received it first. The argument apparently carried the day, and in successive years it went to Edward Teller (1962) and Robert Oppenheimer (1963). (Richard Garwin, unpublished notes, used with permission.)

Oppenheimer received the award from the hands of President Lyndon Johnson.

impromptu hallway encounters were fruitful. But no formal courses were offered and no degrees awarded.

Besides his academic year work at IAS and his summertime work with Jason, Dyson was an active member of the physics community. He frequently published articles in a diverse range of journals. He often attended meetings of the American Physical Society and served on a committee of the American Institute of Physics overseeing the translation of physics journals (mostly Russian) into English. He traveled to numerous meetings or seminars or award ceremonies abroad, including those in Holland, Russia, France (1966), Australia (1967), Britain (1968), Germany and Austria (1969), Italy and Britain (1970), Armenia (1971), Britain (1972), Scotland, Germany, and Spain (1974), Russia (1975), Israel (1977), and so on.

As the need arose, Dyson could help teach a course at nearby Princeton University. The most notable of these was Nuclear Weapons, Strategy, and Arms Control, in the spring of 1976, taught with historian Martin Sherwin (who would with Kai Bird later write an impressive biography of Oppenheimer, *American Prometheus*) and Harold Feiveson, on the faculty of Princeton's Woodrow Wilson School of Public and International Affairs.

One of the enrolled undergraduates, John Phillips, came to Dyson for tutelage. For his term paper in the class, Phillips attempted to design an atom bomb. Without revealing any of the restricted nuclear knowledge in his own head, Professor Dyson tried to steer his young protégé in the right direction. Phillips's personal observations of Dyson include the following: Dyson wore oversize galoshes in the snow, had sympathetic eyes, was patient, and wanted to be called by his first name.[20]

From nonclassified government documents, freely available to anyone, Phillips proceeded to gather a primer of frightening specificity, showing step by step how to build a nuclear bomb. Dyson was appalled at the amount of dangerous information freely available, and suggested, perhaps jokingly, that the paper be burned. He gave Phillips an A in the course.[21]

Only months later, when the *Trenton Times* ran a story about Phillips's project, did the whole affair flash into prominence. Phillips, and Dyson too, were suddenly thrust into a flood of publicity, with journalists and several shady individuals with undisclosed affiliations from around the world seeking interviews. Dyson was proud of Phillips for responsibly handling his short-lived fame as "The A–Bomb Kid." Dyson was not proud of the way newspapers pumped up the drama.[22]

COLLABORATORS

The exercise of mathematics is often a solitary pursuit. Indeed some of Dyson's happiest intellectual labors were performed alone—as a boy in a tree reading, in the family cottage near the Isle of Wight solving equations, or on a bus crossing Nebraska imagining electron–photon interactions.

But for two important rounds of mathematical physics research, Dyson was to pair up with just the right collaborator. The first of these partnerships helped establish a new branch of statistical mechanics. Pioneered in the nineteenth century by Ludwig Boltzmann and James Clerk Maxwell, statistical mechanics is a method for deriving average properties of a large ensemble of objects. A good example is Maxwell's calculation of the spectrum of velocities for molecules in a bottle of gas at a given temperature. Raise the temperature a bit, and the velocities also shift upward.

The statistical problem Dyson now tackled was how to calculate the energies of nucleons (protons and neutrons) inside an atom's nucleus. Princeton physicist Eugene Wigner got Dyson started on the problem in 1959, just as Dyson was leaving Project Orion. One cannot calculate the velocity of every single molecule in a warm gas, and analogously one cannot calculate the quantum energy of nucleons in an excited nucleus. Wigner, however, had attempted an approximate description of the nucleus in the form of an array of parameters—a matrix of numbers, or a spreadsheet—that represented the complicated relations among the energy levels of the nucleus. As a start to understanding those relations one can do no better than guess the relative spacings of nuclear energy levels. These guesses appear as random numbers arranged in the matrix.

Dyson enthusiastically embraced the mathematical beauty of random matrices. In the summer of 1961, working at Brookhaven National Laboratory on Long Island, he wrote a series of papers on this topic in quick succession. In 1962 Dyson invited one of the world's experts on this subject, Madan Lal Mehta, to join him for a year at the Institute. Together they helped firm up the mathematical framework for this kind of statistical mechanics—not unlike what Dyson had done for quantum electrodynamics years before—so that it could be used for other physics topics in addition to the problem of nuclear energy levels.[23] In later decades other theorists were to apply the random matrix approach to such things as disordered solid materials, quantum gravity, and quantum chaos.

The subject of random matrices held Dyson's interest over several decades. The potential mathematical meaning behind random matrices Dyson compares to an iceberg.[24] Above is the tip—the theory is concerned with things like nuclear energy levels. But beneath the surface, he suspects, is much more. One of the most intriguing aspects of random matrix theory is that it seems to be tied to a mathematical issue that has fascinated Dyson since he was a teenager, namely the so-called Riemann zeta function, whose behavior is related to the spacing of prime numbers.[25]

Dyson was invited to spend time in the summer of 1970 at the Scuola Normale Superiore in Pisa, Italy, where an astronomy meeting was scheduled to coincide with his stay. There he was gripped by an impetuous desire to work again on statistical mechanics, the subject that had consumed so much of his time years earlier. Whenever he had the chance he snuck away from his astronomer friends for his illicit tryst with the forbidden topic. He stole to a quiet place, the farthest nook of the library, where he stealthily wrote about his true love—random matrix theory.[26] As late as 2010, Dyson's articles on random matrices were still among the most downloaded of papers from *The Journal of Mathematical Physics*. One corner of this research bears his name in the form of "The Dyson Conjecture."

The Dyson-Mehta partnership was to be followed by a fruitful collaboration between Dyson and Andrew Lenard, a young physicist who visited the Institute during the 1965–66 year. The problem they addressed was one of the most basic in all of science: why is matter stable? They tried to show mathematically, as if they were proving some theorem of geometry, that all the positively and negatively charged particles, all the protons and electrons, in all the atoms that make up a solid object like a bowling ball, should conspire to remain solid and not collapse into a puddle. The explanation also had to account for the fact that two bowling balls could not occupy the same place at the same time.

You'd think by the 1960s that scientists would have worked out the exact explanation, but they hadn't. The mathematics seemed too complicated. Chemical forces, in the form of electromagnetic interactions binding atoms and molecules to each other, naturally keep things stable. But subtle quantum effects were also expected to play a role, and these ideas hadn't yet been formulated into a mathematical model. Two physicists, Michael Fisher and David Ruelle, offered a prize, consisting of a bottle of champagne, to anyone who could deliver a convincing argument.

Lenard brought the stability problem to Dyson's attention. The two men worked together, usually with Dyson trying out ideas standing at a blackboard and with Lenard asking occasional questions.[27] After some months they had themselves the first formal explanation for the stability of matter.

Dyson and Lenard laid out their explanations in two lengthy papers in *The Journal of Mathematical Physics*. The work was good enough to win the champagne. Years later, looking back on this bit of research, Dyson remarked upon the advancing nature of scientific knowledge and how most efforts are eventually superseded. Characteristically, he apologized for him and Lenard taking forty pages of text to say what two later physicists, Elliott Lieb and Walter Thirring, did more elegantly and rigorously in four pages.[28]

A FRIENDLY UNIVERSE

Freeman Dyson was interested in just about every physics problem with a mathematical angle. It's not surprising then that Dyson should add "astronomer" to his résumé. He had, of course, demonstrated a serious interest in things celestial—work on Orion, adaptive optics, Dyson spheres. But now he would become more professionally involved.

In 1962 he wrote a paper describing a hypothetical "gravitational machine," consisting of large masses, such as a pair of stars, surrounded by numerous orbiting lighter objects. The idea behind this paper was to show how gravitational energy could be extracted from such a system and to study the emission of gravity waves. Dyson submitted the article to the Gravity Research Foundation competition. It finished in fourth place that year.

Dyson's growing interest in astronomy was facilitated by a sabbatical year he spent (1967–68) at Yeshiva University in New York City. There he learned astrophysics even as he taught it. Pulsars were a particular area of interest for Dyson and for many other astronomers. Pulsars were mysterious points in deep space casting out bursts of light at regular intervals ranging from seconds all the way down to milliseconds. One of Dyson's first pulsar papers discussed the chance that they could be emitters of measurable gravity waves. The waves, Dyson thought, would be too weak to register at any one moment in terrestrial detectors. But he figured that over time the arriving gravity waves from a powerful pulsar might leave some accumulative trace in the Earth. So he sought access to long-term seismic records from a station in Montana that for many years had monitored nuclear test explosions. Unfortunately for Dyson's scheme, the monitoring data corresponding to actual explosive events had been retained while the much more voluminous and apparently useless monitoring data corresponding to "quiet" times when explosions had not been occurring, exactly what Dyson wanted, had been discarded.[29]

His roving curiosity brought him to question whether the constants of nature are really constant. You'd expect that things like the charge of all electrons, e, or the universal gravitational constant, G, would stay the same. But as we saw with the overthrow of mirror symmetry (parity violation), scientists scrupulously keep looking for discrepancies from prevailing knowledge. Dyson looked into the matter but concluded that over the life of the Earth, e and G couldn't have changed by more than an infinitesimal amount.[30]

When Dyson wasn't doing astronomy he was writing about it. An essay in the September 1971 issue of *Scientific American* is an excellent example of his manifesto-style writing: determined but not dogmatic, thorough but not exhausting. The piece is about the flow of energy through the cosmos and it begins, not surprisingly, with a quote from Dyson's favorite poet, William Blake, including the line, "Energy is the only life and is from the Body; and Reason is the bound or outward circumference."

The article is concerned mainly with explaining why, if gravity is apparently so dominant in the universe, all the visible objects in the sky—stars, planets, galaxies—didn't long ago shrink and merge into nothingness. The answer is that many countervailing forces, what Dyson calls "hang-ups," hold off awhile what seems like an inevitable slide into collapse. Examples include the nuclear reactions inside stars that keep the stars inflated, or the angular motion of planets tracing out orbits around stars, or the revolution of pinwheel galaxies around their own centers.

One of the most important themes of the article, and one that would become an abiding principle for Dyson in coming years, is the status of living things in a universe that appears indifferent to what happens on Earth. Yes, Dyson says, the existence of life on our planet is shaped by the local physical circumstances, such as the fact that we would not be here thinking about all this if the Earth were a bit closer or further from the sun or if those nuclear reactions fizzing away in the sun were a little stronger or weaker.

Life depends on energy, but in some sense maybe energy depends on life:

> It would not be surprising if it should turn out that the origin and destiny of the energy in the universe cannot be completely understood in isolation from the phenomena of life and consciousness.[31]

Dyson was not yet exactly subscribing to what has come to be known as the Anthropic Principle, since he was not restricting his proposition to thinking creatures, or at least not to *Homo sapiens*, but to life in general.

Speaking from the secure position of a tenured spot at the Institute for Advanced Study and holding a consummate scientific reputation, Dyson was here tentatively launching a career as a science prophet, not in the sense that he could accurately foresee the future but rather that he was pointing to some kind of reality that hadn't properly been appreciated. In the *Scientific American* piece he allowed himself to say such things as "I believe the universe is friendly," and that he can "look to the sky with hopeful eyes." These were to become typical Dyson nostrums. He wanted to do more than inform his readers. At the risk of being saccharine he sought to persuade and inspire.

In finishing his article and wanting to underscore his hope that we take comfort in the fresh knowledge that science supplies, Dyson let Blake have the final word:

> If the doors of perception were cleansed every thing would appear to man as it is, infinite, for man has closed himself up, till he sees all things thro' narrow chinks of his cavern.[32]

BUSIEST DECADE

Looking back on his astronomy career, Freeman Dyson conceded that much of his work was ephemeral.[33] He was a cheerleader and not a practitioner:

A large fraction of theoretical papers in astrophysics, including mine, are imaginative speculations based on crude approximations. They are quickly written and quickly forgotten. I did not find in astrophysics any opportunities to employ elegant mathematics. In this field my tastes and my talents remained orthogonal. My love of observational detail and my talent for exact mathematics were never effectively combined.[34]

By almost all measures, though, Freeman Dyson was a successful scientist. Honors were piling up. He had been elected a member of the Royal Society in 1952, before he'd even turned thirty. America's most prestigious science club, the National Academy, gave him membership in 1964, having been nominated by Yang and Oppenheimer. He had earned no Ph.D. (and was proud of it) for regular graduate work, but was now starting to receive honorary doctorates: from Yeshiva in 1966 and Glasgow and Princeton in 1974. Dozens more were to follow. The U.S. Congress thought enough of his commonsense views on the impact of science and technology to invite him three times to testify: about the test ban treaty in 1963, about missile defense in 1969, and about DNA research in 1977.

Dyson did not share the 1965 Nobel Prize in physics but he was acquiring many of the rest of the awards worth having. In 1965 the American Institute of Physics and the American Physical Society gave him the Dannie Heineman Prize for mathematical physics. In 1966 he received the Lorentz Medal of the Royal Netherlands Academy. On and on: in 1968 the Hughes Medal of the Royal Society, in 1969 the Max Planck Medal of the German Physical Society, in 1970 the J. Robert Oppenheimer Memorial Prize of the Center for Theoretical Studies in Miami, and in 1977 the Harvey Prize of the Technion in Israel. The citations for most of these awards refer, of course, to Dyson's QED work of the 1940s, but some also referred to the other subjects on which Dyson had published important papers.*

---

*Dyson's interests and talents reverberated through a kaleidoscope of cultural areas. Here, in a randomly pairwise list, are some of the publications that have carried his writing: *Review of Modern Physics* and *The New Republic*; *Journal of the American Medical Association* and *The Physics of Fluids*; *The Tolstoy Studies Journal* and the *American Journal of Physics*; *Nature* and *The Atlantic*; *The Journal of Mathematical Physics* and *The New Yorker*; *Science* and *The Christian Science Monitor*; *Journal of the Optical Society* and *Foreign Affairs*; *Astrophysical Journal* and *Harper's Magazine*; *Journal of the Statistical Society* and *The New York Times*; *Technology Review* and *The Baltimore Sun*; *Popular Science*; and *The Proceedings of the American Philosophical Society*. Who else in modern life has such disparate interests?

The decade portrayed in this chapter, the mid-1960s to the mid-1970s, was arguably the busiest in Dyson's professional career. He was the Mozart or Bach of physics, prolifically composing pieces of all sorts—on magnets, fluids, pulsars, gravity waves, statistical mechanics, cosmology, extraterrestrial intelligence, the fundamental physical constants, and the stability of matter. Through his involvement with the Jasons he participated in work on adaptive optics, climate change, laser propulsion, missile defense, and nuclear weapons. He continued to do work in the area of pure mathematics. One such paper touched upon work performed sixty years earlier by one of Dyson's teachers, Cambridge mathematician John Littlewood. Littlewood was then still alive and regarded Dyson's paper (along with its dedication to Littlewood) as the greatest compliment he had ever received.[35]

There is often in hyper-achievers the sense that even more and better work could have been accomplished. Dyson had reached his fifties and was no longer the precocious youngster. People expected him to write brilliant papers, which he did. But he wasn't, as he had been with QED, at the very forefront of physics. Plenty of other scientists wrote brilliant papers. Some of the most brilliant were by his colleagues at the Institute. Dyson felt that he was no longer as smart as some of the guys down the hall.[36] Was this the beginning of some kind of recessional?

Dyson didn't realize it at the time, but the first half of his career, the scientific phase, was running out. The second half, the part of his career that tapped accumulated wisdom, was about to begin.

13. Science and Sublime

Dyson as Essayist
(1975–1985)

He hadn't seen the boy in years. Actually he wasn't a boy anymore but a man. He'd left the family and made something of himself. George Dyson now lived on the parcels of land in the channel of water between Vancouver Island and the British Columbia mainland. He lived simply, did odd jobs in the area, and had fulfilled his dream of building a large kayak.

Freeman Dyson wanted to visit his son, and so he traveled north, along with his daughter Emily. The ensuing miniature Dyson reunion was documented in a curious book called *The Starship and the Canoe* by Kenneth Brower, the brother of one of George's Berkeley friends. At the heart of the book are the contrasts between two men, George and Freeman; between two building projects, Saturn-bound Orion and ocean-going kayak; and between two lifestyles, the Princeton life of research and lectures and the Northwest outdoor life centered on woodland and nautical adventure. Brower's book was more profile than biography, since its time frame was so focused. Its story culminated with an incisive view of the week-long meeting of father, daughter, and son. At the time of this encounter in August 1975 George was twenty-two, Freeman fifty-one, and Emily fourteen.

Both Brower's account and Freeman's account—for he too would write up his impressions—began diplomatically with descriptions of the rugged, misty conifer environment of the Pacific Northwest, where grit, resourcefulness, and a desire to be away from the trappings of civilization are primary.

Freeman, more used to teas at the Institute, was impressed by the ability of the men and women on these islands to use and retool heavy powered machines as required. He admired the cheerfulness of young couples adapting to simple conditions and raising children in a near-wilderness. He appreciated their pluck. "These are precisely the people we shall need for homesteading the asteroids," he thought, illustrating the point that Freeman's space mission thinking was present even here—we should say especially here—in a rough-hewn, woodsmoke-scented cabin in the middle of the Queen Charlotte Strait.[1] Maybe this, more than the high-tech sets used in *2001: A Space Odyssey,* is what a human homestead on the moons of Jupiter might look like a century hence, with suitable provisions for high-vacuum and low-gravity conditions.

In his role as field anthropologist, Brower tried not to intrude on the delicate process of family reacquaintance and yet remain alert to meaningful nuances amid the interplay of words. For instance, George asked Freeman whether on Freeman's recent visit to Europe he had seen evidence that the Dyson clan was faring well. No, came the answer, the Dysons seemed to be dwindling. "Not that the father cared," said Brower in his summary. "The genes survived, said the father of five daughters, and that, he supposed, was the important thing."[2] The father, in turn, asked the son whether he would help to perpetuate the Dysons. "Not so many," George said, smiling. "One or two maybe."[3]

Another poignant moment underscoring the continuing differences between the Princeton intellectual and the Vancouver outdoorsman came when everyone was sitting by lantern light around a kitchen table and a marijuana cigarette began circulating. George offered it to Freeman, who declined with hardness in his voice. "The Dysons, father and son, had narrowed the gap, but each at this moment had come to a final frontier of his territory," Brower observed, "and could go no farther. They would continue to orbit each other at this distance."[4]

Freeman's account of the island sojourn does not include the marijuana moment, but both his and Brower's tellings do relate the episode of the capsized boat. On the last full day of the visit, everyone was talking near the shore when they noticed that a mile out a small boat was laboring against the powerful tidal flow. When the boat disappeared, George Dyson and Ken Brower reacted instantly. They hopped in a motorboat, shot out to the churning water, heroically plucked two men from the ocean, and fetched them back to land. The rescued men, nearly dead from hypothermia, were further revived by a hot breakfast of George's pancakes. As things settled down, Freeman talked with one of the survivors, who asked about Dyson's work and accomplishments as a scientist back east. "It seems to me now," Freeman told the man in the spirit of this exhilarating moment, "the best thing I ever did in Princeton was to raise that boy."[5]

BORN WRITER

Indeed Dyson had done many fine things in Princeton. Freeman was the father of Esther, George, Dorothy, Emily, Mia, and Rebecca. Of course, he is known chiefly as a man of consequence in the science world. In the few months before his Vancouver adventure, he had crammed in a lot: finished up a sabbatical year (1974–75) at the Max Planck Institute in Munich, where he did mostly astronomy research; obliged the navy by studying submarine noise with his Jason colleagues; got his adaptive optics work declassified by the military; and grappled with land-sea-and-air carbon dioxide estimates at Oak Ridge. In the few months after Vancouver he would again study magnets, would travel to an observatory in the Caucasus Mountains, and would be asked by the Phi Beta Kappa organization to undertake a program of lectures at eight colleges in places like Idaho, Georgia, and Oregon.

Coming between these two batches of scientific undertakings, and only a few weeks after Vancouver, an innocuous offer arrived from the Sloan Foundation. They wanted Dyson to write an autobiographical book. In making this overture Sloan said that its goal was to promote a greater public understanding of science or, to be more precise, a better understanding of the scientific enterprise as a human process. If not all the complexities of science (quantum field theory, say) could be conveyed in simple terms, at least the efforts to carry out science were to be laid out for appreciation—the hopes, the setbacks, the practical accomplishments, the rewards, and disappointments.[6] Sloan asked several other scientists to tell their tales too, such as physician and writer Lewis Thomas and biologist Francis Crick.

By this point, Dyson was a seasoned writer of popular articles in *Scientific American, The New Yorker, Time, The Atlantic, The New Republic,* and *The New York Times.* He would now accelerate the transition from research to writing. He justified his decision by quoting an assertion of his Cambridge teacher G. H. Hardy—"Young men should prove theorems, old men should write books."[7] Dyson was still capable of original research, but indeed hereafter his science production would slow while his writing production would increase. There would be ample reward for the shift. Accepting Sloan's offer was to be a pivotal development in Dyson's life. "Life begins at fifty-five," he said later in a sprightly mood, "the age at which I published my first book."[8]

In his previous writings Dyson had shown a strong grasp of history, and not just science history. Indeed his command of past events was confident enough and large enough that he could allow himself the luxury of being philosophical. After all, many of the chapters in the book were to be autobiographical, and drawing out lessons from life's episodes was to become one of Dyson's favorite pastimes. Like a great novelist, he offered up a panoramic morality play—about science, technology, war, and exploration. His dramatis personae, the characters who turn up repeatedly in his pages, are often polymaths like Dyson himself: H. G. Wells, who combines a scientist's and a novelist's visions; Hans Bethe, kindly and astute; Edward Teller, mercurial, brilliant, devastating; Robert Oppenheimer, Faustian, heroic and tragic; Ted Taylor, the most ethical great man Dyson ever met; and Richard Feynman, bon vivant and effervescent thinker.

The name of Dyson's book, *Disturbing the Universe*, was taken from a line in T. S. Eliot's poem "The Love Song of J. Alfred Prufrock." The protagonist in Eliot's poem is timid and mostly doesn't dare to disturb anything. The protagonist in Dyson's book, himself, does dare to create a disturbance, or at least to question the status quo. He declares that his mission in writing *Disturbing the Universe* is to be an apostle of science to the world of nonscientists. He intends to examine the ethical component of science, especially as it applies to a spectrum of venerable human issues, "war and peace, freedom and responsibility, hope and despair."[9] Dyson's approach to describing the ethical side of science is not to use equations but to tell stories. His approach will be literary, not analytical.

Most of the chapters run in chronological order through Dyson's life. In his careful selection of teachable moments, we see a scientific sensibility coming into existence, as the young Dyson grapples with academic interests and career choices. But just as important is the blossoming concern for ethical and historical issues. His presentation is personable. You might get the impression that you were hearing the voice rather than reading the page. It's easy to imagine you were in the presence of an adroit stage performer, like Spalding Gray, the monologist who sat at a simple table, sipped occasionally from a glass of water, and, while keeping direct eye contact with you alone, told tales of charming simplicity.

Dyson's book opens with him at the age of eight up a tree reading a book, *The Magic City* (1910) by Edith Nesbit. The story depicts a Harry Potter sort of orphan who confronts unceasing perils in a phantasmal setting. Dyson identifies three features in Nesbit's book that are also important in his own writing career: searching for adventure, struggling with the consequences of technology, and interpreting prophecies. A sense of adventure and ethical considerations are evident right here in Dyson's first book. The "prophetic" side of his writing would take a while longer to materialize.

What are the indispensable stories he has to tell? His time with Bomber Command, his arrival in the United States, his friendship with Feynman, the agonies of Oppenheimer and Teller, the exhilarations of designing nuclear reactors, nuclear rockets, and nuclear treaties. With its autobiographical arc, *Disturbing the Universe* is the closest thing Dyson would come to an extended narrative. Thereafter he would publish many more books, so it will sound strange to say that he is not really a book writer. What he writes are essays that later become the chapters in booklike collections.

Disturbing the Universe was published in 1979 and was nominated for an American Book Award and later for a National Book Award when it was reissued in paperback. It won mostly admiring reviews. *The New Republic,* perceiving a tragic tone in the book, concentrated on Dyson's experience with Bomber Command, the development of nuclear power and weaponry, and the prospects, good and bad, for manipulating DNA molecules, a field of research then in its relative infancy.[10]

A review in *Science* by astronomer George Field noted that the book quoted poets more often than physicists. Field compared *Disturbing the Universe* to a bestseller from a few years before, Robert Pirsig's *Zen and the Art of Motorcycle Maintenance*, a philosophical look at technology.[11]

Field pointed to the appearance of something unusual in a book about the scientific life—a recourse to the artistic and spiritual side of things. With a whole book at his disposal Dyson took poetic license to say things about science that he had expressed previously only in a muted way. And with dispensation came disputation. It was necessary to pick a fight with a friend.

PURSUING THE SUBLIME

Freeman Dyson has high respect for Steven Weinberg. Not only is Weinberg famous among physicists for helping to unify the known forces of nature into a consolidated mathematical framework. He is also, like Dyson, a notable author. Dyson credits Weinberg's 1977 book, *The First Three Minutes*, with legitimizing the study of the deep past. Firm new ideas about the nature of the early universe, fresh celestial observations to back up the ideas, and Weinberg's confident, clear prose all helped to make it intellectually permissible, even fashionable, to study this subject—the creation of the cosmos—which until recently had been in the province of theologians rather than scientists. Then, in Dyson's view, Weinberg nearly spoiled the whole thing by concluding his exhilarating book by saying this: "The more the universe seems comprehensible, the more it also seems pointless."[12]

In his own book Freeman Dyson took the opposite tack. He liked looking for the point of things. He broached the desirability of retaining a spiritual outlook, or at least of keeping an open mind on issues that can't yet be settled by science: "I do not claim that the architecture of the universe proves the existence of God. I claim only that the architecture of the universe is consistent with the hypothesis that mind plays an essential role in its functioning."[13]

In offering this kind of observation, Dyson knew he was bumping up against many mainstream scientists who insist there is no "life force." As far as we know, even intelligent matter, such as the human brain, operates according to the same physical laws as inanimate matter. Jacques Monod, the prominent microbiologist, is typical of those who insist on a clean break with what he calls "animism." The origin of the human species, Monod argued, is but one chance occurrence in a long evolutionary trail of life in the universe. We must be objective about this. Human consciousness is not privileged, Monod said, and is not in any way mixed up with the intrinsic blueprint of the cosmos, if indeed there is any blueprint. The arrival of *Homo sapiens* might be a marvelous accident, but it is an accident.

Dyson objects mightily to this: "I do not feel like an alien in this universe. The more I examine the universe and study the details of its architecture, the more evidence I find that the universe in some sense must have known that we were coming."[14]

Are there any signs that the presence of humans in any way "disturbs" the universe? For Dyson, exactly such portents seem to appear in the form of poignant dreams. The recurring dream of his standing helpless near the sight of a crashed and burning airplane is an example. He doesn't invoke classic Freudian psychology to interpret the dream as evidence of his guilt or cowardice. He merely mentions the dream several times in his writings, allowing us to form our own opinion. So it is with a pair of dreams Dyson saves for the end of *Disturbing the Universe*. He tells the reader his reason for this: "A dream shows up hidden connections between things that our own waking minds keep in separate compartments."[15]

In the first of the two accounts, Dyson's waking mind is grappling with astronomy. In June 1977 he was in Israel at an astronomy conference, where he and other scientists were arguing about the behavior of galaxies. The visible galactic motions did not seem to conform to the standard laws of physics. Either the laws were inadequate, Dyson said, or an additional phenomenon was at work, perhaps the existence of some so far undetected dark material in or around the galaxies.

Everyone daydreams now and then. So even amid this galactic debate, Dyson found himself thinking of his son, who, at that moment, was on the other side of the world leading a party of twelve tourists along coastal Alaska in a small fleet of kayaks he had built himself.[16] During his brief visit to the Northwest, Freeman had trusted to George's nautical acumen and was sure that this Alaska voyage would go well too.

Late that night, these two frontiers, galaxies and Alaska, got mixed up in Freeman Dyson's sleepy mind. The dreams we have at night can sometimes be scripted in fantastical form from events and thoughts we had during the day, and so it was now. In Freeman's dream he and George are in a two-seat craft. It is not a kayak this time but a small starship. They cruise not through the inlets of Vancouver but along a ramp, out the open roof of a large auditorium, and up into the sky. The father assures us that he trusts his son's expertise. George will know what to do.

They quickly leave the Earth behind and their field of view rapidly enlarges. They see stars and whole galaxies. Then the view gets larger still in the biggest possible way. The galaxies are all receding from each other; apparently the two men are seeing the noticeable expansion of the universe, the first humans to be privileged with a direct experience of the big bang.[17] This imaginary journey could have been plucked from Olaf Stapledon's novel *Star Maker*.

In relating this slumbering vision Dyson does not indulge in over-interpretation. He doesn't explain that the dream reverses the traditional parent-child roles; he does not assert that the dream denotes a longed-for reconciliation, ending a divide between a rebellious son and a constrictive father. A dream, after all, is a story we tell ourselves when we're asleep and is neither right nor wrong.

In *Disturbing the Universe* Dyson then turns from his dream journey across the galaxies back to his actual journey across Israel. He tells us that he was out driving near the Golan Heights, a pivotal battlefield in the 1967 Arab-Israeli War. The area also possesses biblical significance, and Dyson is fully alert and prepared to be impressed. Dyson has been told that his hotel stands on the same hill where, in one of the more dramatic episodes of the Bible, Elijah asked heaven to rain down punishment upon the false prophets, those attending the god Baal. In the book of I Kings, Elijah wins out over his rival prophets with God's help.

Dyson does not claim to be any kind of prophet. But he has, like Elijah, witnessed majestic things: stars, galaxies, and the big bang expansion of space-time. For Elijah the potent display of God's powers was not enough. His soul craved a more reassuring sign. For Dyson too the display of astrophysical grandeur—as seen from a telescope or even in the form of his space odyssey dream with George—was not enough. He wanted to be a participant.

> *I do not believe that we are tourists in our universe. I do not believe that the universe is mindless. . . . We are not merely spectators; we are actors in the drama of the universe.*[18]

This strikes a chord that will resonate through much of Dyson's later writings and his public speaking. He, unlike most scientists, will always be searching for more than the detector readings or the colorations found in a test tube. He will be looking for a larger meaning in things, even if he can't adequately say what those meanings are.

Certainly while he was in Israel, Dyson looked for as much meaning as he could. On the hill where Elijah had preached Dyson hoped for inspiration. Elijah had been exhausted by the effort of combating the other prophets (arguing against the prevailing views of the day, you might say) and fled to a distant cave. What came next might be considered a dream, since an angel of God came upon Elijah and drew him out of the cave, where he was shown splendid evidence of divine majesty: a mighty fire, a fierce wind, and an earthquake. But then Elijah was vouchsafed a more subtle sign of the Lord in the form of a "still small voice."

The significance of the voice heard by Elijah has been much debated over the years. Dyson seems to think of it as affirming the idea that the most powerful forces in the cosmos are not necessarily geophysical or even astrophysical, but possibly something quieter and ineffable. Here at the end of Dyson's book he makes the argument, rare nowadays for a prominent scientist, that science does not provide the only important knowledge about existence.

Dyson wanted what Elijah had gotten. He wanted to encounter a still small voice. And then he did. Again Dyson doesn't hold back from furnishing a lesson in the form of a dream, as if he were an ancient augurer and not the famous scientist and explicator of quantum electrodynamics. Again he refrains from interpreting the dream. Instead he gives the reader a sequence of sublime images.

In this last dream he dwells not in a cave. Rather he is in his own Princeton kitchen. The meeting with God comes about not because of some angelic summons but through a telephone appointment. Dyson ventures forth not in a small spacecraft with his son but in a sort of celestial elevator with his two youngest daughters. The elevator ascends out of the roof and all the way to heaven, where the three step out into a throne room. Dyson would like to find God since he has questions to ask. He and the girls search about but find nothing until they come up to the throne itself. Here they see an infant and they take turns holding him. With this, Dyson's book comes to a close:

> *In the silence I gradually became aware that the questions I had intended to raise with him have been answered. I put him gently back on his throne and say goodbye. The girls hold my hand and we walk down the steps together.*[19]

Years later, when Dyson was asked about favorite sections from among his own writings over the years, he named these dream sequences from *Disturbing the Universe.*[20]

REPERTORY THEATER

Freeman Dyson might seek the sublime, but he does not look for it in caves. The Dyson household in the 1970s and 1980s was solidly

middle-class. Conversation at the dinner table was not overly intellectual. The Dyson idea of a family vacation was for them to fly to a science meeting or the Jason gathering in Southern California each
summer, where Freeman would work all day, every day, and the others
would go to the beach. Once they kidnapped him. He drove them to
the airport, where they insisted he come with them; they even had a
ticket. So a week in Hawaii was his one vacation.

Freeman was an attentive father, going to sporting events, musical
concerts, and an occasional trip to hear choir music, practically the
only time he would find himself in a church, whenever one of the girls
was performing. He always had a briefcase filled with reports or books
that needed reading. He didn't get angry. He was soft-spoken.

The children were aware that they had a famous father, but weren't
quite sure why. Rebecca once went to hear her father give a public
lecture to see what all the fuss was about. She was impressed by the
full-house audience. She was amazed to hear this man she knew so
well speak so crisply, using such quotable language.[21]

The four younger girls did well in school. For many years there
were at least two or three members of the "Dyson gang" enrolled at
Princeton High School. They grew up and went off to college: Dorothy to the University of California at Davis, Mia to Tufts, and Emily
and Rebecca to Stanford.

Family, friends, work. The bio-graph of an active life is best told
through stories of interpersonal relations and of accomplishments. But
no diet should be all protein. There should be some roughage also. For
the sake of rounding out the human portrait, here is a more prosaic accounting of Dyson activities in the 1980s. The multitalented Mr. Dyson is like a repertory theater company, performing many things in
rotation.

As the new decade began Dyson was fifty-six years old, father of
several grown children and several still in their teenage years. He continued to be a much in demand speaker. In January 1980 the BBC interviewed him about the benefit and dangers of DNA research. In
March he spoke at Rockefeller University about life in the universe.
The next month he gave a talk at the University of Wisconsin about
the relation of biology to physics. His host on that occasion, mathematician Richard Askey, said that Dyson's talk was brilliant and that
people there were talking about it for weeks.[22]

The Dyson repertory for that year consisted of many parallel pursuits. He wrote a review in *The New Republic* about a book of Oppenheimer letters. He received an honorary degree from York University. In June he gave the keynote address at a mental health meeting in New Jersey on the subject of the grappling with the difficulties of life. In October he spoke at a conference at Gustavus Adolphus College in Minnesota. In this talk, entitled "Manchester and Athens," he showed how these two cities represented metaphorically the need in science for both engineering and experimental science (Manchester) and theoretical science and reasoning (Athens).[23] Later in the month he spoke in St. Louis ("Quick Is Beautiful") about the need to be flexible in fostering new technology.[24]

In January 1981 he was in Toronto talking about biology again, while in February he was in Philadelphia discussing priorities in astronomy.[25] In April he visited Texas for a three-day meeting, where he caught up with his old friend Richard Feynman, and the University of Illinois for a talk about the diversity of life.[26] In May it was Yale and the subject of scientists pursuing unfashionable ideas, then a reprise of "Quick Is Beautiful" in Austria. He spoke about life in the universe at Princeton in August and at Cambridge University in November. He appeared on two National Public Television programs: *The Day After Trinity*, about the Manhattan Project and its aftermath, and *Return to Space*. He traveled to Britain to receive an honorary doctorate at the City University of London and to Israel to receive the Wolf Prize for physics, one of the most prestigious awards in that subject.

The Dyson repertory schedule for 1982 included a talk at MIT, the Compton Lecture, about "fighting for freedom with the technologies of death." In March he spoke at a memorial event for Helen Dukas, Albert Einstein's longtime secretary. Besides serving in that important capacity, she had babysat for the Dyson children in the 1960s. Dyson had gently chided her for refusing to be interviewed, thus shutting off an avenue for potential science historians.[27] In April he repeated the unfashionable-research talk at the University of Minnesota. In October he spoke at the Institute for Advanced Study about space. The paperback edition of *Disturbing the Universe* was nominated for the National Book Award. He received an honorary degree at the New School in New York City.

In November he spoke at the Graduate Theological Union in Berkeley. His remarks about interstellar propulsion appeared in a book about extraterrestrial life; his remarks about unfashionable research appeared in a book published in Germany; and his comparison of physics and biology appeared in a Russian publication.

In the mid-1980s he kept up his flow of lectures and articles. *The New Yorker* carried articles that later ended up in Dyson's second book, *Weapons and Hope*. He reviewed two books about arms control for *Science*, and another for *Nature*. He wrote several articles for the science magazine *Omni*.[28] A form of his unfashionable-research talk appeared in the *Mathematical Intelligencer*. Honorary degrees kept coming: Rensselaer Polytechnic Institute and Susquehanna University.

He went on a lecture tour of Japan, speaking about the origins of life. While in Tokyo he met up with Stephen Hawking for a drink and a foray through the city where Hawking was viewed as a celebrity. "I felt as if I were taking a walk through Galilee with Jesus Christ," Dyson said. "Everywhere we went crowds of Japanese silently streamed after us, stretching out their hands to touch Hawking's wheelchair."[29]

Back in the United States, Dyson spoke at a banquet honoring his former Cornell colleague Edwin Salpeter and at a party for his Princeton friend physicist Gerard O'Neill. He delivered the Pick Lecture at the University of Chicago; his topic was missile defense and other issues relating to international peace.[30] He spoke in Detroit about science and religion at a convention of Catholic bishops,[31] at Harvard (the Phi Beta Kappa lecture) about exploration,[32] and at the computer company Analog Devices about how we can't predict future technologies by extrapolating from present-day technology.[33] In 1985 Freeman Dyson returned to the Vancouver area to participate in a Japanese documentary about his 1975 reunion with George.

Much of Dyson's best work in the 1980s, his writing of essays and reviews, was performed at his office or at his house in quaint Princeton. But this man of fanciful visions does not follow a cloistered scholarly regimen. The Dyson repertory impulse does not permit this. Instead Dyson is often at the airport making a connection to yet one more (or two or three) speaking engagements on a dozen topics.

The *nuclear Dyson* wrote an article for *The New York Times* about demystifying nuclear bombs.[34] He wrote a letter to *Physics Today* suggesting alternatives to the gigantic atom smasher called the Superconducting Super Collider, then under construction in Texas, and later abandoned.[35] He wrote a preface to a collection of essays by Oppenheimer.

The *historian Dyson* moderated a meeting of the Princeton Historical

Society about intellectual émigrés in Princeton in the 1930s and 1940s. He reviewed a book about Tolstoy and history.[36] He wrote a review in *The Christian Science Monitor* of a book about George Kennan and spoke at a banquet honoring Kennan.[37] In *The New York Review of Books* he contributed his name to a letter asking Israel to release Palestinian scientist Taysir Aruri.[38]

The *mathematical Dyson* spoke at a meeting devoted to the centennial of the Indian mathematician Srinivasa Ramanujan[39] and wrote several papers for technical journals.

Dyson the public speaker delivered the Danz Lecture, "On Being the Right Size," at the University of Washington.[40] At IBM he spoke about Richard Feynman.[41] At Duke University he gave the Fritz London Memorial Lecture, while at Yale he argued that the current Ph.D. training system in graduate school was cumbersome and did not encourage creative science.[42]

Dyson received honors. His book *Infinite in All Directions* received the Phi Beta Kappa Award. He won the Gemant Award of the American Institute of Physics for conspicuous efforts to bring science to the attention of the general public. He received honorary degrees from DePauw University and Rider College and was made an honorary fellow of his alma mater, Trinity College, Cambridge. He became an associate member of the French Academy.

Dyson the author: Disturbing the Universe was translated into French; *Origins of Life* (his third book) into Italian and Danish; and *Weapons and Hope* into Russian. He continued writing a river of pieces—feature articles, essays, book reviews—in *Physics Today* magazine, where he was, over a period of several decades, perhaps the most frequent outside contributor.

The 1980s was so bustling a decade for him that three more chapters will be needed to tell the tale. Each of these will center upon an issue of great concern to Dyson. Each will entail the preparation of a book by him on that topic. In the first of these chapters the theme will be the specter of nuclear weapons. The chapter after that will look at biology and the history of living organisms from earliest terrestrial times on into the indefinite future. The third will be devoted to Dyson's effort to reconcile science with philosophical and religious viewpoints.

14. Nuclear Slavery

Dyson as Abolitionist
(1980s)

Lying beneath a bush and bleeding from the head, apparently about to be shot dead by the assailants who had just taken his wallet, Dyson was enraptured momentarily by the glimpse of the surrounding greenery and the blue sky overhead. In the late 1930s Freeman Dyson's childhood ended early with the coming of the world war. Now, decades later, here he was again expecting death, most likely within seconds. And yet he felt elated. Here he was, a man of substance, a thick schedule of appointments to keep, otherwise in good health, brought down by a blow to the head, but he felt ecstatic.

He was—absurdly, considering his bloodied condition—thinking of Tolstoy. Like Prince Andrei, wounded at the battle of Austerlitz in *War and Peace*, Dyson disregarded his pain and reveled in the immensity of the cosmos and the goodness of existence. He was ready, right then, to be borne "away on the blue wave of eternity."[1]

He had been on his way to an ordinary business meeting at the National Academy of Sciences in Washington, D.C., but because of the quick, violent intervention of a couple of thugs, had been granted a special insight: even in the midst of death, or near death, one could imagine that life was beautiful. Dyson was good at that, at spotting the secret signature of things. He was adept at unexpectedly finding a larger perspective. Right then, his thought was this: even if an individual were to die the universe would still go on.

Dyson did not die. The muggers relieved him of his money but not his life. A passerby found him in the bushes outside the Interior Department and rescued him. Taken to his destination, Dyson continued to bleed, onto the marble floor of the National Academy. Like Prince Andrei, Dyson recovered from his wounds and was energized by his travail.

The problems of the world went on. The greatest problem, Dyson felt, the greatest threat to the persistence of civilization, was the continuing existence of nuclear weapons in the arsenals of several countries. Famine, drought, war, epidemic had brought down this or that society. But never before had the destruction of hundreds of millions in an afternoon been possible in the past. A convocation of Catholic bishops, distressed at the prospects of nuclear war, declared that this was the first time since Genesis that mankind was capable of undoing God's creation. What could be done about this grave peril? Surely you would need more than the sagacity and artistry of Lev Tolstoy to square off against such an immense problem.

Dyson centered his interest around a basic question: what are nuclear weapons for? His meditation on this query crystallized as a book called *Weapons and Hope*. The book's inscription comes from the pastoral letter prepared by those bishops:

> *Hope is the capacity to live with danger without being overwhelmed by it; hope is the will to struggle against obstacles even when they appear insuperable.*[2]

BOMBS AND POETRY

The Cold War lasted long enough to have evolved through several phases. We saw a bit of the mid-1950s McCarthyite phase in Chapter 6, when Dyson, as a young professor, was pretty much a bystander. The Sputnik phase played out in Chapter 8 when, armed with a high security clearance and the desire to minimize the radioactive effusions from his nuclear-propelled spaceship, Dyson worked with Edward Teller briefly on an unsuccessful effort to design a neutron bomb. During the Cuban Missile Crisis phase of the Cold War (Chapter 10) Dyson had hindered and then helped the passage of a limited nuclear test ban treaty. He wrote a Jason report about the prospective use of tactical nuclear devices in Vietnam (Chapter 11). Indeed, because of his annual Jason summer study group meetings, Dyson's intimate connection to the technology of nuclear weapons grew but was largely out of sight, within the cloistered councils of Jason.

For decades the spiral of nuclear arms seemed overwhelming. Through heroic efforts the open-air testing of nuclear bombs was at last halted, but the bombs themselves were still around. In 1945 the inventory could be counted on one hand: the one tested in New Mexico in July, the two used on the Japanese cities in August, and one or two more on the way. By 1950 the inventory had risen above 100. The Russians did their best to keep pace. Eventually the combined stockpile would number in the tens of thousands. Quantitatively, the U.S. nuclear portfolio peaked in the 1960s. Thereafter a different race began, a qualitative race to produce more accurate and reliable warheads and missiles. The freeze movement sought an end to both the qualitative and quantitative races.[3]

Ostensibly the Western attitude was the same in the 1980s as it had been in 1950s: if our adversary had nuclear bombs then we would need to have them too. The bombs were evil—millions would die—but a necessary evil. In a dangerous world, where Communist advances threatened Western democracy, the United States and its allies needed the deterrent of a nuclear cudgel.

In order to examine the logic of these arguments Dyson compared the necessary evil of modern nuclear weaponry with the chattel slavery of previous centuries, which was also viewed by many as a necessary evil. Dyson was impressed with the role of the Quakers in ending slavery in British colonies. The Quakers had brought several important qualities to bear: moral conviction (slavery was evil, so they opposed it); patience (keep up the struggle, for decades if necessary); objectivity (employ accurate facts); and a willingness to compromise (the Quakers sought first the end of the trade in slaves and later of slavery itself).[4]

Dyson now applied these principles to the crusade against nuclear weapons. He did not become a Quaker, but in 1980 he did join the Coalition for Nuclear Disarmament, a group of concerned citizens in Princeton, and served on its research committee. Almost immediately the need for compromise arose. Within the coalition, some like Dyson wanted to promote a policy of no-first-use, meaning that the United States should pledge that it would never be the first to use nuclear weapons in the case of armed hostilities. Another faction felt that a more practical approach to arms reduction was to seek a freeze in nuclear weapons, meaning a treaty that would keep the number of weapons from going up. The rationale here was that the public could at least grasp the idea of a freeze, a ceiling in the number of nukes, whereas the no-first-use concept was nebulous. The freeze proposal was adopted.*

While Dyson recognized the important symbolism of the 1982 referendum, he felt that a nuclear freeze was only a short-term tactic. What he really wanted was a clearer concept, a more thorough enunciation of what the weapons were for. This, combined with a better understanding of the Soviet position, would be the starting point for true arms reductions, he felt. History would be his guide.

For example, the controlling concept governing Britain's foreign policy for centuries was the need to dominate the coastal waters between itself and continental Europe. Against a succession of adversaries—Spain, Holland, France, Germany, and then Russia—the sea lanes had to be, and were, controlled by the Royal Navy.[5]

Dyson's friend, diplomat and historian George Kennan, has mentioned analogous strategic concepts shaping nineteenth-century America, principally the Monroe Doctrine (checking European influence in the Western Hemisphere) and Manifest Destiny (the idea that the United States would fill out the space between the Atlantic and Pacific oceans). But at the end of the nineteenth century, Kennan suggested, a pretentious element crept into American foreign policy. This moralizing tendency, which said in effect that America knew better than other nations what was right, was thereafter going to be an element in U.S. actions around the world.[6]

When it came time for Kennan to apply his sense of pragmatism to the actual formulation of policy, as a senior planner in the State Department in 1947, his chosen concept for America's role in the post-world-war world—the equivalent of Britain's safeguard of coastal waters—was a doctrine that sought to guarantee absolutely the free-

---

*In 1981 the Reverend Robert Moore, a local clergyman, became the executive director of the coalition. His practical goal was formulating the nuclear freeze idea as a referendum to be put on ballots. In fact the initiative was put to a vote in ten states during the election of 1982 and won in nine of the ten. In New Jersey it carried with a margin of two to one. Rev. Moore organized a lobbying meeting in Washington, D.C., bringing 600 freeze supporters to meet with New Jersey's congressional delegation, most of whom declared they were in favor of the freeze idea.

Dyson believes the public voicing of opinion had a palpable effect. Fourteen of fifteen New Jersey representatives in Congress voted against a proposed multiple warhead missile program. (W&H, p. 235) Nevertheless, the missile program was approved by Congress. The freeze movement began to lose momentum. Rev. Moore felt that many in the coalition did not take a long enough view, and that it was impractical to expect results too soon. He agreed with Dyson's precepts of moral conviction, persistence, objectivity, and compromise. Thirty years later Moore was still director of the coalition. (PFS interview with Rev. Robert Moore.)

dom and economic power of three important nations—West Germany, Britain, and Japan—against Soviet aggression.

The concept that actually emerged, "containment," although using some of Kennan's ideas, would be broadly interpreted to mean that the United States should combat Communist expansion wherever it appeared, including Cuba, Korea, and Vietnam, regardless of whether or not vital U.S. interests were at stake in these places.

Using Kennan's concept as a model, Dyson now tried to settle upon a central concept of his own for the basing and use of American nuclear weapons. The prevailing nuclear reality was usually called "assured destruction," a phrase coming from the Vietnam War pronouncements of Defense Secretary Robert McNamara, who solemnly said that America's chief strategic requirement was that the United States should always have the capability of destroying an adversary (sometimes he specifically named the Soviet Union) with nuclear warheads even if the United States itself had sustained a first strike.[7] This was America's nuclear Monroe Doctrine. A secondary doctrine held that under some circumstances the United States might wage a limited nuclear war.

You'd expect that the Soviets would hold symmetric views, but Dyson argued that the Soviets rejected both of the U.S. nuclear doctrines of assured destruction and limited war. Dyson, who could read Russian and who was a student of Russian military publications, felt that the central Russian military ethos came out of *War and Peace*. In the Napoleonic campaigns so colorfully depicted by Tolstoy, the Russian forces won by grinding down and outlasting the French forces. Their attitude was this: we will beat you in the end; we will lose battles but win the war; we will live to see your funeral; we will bury you with our economic might. If necessary, we will outlast you in war. This was in fact Nikita Khrushchev's blunt assertion hurled at the United States in 1962. If they had to, the Soviets would "bury" the Americans, meaning, in the Russian vernacular, that they would live long enough to outlast their adversary. Their strategy, formulated into a doctrine called counterforce was enunciated clearly in 1971 by the Soviet defense minister, Marshal Andrei Grechko. Its official aim was not to target American cities and citizens per se. Rather it would be to attack America's weapons and soldiers if war began.[8]

The U.S. policy was officially also to strike at military targets. Even if in practice the rival concepts would likely result in the same thing, namely the deaths of millions, the outlook of the two positions is very different. America says to Russia: if you try anything we will destroy you. And Russia says to America: if you try anything we will outlive you. In Dyson's assessment, the U.S. assured destruction approach works better if the nuclear war is short and predictable; the Russian counterforce approach works better if the war is lengthy and subject to many unpredictable events.[9]

As for a limited war, one supposedly involving the exchange of a few small nuclear blasts, the Russians assured the Americans that the introduction of *any* explosion could, and probably would, rapidly escalate to a full-scale broadside of H-bombs. The American limited war doctrine necessarily enfolds a first-use policy. That is, the United States reserves the right to be the first to attack an opponent with nuclear weapons. Dyson found this unsound for three reasons: it was aggressive and provocative, making effective negotiations impossible; it was basically immoral, since the unloosing of even small nukes meant high civilian casualties; and it was suicidal, since it would trigger an automatic Russian counterstrike.[10]

Dyson maintained that some American analysts of Soviet behavior developed a distorted impression because they insisted on assessing Soviet psychology from a Western historical perspective. It was irresponsible to view the Soviets, or any adversary, as if they were Martians. Dyson's experience had taught him that when it comes to history and warfare, the Russians saw themselves as victims. Vikings, Mongols, Teutons, Napoléon, and the Nazis had, in a grim roll of centuries, invaded Russia and later been ejected.[11] How the Russians dealt with Napoleon in 1812 and Hitler in 1943, Dyson said, influenced how they viewed potential invaders at the present time:

> The American strategy of deterrence, sufficiency, and retaliation is a purely nuclear strategy having nothing to do with war as it has been waged in the past. The Soviet strategy of victory, superiority, and offensive action is a continuation of the historical process by which Russia over the centuries repelled invaders from her territory. Both strategies have advantages and disadvantages. Neither is aggressive in intention. Both are to me equally frightening, because both make the survival of civilization depend on people behaving reasonably.[12]

For Dyson, thinking through important issues, delivering public lectures, and formulating polished written essays are all part of a continuum. In this case the issue was the quest for a concept of nuclear weapons. His most prominent effort to answer the question of what these weapons are for was the Tanner Lectures, delivered at Oxford University in May of 1982. The written version, appearing in 1983, was called "Bombs and Poetry." The "poetry" part referred to Dyson's penchant for quoting from world literature, that "great storehouse where meanings distilled by all kinds of people out of all kinds of experience are presented." The book included meaningful excerpts from a spectrum of poetical writing—W. H. Auden, C. S. Lewis, T. S. Eliot, *The Bhagavad Gita*, Shakespeare, Wilfred Owen, T. E. Lawrence, George Herbert, Bertolt Brecht, and multiple entries from William Blake.[13] These lectures, which form Dyson's nuclear manifesto, appeared later as chapters in *Weapons and Hope*.

LIVE AND LET LIVE

In the years after World War II, the central national security concern of the United States and the Soviet Union was amassing nuclear weapons and contemplating their use. Historian Garry Wills draws attention to the consequences of this nuclear buildup. The network of off-limits labs, sophisticated surveillance and espionage, and the creation of special agencies and protocols for guarding secrets, Wills argues, constituted a new entity, a national security state. The "care and feeding" of the bomb (airports, security, radars, satellites, fuel procurement and enrichment) became a mini-government of its own. The U.S. president, being on permanent alert, was granted wide new powers. "He became, mainly, the Commander in Chief, since he could loose the whole military force of the nation in an instant."[14]

Dyson saw this historic changeover as it unfolded. He continued to search for a coherent plan for what to do with nuclear weapons. Now, it's not as though the White House or the State Department was asking for his opinion. Except for his involvement with Jason, he wasn't part of the government. Yet, he felt compelled to formulate some kind of alternative to both the U.S. and USSR doctrines. He adapted an outlook set forth by his friend the military expert Donald Brennan. Brennan suggested a military version of the Golden Rule—that for any plausibly feasible Soviet attack, we should be able to do at least as badly unto the Soviets as they had done unto us. To this Brennan added something hopeful:

The second principle is that we should prefer live Americans to dead Russians, whenever a choice between the two presents itself. The Soviets may be expected to prefer live Russians to dead Americans, and therein resides the basis for an important common interest; we may both prefer live Americans and live Russians.[15]

This concept, which Dyson embraced as his preferred nuclear philosophy, he called live and let live. It incorporated several practical attitudes: no, we don't have to trust the Russians; no, we don't have to doubt their territorial ambitions; and yes, we've avoided nuclear war so far, but some episodes, such as the Cuban Missile Crisis of 1962, have come close to triggering catastrophe. Dyson's more streamlined approach to negotiations, looking forward to a day when the Cold War would be over, was to regard nuclear weapons as bargaining chips rather than desirable military assets.[16]

The goal of a live-and-let-live concept was to move away from nuclear slavery. Dyson wanted the United States to persuade by example, not by force. On the technology side, for example, the U.S. stopped building larger warheads, and so did the Soviets. The U.S. stopped deploying extensive missile defense systems (in the 1960s and 1970s), and so did the Soviets. Soviet leaders do not always wish to listen to our diplomacy, Dyson argued, but they do listen to our technology.[17]

The harder part of nuclear abolitionism, Dyson believed, was to convince people that movement is possible, that we are not irremediably doomed, that our lives have a meaning and a purpose, and that we can still choose to be masters our own fates.[18] The embrace of nuclear weapons wasn't irrevocable. We needn't commit to a perpetual doctrine of nuclear belligerence.

In mid-nineteenth-century America most citizens would have thought slavery was irremediably a fact of life. It was woven into society, at least in the Southern states, and wasn't going to change. The end of slavery will never arrive, most would have thought. A majority of Americans, even those in the North, even those who disliked slavery, were against abolitionism. The existence of slavery, bad though it might be, was enshrined in the Constitution. To be an abolitionist was regarded by some to be a kind of anarchist. To insist on the abolition of slavery would tear apart the union of American states. Ralph Waldo Emerson, writing in his journal in the 1840s and 1850s, expressed both his loathing for slavery and his reluctance to endure the consuming task of ending it.[19]

A consequence of Dyson's live-and-let-live concept was his embrace of the no-first-use principle. And here Dyson parted from some of his friends, such as Stanford physicist Sidney Drell. Dyson credits Drell (who for many years was the deputy director of the Stanford Linear Accelerator Center) with giving him an excellent education in the technology and politics of military hardware over many years of Jason work together.[20]

The no–first-use idea sounds good, but would it work under duress? Drell has worked to reduce the threat of nuclear war but views a no-first-use pledge as an unfortunate reduction in the options of political and military strategists when war breaks out. Back in the days when Europe was divided by the Iron Curtain, the nightmare of military planners was a hypothetical Russian armored thrust from East Germany into West Germany. The only way to counter the large Soviet superiority in tanks and combat troops, short of building up Western conventional forces, would be (the argument went) to hurl small nuclear explosives at the invaders, while hoping to keep collateral damage to civilians and buildings to a minimum. To which Dyson said: first, there will be plenty of collateral damage; and second, by using nuclear weapons of any kind we might well initiate a larger exchange of nuclear salvos. If we wish to present a credible deterrent we just have to build up a conventionally armed defensive force.

Weapons and Hope, Dyson's book enunciating his nuclear and defense ideas, made it to the *New York Times* bestseller list. In 1985 it won the National Book Critics Circle Award for general nonfiction. The book was generally well received by critics. Dyson's friend Frank von Hippel, also a physicist and an expert on nuclear matters, praised the book's technical competency, its moral stance, and its wide historical perspective. But he questioned the efficacy of Dyson's advocacy of a nonnuclear defense in the face of a nuclear threat.[21]

Dyson's antinuclear crusade was part of a more comprehensive David-vs.-Goliath philosophy, according to which (he asserts) ethical behavior and a strong defense are compatible; defense is good and offense bad; moral arguments can certainly be made against nukes (since nukes have genocidal repercussions) but military arguments—to the effect that the weapons are dangerous even to their owners—are more practical; and having imperfectly verifiable treaties is generally better than having no treaties.[22]

Dyson's liking for defensive weaponry extended even to the idea of the Strategic Defense Initiative, the space- and land-based missile interception system proposed by President Reagan in 1983. Disliked by most physicists, SDI was, in Dyson's opinion, a technically flawed but possibly workable venture. In 1984, he and his friend Edward Teller visited the head of SDI, General James Abrahamson, to urge him to lift the shroud of secrecy over the program. In that way technical progress could benefit from the criticism and fresh ideas needed for highly complex engineering projects. The general promised that the secrecy would indeed be lifted. The secrecy, however, remained, and the program foundered over technological failure.[23]

ILIAD AND ODYSSEY

Freeman Dyson was well placed to act as a middleman in the great debate between those actively working to reduce nuclear stockpiles and those who insisted that the stockpiles were a necessary deterrent against aggression by hostile powers. He attended antinuke church meetings and wrote critical essays in prominent publications. At the same time however, he was owing to his Jason affiliation, advising the generals who maintained the stockpiles. He was, in effect, still a part of Bomber Command, and always would be.

In July 1989 he traveled to Fairchild Air Force Base in Spokane, located in the lovely eastern part of Washington state. Climbing through one of the B-52 bombers kept on alert Dyson felt that the year could have been 1945. Just as in the days of Bomber Command, the crew size was seven and their jobs were still pretty much the same. One big thing was different: the nature of the bomb stored on board.

Dyson sat in the commander's seat and fingered the red button, which, when supplied with a supplementary activation signal authorizing use, released the bombs. Touching the button inspired poignant insights. For the red button even to exist there must necessarily be an immense bureaucratic infrastructure supporting bomber, bombs, pilot training, and fail-safe mechanisms—the sort of national security state outlined by Garry Wills. The regular drills and alerts were highly elaborate forms of ritual combat. They reminded Dyson of the Samurai's stylized exercises. The Samurai prepares often but fights seldom.[24]

Dyson had journeyed to this bastion of the Strategic Air Command as part of a site visit for Jason members. The rationale was that in order to advise the government on security matters it was good to see things in the field, up close. At Fairchild you couldn't get any closer. Dyson had touched the red button that releases the bombs, and then he touched the bombs themselves. He'd modeled the explosive effect of bombs and had been himself briefly a bomb designer, but he'd never before stood next to the actual thing.[25] He walked into a room where dozens of hydrogen bombs lay about on the floor.[26] He felt that it was important to meet these monsters.[27]

Spending a day with the bomber crew, Dyson was reassured to see that conditions were nothing like those depicted in *Dr. Strangelove.* The pilots viewed their job professionally and were not swaggeringly eager to sally forth and lay waste to the Soviet Union. The death of millions did not seem to be in the offing. But the fact that the on-alert B-52s were there at all, ready with two minutes notice to begin a flight that delivered a payload that would light up the sky and scatter bodies and buildings for hundreds of miles around, was more than enough to remind visitors that our present civilization is not so far separated from the ancient Greeks and Trojans. Despite our many modern inventions and medical procedures we still have many things in common with Bronze Age cultures.

Dyson is not fatalistic about this. The human nervous system or hormonal makeup might not have changed much in 3,000 years, but this doesn't mean we, as a species, are doomed to incessant warfare. We don't have to accept a fate of nuclear destruction. In trying to find a way out of the nuclear labyrinth we've made for ourselves we can re-sort to political measures, such as negotiating treaties and shifting to a nonnuclear defense.

Searching for perspective on the vital issue of survival, Dyson, as he so often did, turned to literature. He pointed to two of the earliest and greatest works in the Western canon, Homer's *Iliad* and *Odyssey*, to il-lustrate his point about coping with adversity on a colossal scale. The Trojan War inspired these two epic poems, one about glorious deeds that end in death, the other about clever deeds that end in a homecom-ing. The hero of the first, Achilles, wins renown but is, at the end of the *Iliad*, destined to die young. The hero of the second, Odysseus, performs most of his daring feats in private and is, at the end of the *Odyssey*, restored to home and family. The lesson that Dyson takes from these works of literature is that the business of society is not trag-edy but survival.[28]

Dyson's own odyssey among the armed camps of the U.S. arsenal took him to Long Beach, California, to the missile cruiser USS *Princeton*. Although he was impressed with the ship and crew, the visit prompted him to declare that the navy, with its own missiles, was as much a part of the strategic bombing business as the air force. Moreover, he argued that the arms race was fueled not only by the American-Soviet rivalry but also by the rivalry between the navy and air force of the United States.[29] Dyson saw a further infra-rivalry within the navy itself—between its submarine fleet, armed with nuclear-tipped Trident missiles, and its surface fleet, some of which carried nuclear Tomahawk cruise missiles.

Dyson visited the General Dynamics factory, where Tomahawk cruise missiles are manufactured. Again he was impressed with the professionalism of the workers and the pride they took in their product. On this occasion Dyson was accompanied by Sidney Drell, who said "These people build cruise missiles the way Stradivarius built violins." This made Dyson wonder why the workers couldn't just build violins.[30]

His thoughts about the actual use of nuclear bombs were made more vivid by a visit to Hiroshima in 1985 as part of a lecture tour of Japan. "Coming to Hiroshima," Dyson said, "we feel guilt not so much for the slaughter of 1945 as for our persistence in the same habits of thought and action which made that slaughter inevitable and now may lead us, if we are unlucky, to slaughter on an even grander scale."[31]

How grand? How bad could the slaughter be? A classified report from 1960, relatively early in the strategic buildup of America's nuclear arsenal, laid out the potential lethal details. The Single Integrated Operational Plan (SIOP) was the master blueprint for launching a comprehensive attack on targets in countries ruled by Communist governments, including the USSR, China, and those of Eastern Europe. As the years went by many more thousands of nuclear weapons would enter the stockpile, allowing still more cities to be targeted. In 1980 the collective U.S. and USSR stockpiles amounted to the equivalent of a million Hiroshimas.[32]

The plan for 1960 was devastating enough. The armaments and aims for the maximum U.S. mission were as follows: 3,500 nuclear bombs, carried by 800 planes, delivered to 1,000 ground-zero targets, would produce an estimated 285 million prompt deaths. The eventual death count might have gone as high as 425 million.[33] President Eisenhower, the man who had launched the D–Day invasion in 1944, was himself startled when he saw SIOP. The numbers "frighten the devil out of me," he said. President Kennedy, when it was his turn to see SIOP, wasn't any more pleased: "And we call ourselves the human race," he said.[34]

While in Hiroshima, Freeman Dyson's resolve to work for total abolition of nuclear weapons hardened.[35]

BERLIN WALL TIME

And then it was over. Not the existence of nuclear weapons. They would persist indefinitely. What ended was the formal footing of the Cold War. The recessional began in the 1980s in places like Poland and Czechoslovakia, where disenchantment with Communism was becoming more common, and then within the Soviet Union itself. In 1989 the Berlin Wall came down. In 1991 the Hammer and Sickle flag, the symbol of the Soviet Union, was withdrawn from atop the Kremlin. Many of the bombers were taken off alert. "The world of strategic bombing changed more in 1991 than in the previous forty-five years," Dyson said.[36] It might be hard for a person born after about 1980 to appreciate the magnitude of the nuclear peril—as portrayed in the SIOP report—and how it shaped government policy during the Cold War.

Was the Cold War really over? A Jason study in the mid-1990s anatomized the end of the nuclear arms race. The "science" phase of the arms race ended as early as the 1960s, with the help of the limited test ban treaty in 1963. The military phase dissipated, with the help of the Anti-Ballistic Missile Treaty and the Strategic Arms Limitation Talks treaties, in the 1970s and 1980s. Even the political phase of the arms race started to wind down in the 1980s, with the help of the START treaty, when both sides, East and West, realized that an immense inventory of nuclear materials was not only expensive to maintain, but represented a potential environmental disaster and security risk.[37]

Had the possession of nuclear weapons all those years made the world safer? Dyson thinks not, but recognizes that his is a minority view. At one meeting he attended (of mostly physicists) when the proposition was put to a show of hands, Dyson was one of the few who signified that he would feel safer if nuclear bombs disappeared all together. Sadly, he had to admit, even most of his "liberal and enlightened" friends, in the United States and in other countries, "do not believe that abolition would be desirable, even if it were possible."[38]

In the past, to contradict a majority of politicians *and* a majority of one's fellow scientists on a topic of such overriding importance to national security would land a person in jail, or at least earn (from the government) an official rebuke or (from scientific colleagues) impatience or condescension or indifference. But not in this case. Freeman Dyson, by force of his cheerful courtesy, thoughtful remarks about his critics, and his imaginatively argued views, has maintained the respect of his adversaries. In January 1995 he received the Department of Energy's Enrico Fermi Award, the most prestigious honor given by the U.S. government for a lifetime contribution to nuclear matters and for his broad career in science and letters.[39]

In the early 1960s Dyson headed the Federation of American Scientists. The man who headed the FAS forty years later, Charles Ferguson, was a junior officer serving on a ballistic missile submarine in the U.S. Navy in the 1980s. Ferguson read *Weapons and Hope* and was impressed by the argument that society didn't have to be held perpetually in bondage to nuclear slavery. "One of the reasons I am now heading FAS is due to Dyson's *Weapons and Hope*," Ferguson said.[40]

Each year in August, on the anniversary of the Hiroshima bombing, the Coalition for Peace Action (the new name for the Coalition for Nuclear Disarmament) holds a commemoration, which has often occurred at the Institute of Advanced Study where, by virtue of Dyson's faculty status, they were allowed to congregate. Just like the commemoration each year in Hiroshima itself, the Princeton observance is marked by a simple ceremony in which candles are lit at nightfall and launched on tiny rafts out onto water. The candles float about the bucolic pond lying behind the Institute buildings.[41] Dyson attends as often as he can. Sometimes he is fresh from his customary summertime attendance at Jason's deliberations in California, which often deal with the stewardship of America's nuclear arsenal. The arsenal, though smaller than it was, is still enormous.

When Dyson was selecting essays to include in one of his books, he chose to retain his description of those visits to the missile cruiser and to the bomber base. As a relic of the Cold War, the essays might be out of date, he explained, but he wanted them around anyway as a sort of memorial—the nuclear equivalent of the War Memorial at Winchester College—and as a sign that we have further to go.[42]

15. The Arc of Life

Dyson as Biologist

(1980S AND 1990S)

When Freeman Dyson met Francis Crick in 1945, Crick was actually in a modest mood. The war was just over but both were still nominally associated with the armed forces, Crick with the navy and Dyson with the air force. Both were at a loss as to what to do with themselves. Crick was depressed, since he felt the war had drained away his chances for making a brilliant career in physics, and felt he was too old to start over in a new field.

In 1946 the two met again. By this time Dyson had left mathematics for physics and Crick had left physics for biology. Dyson agreed that biology was exciting, but he estimated that physics would remain the premier science for at least another twenty years. You really ought to stick with physics, Dyson argued. Crick ignored his advice.[1] In the following half decade or so, both young men were to do their most famous work, Dyson with quantum fields and Crick with chromosomes. And if in the years after that biology overtook physics in preeminence it was partly because of Crick's work with James Watson in deciphering the structure and then the function of the genetic molecule deoxyribonucleic acid (DNA).

Dyson himself came over to biology in the 1980s, at least part-time. He drew inspiration from another quantum physicist, Erwin Schrödinger, who in 1945 published a brief book with the provocative title *What Is Life?* Twenty years before that Schrödinger had helped to tease out the quantum nature of atoms, but in 1945 he was a refugee in Ireland during World War II. He did not do experiments and did not generate new factual information about biology. His chief service was to ask pesky questions about the central role of chromosomes.

Dyson would also write a pithy biology book that asked more questions than it answered. It too would have a provocative name: *Origins of Life*. It too was filled with interesting speculations but no new biological facts.

As a bookend to this topic of origins Dyson would, decades later, engage in a profound debate over the possible demise of life in the distant future. We'll look at these prospective starts and stops and what Dyson has to say about everything that comes in between.

HANGING ON

It's not as though physics wasn't fun anymore. But Freeman Dyson really liked biology too. His interest had been nudged along by a sabbatical year (1964–65) spent at the relatively new San Diego branch of the University of California. In numerous discussions with biochemist Leslie Orgel, Dyson became attracted to the crucial question of how, 4 billion years ago, living cells emerged from nonliving chemicals.

Later, at a 1981 meeting at Cambridge University, he was part of an ecumenical group of biologists, chemists, physicists, and mathematicians that pored over the problem of early life. A few years after that, in 1985, Dyson was asked back to Cambridge, and now he came armed with more ideas, more equations, more speculations. He delivered a series of talks, the Tarner Lectures, which were to grow into another Dysonian manifesto.

These are some of the milestones he identifies along the trajectory of life, as it has existed on our planet and as it might be in the cosmos into the distant future.

RNA Life

Which came first, the chicken or the egg? The molecular equivalent of this question is to ask which came first, the nuclei acids that constitute the blueprint for making all the biomolecules in a living cell or the proteins that help to process the nutrients in the cell's environment and build the cell's own substance? Many biologists believe that the nucleic acids, and specifically RNA, came first. Why RNA, which in many modern cells acts as a sort of handmaid for DNA in that it carries the genetic instructions from DNA out into the other parts of the cell, and not DNA itself? Because RNA, while it acts like DNA in being able to encode genetic information, also has been found to act like proteins, including the ability to serve as an enzyme, the class of molecule that brokers many of the central chemical reactions in the cell.

Owing to the work of Leslie Orgel, Francis Crick, and Carl Woese, the RNA-first theory gained support. Their origin of life scenario was this: in the beginning there was RNA.

Dyson did not like this explanation and in typical fashion set off to explain things in a different way. RNA, he argued, is too sophisticated to have started things off. In modern cells a human chromosome can contain millions of molecular units (nucleotides). Replication of such a complex object in the early Wild West phase of life could easily have involved many wrong turns. These errors, Dyson maintained, would have crippled the effectiveness of the cell and its offspring down through many generations. The errors would likely multiply at each iteration. Reproduction had to be more tolerant of errors.

Minimal Life

The earliest cells had to be simpler to survive. Homeostasis, the process of enduring from moment to moment in some stable condition, was paramount. Hanging on to life, scratching out an existence, was to be the theme of Dyson's explanations for how life came into being and how it persisted. An earlier idea, by the Russian biologist Alexander Oparin, who believed that primitive cells developed first, followed by enzymes, followed by genes, was just what Dyson wanted.[2]

What does it mean for a thing to be "alive"? Minimum requirements would seem to include an enclosing surface (a membrane), some functioning innards, and an ability to reproduce. (Some entities like viruses challenge even this simple specification.) Reproduction of the protocells didn't have to be exact. Offspring would emerge when the cell got fat and had been jostled by some event in its surroundings, such as a quickening change in temperature or turbulence, causing the cell to break in two. The daughter cells might have been different from the parent, but so what? It's not as though a true lineage was important. Species didn't yet exist.

Life as a Computer

Dyson began to write up his ideas. He reached for a handy metaphor by invoking John von Neumann, his late colleague at the Institute for Advanced Study. Comparing a biological cell to a computer, Dyson suggested that the nucleic acids that encode information are like software, while the proteins that process that information are the cell's hardware. The proteins, in complex organisms, serve as the primary participants in sustaining metabolism, in keeping the nervous system humming, in keeping the immune system alert, in maintaining the endocrine system of hormones, and in deploying a host of fundamental housekeeping functions.

Dyson argued that at a bare minimum we can imagine a computer running in some hardwired way. We can imagine hardware without software but cannot imagine software having a meaning without any underlying hardware on which to operate. So it was with early rudimentary cells. The processing of chemicals was essential; the execution of exact genetic instructions was not. The accurate transcription of instructions, as if from a downloaded piece of software, was too great a luxury. Dyson set out to create a model backed up by mathematics that could account for his saga of early life.

Life Begins Twice

Act I in Dyson's theater of life presents the lawless, pioneering phase. No fancy replication, just homeostasis, hanging on to life. Maintaining a distinction between yourself and all the other chemicals in your neighborhood was the bare fact of life. Early proto-cells had to eat those chemicals to stay alive. Metabolism—using fuel to build cells—was the game. Reproduction was crude. Many errors, many failed experiments, many nonsustainable trial configurations resulted. Death was an important process. The failures far outnumbered the successes.

Act II was about the rise of the replicators. Rudimentary RNA might have survived on its own, with its own membrane or as a parasite within cells. Thus with the help of the metabolizers and with enough time, early RNA could master the art of exact or near-exact replication. This constituted the second origin of life. Possibly the proto-RNA could return the favor by taking an active, even genetic, role in the lives of the metabolizing cell. RNA, Dyson argued, was a sort of benign disease within cells.

Act III in Dyson's drama was the symbiotic coming together of the metabolizers and the replicators. Dyson cited biologist Lynn Margulis's work in explaining how some components within the modern cell, such as the mitochondria, began as separate self-sufficient organisms before being incorporated into other cells. Thereafter they thrived and worked to the mutual advantage of themselves and their hosts; likewise, RNA, beginning as an invader, then as a parasite, became a full and useful citizen of the cell.

The RNA might splinter off a version of itself that later turned into DNA. The cells would come to own a genome, a stock of genetic information that helped operate the cell on a more businesslike footing, especially the consistent production of proteins, just as early post-British America, consisting of a loose affiliation of states under the Articles of Confederation, was replaced by a more stable union under a federal constitution.

And what about that genome? Biologist Carl Woese holds that in those early days of life, cells did not hoard their genetic material, but rather shared it around freely. Dyson, adopting this view, extended his computer hardware-software metaphor. He refers to this early epoch of life as being typified by the exchange of "open-source software," that is, the free exchange of genetic information among many types of cells. Woese argued that this epoch was characterized by a pre-Darwin type of evolution, one in which genetic material moved horizontally among cells rather than vertically down through a lineage of generations.

In laying out his scheme for the great experiment of life, Dyson the biologist called upon the talents of two of his intimate colleagues, Dyson the mathematician and Dyson the physicist. He drew upon statistical mechanics and upon his former work with the alignment of atoms in a magnet. It all had to be numerically rigorous. The Tarner Lectures at Cambridge (appearing later in book form as *Origins of Life*) represent the only time when, in a presentation aimed at the general public, Dyson used equations, lots of them. These formulas embodied the mathematical machinery whereby, in one of the most crucial chemical experiments of all time, un-alive molecules cycled through trillions of trials until they had assembled themselves into living cells.

Garden of Eden

Dyson illustrated the mystery of life with a graph. The horizontal axis corresponded to the increasing complexity of the chains of molecules. The vertical axis represented the effectiveness of the molecules' enzyme action, depicting how well metabolism proceeded. The graph divided into three zones. The upper left Dyson called the "garden of Eden." Here the combination of complexity and effectiveness was so great that the organisms never died. This was the realm of immortality.

The lower right part of the graph was the absolute elsewhere, the dead zone. Here, through a combination of insufficient enzyme effectiveness or the wrong number of constituent molecules, the cells were not well adapted to their environment. They could not maintain homeostasis. And in the middle estate, between death and immortality, was life. Here the cells lived for a while, grew, reproduced, and then died.[3]

This was not the end of the story but the beginning. Only here, at the point where Dyson's model had finished its job by establishing a semi-stable population of enzyme-based or protein-based confederations of molecules, could the nucleotides enter the picture. Only then, when the pinpoint-replicating molecules implanted themselves into the sloppy but established primitive metabolizing proto-cells, could the smart process of genetic inheritance take hold and the era of modern cells begin. Only after the wide-open period of open-access software sharing, in which RNA and then DNA codes were tried out in a variety of cell types, could the next big biological experiment begin.

To summarize Dyson's toy model of life: as a starting point for life he favored homeostasis (a confederation of molecules roughly reproducing) over replication (exact duplication); the diversity of architecture over uniformity (which would come later); the flexibility of function (the ability of the proto-cells to do things) over the tyranny (or, as biologist Richard Dawkins insisted, the selfishness) of genes; and the ability of the whole organism to tolerate errors rather than insisting on the exact precision of components.[4]

What did biologists think of Dyson's theory? Not very much, as he himself admits.[5] The versatility of the RNA-first theory of the origin of life is just too tempting. Carl Woese, however, says that the metabolism-first idea is not necessarily wrong, and that Dyson has done a good service in drawing attention to the importance of homeostasis.[6] He does, however, question Dyson's use of the word "error" to characterize the less than perfect replication of life molecules. After all, what does "error" mean at this early point in biological history? If a bit of chemistry works, it works. That the organisms reproduced at all is more important than fidelity to a particular genetic plan.

Dyson has little to say about later pilgrimages of life from its home base, possibly in some relatively warm coastal shallow or near a deep-sea thermal vent, into the outer space of cold ocean water, or later still from water onto dry land or, billions of years along, the emigration of *Homo sapiens* out of Africa into the wilds of Eurasia.

HOMESTEADING

When Freeman Dyson feels strongly enough about something he plants his feet and declares himself. He writes a manifesto. He wrote one on the subject of nuclear-powered space exploration during his Orion days (1958). He wrote one on the subject of climate change during one summer at Oak Ridge (1974). His book *Weapons and Hope* (1984) set forth an expansive view of war and peace, and *Origins of Life* (1985) offered his hypothesis about the emergence of living things from the primordial kettle of nonliving chemicals. The advent of life—a crew of chemicals venturing forth in its membrane spacecraft—was a counterpoint between two tendencies, the selfish but exacting government imposed by replication molecules and the flexible homeostasis kept going by metabolizing molecules.[7]

Dyson's grandest manifesto, the clearest summation of what he was up to in the 1980s—indeed the most compact statement of what he has been striving for in his writings ever since—appeared in his next book, *Infinite in All Directions* (1988). There he openly declared that he was preaching a sermon. It came to this:

> *My message is the unbounded prodigality of life and the consequent unboundedness of human destiny. As a working hypothesis to explain the riddle of our existence, I propose that our universe is the most interesting of all possible universes, and our fate as human beings to make it so.*[8]

Dyson is aware that with his phrase "most interesting of all possible universes," he risks sounding like the fictional character Dr. Pangloss in Voltaire's comic novel, *Candide*. Pangloss's slogan, "this is the best of all possible worlds," is supposed to ameliorate our bewilderment over a life often filled with catastrophes. Dyson, having lived through world war and cold war, doesn't pretend this is a benign universe, only that it is interesting. What he means by interesting we shall see in due course.

The first part of Dyson's message, about the prodigality of life, refers to the millions of species inhabiting our planet. Following the early open-source, or pre-Darwin era of development, when biological architecture was freely adapted by organisms, a proprietary era set in, a time when some groups of cells—the first species—began to hoard their genes; to be exact we can say that certain genes were applicable only for select species of organisms. This, according to Carl Woese, marked the advent of the Darwin interlude.

Billions of years later, with the emergence of humans and their vast overlay of technological artifacts, including the ability to alter climate and radically influence other species and ecosystems on a worldwide basis, humans have entered a post-Darwin phase of evolution. This boisterous percolation of human culture, says Dyson, operates a thousand times faster than ordinary biological evolution. Dyson largely skips the Darwinian phase, the mainstay of evolutionary biology, in order to concentrate on events in the post-Darwin era. This is where his interest lies. This is where human destiny unfolds.

Humans in Space

The second panel in Dyson's triptych of messages, the unboundedness of human destiny, refers to the vast history of emigration, starting with our species moving from its apparent roots in Africa, out into Asia and Europe, followed thousands of years later by a flow by foot across the Bering land bridge into the Americas and later still the Polynesian dispersal by canoe into the Pacific archipelagos. Finally came the European sailings across the Atlantic and Indian oceans, a process that for good and bad reconnected all the races of the world.

This odyssey was just the beginning. The cultures and nations are far from reaching equilibrium and there remain ample opportunities for Panglossian catastrophe through starvation, nuclear war, and climate radicalization. But the next step in the cosmic human destiny is to explore and then inhabit selected outlying precincts of our solar system. Reckoned in terms of past human explorations and emigrations, the off-Earth enterprise is still at an early stage. Apollo technology brought men to the Moon. Since then we have backtracked, doing no more than dispatching a few astronauts at a time to a station held in fixed Earth orbit.

What comes after that? Dyson's friend, Princeton physicist Gerard O'Neill, suggested building cylindrical space stations, big enough to accommodate cities and agriculture, and gently rotating so as to provide a sense of gravity to those positioned around the edge, a situation not unlike the crew compartment on *2001: A Space Odyssey*. For Dyson the O'Neill cylinders were too big and too small at the same time. Parked in the inner solar system, they weren't ambitious enough. On the other hand, they would be too expensive for what they did, acting as a mere suburb to Earth. Dyson wanted something cheaper, like a spacefaring equivalent of the *Mayflower*, something that could appeal to the intrepid outdoorsmen like George Dyson and his Vancouver friends.[9]

For the time being humans will have to stay put. We could meanwhile proceed with a personless search for life that's already out there. Much scientific information can be gained relatively cheaply. One of the biggest goals of these missions—indeed one of the most stirring aims in all of science—would be the identification of extraterrestrial life. For many years now Dyson has enthusiastically written about how and where to look for off-Earth life.

Canterbury Tales

Some places seem more likely than others to harbor life. Jupiter's moon Europa, for example, probably has a deepwater ocean, insulated from above by an icy crust and warmed from below by a tidal force operating between planet and moon. It would be difficult to land a craft on Europa and bore down through thick icepack. A better chance for seeing Europan fish, Dyson argues, is to imagine that a meteorite strike might temporarily break the ice and splash some aquatic creatures into space, much as strikes on Mars have sprung rocks into space, some of which have found their way to Earth. Dyson says that we should look for such freeze-dried fish in the diaphanous ring of material that surrounds Jupiter.[10]

Some prospecting for life can be done with telescopes on Earth or with visiting probes for a close-up inspection. Previously such visits to the various neighborhoods of the solar system—*Magellan* at Venus, *Rover* and *Viking* on Mars, *Galileo* at Jupiter, *Cassini* at Saturn, and the *Voyagers* and *Pioneers* in the outer portions and beyond—have radioed back much information about the local environment, but so far no evidence for life has presented itself. Finding life out there isn't going to be easy. The pilgrimage bringing ourselves or other life forms to the outer solar system will require even more time.

Geoffrey Chaucer's medieval poem depicted a guide leading a party of pilgrims toward the saint's shrine. Along the way they entertained themselves with stories. Well, Dyson is the Chaucer of interplanetary space. While we immigrate into space in slow motion, as it were, he tells stories. His stories take the form of thought experiments. Favoring a cheap-quick-small approach to exploration rather than using expensive-slow-large space missions, he asked why, instead of 1-ton spacecraft, we couldn't have 1-kilogram craft? Instead of heavy rocket propellant and a bulky engine, why not use something light—a skimpy but sturdy broadly deployed sail for catching the thrust of the sun's light. A kilogram-sized craft would need only a 30-meter-square sail in order to achieve speeds for reaching Uranus in a few years.

You can get to Uranus the old way or you can get there the new way. The old way was to use chemical rockets to boost the 1-ton *Voyager 2* craft and a nine-year travel time for a one-flyby view. Dyson considered *Voyager* to have been a good mission and it had just passed Uranus at the time of his writing about it. Contrast now what a follow-up mission could be. His 1-kg craft would not merely fly by but would linger. It would have the leisure to scrutinize the planet and its trove of moons.

Dyson never insists that his vision of the future will be accurate. He always attaches a disclaimer: This is one of many things that could happen. Don't complain if it doesn't happen this particular way. With my scientific knowledge of the world, I am saying that certain things are possible, things involving fast ships, and observations. I make these predictions as an entertainment, as an exercise in creative scientific thinking, in the spirit of Project Orion.

Astrochicken

Dyson's signature proposal came at a 1988 lecture at the University of Washington. He called his kilogram craft "Astrochicken," since it is about the size of a chicken. It would not be built but grown.[11] It would be organized biologically and its blueprints would be written in the digital language understood by DNA. It employs a symbiosis of plant and animal and electronic components. The plant part provides a basic life-support system using photosynthesis for producing energy. The animal part provides sensors and nerves and muscles for observing, ori-enting, and navigating. Finally, the electronic part is there to receive instructions from Earth and to transmit back to Earth what it learns.[12] What would happen when Astrochicken got to Uranus? It would keep up its energy level by grazing on ice and organic materials available in Uranus's rings.

Inspect the planets and moons, sure, but a more likely place to find life, Dyson argues, is on asteroids and comets, for the simple reason that these small denizens of deep space account for more total surface area than the planets. Dyson is so sure of himself that he offered a $100 bet that the first extraterrestrial life discovered will reside not on a planet but on an asteroid or comet.[13] But what kind of organism could live on a comet? One that must tolerate vacuum, low temperatures, and low gravity. It won't be easy, but it is conceivable.[14]

Indeed, the movement of life on Europa from a subsurface aqueous environment into a vacuum environment above the crust might be less arduous than the movement of terrestrial life onto dry land after 3 billion years in the sea, Dyson argues.[15] He illustrates his point by examples from an 1895 science fiction novel, *Dreams of Earth and Sky,* by Konstantin Tsiolkovsky. In this story creatures live in airless space. They accomplish this by being part plant and part animal—with airtight skin and winglike limbs that act as solar collectors.

Dyson not only proposes the style of the organism but also the manner of its detection. He believes we could find such peeping, light-gathering organisms through "pit lamping," a name deriving from a form of nocturnal stalking in which human hunters spot their prey by the use of head-mounted lamps worn by miners; the light reflects from the victim's eyes in a focused return beam. This eye light shows up as bright spots against a dark background. Dyson suggests that we go pit lamping for life in the outer solar system.[16] The sun shines into the distance, and we look for a telltale deer-in-the-headlight fixed stare back.

Dyson Trees

In the cold parts of the solar system it helps if creatures are warm-blooded. After all, Dyson says, polar bears survive in Arctic regions devoid of plants. They keep their blood warm by eating seals. On a comet, warm-blooded plants would have to eat sunlight by evolving advanced solar collection arrays, including lenslike structures for focusing meager sunlight onto efficient receiver-like tissue. Comets might be cold but they are water-rich. If the plants put down sufficient roots nutrients could be mined from below. With gravity so low, the plants might grow as tall as they liked, perhaps reaching a scale as large as the comet itself. Maybe bigger. Dyson foresees 100-mile-long trees sprouting from ten-mile-wide comets. In low gravity there is no reason why trees can't attain mega-Sequoia proportions. These hypothetical horticultural wonders, sometimes referred to now as "Dyson trees," have figured in several novels.[17]

But who needs novelists when Dyson's own writing is so vivid in evoking the trek of women and men out to the abode of comets. For all his talk about the remote detection of life or the dispatch of spacecraft to check on habitats in the far corners of the solar system, Dyson continues to harbor hopes, or at least dreams, of *Homo sapiens* boldly going forth to these places to look and perchance to live. Dyson trees could furnish both fuel and shelter for human settlers. "When humans come to live on the comets, they will find themselves returning to the arboreal existence of their ancestors."[18]

Oort Archipelago

Like a person daydreaming of buying land in a beautiful but forlorn location in order to put up a holiday hideaway, Dyson has his eye on the Kuiper Belt, the girdle of comets and small bodies that ply mostly outside the orbit of Pluto. Indeed, having been demoted from planetary status, Pluto is itself now considered a Kuiper object. Dyson is also intrigued by the still further out Oort Cloud, a swath of small parcels, billions of them, with a large collective surface area.[19]

Dyson sees the Kuiper and Oort assemblies as something like the Alaska-Canada Inside Passage, a vast archipelago where homesteaders from Earth might make a go of it.[20] The reasons for such a risky migration might be biological or political—such as escaping devastation or overcrowding on Earth, or mining minerals, or for seeking sheer adventure. Again, whenever Dyson discusses such fond ideas he is careful to say that he is not making a specific prediction. He is only speculating that certain kinds of living could happen. The laws of physics and biology do not forbid them. Like the first proto-cells on Earth who hung on to existence by agglomerating useful molecules while luxuriating in nutrient-rich tide pools or at the margins of warm mid-ocean vents, twenty-second-century Kuiper Belt city-states might grow by accretion of celestial objects tethered together, much as Indonesia grew by stitching together islands.[21]

Beyond that, what? Well, then it's off to other stars and across the galaxy with transportation technology that hasn't been invented yet. More unfathomable than the rocket design is the social fabric that could hold together a community on treks far more arduous than those of the biblical Israelites across Sinai or Paleo-Siberians over the Bering land bridge.

But intelligence, viewed over a wide enough breadth, is patient. "Mind has waited for 3 billion years on this planet before composing its first string quartet," says Dyson. "It may have to wait for another 3 billion years before it spreads all over the galaxy."[22]

PERSISTENCE

The third part of Dyson's grand message—the bit about this being the most interesting of universes—concerns the relation between life and the cosmos. Dyson chafes at jurisdictional boundaries, such as the one that separates cosmology from biology. He finds it a pity that the overall theory of biology, consisting of Darwin's evolution by natural selection plus modern genetics, and the overall theory of cosmology, consisting of the big bang model supplemented with quantum mechanics and general relativity, have progressed in past decades pretty much without reference to each other.

The only life we know about, here on Earth, came along about 4 billion years ago, some 10 billion years after the big bang moment. So it's hard to say what connection there is between the origin of life and the origins of the visible universe itself. These are difficult questions for scientists to grapple with. Indeed they have not always been viewed as scientific issues at all, but something more appropriate for theologians.

Late Life

If the respectability of the study of cosmic origins was established by the publication of Steven Weinberg's *The First Three Minutes* in 1977, how about the last three minutes? How about the study of the remote future of the cosmos? Not yet a legitimate scientific enterprise, the indefinite future had long been in the hands of theologians and novelists like Olaf Stapledon. Dyson sniffed an opportunity.[23]

In 1978 he gave the Arthur Lectures at New York University on the topic "Time and Its Mysteries." His particular twist on this assignment was to speak about time and biology. Not the biology of the past 4 billion years, nor the biology of our current human cultural era, not even the future out to the comet-dwelling era of Dyson trees. Instead he talked about life a billion trillion trillion years from now.

Dyson doesn't pretend to predict what will happen. He is a great extrapolator. He paints the future. His palette consists of thermodynamic lore, phase transitions, the trajectories of celestial objects, and the decay of nuclei. The portrait he draws of the geriatric universe is more diaphanous than the emptiest landscapes of Monet or Turner.

What does physics say about the far future? First, there will be inevitably a series of deaths. Our own sun, having exhausted much of its internal nuclear fuel over the next few billion years, will actually expand for a while, enveloping and burning Earth. Later still the sun will shrink to the status of a white dwarf star. Given enough time, and in Dyson's Arthur Lectures there was lots of time, many slow or rare processes come to pass. To express so colossal a chronology we must use exponential notation. In this convention a million—1,000,000, a one followed by six zeros—is written as 10^6. A trillion—1,000,000,000,000—is written as 10^{12}. The strung-out phenomena of the universe include, in Dyson's estimation, the detachment of planets from stars (10^{15} years from now), the detachment of stars from galaxies (10^{19} years), and the growth and then evaporation of black holes into a thin gas of particles and radiation (10^{64} years).[24]

The big biology-cosmology questions are: Can life persist into these extreme times? And if life survives will consciousness still be active? Will intelligible communications continue even as the universe expands, making it harder and harder to harvest matter and energy? Early life, typified by the pilgrimage away from ocean vents, may have found temperatures to be a bit warm. Current life, at least for human habitation on Earth, finds temperatures just about right. Future life, in whatever form it takes, will find the thermostat turned way down.

String Quartets

To Dyson's surprise, his NYU host submitted the lecture notes to the prestigious journal *Review of Modern Physics*.[25] To his greater surprise, the editors accepted the piece.[26] It became for many years the main scientific description of the physics of Deep Time.

Dyson is an optimist. He finds that eternal life and finite energy are compatible providing that certain modifications to life come about. First some bad news: life and intelligence tied inextricably to ordinary matter, such as the biomolecules that compose our bodies and brains—requiring warmth and liquid water to function well—will not endure. Life will have to take a radically different form. Even the Martian invaders imagined by Stapledon as a cloud of tiny organisms are too matter-bound. Life has to be simpler, maybe no more than waves passing through a mist of micron-sized dust grains. It's hard to imagine how such a pulse could be alive, much less carry on communications. But then, as Dyson points out, we wouldn't have predicted the architecture of a bacterium if we didn't already know it.[27]

The scope of late life Dyson provides in his landmark *Review of Modern Physics* article far transcends his previous ponderings over the riddle of existence. Forget nuclear test bans and Project Orion and homesteading the Kuiper Belt. Forget even the advanced degree of civilization needed to construct Dyson spheres that intercept and use the entire energy emission of a star. At this point in the far future, the existence of life itself, anywhere and everywhere, is at stake. The kind of life forms embodied in dust clouds (a "Dyson swarm" as we might call it) is far more advanced. It would have to be if it were frantically going to scrounge energy in an expanding and cooling universe.

Dyson does the math. He sets out formulas for calculating the energy consumed and later dissipated by the swarm society. This minimum energy is proportional to the square of the creature's temperature and to its "complexity." Complexity, essentially the same as consciousness, is related to "the amount of information that must be processed in order to keep the creature alive long enough to say '*cogito, ergo sum.*'"[28]

Dyson calculates that the complexity value for a human being to produce one second's worth of consciousness is 10^{23} bits of information. For the entire human race, one second of consciousness is encapsulated in the form of 10^{33} bits. The bigger the consciousness, the bigger the energy requirement. To keep ahead of the inexorable expansion of space-time and the dilution of energy resources, the swarm would have to reduce its temperature or reduce its level of consciousness. But even this, he sadly concludes, won't be enough for life to endure indefinitely.[29]

Hibernation

Wait. Dyson comes up with an alternative. The creature can hibernate. It can slow its thinking process to a halt and wake up later. In this way, taking ever longer naps, it can conserve energy.

But what about the quality of life? We're no longer talking about owning a fine home, dining well, and reading a good book. However, it wouldn't be much fun if, as the eons crept past, the creature would have to surrender its mental faculties in an effort to economize on memory space. After all, the third part of Dyson's grand manifesto, the third part of the message he has come to preach, is that the universe is interesting in a meaningful way (a sentiment to be explored in the next chapter) and that the presence of humans, or at least some strain of intelligent creatures, should be around to help make things interesting.

Analog vs. Digital

For a full life, Dyson says, you should have a growing memory, one that can accommodate new experience while retaining the old. This can be performed if the creature forswears digital memory—the form of data storage used in most present computers, in which information is represented by strings of 0s and 1s—in favor of analog memory. Dyson provides an example of what this means: information can be associated with, say, the apparent angle between two distant stars.[30] With this understood, intelligent life might hang on.

Dyson maintained this view of persistent life for many years. Then in the late 1990s, new observations changed the picture. For decades the majority opinion among cosmologists was that the expansion of the universe could follow one of two courses: either the expansion would continue at an ever slower rate (owing to the mutual gravitational tug of galaxies upon each other) or would even reverse, causing the galaxies to come back into closer proximity, eventually bringing about a grand crunch, a big bang in reverse.

Well, new telescope measurements seemed to upend this view. Neither scenario was cogent anymore. Measurements of remote supernovas now suggested that the rate of expansion is not slowing, not reversing, but growing. The big bang is accelerating. The overall thinning of energy resources is actually speeding up. The universe as a place to live is becoming impoverished at a much greater rate than we had earlier thought.

Lawrence Krauss, a physicist at Arizona State University, deduces that space is expanding so rapidly that galaxies will eventually accelerate away from our view. They will vanish from sight. Krauss calls this the "worst of all possible universes." He and Glenn Starkman, a physicist at Case Western Reserve University, determine that we don't even have to wait all that long for the thinning of the universe to be dire:

"Within two trillion years, well before the last stars in the universe die, all objects outside our own cluster of galaxies will no longer be observable or accessible. There will be no new worlds to conquer, literally. We will truly be alone in the universe."[31]

Dyson's optimism about the eternal persistence of life would seem to be trumped by the emptying of space. Even with ever longer periods of hibernation, there wouldn't be enough energy, much less coffee, to wake up to. Intelligent creatures would have trouble finding food, much less having meaningful conversations.

Edward Witten, Dyson's colleague at the Institute for Advanced Study, doesn't like the idea of an accelerating universe: "It's definitely the strangest experimental finding since I've been in physics," Witten has said. And yet the facts are the facts, until overwritten by later observations. "People find it difficult to accept," said Witten. "I've stopped expecting the finding to be proved wrong, but it's an extremely uncomfortable finding."[32]

Krauss and Starkman identify themselves as "frustrated optimists." They suspect that memory and consciousness will probably turn out to be digital and not analog, and under the current understanding of the accelerating expansion of the universe, life cannot persist indefinitely.[33]

Meanwhile Dyson does not give up. Astronomers have changed their mind about the general mechanism of the universe many times before, he says. Some new mechanism might still turn up—wormholes through space-time—that allow resources to be found for the continuation of life.[34]

Dyson is irrepressibly the optimist or (as some suspect) the wishful thinker. He regards himself as a scientific humanist in the tradition of H. G. Wells. As a young boy at school, Dyson took refuge in a library where he read Wells's adventure stories. As an elderly man, Dyson takes refuge in Wells's expansive view of the human presence in the cosmos. Dyson singles out the opening lines of Wells's *Outline of History*: "Not only is Space from the point of view of life and humanity empty, but Time is empty also. Life is like a little glow, scarcely kindled yet, in these void immensities." For Dyson's purposes, it is necessary to view the arc of life as being open-ended: "It was important for Wells, and for me, that the stage is large and humanity small. An awareness of our smallness may help to redeem us from the arrogance which is the besetting sin of scientists."[35]

16. God and Man at Princeton

Dyson as Preacher

(1985–2000)

AROUND THE DYSON SPHERE

When Freeman Dyson reached his canonical three-score-and-ten, the retirement age for professors at the Institute for Advance Study, his friends and colleagues held a festival in his honor, they had no shortage of topics to cover. This grand event, called "Around the Dyson Sphere," took place over two days, April 8–9, 1994. The two organizers were professors at the Institute, Frank Wilczek, later to win a Nobel Prize, and Edward Witten, the chief proponent of string theory and a winner of the Fields Medal, the most prestigious award in mathematics.

The program of talks, tied to phases in Dyson's career, spanned a variety of science and technology subjects: quantum field theory, gravity, missile defense, stability of matter, adaptive optics and telescopes, magnets, the imaging of biomolecules, evolution, pure mathematics, arms control, and the formulation of federal science policy. Dyson was on hand for these talks and good-naturedly commented as the speakers progressed.

The daytime talks were technical in nature, but the after-dinner remarks were convivial, and anecdotes flowed. For example, physicist and *New Yorker* writer Jeremy Bernstein, who in the mid-1950s had been a short-term visitor to the Institute, recalled seeing Dyson reading the Bible in Russian and (while both of them were working on the Orion project) Dyson being arrested one day when the guards mistook him for an intruder; Dyson had broken his eyeglasses and was wearing snorkeling goggles while walking around in the bright sunshine.

239

Abraham Pais, like Dyson a theoretical physicist and young professor at the Institute in the 1950s, commended Dyson for helping to make clear many difficult physics concepts, complimented him for being a contrarian, and congratulated him for having found the right mate in Imme Jung. Former Institute director Marvin Goldberger, a member of Jason and a theoretical physicist, asserted (in a letter read out at the dinner) that Dyson had not had many physics collaborators over the years because "he thinks faster than others." "He might be wrong," said Goldberger of Dyson, "but never boring." Marvin Goldberger's wife, Mildred, who had met Dyson many times at Princeton and at summertime Jason meetings, said that Dyson was always respectful of women. He talked to them at parties with interest, she said. He didn't need to drop the names of important friends. He didn't need to be one-up on other people.

Dyson's daughter Esther was one of the last to speak. She had the impression, growing up, that for all of his accomplishments the thing Freeman Dyson was most proud about was his children. "And now his grandchildren," she added. "He is optimistic but clear-eyed. I've never met anyone more tolerant or understanding." At the end of the evening, the guest of honor thanked his friends at the Institute ("Where they have been pampering me for forty years") and at Jason. He was glad to have been a part of both the worlds of science and action.

Freeman thanked Esther for introducing him into still another world, the world of business. And as for his amazing variety of interests, this he attributed to his short attention span. He could never stay focused on one topic for very long before moving on to another.[1]

Further honors were heaped upon Freeman Dyson. He received the Matteucci Medal (1989) of the Italian National Academy of Sciences; the Antonio Feltrinelli Prize (1990), given by the Accademia dei Lincei; the Oersted Medal (1991), the highest award of the American Association of Physics Teachers; the Lewis Thomas Prize (1996), given by the Rockefeller University for literary efforts by a scientist; and the Burton Award (1999), given by the American Physical Society for work accentuating the role of physics in society. Honorary degrees from colleges kept arriving: Rider College (1989), Bates (1991), Haverford (1991), Dartmouth (1995), ETH Zurich (1995), Scuola Normale Superiore Pisa (1996), University of Puget Sound (1997), Oxford (1997), and Clarkson (1998).

Dyson had done well at the Institute. Privately he wondered if he hadn't been in a rut by staying in Princeton for so long.[2] Getting out into the bustle of a university might have been good for him. He felt, however, that his children wouldn't have wanted the change. Imme Jung isn't sure about this view. She and her children speculate that it was Freeman himself who wanted to stay. "He's married to the Institute," Imme said. "He'll never leave."[3]

He had been at the Institute as professor for forty years, and was going to continue working there under the designation of professor emeritus, keeping his office, with its splendid view of a sprawling grassy space and an immense oak. His office was room number 292 in a building that now bears the name of the mayor of New York—Bloomberg Hall—a generous donor to the Institute. The office across the hall was occupied by Ed Witten. By craning your neck out at the window of Dyson's room you could see Einstein's office (now occupied by another professor) in Fuld Hall. The other faculty for the School of Natural Sciences at the Institute at this time were Stephen Adler, Piet Hut, and John Bahcall. Dyson was friendly with his colleagues but generally worked alone.

Although his main work at this point in the mid-1990s was writing book reviews and giving public lectures, he was still interested in mathematical physics. He was then assembling a volume of his select scientific papers, which would be published in 1996. Alongside the papers, Dyson provided a running annotation year by year of his research interests and a generous inclusion of biographical material. He had also, a few years before, published a collection of works (mostly a scrapbook of lecture transcripts and book reviews) from across sixty years. This book, *From Eros to Gaia*, led off with his schoolboy fantasy from 1933, "Sir Phillip Roberts's Erolunar Collision."

The house on Battle Road Circle had nearly emptied out. The four younger daughters were in or already out of graduate school: Dorothy in veterinary school at the University of California at Davis, Emily in medical school at the University of California at San Diego, Mia at the Princeton Theological Seminary, and Rebecca (like her sister Emily) at the UCSD medical school. Grandchildren were starting to arrive.

Imme didn't have the girls to fuss over anymore. Instead she had flowers. She spent many hours in the garden out back. Her long-distance running became ever more serious. She ran and won. For her age group she came in first at the San Francisco Marathon in 1987 and the Boston Marathon in 1996. Although still a German citizen, she (along with her husband) was interested in political affairs, and often contributed to the campaigns of various Democrat candidates, especially Representative Rush Holt, one of the few physicists in Congress.

George's boat building continued. But he had also made himself into a writer. In 1986 he published a book, *Baidarka*, about kayaks, the Aleuts who had built them, and about his own experiences on land and water. He holds the record for building the longest kayak, a craft forty-eight feet long and holding six people. His interest in science and technology history led to his second book, *Darwin Among the Machines* (1998), about the evolution of computers, particularly John von Neumann's contributions.

Esther, the oldest of Freeman Dyson's children, was increasingly coming into the public eye. Having worked as a reporter on investments and high-tech products, she bought out her employer in 1983 and established a company called EDventure. She became interested in business possibilities in Eastern Europe, which was undergoing tumultuous changes before and after the end of the Cold War. She was one of the first to chronicle and champion the rise of the Internet. Her monthly newsletter culminated in a book, *Release 2.0*, in 1997. She wrote columns for *The New York Times* and organized a number of notable computer and Internet meetings under the name PC Forum. These forums, usually held in winter in warm places like Arizona, provided the occasion for Dyson family reunions.[4] Sometimes all six Dyson siblings would be present, and several grandchildren.[5]

Freeman's brood was fairly fledged. He would have even more time to pore over writing projects, especially in areas that had stood outside the purview of the retirement events. Although spread out across two days, "Around the Dyson Sphere" could not examine all of Dyson's primary interests. Unfortunately, what they left out—Dyson's expansive writing about the connection of science to social concerns such as religion, art, philosophy, and ethics—had become an essential part of his status as a public figure. How could you slot topics like theology and ethics in with talks about spin waves and quantum field theory? So, to finish the journey around the Dyson sphere, we're going to look at these overlooked subjects.

NATURAL THEOLOGY

"The more the universe seems comprehensible, the more it also seems pointless." There is no better way to look at Dyson's cultural writing career than to return to Steven Weinberg's assertion in his book *The First Three Minutes*, a phrase now raised to the status of an aphorism. Addressing or refuting the alleged "pointlessness" of the universe was going to be one of Dyson's primary occupations hereafter, part of his effort to reconcile scientific with spiritual knowledge.

Dyson considers that both forms of knowledge provide valuable windows on the world. You can't really look out of both windows at the same time but both windows allow you to see aspects of the world not visible to the other. Dyson is not a conventionally religious man himself—religion is more a way of life than a set of beliefs he likes to say—but he feels that the great spiritual traditions such as Buddhism, Hinduism, Islam, or Christianity offer a fruitful way of contemplating the "point" of the universe.

The Gifford Lectures, delivered by Dyson in April and November of 1985 in Scotland, were to be a primary showcase for his thoughts on this matter. Instituted in order to explore the subject of natural theology, the lectures are given intermittently at Scottish universities in Glasgow, Aberdeen, Edinburgh, and St. Andrews. Gifford speakers over the years have addressed a variety of circumstances underlying human existence. Notable examples include Hannah Arendt, whose books looked at the nature of evil; Niels Bohr, who presided over the establishment of the quantum description of reality; Roger Penrose, who ventured to relate the wellsprings of consciousness with quantum behavior and with gravity; and William James, one of the founders of modern psychology and whose Gifford Lectures provided a catalog of case histories of exalted mental behavior. Gifford speakers have even included Richard Dawkins, biologist and militant atheist, best known for promulgating the idea that competition among selfish genes, not the unfolding of God's plan, established and governed the landscape of living organisms on Earth.

In practice, Gifford lectures have taken wide latitude in their interpretation of "natural philosophy." When it was Freeman Dyson's turn to lecture, he seized the opportunity as a bully pulpit. He came to Scotland to preach.[6]

Arriving in Aberdeen in April and November of 1985 he met with foul weather. Still, he paused to notice that the city was covered with daffodils in April and roses in November.[7] Free to create his own form of natural theology, and always eager to enlarge the scope of permissible discussion, Dyson spoke of some things he believed but couldn't prove: "I believe that we are here to some purpose, that the purpose has something to do with the future, and that it transcends altogether the limits of our present knowledge and understanding."[8]

Dyson spoke of poetry. The works of Blake and Eliot and Dylan Thomas gave him access to beauty and to the sublime. Many scientists generally view art as a pleasurable and creative way of depicting reality. Appreciating a poem, Samuel Taylor Coleridge said, involved a momentary willing suspension of disbelief.

Religion, however, is another matter. It involves a fervent, permanent belief in supernatural things. In general scientists are suspicious. Richard Dawkins, for example, argues that religion is founded on superstition and that religious thinking is antithetical to rationalism and scientific thinking. He cites a 1998 U.S. National Academy of Sciences study of its own members showing that only 7 percent believed in a God.[9]

Can science and religion coexist peaceably? Dyson says yes. To support his claim, he looks at five test cases, a thicket of quarrelsome issues over which science and religion would seem to scrape roughly up against each other. Together, Dyson's lectures on these subjects form yet another of his manifestos. They are the heart of his Gifford presentation and the centerpiece of his book, *Infinite in All Directions*. Here are the five areas of possibly intractable confrontations. Let's see what Dyson and those who disagree with him have to say.

1. The origins of life. Dyson's own escapades as a biologist illustrate the issues involved. Whether they were loose confederations of chemicals (Dyson's view) or more disciplined blobs governed by replicating nucleotides (the majority view), the earliest living entities were subject to chance chemical encounters. At the even deeper level of atoms, matter is subject to quantum uncertainty—think of that sea of virtual particles splashing about inside every atom.

What kind of God would stand behind such an indeterminate universe, one in which every microscopic fork in the road was, in effect, governed by statistical likelihood rather than exactitude? Dyson was no theologian, he protested, but an appropriate God for the job would be one that was himself (or herself or itself) in doubt as to the outcome of these micro-branchings of history. So, to reconcile science and religion on the origin of life, Dyson says, imagine a God who is not omniscient but who learns as he goes along, just as we humans do.[10] Instead of adapting our scientific views to a fixed idea of divinity, Dyson cheerfully offers to devise a theology that fits in with the observed properties of nature.

2. Free will. The traditional conundrum of human choice—how can we freely decide things if God has decided for us in advance—might well be eased if (on the theological front) God were to be bound (on the atomic front) by the fuzziness in knowledge imposed by Heisenberg's principle of quantum uncertainty. In order to believe both in God and in free will Dyson suggests that God was less than omnipotent.[11]

For those who prefer a scientific, and not a theological, explanation of free will, Dyson is ready. He holds that the psychological appearance of free will, the feeling that at least for part of the time we're in charge of the thoughts that come into our minds, stems from the intrinsic quantum uncertainty of atoms. Our minds are associated with brains made from atoms. Our brains are machines for processing "free will" at the atom level into free will at the human level. Consciousness, Dyson argues, is not merely an emergent state arising passively from chemical reactions. In effect, mind invades matter, at least the matter in our brains. Does this make Dyson an animist—one who believes that brute matter is filled with some kind of animating spirit? Yes, it does. And Dyson is proud to say it:

> *I cannot help thinking that our awareness of our own brains has something to do with the process we call "observation" in atomic physics. That is to say, I think our consciousness is not just a passive epiphenomenon carried along by the chemical events in our brains, but is an active agent forcing the molecular complexes to make choices between one quantum state and another.*[12]

Lawrence Krauss, who jousted with Dyson about the prospects for life in the late universe, also disagrees with him about free will. Krauss, and many other scientists, see free will as an illusion, a useful illusion for the sake of our self-esteem. True, our knowledge of atoms as reflected in the measurements we make seems to be subject to uncertainty, Krauss says. We don't know precisely what goes on inside an atom. But he insists that the electron is still subject to the exact equations of quantum reality. Scientists might not know where the electron is but the quantum rules do.[13]

EIGHTEENTH-CENTURY MAN

3. Teleology. Aristotle said that earthly matter consisted of four elements. Earth, water, air, and fire each had a sort of disposition of its own. Each wanted to be in *its* proper location in the cosmos. This was a teleological explanation: an object moved because it had an inherent purpose to move there. *Meaningfulness* was at the heart of his scheme.

Modern scientists don't think this way anymore. They now explain that matter moves because some inanimate force, such as gravity, nudges it along. Objects are not alive. They don't have volition. There is no "meaning" in the fact that Venus's orbit around the sun lies outside Mercury's orbit.

The essence of science is to be impartial and unimpassioned. Account for facts. Other than this, there is no right or wrong. "Any mingling of knowledge with values is unlawful, forbidden." So says Jacques Monod as quoted by Freeman Dyson.[14] Dyson is impatient with this dogma. "Monad was one of the seminal minds in the flowering of molecular biology in this century," said Dyson. "It takes some courage to defy his anathema. But I will defy him and encourage others to do so."[15]

The anathema against value judgments in science, Dyson believes, began with the struggle over the Darwinian revolution, especially as it pertained to the place of humans in the hierarchy of the world. On one side were evolutionary biologists such as Thomas Huxley, who sought to limit the role of religious sentiment in scientific argument. On the other side were the forces of moralism, led by Anglican bishop Samuel Wilberforce. This battle was won eventually by those who, lamentably in Dyson's view, battle against any value judgments in science. The result of this science-religion conflict, he believes, soured the intellectual life of the nineteenth century and still, in our time, impedes a freer exploration of the universe.

It wasn't always so. Some of the greatest scientists, such as Isaac Newton, were deeply religious and allowed their religious impulses to guide some of their best scientific research even if, when it came time to publish that research, spiritual motivations were often left unsaid. Another example Dyson offered was Thomas Wright, who, in 1750, proposed the basic structure of the Milky Way that we know today. Wright said that the faint smudges in the sky known as nebulae might actually be clumps of stars, now called galaxies, like the Milky Way. Some decades later William Herschel added much more observational evidence for Wright's findings.

Dyson was particularly pleased by Wright's mixing of knowledge and values. Wright, having spoken of the many stars, worlds, and galaxies making up the cosmos, went on to ponder the grander scheme at work in the sky:

> *In this great celestial creation, the catastrophe of a world, such as ours, or even the total dissolution of a system of worlds, may possibly be no more to the great Author of Nature, than the most common accident in life with us, and in all probability such final and general Doomsdays may be as frequent there as even Birthdays or mortality with us upon the earth. This idea has something so cheerful in it, that I own I can never look upon the stars without wondering why the whole world does not become astronomers.*[16]

Dyson weighs Wright's wondrous pondering of the heavens against Monod's unlawful mixing of knowledge and values or Weinberg's sense of the universe seeming to be pointless. If Monod and Weinberg speak for the twentieth century, Dyson would prefer to be of the eighteenth century.[17]

4. Argument from design. Does the universe have a design? Does it have an author? Dyson regards this as another polarizing issue dividing those who deem either faith or reason to be all-important. Science mostly ignores the "authorship" question and looks for facts around which to build richly structured explanations. For the layout of the cosmos as a whole, there is big bang cosmology. For the makeup of ordinary matter, there are physical and chemical theories about quarks, protons, atoms, molecules, and the forces that bind them among each other. The centerpiece of modern geology is the idea of immense crustal tectonic plates floating about and banging together on an underlying sea of heavier mantle material within the Earth. In biology, the overarching framework is Darwin's theory of evolution, supplemented in more recent decades with observations from molecular biology, including the study and manipulation of DNA. In all these branches of science "design" is an inanimate impulse that emerges from the messy commerce among observable things—galaxies, atoms, continents, molecules, bacteria.

Dyson isn't forsaking the grand frameworks of conventional science, is he? Of course not. Looking through the scientific window at the universe has brought incalculable benefits to our lives and our understanding. What Dyson says is: don't forget that other windows are available for viewing the universe. Other people, those who avidly look at the world through the window of religion, are very much interested in the question of authorship. For them design is not serendipitous but the deliberate creation of a divine author.

5. *Final aims.* The same year Dyson gave his series of lectures in Aberdeen another American scientist offered rival Gifford Lectures on the diagonally opposite side of Scotland in Glasgow. Carl Sagan, in his Gifford Lectures, allowed that science and religion needn't be in conflict. But he didn't necessarily admit that he, Carl Sagan himself, felt a need for religion. He remained, occupationally and intellectually, firmly on the side of traditional science. He steadfastly argued that he could not prove the existence or nonexistence of God and neither could anyone else. Until he was shown some palpable proof that could pass scientific scrutiny, then he would not be persuaded. Firmly but enthusiastically he argued that the mighty achievements of science and the knowledge of the universe, applying to things from microbes on up to the size of galaxies, gained by scientific means afforded all the edifying sense of wonder that he could hope for. He had no need of metaphysical speculations. The more we know of the cosmos, Sagan said, the more puny our gods and religion seem: "And in fact a general problem with much of Western theology, in my view, is that the God portrayed is too small. It is a god of a tiny world and not a god of a galaxy, much less of a universe."[18]

Dyson, in Aberdeen, said something different. Although no less scientific than Sagan in the pursuit of facts in support of well-reasoned hypotheses, Dyson argued that the final aim or the ultimate purpose in the cosmos, if there is one, lies beyond our intellectual reach:

> *The choice of laws of nature, and the choice of initial conditions for the universe, are questions belonging to meta-science and not to sci-*

ence. Science is restricted to the explanation of phenomena within the universe. Teleology is not forbidden when explanations go beyond science into meta-science.[19]

Why do this sort of recalibration? So that we can rescue the idea of purpose. Dyson freed himself of having to explain the seeming favoritism that God might have toward the human race—entailing the tuning of the circumstances of the big bang and the laws of nature to just the right levels to favor the advent of living organisms, and later of thinking organisms—by locating those circumstances and those laws outside the universe in some absolute elsewhere, outside the purview of science.

The 1902 book that came out of William James's Gifford Lectures was entitled *The Varieties of Religious Experience*. It became a classic text on the subjects of psychology and spiritual thinking. Dyson has owned a copy of this book since he was fifteen years old, and James is probably the greatest influence on Dyson's thinking about religion.[20] James was the Oliver Sacks of the early twentieth century. A physician, philosopher, and writer, James didn't take theology seriously, but he did take seriously the accounts of individual religious experiences. This was his summary view: the religious life is "having the belief that there is some unseen order, and that our supreme good lies in harmoniously adjusting thereto."[21]

Sagan also made use of James. He adapted James's title, calling his Gifford presentation "*The Varieties of Scientific Experience*." Science was enough for Sagan. His commandment was "Thou shalt understand the world. Figure things out."[22]

COMPLEMENTARITY

The philosopher Daniel Dennett and others have argued that religion is a natural aspect of human existence, a belief system that competes with other belief systems in helping human societies to survive. These beliefs, or at least the belief in belief as Dennett says, can evolve over time and can be assessed as to how successful they are in making the society flourish or not.[23] As such, religion is a spell with powerful influence over human culture. When the articles of religious faith are put to a more rationalistic test—for example, is a man walking on water in accord with the known laws of gravity?—they exercise less power.

In reviewing Dennett's book *Breaking the Spell*, Dyson concedes the point that religion is a natural phenomenon. But he goes on to insist that society would be the poorer for losing religion:

> *As human beings, we are groping for knowledge and understanding of the strange universe into which we are born. We have many ways of understanding, of which science is only one. Our thought processes are only partially based on logic, and are inextricably mixed with emotions and desires and social interactions. We cannot live as isolated intelligences, but only as members of a working community. Our ways of understanding have been collective, beginning with the stories that we told one another around the fire when we lived in caves. Our ways today are still collective, including literature, history, art, music, religion, and science. Science is a particular bunch of tools that have been conspicuously successful for understanding and manipulating the material universe. Religion is another bunch of tools, giving us hints of a mental spiritual universe that transcends the material universe.*[24]

Dyson is thus a sort of transcendentalist. Like Ralph Waldo Emerson and other members of the Transcendentalist Club in New England in the 1830s, Dyson wants to employ knowledge gained from a variety of sources—science, literature, nature, and spirituality (not necessarily organized religion) to appreciate and understand the world.

Dyson is not so much seeking religious experience, at least not from traditional denominations, as he is spiritual experience. He and Emerson subscribe to science as a valid route to knowledge, and both feel that science is not enough. Both chafe at the smugness of science and its exclusive reliance on a materialistic viewpoint. Here is Emerson in 1841, from his famous essay on transcendentalism:

> *The materialist, secure in the certainty of sensation, mocks at the fine-spun theories, at star gazers, and dreamers, and believes that his life is solid, that he at least takes nothing for granted, but knows where he stands, and what he does. Yet how easy it is to show him that he also is a phantom walking and working amid phantoms, and that he need only ask a question or two beyond his daily questions to find his solid universe growing dim and impalpable before his sense.*[25]

Dyson's omnivorous pursuit of this multiplicity motivates some of his most sparkling writing, and brings him invitations to speak at places around the world.

At Cambridge University in September 1992, for example, scientists and philosophers met to discuss the subject of reductionism, the general process of understanding the whole by examining the parts. This approach to knowledge—such as studying atoms in order to understand bulk material or studying cells in order to understand the body—has led to spectacular progress in science. Yet, the meeting was contentious.

Dyson was indignant: "A reductionist philosophy," he said, "arbitrarily proclaiming that the growth of understanding must go only in one direction [upward from the parts to the whole rather than from the whole to the parts] makes no scientific sense. Indeed, dogmatic beliefs of any kind have no place in science."[26]

The announced subject of the Cambridge meeting might have been reductionism, but the argument at times hinged on the relation of science and religion. Chemist and writer Peter Atkins was also indignant: "Only the religious—among whom I include not merely the prejudiced but also the underinformed—hope that there is a dark corner of the physical universe, or of the universe of experience, that science can never hope to illuminate."[27]

Dyson embraced science, but felt we needed more: "To my mind the history of science is most illuminating when the frailties of human actors are put into juxtaposition with the transcendence of nature's laws.[28] Atkins: "Religion says that the world is too big for our comprehension. Science says that it *can* tackle the big questions."[29]

Dyson objects to the extreme form of reductionism, a view that seems to say that "all forms of knowledge, from physics and chemistry to psychology and philosophy and sociology and history and ethics and religion, can be reduced to science. Whatever cannot be reduced to science is not knowledge."[30] In Dyson's opinion, valid knowledge comes in many forms: a perception of good and evil, an appreciation for art, and the appraisal of life through everyday experience or through religious feelings all offer alternative windows for viewing the world.

Like Niels Bohr's complementarity principle, which says that physical matter can be viewed as collections of particles or as trains of waves—but not at the same time—so the rest of the universe can be viewed in multiple ways. "The final frame of traditional theology and the formal frame of traditional science are both too narrow to comprehend the total of human experience. . . . Theology excludes differential equations, and science excludes the idea of the sacred."[31]

THEOFICTION

Dyson is, like Emerson, a stargazer and a dreamer. Dyson is familiar with many of the sacred books, especially the Hebrew-Christian Bible. Another storehouse of religious ideas for him comes from his reading of certain science fiction authors. Yes, science fiction, that genre so loved by readers and belittled by mainstream literary critics. Flying through the outer reaches of the galaxy, in an imaginative sense, came naturally to Freeman Dyson. "Science is my territory," he said, "but science fiction is the landscape of my dreams."[32] Dyson's preference among sci-fi books is for those that use the future or outer space settings as occasions for exploring theological themes. Dyson's name for this subgenre is "theofiction."[33]

Dante's *Commedia* and John Milton's *Paradise Lost* are examples of early theofiction. These works might not at first seem like science fiction. But they do both involve journeys through space, and are works of great artistry and spirituality, and they do take notice of the geologic and astronomical lore of their day.

Undoubtedly Dyson's archetype for theofictional writing is Olaf Stapledon. When it came time to reissue Stapledon's masterpiece, *Star Maker* (originally published in 1937), the editor asked Dyson to write a Preface, which he did.

Star Maker begins in down-to-earth fashion with a narrator sitting on a hill contemplating his life and gazing at the night sky. Then, by dreaming or by some unexplained form of disembodied flight, he finds himself out with the stars. Through the further technological mechanism of radio-based telepathy, the narrator acquires the ability to listen in on the minds of human-level creatures and indeed co-inhabit their consciences. After some initial awkwardness, the narrator—while recurringly speaking to us as an individual—gradually takes on the mental attributes of a succession of alien beings. Some of these beings join him in his journey, and they constitute a collective mind of growing experience and perspective.

Star Maker is impressively ambitious but almost impossible to read as a piece of fiction. Except for the narrator, the book contains no characters in the conventional sense and no story line other than the incessant journeying through the cosmos in search of more experience and the prospect of glimpsing the Star Maker, the putative creator of the universe. The book's scope gets wider and wider at a dizzying rate. Centuries, millennia, and eons go by. We are shown myriads of world civilizations, then empires of worlds, then civilizations on the galactic scale, then intergalactic organizations. Worlds, stars, galaxies, even primordial gas nebulae possess consciousness. These "minded" worlds and stars themselves form federations and conduct wars.

The book culminates in a meeting between the narrator and the Star Maker, the maker of all that is. The narrator has by this point appropriated to himself essentially the mindedness of all creatures in the cosmos, and yet he is not equal to the majesty and awfulness of the deity. Although worthy of being worshipped, the Star Maker is capricious, interested (selfishly, we might say) in creating universe after universe in experimental fashion, each time trying out a different configuration of physical and biological laws, with a consequential spectrum of intelligent creatures and their respective inevitably ephemeral civilizations.

In his Preface to this visionary theological saga, Dyson compares Stapledon's fictional panoply of alternative universes, each with its own attributes (for example, one universe might have space but not time, another has extra dimensions) with some current scientific cosmology theories. For instance, physicist Lee Smolin has explained the apparently fine-tuned aspects of our universe—the laws of nature, such as the strength of interactions inside the sun, seem to be just right for fostering life on Earth—by suggesting that ours is just one of many universes, maybe an infinite number, each with its own set of physical laws. In a very loose analogy with Darwin's process of natural selection, some universes in Smolin's scheme survive longer than others, and some are therefore hospitable (or hostile) to the presence of living or intelligent creatures.[34]

Dyson compares *Star Maker* with that classic theofiction poem of 700 years ago, Dante's *Commedia*. Like Dante, Stapledon offers an inferno (the part of the book devoted to the ceaseless cycles of warfare in world after world), a purgatorio (the era when the worlds and galaxies begin to put aside their petty feuds and learn to coexist), and a paradiso (when the narrator meets and is overawed by the deity).

Freeman Dyson is Stapledon's greatest fan. From Stapledon, Dyson borrowed ideas of scientific interest (such as Dyson spheres), visions of gliding through space (motivating Dyson's work on Orion), and an appreciation for the diversity of life in the cosmos. Dyson's greatest borrowing from Stapledon seems to be the idea of a Star Maker–like deity, one who doesn't know everything and who learns as he goes along. This type of generic god is not unlike the one Dyson had in mind in laying out his five-step exploration of natural theology in his Gifford Lectures.

Dyson later learned that exactly such a theology, one featuring a non-omniscient, non-omnipotent god—had been promulgated by a sixteenth-century Italian-born theologian named Faustus Socinus.[35] Socinus, who spent most of his writing career in Poland, was a sort of Unitarian (disbelieving in the essential divinity of Christ). He promoted reason over superstition and was against war and killing of all kinds. The Catholic Church of Poland made things difficult for him.

Although Dyson admits to being only an amateur theologian—indeed, most of the time he seems to have very little patience for the subject—he has taken care to formulate a working hypothesis about what a grand spirit could be like, if such a thing exists at all. He combined Socinus's idea of a less than mighty experimental god with Stapledon's idea of a growing intergalactic, sympathetic, collective consciousness, a sort of adult version of his youthful Cosmic Unity idea:

> I do not make any clear distinction between mind and God. God is what mind becomes when it has passed beyond the scale of our comprehension. God may be considered to be either a world-soul or a collection of world-souls. We are the chief inlets of God on this planet at the present stage of development. We may later grow with him as he grows, or we may be left behind.[36]

Emily Dickinson anticipated (in Poem 632) this kind of meta-scientific theology in just a few lines of poetry:

> The Brain — is wider than the Sky —
> For — put them side by side —
> The one the other will contain
> With ease — and You — beside —

The Brain is deeper than the sea —
For — hold them — Blue to Blue —
The one the other will absorb —
As Sponges — Buckets — do —

The Brain is just the weight of God —
For — Heft them — Pound for Pound —
And they will differ — if they do —
As Syllable from Sound —

SOCIAL JUSTICE

For Freeman Dyson, religion is not a body of beliefs but a way of life—a literary and an ethical thing. Combine this with his adage that with knowledge comes responsibility, and you arrive at Dyson's motivation for working in the public interest.

In this respect, his career resembles that of the British scientist John Burdon Sanderson Haldane. Like Dyson, Haldane was precocious at mathematics, loved the arts, but made his name in science. Both worked on bombs: Haldane devised gun-launched grenades during World War I, while Dyson worked for Bomber Command in World War II. Both were government advisors: Haldane working with the Royal Navy on how to escape from sunken submarines, Dyson with the Royal Air Force on how to escape from falling airplanes. Both wrote essays about the future of science, especially biotechnology. Haldane predicted, for example, that someday many human births would come about by means of ectogenesis, meaning fertilization and even gestation outside the mother's body. He was much criticized for these daring predictions, which he published in 1924 in a booklet called *Daedalus; or Science and the Future.*

Although a notable genetic biologist, J. B. S. Haldane had by the 1930s become better known for his writing popularizing science and showing how it benefits society. As for Freeman Dyson, he too has become better known, by the public, for his essays and books than for his scientific research. His two books most in the Haldane spirit are *Imagined Worlds* (1997) and *The Sun, the Genome, and the Internet* (1999).

Imagined Worlds, like many of Dyson's works, began with a specific occasion, a series of lectures given in Jerusalem in 1995 about science and ethics. Many of the essays in this book show how science and technology can help or hinder the goal of arriving at a just society, one in which poor people have a chance to catch up to rich people.

Must science benefit the race? Isn't it enough that scientists are driven by curiosity to explore the unknown? If this results in practical benefits, so much the better. But surely we shouldn't insist on science being useful, much less requiring that it help in the moral task of telling right from wrong. Dyson disagrees. He believes science *can* play such roles. Science and values should not, as Jacques Monod desired, be held apart.

Steven Weinberg, siding with Monod, doesn't like mixing fact finding—which science does well—with fault finding. "Science can never explain any moral principle," said Weinberg. "There seems to be an unbridgeable gulf between 'is' questions from 'ought' questions."[37]

Jacob Bronowski sides with Dyson. Like Dyson, Bronowski was a Cambridge-educated mathematician interested in poetry who later turned to biology and became better known for his writing and lecturing than for his research. Bronowski actually edited a Cambridge literary magazine in the 1930s. In Bronowski's book *Science and Human Values* he tried vigorously to undo the compartmentalization of science away from the rest of society:

> There are, I hold, no atomic facts. In the language of science, every fact is a field—a crisscross of implications, those that lead to it and those that lead from it. . . . Scientific facts are never discovered by an individual, but by a community of instrument makers, theorists, engineers, and editors of journals where results are published. Scientists continually exercise value judgments—they subscribe to a social convention of truthfulness that is something like the Hippocratic oath. . . . Science is not a mechanism but a human progress, and not a set of findings but the search for them. Those who think that science is ethically neutral confuse the findings of science, which are, with the activity of science, which is not.[38]

It would be nice if we had the social equivalent of adaptive optics, analogous to what astronomers do to make celestial images sharper. This would allow us to take human problems and, with a clever momentary adjustment of lots of tiny mirrors, make a sequence of corrections that bring lives into ethical focus. We don't have such a process, but people like Bronowski and Haldane urge us to give it a try.

Dyson has practical suggestions to make. *The Sun, the Genome, and the Internet* has as its subtitle *Tools of Scientific Revolutions*. Here Dyson updated his Haldane-like short list of technologies most likely to help society. In the early 1980s Dyson's troika had consisted of genetics, space, and artificial intelligence. By the end of the 1990s this threesome had been replaced by biotechnology, solar energy, and the Internet. The book's tone is generally moralistic: market forces aren't enough to create a better society. Ethical considerations must drive technological decisions. The emphasis in this series of articles is on a quicker-smaller-cheaper approach to technology, whether in designing new medicines or in propelling spacecraft to distant planets. He wants to bring profitable industry to small towns, not in the form of heavy machines and energy-intensive factories, but in the form of small-scale but significant enterprises. Dyson hopes that society can exploit mobile, quickly advancing, economical technologies to level the playing field in life, to slow or reverse the migration from villages to overcrowded cities. He hopes that rural Mexican villages can become as wealthy as Princeton.[39] He knows this won't happen overnight.

Dyson's crusading zeal is long-standing. Another anonymous entry in the "Chamber Annals," the ledger where schoolboys at Winchester College could write about their fellow students, said of Dyson (then seventeen years old): "He never did anything unless it would (ultimately of course) benefit the race."

The Prodigal Son

The year after the retirement festival event at the Institute for Advanced Study, Winchester College also held a Dyson event. This was appropriate, since in terms of years spent in residence, the place with the greatest claim on Dyson, after Princeton, New Jersey, was his hometown of Winchester, England. Winchester was the place where he blossomed in mathematics and where in fell in love with literature.

In May 1995 Dyson received the highest honor for a Wykehamist, the name for a graduate of Winchester College: he was met *Ad Portas* (at the gate) of the school's central courtyard. There, on the cobbled square amid fourteenth-century brick walls, surrounded by the assembled robed students and faculty of the college, the Prefect of Hall—the senior student—commended Dyson, first in Latin and then in English, for his wide-ranging career. Dyson responded with a speech of his own.

He did what speakers are supposed to do. He put his audience at ease by telling them a nice tale of his childhood days sporting through the medieval halls and over the manicured lawns. As a college brat, the son of a teacher at the school, his pleasant memories of the place began long before he was a student. He quoted his mother: "Education is what is left over after you have forgotten everything you ever learned." In that sense, Dyson said, the most valuable education he'd gotten at the college was a feeling for style. He was referring to the classical authors taught at the school, such as Tacitus and Horace, but he might also have had in mind the style of his admired thinkers such as Feynman and Stapledon.

The rest of Dyson's speech was not what his audience had been expecting. He reminded them that the 1930s (his years at Winchester), like the 1960s, was a time of student rebellion against received ideas. He loved Winchester College, he said, for fostering friendships and for demanding intellectual rigor from its students. But he felt other emotions too:

> I hated the College for perpetuating the privilege of the ruling class. I hated it because it separated me from the mass of English people outside the sacred walls. I left the College in 1941 with the battle between love and hatred unresolved. I was not a loyal Wykemhamist. I left England and was glad to raise my children in America, partly to escape from the culture of boarding schools in which I had grown up. I sent my children to an American public day-school and did not need to think about sending them to Winchester.[40]

If Dyson had dismayed his listeners, he quickly made amends. He admitted that after fifty years, the hate was gone and only the love remained. He praised Winchester for its emphasis on academic excellence and for not being merely a "training ground for the rulers of a vanished empire." He regularly read the school newsletter, and was happy to see that the virtues that had made Winchester such an exemplary institution were still at work: insisting on unsparing honesty, maintaining historical perspective, and promulgating a splendid literary style.

Dyson had come back to Winchester, he said, as a prodigal son. "You are forgiving me for my disloyalty, for abandoning King and country at a time of hardship and rationed bread, for going away to live among the fleshpots of America. I am profoundly grateful for your forgiveness." He was again proud to be a Wykehamist.

CATHEDRAL

Freeman Dyson's winning the Templeton Prize took many people by surprise, including Dyson himself. At that time the Templeton Foundation gave its yearly prize for "progress in religion" and pegged the monetary value of the prize to be slightly ahead of that for the Nobel Prize. On May 9, 2000, Prince Philip, presented the prize to Dyson at a private ceremony at Buckingham Palace. This was followed a week later by a public ceremony at the National Cathedral in Washington, D.C. In receiving a million dollars, Dyson may have lost his amateur status as a theologian.

The National Cathedral is the largest and most resonant Gothic space in Washington. In Dyson's acceptance speech he sounded the themes that presumably had won him the award: that good works, such as helping the poor, are better than volumes of theology; that both science and religion are exciting because they grapple with mysteries; that God and mind, to his way of thinking, are one and actively present simultaneously at the microscopic level of atoms, at the macroscopic level of human beings, and at the cosmic level of the universe itself; that green technology, such as biotech and solar power, is reexerting its primacy over gray technology, such as machines and fossil fuels; that the marketing of high-tech goods and the capitalist system in general, useful as they may be, must be tempered by ethics; that this attention to social justice will both help to alleviate human misery and enlarge the global economy; and that we must utilize both windows, science and religion, if we're going to get a better view of our immense universe.[41]

How can you win a religion award and not be religious? Dyson's family upbringing had been middle-brow, nondogmatic Anglican. He claimed to have had no intense religious experiences during his long life, with the exception of his fervent and short-lived invention of Cosmic Unity as a fourteen-year-old. When he attends a church service, it is really "more for the music and the fellowship than for what you actually learn." He views the Christian Bible as literature.[42]

Was Dyson the new Haldane, promoting an ethical role for science? Was he the new Emerson, promoting a transcendental view of the world, one which said that vast realms of reality lay outside the scope of science? Was he a new William James urging us to appreciate the religious frame of mine? Or was he trying to take science backward? Was he trying to reinstate the eighteenth- or seventeenth-century collaboration of scientific and religious feeling? Was he actually saying that atoms behaved as if they had a life of their own rather than being inanimate objects buffeted by inanimate forces? Doesn't this un-install the materialist perspective that has brought so much clarity into the study of chemistry, physics, and biology over the past three centuries?

Plenty of his fellow scientists, even those who respect his research achievements or his ethical outlook, wonder about Dyson's love affair with religious sensibilities. Richard Dawkins, for example, reacted to Dyson's Templeton speech with mockery. He felt that Dyson's high stature, coupled with his perceived alliance with religion, would only encourage a belief in superstition. Dyson responded by lamenting Dawkins's harsh tone toward religion, which could drive away some students who might otherwise have considered scientific careers. Dawkins, famous for his own rigorous theory of the universe—the biological side of it, anyway—as being built from the ground up from patently inanimate atoms and ruthlessly selfish genes, questions Dyson's equating of God and mind. Dawkins, author of a book called *The God Delusion*, asks Dyson for evidence of God's existence. Dawkins much prefers Einstein's agnostic formula for God: "a name we give to that which we don't yet understand."[43]

What kind of a theologian is Dyson? Dawkins helpfully outlines a spectrum of theological perspectives. A theist, Dawkins says, believes in a supernatural intelligence that created the world and who goes on intervening in human affairs. A deist, on Dawkins's chart, also requires a supernatural creator, but one who does not intervene in subsequent times. A pantheist—Spinoza and Einstein are examples—does not see a supernatural God at work, but uses the word God as a metaphor for nature or for the universe. "Pantheism is sexed-up atheism," says Dawkins. "Deism is watered-down theism."[44] By these rules, Dyson should probably be placed somewhere between a pantheist and a deist whose God is a kind of meta-scientific, collective consciousness.

Dyson teems with metaphors for this consciousness: "The universe is like a fertile soil spread out all around us, ready for the seeds of mind to sprout and grow. Ultimately, late or soon, mind . . . will come into its heritage."[45]

What a strange career Dyson has had. Many people knew of the mathematician but not the engineer. Some had read of Dyson the physicist but not Dyson the diplomat. They had read *Disturbing the Universe* but not *Infinite in All Directions*. They might have known about Orion and TRIGA but not about Socinus. Then came the Templeton Prize. If for the sake of argument we could consider it to be the theological equivalent of the Nobel Prize, then Dyson's Nobel-worthy work would have been his Gifford Lectures in Aberdeen, and his essays collected into books over the previous twenty years.

Dyson had not won the million-dollar physics Nobel for his work in explaining away the infinities that arise when you get closer and closer to an electron, an accomplishment relying on an artful redefinition of the mass and charge of the electron. But he *had* won the comparably endowed prize for explaining the disparities that arise when you use science to explain the whole universe, physical and moral. Dyson's attempt at smoothing over potential conflicts between science and religion had swept the apparent incompatibility not under the carpet but out beyond the edge of the universe.

Emerson, 150 years ago, outlined a position similar to Dyson's: "The human mind seems a lens formed to concentrate the rays of the Divine laws to a focus, which shall be the personality of God. But that focus falls so far into the infinite that the form or person of God is not within the ken of mind."[46]

17. Splintering the Species

Dyson as Heretic

(1990–2010)

Does Freeman Dyson tell the truth? Not that we expect him to tell falsehoods, but does he, in the moral sense, speak true? Does he see things, inconvenient facts that others overlook?

On several important topics, as we'll see, he is out of step with mainstream scientific opinion. About the origin of life, about carbon dioxide emissions, about the desirability of human space travel, or about reconciling religion and science, Dyson is heretical. If possible he avoids being part of a majority.[1]

We might admire him for his courage to be different, but is he *right*? Is he seeing the true essence of these issues? Is he speaking truth to power? Is he a prophet, or is he just a cranky old man freed by tenure and now by retirement to say anything he wants?

Indeed, he allows himself to say in print what others might hold back. Some of what he says is disagreeable, although he himself is not a disagreeable personality. Lawrence Krauss has enormous respect for Dyson, but found that during their friendly arguments over cosmology Dyson seemed instinctively to take issue with most prevailing opinions about the universe.[2] Princeton physicist William Happer observes that at Jason meetings if a vote is being taken on some proposition and if a lone voice stands against the majority, that dissenter will usually be Dyson. But Happer sees Dyson as a hero for holding to his opposition opinions, especially on the issue of climate change, about which Dyson and Happer share many views.

Another Jason, Henry Abarbanel, is amused by Dyson's contrariety, but says that Dyson is never dogmatic. Rather, he is soft-spoken, patient in hearing others' views, unfailingly polite, almost shy.

263

Nevertheless, once Dyson begins to speak, he likes to lay out a clear case. Abarbanel insists that Dyson's waywardness isn't objectionable if you stop to examine his line of reasoning. That's exactly what we'll do in this chapter.

A person who goes against consensus on important issues is called a heretic. If, furthermore, the contrarian vision proves to be apt—if the heretical portent comes to pass—then we call him a prophet. Prophecy is retrospective.

Our modern cliché image of prophecy is of a gnarled man with long beard holding burnable views who foretells unpleasant events. Dyson denies being a prophet. He disdains "futurology" as a bogus science. Knowing many scientific and engineering principles, he does, however, try to arrive at some estimations of where present science and technology are taking us. This chapter will consequently investigate his provisional status as a prophet, at least in the generic sense of him being a person who, at the risk of being ostracized or taken as a fool, attempts to speak true.

What is truth? Daniel Dennett argues that scientists try to settle the truth of a dispute with facts and further statistical analysis. Experiments are for "discovering the truth (not the capital 'T' truth about everything, but just the ho-hum truth about this particular little factual disagreement)."[3] Dyson certainly revels in these little-t truths—such as measuring the whereabouts of an electron with a detector—but he doesn't shy away from large-T truths.

The Bible is filled with stories about the search for Truth. The Hebrew prophets held a vision of what a just society should be and presumed to tell others what God expects of people. Amos, Hosea, Jeremiah, and Isaiah spoke during the centuries when the kingdoms of Israel and Judah were menaced by the Assyrian and Babylonian empires to the north and east. But the real problem, as the Hebrew prophets saw the matter, was the backsliding of the Israelite tribes. In their religious observance they devoted too much attention to ritual and not enough to righteousness. The prophets didn't so much "prophesy" the future as anticipate the disasters coming about through the short-sighted actions of the nation. The prophets weren't magicians, but they were inspired to enunciate a vision of a better life and how to achieve it.

The Hebrew prophets dispensed their visions from places like the temple in Jerusalem or the Ishtar Gate in Babylon. Freeman Dyson's platform for speaking truth, since the mid-1990s, has been *The New*

York Review of Books (NYRB). This is the finest literary publication in the United States because it recruits the best writers to review the best books. Actually not all of the books have to be the best but only good enough to prompt a lively 4,000-word sally by a reviewer who is frequently more interesting to read than the book under scrutiny. So it is with many of the reviews by Dyson.

Dyson does more than review. He preaches, gently but persistently. It's time now to see how his long-ruminated considered opinions have coalesced into several set piece sermons. It's time to start summing up Reverend Dyson's career. What hand of heretic or prophet is he? Assyria no longer looms as a threat. Instead, other challenging issues absorb his interest. We'll look at four topics where Dyson presents not just views but visions: consciousness, climate, biotech, and the prospective peopling of the solar system.

EXTRAORDINARY KNOWING

Freeman Dyson had read about Uri Geller and wanted to see him in action. So in 1973 he and his family came to the show in San Diego. Geller advertised an ability to bend spoons and keys through psychic force, a claim that could fill an auditorium with curious people.

When Geller asked for a volunteer, Dyson's twelve-year-old daughter, Emily, gamely went up on stage with a key she'd brought from home. Geller held the key briefly, gave it back to Emily and, while she waited there patiently, he went on to explain how he could interfere with the atoms in the key using his special powers. When Emily was asked to produce the key again, there it was, bent! The performance continued with Geller undertaking further astonishing things with volunteers. Then he left.

The second half of the show fell to James Randi, a magician who goes by the name of the Amazing Randi. Randi proceeded to do the same things Geller had done, such as bending keys. The difference was that Randi explained how it was done. An able magician can palm the volunteer's key and return a substitute. Then, while talking to the audience, he secretly bends the key. Through further sleight of hand he returns the original key to the volunteer, who, along with the audience, is amazed when the now bent key is revealed.

Dyson related this anecdote many years later in a *NYRB* review of the book *Debunked!* by Henri Broch, whom Dyson identifies as the

French equivalent to the Amazing Randi, and Georges Charpak, a Nobel Prize–winning physicist. The book recounts examples of faulty statistical reasoning or outright fraud in the making of paranormal claims about otherwise unexplained phenomena, especially in the area of extrasensory perception (ESP). Dyson makes it plain that he approves of scientific proof and disapproves of fraud.[4]

Then he does something unexpected. After praising Charpak and Broch for their rigor, Dyson criticizes them for going too far. They go too far in dismissing paranormal phenomena, a category that includes such things as ESP. Dyson concedes that no scientific experiment has found evidence for ESP so far. But that doesn't mean it can't exist. Telepathy, communication between minds without the use of the five known senses, has not yet swayed the dials of scientific metering equipment. Maybe the equipment is unsuitable or ESP is too evanescent to be captured by scientific means.[5] Dyson gently chides the authors of *Debunked!* for not admitting these possibilities.

This is not what scientists want to hear—that certain phenomena are out of reach of measurement. Indeed, the history of science provides a high-contrast map of staked-out physical, chemical, biological, and psychological territory. One can say thousands of things about genes, volcanoes, electrons, and polar bears. Dyson himself has contributed to this cornucopia of knowledge. But not everything can be mapped, especially in the mental universe. How do you measure love or fear or jealousy?

Actually, Dyson doesn't say that there are subjects off limits to science, subjects that aren't open to scientific scrutiny. Rather, for many subjects there may be other ways of knowing that are perpendicular to the ways of science. His invocation of Niels Bohr's complementarity concept is crucial in the case of ESP. Just as light can be studied as waves and as particles but not both ways at the same time, so mental phenomena, Dyson argues, can be viewed with science, and with other means (art, religion, and so on), but not at the same time.[6] Emily Dickinson's poem about the brain doesn't help the neurologist; conversely, brain surgery says nothing about the insights inspired by Dickinson's poem. But together we get a fuller picture of the mental universe.

Dyson tells us in a postscript that his *NYRB* article called forth numerous letters to the editor, many from scientists outraged that he should have allowed that telepathy might exist, and many from ESP believers outraged by his assertion that proof of telepathy was still lacking. Thus Dyson remains happily in the middle, scorned, or at least questioned, by partisans on both sides. Niels Bohr's quantum principle of complementarity engendered a school of thought, referred to as the Copenhagen interpretation of quantum reality. By contrast, Dyson's principle of mental complementarity has few followers. His regard for the ineluctability of conscious activity will not likely be referred to as the "Princeton interpretation."

As a concession to orthodox scientific thinking, Dyson can cast his notion of ESP into practical technology. If you prefer thinking of ESP as being implemented with transmitters and receivers implanted in human brains, he can oblige you. A fleet of a hundred thousand implanted devices, he suggests, could dispatch the signals sent out by the hundred billion neurons making up a typical brain. All we needed, but didn't yet have, was the mechanism for converting neural signals into radio signals and the means for embedding so vast a broadcast array within sensitive brain tissue. "A society bonded by radiotelepathy," he says, "would experience human life in a totally new way."[7]

Speaking in these terms—implanted transmitters, bandwidth, and neurology—Dyson can sound reassuringly scientific. But in his earlier *NYRB* piece he wrapped up his discussion, seemingly with a note of pride, by disclosing that one of his grandmothers had been a "notorious and successful faith healer." He neglected to define what he meant by "successful" faith healing.[8]

Dyson contributed a Foreword to a 2007 book called *Extraordinary Knowing: Science, Skepticism, and the Inexplicable Powers of the Human Mind* by Elizabeth Lloyd Mayer. The book provides a history of ESP. Dyson is of two minds. As a scientist, he informs us, he doesn't believe the stories in the book. As a human being, however, he wants to believe. As a scientist he would have to suspect fraud or misguided interpretations of the purported paranormal events. As a human being he finds some of the stories convincing. "My own position," he tells us, is "that ESP is real, as the anecdotal evidence suggests, but cannot be tested with the clumsy tools of science."[9]

This is the heretical Dyson. Here and in other cases like this, in the opinion of some scientists, Dyson crosses the boundary of credulity. Has he become too much the theofictionist? Has he taken the novels of Olaf Stapledon and tales of Martian telepathy too much to heart? Others will say that by keeping an open mind, he is upholding the true spirit of science. Depending on whether or not you accept Dyson's vision of reality as valid, he is a prophet or a crank.

WETTER SAHARA, WARMER SIBERIA

Is Freeman Dyson a prophet? Does he speak true? We won't be able to decide until we see some of his visions borne out. Colonizing comets? Artificial intelligence? Origin of life? Too early to tell. Will the U.S. nuclear weapon inventory be reduced to zero? Possibly. Does extrasensory perception operate within or rather among human minds? It might take decades or centuries to answer. And that's the trouble with prophetical orations. It can take a lot of time, a biblical amount of time, to settle the issue of truth.

The specter of climate change approximates an end-of-days topic of seemingly biblical proportion. Dyson's heretical view of ESP is hidden away in obscure publications. Not so his heretical view of climate change. If you didn't know who Freeman Dyson was before, you got to know him when his face appeared on the March 29, 2009, cover of *The New York Times Magazine.*

The article inside was devoted mostly to portraying Dyson as a kindly gent, still active in scientific and public affairs at the age of eighty-five, fully alert, anything but senile, beloved and respected by friends and colleagues. But in the course of the interview, climate questions were asked and climate opinions were given, and it's as if the whole rest of the man's career didn't exist. Quantum science, test ban treaties, reactor engineering, tactical nukes in Vietnam, theofiction: none of that mattered. He was a climate skeptic. He wasn't sure that the dire warnings issued by the "experts" were believable. That's all many people knew about him.

How could a guy with such a splendid record of achievement, of wide experience, of vast perspective, arrive at such an unexpected and unorthodox attitude about climate? How could this liberal, antinuclear, Democrat-voting, good-deed-doing crusader side with the climate weirdos? At least on this topic he had become the heresiarch, the heretic in chief.

The profile naturally provoked letters to the editor of the *Times.* Dyson's writings in *The New York Review of Books* provoked letters. And now that there was a blogosphere, hundreds of worked-up amateur writers could also tender their opinions. To many Dyson was courageous, to many more a fool.

In a post-profile profile, Dyson was unapologetic. He was peeved because the *Times* had distorted his interest in the matter. The subject of global warming represented only a small part of his interests, he said. He didn't want a leading role in the climate debate. That was the job for younger researchers. He would, however, not shy away from stating his views on so important an issue. As if to prove the point, he provided just the kind of juicy quote guaranteed to keep the controversy smoldering. He was glad that some developing nations had decided to become rich, even if this meant a greater embrace of fossil fuels.[10] "I'm happy every time the Chinese and Indians make a strong statement about going ahead with burning coal."[11] He points to the economic resurgence of China—fueled by an immense energy expenditure—as being the "most important improvement in the human condition in the last half century."[12]

What bothered him most was what he perceived as a growing intolerance for unorthodox opinions among his scientific colleagues. Some scientists who should have maintained a rigorous standard of proof when it came to interpreting data were being led astray by charismatic figures, and then blamed others who did not join them. Dyson asserted that former vice president Al Gore—whose movie *An Inconvenient Truth* had been a cause célèbre the year before—was not just being alarmist but had become the chief propagandist for or the high priest of a secular religion, the religion of climate change, a belief system in which scientific facts are trumped by politics. Au contraire: some say that it is Dyson who ignores or misinterprets the facts.

How did he end up on the wrong side, as many of his scientific friends would say, of the carbon issue? Not surprisingly, the route by which Dyson came to hold his climate views is complicated. First of all, Dyson does not believe that the climate issue is a gigantic hoax. He does not deny that carbon dioxide levels in the atmosphere are rising and that human activity is largely to blame. He does not deny that climate is changing or that some bad consequences will follow, such as a rise in sea level and population dislocation. He does say, however, that some of the changes might be good. Warmer temperatures would, for example, extend the growing season in many places.

His main objection to the consensus scientific view, encapsulated in the reports of the Intergovernmental Panel on Climate Change, is that it rests on poor data and faulty computer models. Dyson suggests that computer simulations of climate, long-term weather, do an able job of accounting for carbon dioxide uptake in the sky and in the oceans but not in that other vast terrestrial sheath, the biosphere. We should be accurately measuring the worldwide growth of soil. Extra soil would retain extra CO_2. Dyson argues that forecasts of dire climate consequences—intensified droughts, floods, sea-level rise—are not sufficiently firm to justify the large expenditures needed to slow carbon emissions by doing such things as junking coal-fired power plants.

But couldn't we carry out those mitigation plans anyway, even if the models aren't quite right? Shouldn't we be cautious on a matter of such great importance? After all, we all take out fire insurance on our homes, even though the chance of our homes burning down is small. Dyson's answer to this objection is that undertaking an extensive and expensive program of carbon mitigation will distract society from other ills that loom larger: hunger, public health, literacy, poverty, corruption, and war. Each year millions succumb to these blights.

In the years leading up to the *New York Times* piece, Dyson published numerous review articles guardedly expressing his climate views. Only when the *Times* piece appeared, however, did his apostasy become well known. Amid the furor that followed were many assertions that although Dyson might be smart, he wasn't smart on *this* topic, and that he should mind his own business.

This turns out to be untrue. Recall that as early as 1972 and for several summers thereafter, he worked at Oak Ridge National Laboratory with colleagues such as Jack Gibbons (later President Clinton's science advisor) on early computer climate modeling. Doubts arose in his mind even then about the efficacy of modeling and the quality of soil data. He disagreed with his Jason colleagues over the same issues. This is when he became a climate heretic. He felt that the carbon problem, as it was beginning to form in scientific circles if not yet in the larger social consciousness, had more to do with soil management than with atmospheric mitigation.

He differed strongly enough from his Oak Ridge associates that he wrote a manifesto about his agricultural scheme.[13] In a research paper in 1977 in a journal called *Energy*, he suggested that a hypothetical rise in atmospheric CO_2 might be addressed by capturing it with trees or swamp plants bioengineered to grow larger roots. The roots, he said, would incorporate the CO_2. This carbon would stay put in the form of new topsoil.[14]

But maybe we don't need to worry, since the extra CO_2 and the rising warmth it brings might be a positive benefit. Can this be true? Can such a colossal intervention in nature be good for anyone? Dyson has been rehearsing an answer for several decades. Actually, one of his fullest treatments of the subject came very early, as a 1974 speech at an energy meeting in Madrid. He pointed to several examples of past or future environmental modification. We saw these examples in Chapter 11: a greener England, a wetter Sahara, and a warmer Siberia, and a possible doubling of the arable land on Earth.[15]

Global warming, Dyson likes to point out, is not global. Warming is much more pronounced in dry places than in wet places, in cold places more than in warm places, in polar areas more than in tropical areas, at night more than during the day, at high elevations more than in lowlands, and in winter more than in summer.[16] These disparities make climate change hard to pin down as being *one* thing, a single thing to be dreaded or corrected at great cost. How can we cure the patient if we haven't yet diagnosed the illness?

Vigilant scientists and engineers have learned to look for the hidden costs or unintended consequences of new technology. Dyson likes to add that there are also hidden costs of saying *no* to certain innovations—whether in the development of new medicines or the introduction of new crops or the deployment of new modes of transportation.

Remaking nature is exactly what the human species has been doing since the advent of agriculture 12,000 years ago, Dyson insists. Animal husbandry, the culling of grain species, in vitro fertilization, the diversion of rivers, the burning of forests, are just a few of the large-scale human interventions. Many of the highly regarded plant and animal species in England now are nonnative. Pollution and other technological depredations are still problems in some areas, but major strides have been made in cleaning up cities and rivers. England is again a pretty good place in which to live despite many layers of artificiality.

Carbon Humanism

> "First comes feeding, then morality"
> *The Threepenny Opera,* BERTOLT BRECHT

But what if greenhouse warming does *not* result smoothly in an agricultural cornucopia in Siberia and the Sahara? And what if bioengineering and other carbon mitigation schemes aren't up to handling the great carbon burden? Well, then we might just have to confront a great social divide, one not mentioned in the *Times* article.

This is the prospective conflict between naturalists and humanists. These two communities overlap considerably, and many adherents would be reluctant to have to decide between these two worthy isms. In Dyson's view, feeding people comes first:

> *If people do not have enough to eat, we cannot expect them to put much effort into protecting the biosphere. In the long run, preservation of the biosphere will only be possible if people everywhere have a decent standard of living. The humanist ethic does not regard an increase of carbon dioxide in the atmosphere as evil, if the increase is associated with worldwide economic prosperity, and if the poorer half of humanity gets its fair share of the benefits.*[17]

Can it be that simple? The Chinese burn coal to make electricity, while on the other side of the Pacific, Americans would capture carbon dioxide to make dirt? Isn't Dyson being shortsighted? By feeding those alive now by burning more coal, aren't we choking those alive a hundred years from now? Dyson's answer to this objection is often to say that unanticipated technological innovations and new scientific insights will rescue us from seemingly intractable problems.

Should we count on these future innovations? Many scientists, even those who consider themselves as Dyson's friends, say that his optimism is misplaced, and that he overestimates the ability of bioengineering to produce plants that store more carbon in their roots. One recent study published in the journal *Science,* for example, shows that crop yield does *not* necessarily go up for increased levels of CO_2.[18] Some critics go further and say that Dyson gets facts wrong. Computer models, they say, are much better nowadays than they were during Dyson's summers at Oak Ridge.

As a scientist, Dyson ought to amend his views as new information becomes available. But the heretic is not recanting. No new carbon data or improved climate models have persuaded him to change his mind. He sticks to his food-first imperative. We can try to reduce our use of fossil fuels, he says, but if the unwelcome choice lies between people starving or keeping the coal-fired generators running, then we should keep burning coal.

This argument seems all the more contradictory for a man who has several times written and spoken about the differences between what he calls green and gray technology. Gray things include physics, factories, plutonium, and technology in general. Green things include biology, gardens, manure, and children. Dyson usually roots for green over gray. He makes sure to say that gray things are important; gray thinking has facilitated many good things, such as Newton's laws of motion, modern medicine, fast transport, higher literacy, and more food. But in the long run green things hold a higher promise of making the world more livable.

Dyson cannot be exactly a naturalist or humanist. Instead he tries to reconcile them, or at least enunciate the nature of their divergence:

> *Naturalists believe that nature knows best. For them the highest value is to respect the natural order of things. Any gross human disruption of the natural environment is evil. Excessive burning of fossil fuels is evil. Changing nature's desert, either the Sahara desert or the ocean desert, into a managed ecosystem where giraffes or tuna fish may flourish, is likewise evil. Nature knows best, and anything we do to improve upon Nature will only bring trouble.*

And humanists?

> *The humanist ethic begins with the belief that humans are an essential part of nature. Through human minds the biosphere has acquired the capacity to steer its own evolution, and now we are in charge. Humans have the right and the duty to reconstruct nature so that humans and the biosphere can both survive and prosper. For humanists, the highest value is harmonious coexistence between humans and nature. The greatest evils are poverty, underdevelopment, unemployment, disease, and hunger, all the conditions that deprive people of opportunities and limit their freedoms. . . . The humanist ethic accepts the responsibility to guide the evolution of the planet.*[19]

Does it have to be humanist or environmentalist? We'd like to say this is a false dichotomy. But then wouldn't we too, like Dyson, be guilty of wishful thinking, hoping or expecting that technological fixes, such as wonderful alternative energy sources that allow us to cut back on the use of fossil fuel, will rescue us from having to choose between mass starvation and climate catastrophe?

Current scientific evidence suggests Dyson is almost surely wrong about the good consequences of climate change outweighing the bad. But he is not wrong to insist that two billion Chinese and Indians should aspire to live as well as Westerners. How to accommodate these aspirations into a working model for global civilization will probably be more difficult even than reducing carbon dioxide emissions.

One can compare Dyson's climate dilemma to another drama. In Henrik Ibsen's 1882 play, *An Enemy of the People*, set in a small Norwegian town, a moralistic doctor helps to develop a system of therapeutic baths that will soon bring wealth to the citizens in the form of a lucrative tourist trade. Then the doctor discovers that the water system is polluted. He takes this news to his brother, the town's mayor. The doctor is shocked when the mayor tells him to keep the news to himself. The doctor does not keep it to himself and instead indignantly goes to the public with his admittedly unwelcome revelation. Rather than being acclaimed for his honesty, he is shunned as a troublemaker.

If we were recasting the climate story as the pursuit or questioning of inconvenient scientific truths, how would we assign the parts of mayor and doctor? If John Adams were to write an opera called *Doctor Climate*, what part would we give to Freeman Dyson and which to Al Gore?

Of course this is a silly comparison to make. Both Gore and Dyson seem to be honestly confronting the same set of facts. Neither of them is an enemy of the people. Many humanists and naturalists alike have respect for the accomplishments and courage of both the former vice president and the professor. But can Dyson and Gore both be right on the issue of climate change? It could be more apt to say that one of them doesn't necessarily have to be wrong. The uncomfortable reality here is that because of the importance of this issue, something will have to happen. Long before definitive scientific facts can be delivered, legislators, businesses, and citizens will have to decide on a course of action.

PET DINOSAURS

If you find Dyson's climate views discomforting, wait until you see what he says about biotechnology. Prophecy and heresy go together. Heretics diverge from orthodoxy. They are splinterers. Heretics are also prophets if, in the course of time, their vision is vindicated. Many are heretics, few prove prophets.

Prophets look for signs of change wherever they can. In a lecture at Boston University in 2005 Freeman Dyson recalls taking his grandson to a reptile exposition in San Diego. Like a dog show or an automotive show, a variety of new reptile types, specially bred, were on display at the expo. That day, Dyson's immediate preoccupation was escaping without having to buy his grandson a snake. But the occasion of his visit inspired a *New York Review* essay about the pace of biotechnology developments.

Dyson likes to view the world in terms of doublets: theorists and experimentalists, concepts and tools, naturalists and humanists. One of his favorite dichotomies, as we have seen, is the division of technology into green and gray. Both parts of this duet are necessary. In the history of technology and science, many gray revolutions are evident. The semiconducting world of electronics and its offspring, the Internet and email, are all around us. Physics-based science and gray-based technology are still powerful.

But biology had become larger than physics in terms of its impact on the economy, larger in its immediate contribution to human welfare, and potentially more portentous in its implications for ethics.[20]

Dyson looks at the growth of the immense computer game industry, enabled by the advent of the personal computer, as being a foretaste of our new biological world. This new market won't just be for scientists at elite labs. Dyson expects bio amateurs to get involved the way amateur astronomers, with their sophisticated scopes and software, contribute to making modest celestial discoveries.[21] Popular biotech gaming can be bigger than that:

> *The final step in the domestication of biotechnology will be biotech games, designed like computer games for children down to kindergarten age but played with real eggs and seeds rather than with images on a screen. Playing such games, kids will acquire an intimate feeling for the organisms that they are growing. The winner could be the kid whose seed grows the prickliest cactus, or the kid whose egg*

*hatches the cutest dinosaur. These games will be messy and possibly
dangerous.*[22]

Cutest dinosaur? For those who would be conjuring up the horrors
of *Jurassic Park* unfolding in their own basements, Dyson offers an ad-
dendum. "Rules and regulations will be needed to make sure our kids
do not endanger themselves and others. The dangers of biotechnology
are real and serious."[23] His caveat seems rather matter-of-fact. Should
we be alarmed? What are the rules? Who makes the rules? Who en-
forces the rules about dinosaurs in the home?

Dyson once sat on a committee of citizens in Princeton appointed
to assess the relative hazards and benefits of genetic research at the local
university. In the end they decided that the research should proceed.[24]
Dyson doesn't pretend there are no problems ahead. He regards the
discovery of DNA manipulation techniques to be just as significant for
biologists as the discovery of fission was for physicists.[25] "Whoever can
read the DNA language can also learn to write it."[26] Dyson has spent
years trying to head off a nuclear war, but even he figures that a nucleic
war, one exploiting biological manipulations in some fiendish way—
of the kind described by H. G. Wells in his novel *The Island of Doctor
Moreau*—could be worse.[27]

Biotech is here now whether you like it or not. One of the most controversial biotech topics is genetically modified (GM) food. Dr. Moreau
did his experiments on a remote Pacific island and Dyson's pet dinosaurs won't be escaping from apartments into Central Park this year.
But "frankenfood," as GM food is sometimes called, is available to
consumers right now at the corner grocery, at least in the United States.

GM food was a prime topic of discussion at the January 2001 meeting of the World Economic Forum, held annually for many years in
Davos, Switzerland. Here, on a mountaintop retreat, the same one depicted in Thomas Mann's novel *The Magic Mountain*, lords of finance and
heads of state gather. The celebrities are supplemented with artists and
scientists who, as Dyson points out, are there to provide entertainment.
The 2001 meeting featured a food fight between Europe and Africa. In
Dyson's characterization of the dispute, many Europeans stood against
genetically modified food, since they saw biotech innovation primarily
in terms of the potential for catastrophe, such as the release of difficult-
to-reverse biological forces into a fragile ecology. Even a tiny chance of
disaster, they maintained, was too risky, considering the stakes.

Wearing a necktie even when he hiked,
FJD contemplates the view up. Near June
Lake, east of Yosemite National Park, part
of the Sierra trip, 1955.

Self portrait of Verena Huber Dyson, 1955. A serious photographer, with a darkroom set up in the home, she was contemplating a return to mathematics research.

TOP First Christmas in the new house on Battle Road Circle, only a few blocks from the Institute for Advanced Study in Princeton, where FJD was a professor. The Dyson family in 1956 included (left to right) Freeman, Esther, Verena, George, and Katarina. A month later the family fell apart.

ABOVE Imme Jung, the second Mrs. Dyson, with baby Mia, c. 1964, in Germany. As her four daughters were growing up, Imme would take them to visit her family in Germany, many times to help celebrate her own mother's birthday. FJD would sometimes attend.

OPPOSITE TOP FJD receives the Templeton Prize from Prince Philip at Buckingham Palace, London, May 9, 2000. Dyson was surprised to win the prize. The exact nature of the prize had changed over the years, but generally it had been given to a person who has helped to foster spiritual or religious values. Many recent winners have been scientists. Dyson, writes occasionally about spiritual values, but doesn't consider himself to be conventionally religious.

OPPOSITE BOTTOM FJD with his grandson Randy Reid, son of Dorothy Dyson, winter 2012, northern California. Randy is building a telescope, which shortly thereafter was used to record some fine pictures of the moon. FJD and his wife try to visit their children and grandchildren as often as they can.

ABOVE Son George Dyson, stepdaughter Katarina Halm, and father Freeman Dyson in Vancouver, c. 2000. FJD and Katarina speak frequently on the phone. She can still recite poems they discussed with each other more than fifty years before.

TOP Verena Huber Dyson in 2006. After being divorced from FJD in 1958 she never remarried. She had a long career as a mathematician and philosopher.

ABOVE Imme Dyson and her four daughters, Dorothy, Emily, Rebecca, and Mia, in San Francisco, October 2009, at the Susan Komen 60-Mile Walk.

TOP FJD looks at his 2007 Christmas present from Esther, a kit which can be used to produce a partial genetic map from a saliva sample. Esther gave kits to more than twenty Dyson family members.

ABOVE Meeting in Greenland, June 2007, where the subject of discussion was not the melting of the iceshelf but rather the nature of artificial life. FJD is just left of center, with a white shirt. Three people to his left is Steven Chu, then director of the Lawrence Berkeley National Laboratory and later U.S. Energy Secretary.

TOP LEFT FJD in 2008 at a celebration of his eighty-fifth birthday at a fluid-dynamics conference at Rutgers University. At this meeting, which he attends almost every year, he mingles with a set of long-standing friends working in that research field. He has several such sets of friends associated with his many interests. His priorities in life, he once said, were family first, friends second, work third.

LOWER LEFT Imme and Freeman at Star City, the cosmonaut training center outside Moscow where a ceremonial yurt had been used in preparing cosmonauts for their eventual landing in Kazakhstan. Esther Dyson had trained as a backup cosmonaut for a space mission in 2009, and Imme and Freeman were part of the small entourage allowed to view the launch. In the end Esther did not fly. On the way home, Freeman gave a lecture in Moscow.

RIGHT FJD with his youngest grandchild: Freeman John Dyson holds Jack Freeman Dyson, 2010. FJD has five daughters and one son, and the son (George) himself has a daughter but no sons, so it might seem that the Dyson name would peter out. However, FJD's daughter Rebecca Dyson (Jack's mother) decided, with her husband, that their children would retain the Dyson name. FJD's necktie was once owned by Albert Einstein.

Many Africans, by contrast, saw the problem in terms of the present danger of malnutrition. Feeding a burgeoning population is a problem needing solution now. Dyson felt that genetic modifications in food would help alleviate the palpable ecological problems already under way in Africa now: overgrazing, pollution of water supplies, lack of hygiene, and overcrowding in cities.[28]

Prophets like to dispute with other prophets. At Davos the specter of edible biotech reached a high point in the matched talks by Dyson and computer designer Bill Joy, founder of Sun Microsystems. Joy argued that high technology, including the machines he himself had invented, might be creating conditions under which determined madmen or small terrorist groups could contrive weapons of great destructiveness. These deadly instruments wouldn't necessarily depend on explosions but rather on rapidly dispersed chemical or biological agents.

The greater danger might come, Joy intimated, not from renegades with deliberate malice in mind but rather from well-meaning scientists inadvertently unleashing hazardous organisms into the ecosphere in the form of nanoscopic materials or ingested substances containing microbes that could later result in cancer.[29]

Dyson urged strict guidelines for biotech work. Such guidelines have been in place for several decades, he pointed out, ever since the first recombinant DNA work in the 1970s, experiments in which segments of genetic material were removed from or added to a chromosome. The main impetus behind the research was not to produce games or frivolously spawn new forms of pets but to understand disease and to feed starving people.

In the spring of 1997 Dyson gave a series of lectures at the New York Public Library about tools that underlay progress in science. He expected these tools to help level the playing field between poor rural and rich urban societies. This became a central concern of his—how science and engineering could help to further social justice by narrowing the gap between haves and have-nots and an important theme of his book *The Sun, the Genome, and the Internet.*

Genetically enhanced food is just one component of the biotech revolution. Why not turn the creatures of the Earth into factories? Grow flowers with silicon leaves that could harvest sunlight at 15 percent efficiency rather than plants with green leaves yielding only 1 percent. Bioengineer worms that can mine metals from the earth, or termites that eat junked autos, or trees that turn sunlight directly into fuel.[30]

Early biotech inventions are evident. Human population skyrocketed over the past century and a half owing to better sanitation, the introduction of antibiotics, and the advent of artificial fertilizer. According to Princeton biologist Lee Silver, half of the nitrogen passing through human bodies comes from food grown using that fertilizer, which is processed in factories chemically extracting nitrogen from air.[31] Millions would starve in the absence of this biotech invention.

Dyson credits Silver with teaching him a lot about the awesome implications of genetic research. Tinkering with animal chromosomes, for example, allows animals to manufacture parts or substances for human bodies. Bacteria began making human insulin in the 1980s. Silver predicts that pigs will one day manufacture human skin, while cows will produce human blood.[32] With cloning and stem cell technology, we'll be able to grow simple human organs, such as livers, within the next ten years or so, Silver estimates; complex organs, such as the heart, will take longer.[33]

In 1999 Dyson spent a semester at Gustavus Adolphus, a small Christian-oriented college in Minnesota. Most of the students taking the class, "Genetics and the Moral Universe," were biology majors. Class discussion, not surprisingly, took up bioethics issues such as human cloning, organ donation, denying expensive medical procedures for very old patients, and moving genes from one species to another.

One of the professors who taught this course with Dyson, chemist Lawrence Potts, remembers Dyson's modesty, humility, and gentleness. Ever in demand as a speaker, Dyson had to make frequent departures from the campus. It was Potts's pleasurable task to take Dyson to and from the airport. On these drives the men spoke about many things: how to care for aging parents, how to raise children, and how science kept changing. Whenever he attended meetings of the American Physical Society, Dyson enjoyed watching odd sessions where speakers would describe perpetual motion or faster-than-light-speed travel.[34]

MEET VICTOR FRANKENSTEIN

Bioethics classes taught in colleges can go only so far in allaying concerns about biotech advances. Lingering worries, even dread, still cling to the notion that somewhere, most likely in a dank basement laboratory, some infernal adjustment is proceeding. It's one thing to tinker with the genetic makeup of pine trees. But now they're going to do it with humans.

Mary Shelley, beside the shores of Lake Geneva and urged on by her husband, Percy Shelley, and his friend Lord Byron, conceived of a yarn about a scientist (is he mad?) who makes an artificial man from (exhumed) parts of other men and then jump-starts his (or should it be "its"?) nervous system by siphoning electricity from a thunderstorm. The exhumations are a matter for the civic authorities but bestowing the spark of life is surely only for God alone. Twitching the patchwork cadaver into living flesh is what made Dr. Frankenstein's Promethean action blasphemous. Frankenstein suffered grievously for it.

Modern biologists don't use atmospheric electricity to create life. Instead of secretly stitching sundry organs from a crypt, they delicately restitch genes in government-funded labs. Freeman Dyson's practical involvement in this work is peripheral. The one time he actually used DNA manipulation equipment, as part of a Jason site visit, his trial experiment failed.[35]

Dyson points to Silver's particular expertise, extending genetic biology to human reproduction, a subject Silver calls "reprogenetics," in underscoring the solemn importance of biotech. One of the most powerful human instincts is the desire by couples to have children. One of the great triumphs of fertility science was the development of in vitro fertilization. Millions of healthy babies have been conceived this way, babies that would probably not have come to life otherwise. There was a time when such human fertilization outside the womb was considered by many to be immoral. Now the process is routine.

What about the use of genetic science to combat disease by manipulating the fertilized egg cell through the selective removal or substitution of genes implicated in specific diseases?[36] Curing disease sounds like a good thing. How about using genetic science to produce "superior" children. What if substituting certain genes would result in higher intelligence or beauty? Are we now in a position to play God and make the human race into anything we want? Would only rich families be able to afford this expensive form of eugenics? The next step after that would be do-it-yourself genetic kits. "Having reprogenetic babies at home," Dyson said, "might become a popular hobby, like desk-top publishing today."[37] Writing genomes will become an art form, sort of like writing screenplays.[38] Dyson, who revels in this sort of provocative writing, is not necessarily advocating such genetic alterations, especially if they unleash a class war between the rich, who can afford enhancements, and the poor, who cannot.

More disturbing scenarios are out there. Silver says that it is possible for humans and chimps to mate and bear living offspring. One of his female students even offered to donate an egg cell for the sake of attempting such an experiment.[39] No responsible scientist is calling for such experiments, but they remain possibilities.

Dyson says different things on different occasions about altering the human genome. At an invitation-only convocation of scientists he had the following to say about human genetic modifications:

> We would be wise to keep ourselves as much as possible the way we are, and I hope we will be successful in it. I don't see any great likelihood if you monkey around with humans that you'll produce anything much better.[40]

But another time he'll say something else. Biotech tinkering won't just alter the human genome, but splinter it. Reprogenetics will lead to a branching of the human race: "When desires for different ways of living can be translated into reality, the diversity of desires will be translated into a diversity of species."[41]

Along with this splitting Dyson expects irresolvable conflicts to arise. As recently as 30,000 years ago at least two human species (or subspecies) coexisted, *Homo neanderthalensis* and *Homo sapiens*. Interspecies rivalry would probably have been much more pronounced than any intertribal or interdenominational strife of the kind that spurred the Children of Israel out of Egypt or launched the *Mayflower* across the Atlantic.

Dyson likes to end his books with a bang. With *The Sun, the Genome, and the Internet*, he concludes with a vision of multiple human species:

> Sooner or later, the tensions between diverging ways of life must be relieved by emigration, some of us finding new places to live away from the Earth while others stay behind. In the end we must travel the high road into space, to find new worlds to match our new capabilities. To give us room to explore the varieties of mind and body which our genomes can evolve, one planet is not enough.[42]

POLYNESIANS ON PLUTO

Freeman Dyson is a preacher; he brings not brimstone but hope. He speaks about the future not to make specific predictions, not to scare people, but to encourage them. All of Dyson's heresies—nuclear, religious, climate, biotech—can be aggregated into a single grand heresy: that humanity will largely outgrow its home planet and will migrate into the outer parts of the solar system and across the galaxy. What makes this heretical? Isn't space colonization the theme of a thousand romantic science fiction thrillers?

What makes Dyson's off-Earth scenario heretical is that, like the Hebrew prophets, he sees the future as a mixture of glorious adventure and lengthy warfare. Not against some distant foe but against ourselves. He anticipates that as genetic experimentation proceeds, and as the human race occupies new niches in the cosmos—the interplanetary equivalent of Darwin's finches inhabiting the various Galápagos Islands—it will split into numerous breeding species. Not only is one Earth not enough, but apparently one human species is not enough.

In this breathtakingly grand endeavor, there is no such thing as inherent safety as there is in the design of the TRIGA reactor. Whether in terraforming the Earth, rearranging the geology and ecosystems to suit human society, or in refining the human genome, there are great risks. Paraphrasing J. B. S. Haldane on the future of science, Dyson remarked "that the progress of science is destined to bring enormous confusion and misery to mankind unless it is accompanied by progress in ethics."[43]

A prophet must be steadfast. Dyson did not come tardily to his comprehensive view of human development. Much of that vision was present in a 1972 lecture he made at Birbeck College in London. The speech celebrated the reissue of *The World, the Flesh, and the Devil*, a 1929 book by biologist John Desmond Bernal (1901–1971), who, like Dyson, seemed to be ahead of his time in writing about human evolution. Bernal's title referred to an ambitious program to deal with what he saw as the chief constraints on humanity's further development. The first threat consisted of the material conditions of our world, including a finite food supply. The second threat was our own physical mortality. The third was the irrational side of human nature, which often led to strife.

A prophet sometimes invokes other prophets. Dyson, who would later formulate his own list of most pertinent technologies, recounted Bernal's proposed solution. In 1929 Bernal suggested that (1) to surmount material wants on Earth, human colonization of space was necessary; (2) to overcome bodily ailments we should develop artificial implantable organs; and (3) to overcome human irrationality some kind of emotion control was required.[44]

Dyson subscribes to the first two points but disagrees with Bernal on the third. Dyson sees the emotions not as a drawback but as the very heart of what it is to be human: "Human beings cannot be human without a generous endowment of greed and love. . . . The central complexity of human nature lies in our emotions, not in our intelligence."[45]

The human trek out of Africa took thousands of years and it might take that long to plant human colonies on Titan or on comets. Predicting how such a colossal journey will unfold is impossible, and Dyson is sure that qualitative changes will outweigh all quantitative changes we can foresee;[46] biotechnology will trump any mere innovations in rocketry we can imagine;[47] the main problems to be overcome in launching extraplanetary trips will not be economic but spiritual in nature.[48]

Dyson likens himself to the sixteenth-century Englishman Richard Hakluyt. Just as Dyson wrote about cross-galactic schemes from his Princeton armchair, so Hakluyt, from his university post in Oxford, promoted English colonies in the cross-oceanic land that would later be called Virginia.[49] Hakluyt, a true Jason, hoped the Admiralty would enlarge its navigational skills, and he advised Queen Elizabeth to consider the economic and cultural benefits of expanding her realm in North America. Hakluyt urged Englishmen to venture out onto the ocean, but he never went himself, just as Dyson will not be shot into space, much less visit the rings of Saturn, his Orion goal in the 1950s.

For the immediate future space travel is a joke, Dyson says.[50] It will, however, eventually happen. Occasionally his enthusiasm prompts him to make overly specific estimates for achieving cheap space travel—by the year 2085, he once said, as long after Sputnik as the *Mayflower* came after Columbus.[51] But usually he is circumspect, and for good reason. Without knowing the time frame for any of the intermediate steps he can't make hard predictions. He imagines that something like this will happen: we will develop new economical forms of transport, such as solar sailing; we will bioengineer plants that can adapt to low temperatures, gravity, and pressure, and, having sent these plants on ahead, we will eventually shelter in the greenhouses grown by the plants on the surfaces of distant moons and comets.

All this, or something like it, will happen because it must happen, unless the human race destroys itself first right here on Earth. Irresistibly, he reaches for the sublime:

> *This unimaginably great and diverse universe, in which we occupy one fragile bubble of air, is not destined to remain forever silent. It will one day be buzzing with the murmur of innumerable bees, rustling with the flurry of feathered wings, throbbing with the patter of little human feet. The expansion of life, moving out from Earth into its inheritance, is an even greater theme than the expansion of England across the Atlantic. As Hakluyt wrote that there is under our noses the great and ample country of Virginia, I am saying that there is under our noses the territory of nine planets, forty moons, ten thousand asteroids, and a trillion comets.*[52]

And if even that isn't enough real estate, Dyson will tell you how living organisms can hitch a ride on gravitationally ejected comets for journeys to stars beyond our own.[53]

18. Long-Term Thinking

Dyson as Storyteller

What makes for renown? In a biography of Franz Kafka, the literary scholar Reiner Stach succinctly enumerates the factors:

> *The wider the net an individual casts in the world, the greater the likelihood that we will be captivated and impressed. Possessions, achievements, influence, power, sexual partners, descendants, admirers, successors, enemies: it is this horizontal dimension, the social extension of a person's life, that rescues the life from the undertow of anonymity.*[1]

Dyson has cast a wide net. His most palpable legacy is, of course, his family. In 1950 he expressed himself to Verena, his first wife, as wanting six children, and in the end that is what he got. And from these children he has sixteen grandchildren.

Dyson's eldest child, Esther Dyson, is an investor and philanthropist. She lives in Manhattan and travels the world. One of the companies she has backed is called 23andMe, named for the twenty-three pairs of chromosomes packaged within each of the trillions of cells making up the human body. One of the main products sold by 23andMe is a service for reading a specimen of DNA from an individual and then comparing it to similar readings for other people.

As a Christmas present in 2007, Esther gave her extended family the gift of genetic knowledge. She sent test kits (twenty-six in all) to Freeman, Imme, and many of her siblings and nephews and nieces. So, instead of spreading the names of those six children and sixteen grandchildren across a family tree made of mere parchment, something much more quantitative could be displayed. From a sample of saliva an analysis for selected segments of DNA can be formed. Each person's genetic map is unique, but that map reveals the genetic overlap with relatives. On average a child will inherit half of his operative genes from his mother and half from his father. A grandchild and grandparent share genes at the one-fourth level.

Esther is fond of posting family photographs on the Internet via Flickr, a company she supported as an early investor. She also posted some of the results from these DNA scans. This high-precision family history showed, for example, that genetically speaking Marcus Scott, son of Emily Dyson, is a bit more related to his grandfather Freeman (56 percent of Marcus's maternal-related DNA) than to his grandmother Imme (44 percent). Conversely Marcus's brother Mitchell is genetically a bit further from Freeman (43 percent) and closer to Imme (57 percent).[2]

This is the genetic Dyson. How about the current demographical Dyson?

THE DYSONS NOW

George Dyson lives in the port of Bellingham, Washington, about halfway between Seattle and Vancouver. He still builds kayaks and owns an expansive book-lined factory-showroom overlooking the harbor. He is better known now as a historian of science and technology. In addition to *Baidarka* and *Darwin Among the Machines*, he has written *Project Orion* (2006), a book about his father's nuclear rocketship, and *Turing's Cathedral: The Origins of the Digital Universe* (2012). He is divorced and the father of a grown daughter, Lauren.

At holidays Freeman and Imme try to visit as many of the children as possible. Dorothy Dyson is a veterinarian specializing in large animals. She lives in Redding, near the north end of California's central valley. She is divorced and the mother of three: Randall, Donald, and George. Emily is a cardiologist and mother of four: Max, Mitchell, Marcus, and Lucy. She lives in San Diego, not far from where Freeman often brought his family for Jason summer work. Mia is both a nurse and a minister. She lives in Pownal, Maine, and has four children: Bryn, Tess, Liam, and Aidan. Rebecca is a radiologist and lives in Mount Shasta, not far from Dorothy. She too is the mother of four:

Charles, Clara, James, and Jack. Two of Freeman's daughters have undergone treatment for breast cancer.

Verena Huber-Dyson taught mathematics and philosophy at the University of Calgary for many years. In 1988 she became an emerita professor. She now lives in a retirement home not far from George in Bellingham. Verena's daughter Katarina lives in Vancouver. Katrina occasionally talks on the phone with her stepfather. Freeman's other immediate family relative is his sister, Alice. Now in her nineties, she moved in the spring of 2010 into a retirement residence. It fell to Imme to sell the home in Winchester, England, that Sir George and Lady Dyson bought in the early 1950s. Freeman is still close to Alice and visits her once or twice a year.

Freeman Dyson has lived in the same Princeton home since 1956. It sits on a leafy lane not far from the Institute. The homestead includes a large backyard with plentiful flower beds tended scrupulously by Imme. She runs ten miles every day to stay in training. Recently she won a half marathon (for her age group) in Shasta, California. Freeman often accompanies Imme to running events in order to cheer her on. Sometimes he sits in the car reading books.

The interior of the Dyson homestead is darkly paneled. Photographs on the wall include one of Freeman's father, Sir George, conducting a musical work; one is of Freeman at the *Ad Portas* ceremony at Winchester College; and one of him with a daughter on her wedding day.

A framed award meets the visitor upon entry near the stairway leading upstairs. Of all Dyson's awards, which one does he choose for this prominent patch of wall? It's the Oersted Medal, given by the American Association of Physics Teachers. For a man who professes not to like teaching—at least not the supervision of students through the doctorate mill—this might seem like a curious choice. On the other hand, the essence of Dyson's career, through his writing and lecturing, has been to teach.

As this book makes clear, Dyson hasn't had one career, but many. Even now, in his upper eighties, he continues to travel the world, adding to his storehouse of experience. This last chapter surveys recent events in his life and how he neatly compacts his circumspection into a workable philosophical view. Instead of keeping a private diary, he writes public essays for thousands to read. He likes telling stories.

SAN FRANCISCO, 2005

Freeman Dyson once compared himself with historian Barbara Tuchman, whose book *A Distant Mirror* used historical events in fourteenth-century Europe to reflect on events of the twentieth century. Instead of using the past as his mirror Dyson uses the future. His obsession with the future, he explains, is the flip side of his immersion in the past while growing up in the cathedral city of Winchester, where he lived in a home 300 years old and attended a school 600 years old.[3] The school, Winchester College, was built mainly by William of Wykeham, who is mentioned in Tuchman's book. For Dyson, walking the medieval hallways of his school, William was not just a figure in a book but an everyday reality.

Living in Winchester one swims in the past—the Roman, Saxon, Norman, and Tudor past. This only made young Freeman ponder all the harder what the future would look like. Winchester made a historian out of him, a historian of future events. Now obviously you can't accurately write about things that haven't yet happened. It's hard enough to determine past events, at least with the precision available to physicists, who measure atomic properties to a part in a billion. That's because electrons and planets are relatively simple. People and civilizations are more complicated.

What you can do, however, and what Dyson does so well, is to imagine what is possible for the future and what the laws of science allow. One thing Dyson counts on, in writing about the future, is continuity in the basic substance of human nature:

> The past and future are not remote from us. The people of six hundred years back and of six hundred years ahead are people like ourselves. They are our neighbors in the universe. Technology has caused, and will cause, profound changes in styles of life and thought, separating us from our neighbors. All the more precious, then, are the bonds of kinship that tie us all together.[4]

Dyson once found himself at an exhibition of Paleolithic art. The objects were from France but looked, to his eye, as if they were from Japan:

> The exhibit showed us visually that over periods of ten thousand years the distinction between Western and Eastern and African cul-

*ture lose all meaning. Over a time span of a hundred thousand years
we are all Africans. And over a time-span of three hundred million
years we are all amphibians.*[5]

Future calendars might want to include not just days and months
but also millennia.

This kind of thinking is encouraged by the Long Now Foundation,
a group that sponsors discussions of deep history. Long Now was the
host for an event in October 2005 when Esther, George, and Freeman
Dyson all appeared on a public stage together for the first time. The
topic of discussion was billed as "The Difficulty of Looking Ahead."
George introduced his father by giving a short summary of Freeman's
space-related exploits such as his boyhood story about the Erolunar
encounter and his Orion work. Then George showed a clip from an
episode of *Star Trek* in which the Starship *Enterprise* encounters a gigantic mysterious globe that defies all explanation. After some doubtful exchanges about the thing's identity, the truth begins to dawn on
Captain Piccard. "Commander Data," he asks, "could it be a Dyson
sphere?" This clip, which George has used to introduce his father a
couple of times, never fails to bring forth ample laughter and a round
of applause just as Freeman comes on stage.[6]

The Long Now evening was significant too because Freeman's first
wife, Verena Huber-Dyson, was in the audience. Imme had planned it
all. Taking Freeman by the hand, Imme led him over to Verena. He
giggled awkwardly, but the ensuing conversation was friendly and
lasted about five minutes. This was the first time Freeman and Verena
had seen each other in almost half a century.[7]

A few days later, Freeman was a speaker at a meeting across San
Francisco Bay in Berkeley. The meeting celebrated the ninetieth birthday of Charles Townes, winner of the Nobel Prize for work on lasers
and the Templeton Prize for religion and science. Dyson fit his tribute
to Townes into the form of a talk about the future of science, and how
progress depends on collaboration between unifiers and diversifiers.
The standout unifiers, such as Isaac Newton and Albert Einstein, are
profound thinkers who consolidate a wealth of ideas into an elegant,
universalist scientific framework. Their aim is, in effect, a theory of
everything. By contrast, the best diversifiers, such as Enrico Fermi,
uncover new ideas and explore new phenomena. Science needs both
types. Unifiers, says Dyson, "are happy if they can leave the universe

looking a bit simpler than they found it. Diversifiers are people who . . . are happy if they leave the universe a little more complicated than they found it."[8] Dyson, who loves complexity and diversity and mystery, claims to be a diversifier. It's ironic then that Dyson's single greatest professional achievement, helping to formulate the new quantum electrodynamics, was the work of a unifier.

Townes's work with radar, microwaves, lasers, astronomy, and defense issues made him a superb diversifier. He was a tinkerer. No one could be sure how experiments would come out; that's why they were experiments. One can't fully predict what practical uses could be made of discoveries. Indeed, when Townes and others had invented the laser they weren't quite sure at first what do with it.

So how can Dyson talk about the future of science? He can't. No one can. He gripped the lectern as if bracing himself for the historical events coming our way. "The way to learn about the history of science," he said at the end of his talk, "is to stay alive as long as you can and see what happens."

GREENLAND, 2007

When in 1966 Dyson was interviewed by Stanley Kubrick for the segment that was eventually cut from *2001: A Space Odyssey*, Dyson predicted that for pushing space exploration forward advances in an understanding of biology would be more important than advances in electronics. It would be useful, Dyson said then, in historian-of-the-future fashion, to make machines from biological materials.[9] What is a "biological material"?

We still aren't sure. Forty years later Dyson found himself in Greenland at a meeting devoted not to climate change, as you might expect, but to biological materials, although by then the preferred name was synthetic life. The gathering in this exotic place was kept small to about twenty scientists, including Steven Chu, then the director of the Lawrence Berkeley Lab and later U.S. energy secretary.

The Greenland meeting looked at the prospective merging of nano- and biotechnologies for doing such things as re-engineering bacteria to make fuel or tailored pharmaceuticals. Naturally the effort to invent hybrid life-forms had an ethical component, and a session was devoted to scientists playing God. Dyson contributed to all the discussions but was particularly keen on the subject of the potential benefits and dangers of bioengineering as it applied to public health and the food supply.

The consensus report emerging from the meeting pointed to the growing ability to map genomes and to construct deliberate genetic sequences for the purpose of making functioning single-cell facto- ries.[10] Could these scientists predict when bio-factories will come about? No. But only three years after the Greenland meeting, in May of 2010, biotech entrepreneur Craig Venter and his colleagues reported in *Science* that they had created an artificial genome and placed it into an already living bacterium, which then replicated to form a succession of new cells using the assumed genome as blueprint. Venter went so far as to say that the cells constituted "the first self-replicating species we've had on the planet whose parent is a computer."[11]

Biologists were generally impressed with Venter's work, but many did not exactly consider that a living organism had been created from scratch, since the host cell had grown naturally. Asked his rapid opin- ion of Venter's achievement, Dyson said that Venter's experiment had been clumsy but that it was important work, as it was a big step toward creating new forms of life.[12]

Should we make new forms of life? Should humans appropriate the godly role of creator? Dyson the philosopher has declared himself many times: it is part of our human destiny to make this the most in- teresting universe possible, and evidently this involves making more life and spreading life through the cosmos.

LISBON, 2007

Freeman Dyson's career has passed through several phases. First came the *Knaben Physik* phase when, in his mid-twenties, he helped build the new quantum electrodynamics. Then came the Tom Swift phase of gee-whiz engineering in the 1950s: TRIGA, Orion, Dyson spheres. The 1960s to the 1980s was Dyson's Metternich diplomatic phase, fea- turing nuclear treaties, Jason activity, and the Vietnam War. After that came the Emerson phase, featuring elegant essays on dozens of topics. Next came the Jeremiah phase of prophetic-heretical writing and preaching. All of these personas are present in the man in his present historian-philosopher-storyteller phase.

Dyson was invited to a meeting in Lisbon called "Is Science Near- ing Its Limits?" His talk was unsurprisingly entitled, "Science Is

Nowhere Near Its Limits." Look at history, he said. Oswald Spengler, in his 1918 book, *The Decline of the West*, got just about everything wrong, especially scientific things. Spengler argued that physics had played itself out. Instead, within one little decade, Heisenberg's quantum revolution, Einstein's relativity revolution, and Gödel's incompleteness theorem had cracked the bedrock of established knowledge, leading to a new golden age of mathematics and physics.

At least half of Dyson's Lisbon talk was devoted to refuting point for point the assertions of the conference's organizer, George Steiner, who is better known as a literary critic. Steiner argued, for example, that science, with increasing specialization within subdisciplines, was losing its universal language. Look at history, Dyson said again. Many regretted the apparent loss of unity when scientists, in the early nineteenth century, switched from using Latin to using their several national languages. Science got over it.

But what about all those subdisciplines? Dyson granted that many researchers were pursuing ever smaller areas of knowledge. But there is a compensating advantage in the growing internationalism of science, in the availability of new research tools such as Google and Wikipedia, and in the start-up of so many interdisciplinary institutes.[13]

How can science be reaching its limits, Dyson asked, when so many fundamental things—the origin of life, the nature of consciousness, the properties of dark energy—need explaining? "Science is not a collection of truths. It is a continuing exploration of mysteries."[14]

GALÁPAGOS, 2008

Imme and Freeman celebrated their golden wedding anniversary by taking a trip to the Galápagos Islands. This is where scientific history was made. Over geologic ages the finches on these islands had splintered into many species long before Charles Darwin arrived to gaze at them and gain his central insights about natural selection. Still comparatively wild, these volcanic outposts in the Pacific continue to be a laboratory for studying evolution in real time. Can Dyson, or anyone, write the future history of these islands or their birds? No. The swing in weather—dry one year, wet the next—is too great.

Mr. and Mrs. Dyson were there to relax. No lectures this time, no scientific sessions to attend. Imme snorkeled while Freeman read. To human eyes the place is placid and beautiful. But nature is rather cavalier with life and death. From the railing of the cruise ship, the vacationers saw a deadly drama unfold. A sea turtle, one that Imme had viewed earlier that day while she swam in the ocean, was rushed by an orca (that's Freeman's recollection; Imme remembers it as a shark), which easily shattered the turtle's shell, leaving the sea flush with blood and covered with scavenger birds.[15] Death by sea, life by land: the couple strolled for miles past albatrosses sitting on eggs, the males and females taking turns. The birds were as thick, Freeman thought, as humans in Manhattan.

Aside from visiting the Galápagos in person, Freeman converted his observations into writing. In his critique of a book about the place in the *New York Review of Books* he lamented the book's tone, with its prediction that the islands would assume one of two extremes, either as a preserved wilderness free of humans or as a vulgar resort crammed with honeymooners at the density of albatrosses. Which way will it go? Dyson can't be sure, but he believes we can steer a middle course.[16]

KAZAKHSTAN, 2009

In one of Dyson's most important self-chosen roles—prophet of space travel—he has been stymied. He is an armchair explorer, pointing the way across the galaxy but not going there himself. He designed a nuclear spacecraft and hoped to travel personally as far as Saturn. The first steps into deep space, in cosmic terms only baby steps, are into Earth orbit, then the Moon, then further out into the solar system.

Where the father fell short perhaps the daughter could succeed. But first, Esther needed Freeman's advice. She was a rushed businesswoman and didn't have a lot of spare time. She'd helped to found or had invested in such companies as FedEx and the Russian equivalent of Google. She sat on several boards of directors. Her travel schedule took her to another city, if not out of the country, every week. The question was this: should she put this all on hold, she asked her father, in order to go to Russia and train there for six months to be a cosmonaut and possibly be hurled into space from a launch site in Central Asia?

Freeman had long supported his eldest child in whatever she'd attempted. Now he positively glowed. Going into space? His own good-natured frustration at not traveling off Earth had crept into dozens of essays. Here was a chance for his firstborn to arrive at—if not exactly

Saturn—at least low Earth orbit. He was thrilled. She made up her mind to do it.[17]

Even if she came up to full qualification, the odds were against her actually going into orbit. She was to pay $3 million for the training and for the contingency that if the designated tourist-class flier, Charles Simonyi, was unable to proceed then she would go in his stead, and cough up another $30 million or so. All of this was arranged by a company called Space Adventures, in which Esther was an investor. Simonyi, a former Microsoft executive, was a friend of Esther's and also happened to chair the board of directors at the Institute for Advanced Study. He was rich enough and hardy enough to be going now on his second orbital voyage.

In March 2009 Esther and the other cosmonauts went from their training base at Star City near Moscow to the launch facility at Baikonur in Kazakhstan. As part of her space adventure, Esther was allowed a small entourage of bystanders, which included Freeman, Imme, and George Dyson. On this occasion, Simonyi did fly, Esther did not, but all agreed that the effort had been worthwhile.

Other events along the way: Freeman slipped on the ice and smashed himself, leaving blue bruises all around his face. He gave a lecture in Moscow. He and Imme were nearly arrested at the Moscow airport when a bottle containing a mysterious substance was discovered in their luggage. At first they claimed not to know what it was. Later it was recognized to be a ceremonial sample of soil from the space site. Esther, with a million things to bring home, wanted the dirt but didn't have room for it in her own suitcases. It was confiscated.[18]

CHICAGO, 2010

Saxons and Normans built cathedrals in Winchester. Eventually we might build cathedrals on comets, cathedrals made of warm-blooded biological materials, cathedrals providing shelter and food and energy and perhaps some new spiritual nourishment for future space colonists. How and when could this happen? We can't say. Space flights from Kazakhstan and Cape Canaveral only began a few decades ago.

In Chicago Dyson spoke at a meeting called the International Space Development Conference. He shared top billing with a couple of astronauts, including a man who has gone as far away from Earth as any human has ever gone, Buzz Aldrin, the second man to stand on the

Moon. Dyson's speech covered such by now familiar themes as the need for new propulsion systems—how about using lasers? We should not attempt to adapt remote planet or comet surfaces to our human needs, but rather we should adapt human habits to those environments. Ask not how we can change Europa but how Europa can change us.

For doing these things long-term thinking is required, a thing Russians are more inclined to than Americans, an opinion informed by Dyson's pilgrimage to Baikonur and seventy years of studying Russian culture. Esther didn't get to visit the International Space Station, but is confident that she will get into space or at least take a suborbital joyride in the next ten years. She believes that NASA will get out of the "truck driving" part of space travel, the ferrying of supplies up and down. This will allow private entrepreneurs to thrive in the business of hauling freight and paying passengers into suborbital trajectories or low Earth orbit at first and later to more distant destinations like the Moon and even Mars.[19]

Freeman Dyson was the president of the Space Studies Institute, an organization dedicated to the commercialization of space. In response to congressional hearings on a NASA funding bill, Dyson and his fellow SSI officers wrote an open letter calling on Congress to provide funds for "pre-competition research," which would lead to commercial space activities in such areas as launch vehicles, satellite solar power, and even manufacturing and mining on planets and our Moon.[20]

WASHINGTON, 2011

In April 2011 Dyson was the star at another space event. He received the lifetime achievement award of the Arthur C. Clarke Foundation at a banquet in Washington, D.C. Clarke was of course the author of *2001: A Space Odyssey* and other science fiction novels but was also an important early promoter of satellites. The glamour of the manned missions to the Moon helped establish space exploration as an exciting frontier. What made space a successful commercial enterprise, however, was satellites, those ubiquitous overhead sentinels that monitor storms, keep military bases under surveillance, supply customers with their ground locations to within centimeters or less, and transmit television shows around the globe. The foundation's ceremony took place in a large room whose ceiling was hung with full-size satellite specimens as if they were display items in a natural history museum. Indeed, satellites have come to be seen as if they were natural objects, like jungle birds, roosting overhead.

Before the awards part of the evening, a short video of Clarke was shown. Speaking on the occasion of the 1964 World's Fair in New York City, Clarke said that it was impossible to predict the course of technological innovation. The things you can predict now, he said, probably won't happen. The things that will happen you couldn't have imagined. So, Clarke impishly said, if you want to predict the future you have to imagine the unimaginable.

Predicting the unpredictable is one of Freeman Dyson's habits, especially when it comes to the spread of life from Earth to the rest of the solar system. How will this prospective *Mayflower*-scale migration come about? Gray technology will provide space hardware that can transport us to planets and comets. Green technology will provide hardy organisms—eventually including us—adapted to low vacuum, low temperature, and low gravity. To do any of this, however, costs have to come down.

The man speaking before Dyson at the Clarke event hopes to do exactly that. There to accept the foundation's Innovator Award was Elon Musk, who had founded PayPal (a company delivering Internet paying services) and Tesla Motors (featuring sporty all-electric automobiles). Musk was on hand because his third great venture is SpaceX, whose chief products are Falcon, a rocket designed to deliver payloads to Earth orbit more cheaply than NASA has ever done, and Dragon, the first private spacecraft to have orbited Earth and then returned safely. The company expects Dragon to ferry goods and probably astronauts to space stations.

When Dyson finally spoke, the first thing he did was to apologize for being anticlimactic. Elon Musk, Dyson said, was the real thing. Musk delivered a useful product, while he, Dyson, was there only to talk about a dream.

He read his speech in a loud, clear voice, with occasional percussive effects at moments needing emphasis. Dyson's appearance—age accentuating the angularity, with elfin ears pointing up, aquiline nose pointing down, and hair swiping diagonally across the forehead—revealed a man who is old but who, at least audibly, was still the precocious schoolboy, eager to have you hear his prize essay and embrace his vision.

Politely fitting his remarks to the occasion, Dyson began with a story. He spoke of his last encounter with Arthur C. Clarke, at a meeting in Colorado in 2003. Actually Clarke was not present in person. Instead, his 3D holographic image was fed across the world by satellite from Sri Lanka, where he lived, to the hall in Colorado, where Dyson and others could greet him. They too, one at a time, were encoded as holograms for Clarke to see at the other end.

Then Dyson got to the main part of his award acceptance speech. His well-rehearsed theme was his vision of life spreading from Earth into the cosmos, of life invading matter. On this occasion he offered a new enunciation of his spacetraveler's manifesto. He spoke of the "biosphere genome," his name for the collectively mapped genomes of all known species on Earth. He expected this map to be compiled over the next few decades. This would be the most important database on Earth, about a petabyte of data, large but smaller than some commercial information troves such as Google. It would be able to fit onto a storage device the size of an egg. It is this "biosphere egg" that Dyson wants to dispatch into other worlds where, with proper development, it could implant life. Away from competing with nature's own course here on our home planet, a new biosphere could deploy itself at leisure.

Why plant such a seedling on another world—or, more likely, on some lower-gravity object like a passing comet or asteroid? Well, we would do it for the same reason that we plant a bulb in a kitchen window flowerpot: for the beauty or as a bit of decoration, but chiefly we would do it because it represents living things, things to be nurtured.

Understanding the biosphere genome—the total web of life as we know it at the basic level of genes—will, Dyson argues, "be the transforming event of human history in the twenty-first century." This event will be so significant that Dyson gives it a grandiose name: The Turn. The Turn is not the point at which we understand life. It's the point at which we use nature's own tools to design new ecologies and new species. "We will make mistakes" in the process, he admits, but we'll learn from these mistakes. There is no going back. "The future will be different from the past."[21]

PRINCETON, 2013

The man who once claimed to prefer the eighteenth century to the twentieth, at least when it came to fostering ties between scientific and humanistic values, has now lived well into the twenty-first century. Is he slowing down? Dyson in his upper eighties is slower than Dyson in his seventies. But by octogenarian standards he is active.

Dyson has consorted with lots of people in his long life. He has friends he made through Imme's long-distance running events; he has flower friends (Imme and Freeman usually attend the annual Flower Show in Philadelphia); business friends he met through Esther; colleagues at the Institute and nearby Princeton University. He has biologist friends, Peace Action friends, physics friends, and astronomer friends.

He continues to attend Jason's summer meetings in La Jolla, California. He now carries the designation of senior advisor. According to Roy Schwitters, the current chairman of the Jason steering committee, "Dyson's need-to-know status is reviewed periodically. Needless to say, we much value Freeman's continuing contributions." Jason sports an increasing number of non-physicists, and the research topics include more biological and computer subjects. But nuclear stockpile stewardship seems to be the number one concern. The opinion of Jason thinkers is that the warheads in the U.S. arsenal will be viable for the foreseeable future.[22]

Dyson approaches his nineties but goes to work most days. What he sees around his room, when not putting words on his computer screen, are pictures of children and grandchildren, and stacks of papers. Books fill shelves the long length of the room and are piled three feet high from the floor up. Books reside on top of filing cabinets. They include translations of his own compositions: Chinese and Italian versions are visible. The blackboard at the end of the room is covered with equations and the inscription "Do not erase."

The man who gives lectures up and down the land is still shy. When eating lunch, he sometimes sits by himself in the cafeteria. At the 3:30 tea held in the lobby of Fuld Hall, he might stand alone until approached by a young scholar with questions. On some days he is joined by Imme and friends after work at Harry's Bar, the Institute's own watering hole.

His two most recent books are *The Scientist as Rebel* (2006), largely filled with articles from *The New York Review of Books*, and *A Many-Colored Glass* (2007), consisting of lectures delivered at a variety of universities. These pieces generally line up with classic Dysonic interests: nuclear weapons, heretical thinking, biotech, the complementary roles of science and religion in understanding the universe, and of course his essential Mayflowering theme—the destiny of humans, or some subsequent intelligent species, to spread across the galaxy.

Dyson can't seem to say no when asked to write introductions to other people's books. We've seen a few examples already: a new edition of Olaf Stapledon's novel *Star Maker* and a book about ESP. Here are others: a gathering of letters by Richard Feynman; a book about astronomer Thomas Gold; a book of Einstein's writings; a book of Einstein quotations; a book by Clement Durell, Dyson's math teacher at Winchester College, about special relativity; a book about physicist Joseph Rotblat; and a 2010 collection of science essays by other writers.

Dyson, as undertaker, has provided numerous obituaries of great scientists, especially if they were friends of his: Hans Bethe, Paul Dirac, Edward Teller, Robert Oppenheimer, Ted Taylor, and John von Neumann. One of the best of these remembrances was of Princeton physicist John Wheeler, an important quantum thinker and Richard Feynman's graduate advisor. Dyson, as if writing about himself, extolled Wheeler for his complementary virtues of being both conservative and rebel in his research. Wheeler was both an expert calculator of things that could be measured in the lab and a creative dreamer of new ideas; he coined the term "black hole." Wheeler's writing combined the best of prose and poetry. Dyson lets you know that he prefers the poetic side of Wheeler.[23]

The heart of Dyson's writing since the mid-1990s has been his contributions to *The New York Review of Books*. In approaching his reviewing assignment, Dyson paces about the house or office. Then, when he has ordered all his chosen points, he sits and writes out the entire piece. His wife often reads a draft. Here is a sprinkling of late-appearing Dyson reviews and some of the stories he tells along the way.

Writing about Richard Holmes's book *The Age of Wonder*, Dyson said he looked forward to a new Romantic Age when science and the arts would be allies again in exploring the universe. He tells the story of his participation in a festival in Rome featuring scientists and artists.[24]

Reviewing James Gleick's *The Information*, Dyson lamented that as the speed and volume of data flow increased our ability to make sense of it all was being challenged. "It is our task as humans to bring meaning back into this wasteland. As finite creatures who think and feel, we can create islands of meaning in the sea of information."[25] As Dyson likes to say, information is cheap while meaning is expensive.

In a piece about David Deutsch's *The Beginning of Infinity*, about science, philosophy, and human destiny, Dyson says that philosophy can be classified as a branch of science or as a category of literature. He prefers his philosophy to be literary. "Deutsch becomes a true philosopher when he forgets his technical arguments and tells evocative stories."[26]

Dyson's yearning for literary wisdom also shows up in his review of Daniel Kahneman's *Thinking, Fast and Slow,* about how the human mind processes information and arrives at impressions. Dyson likes the book but chides Kahneman for neglecting to mention either Sigmund Freud or William James, whom Dyson regards not as scientists but as artists. Kahneman, Dyson suggests, helped to make psychology an experimental science, while Freud "made psychology a branch of literature, with stories and myths that appeal to the heart rather than to the mind."[27]

Finally, writing about *Lake Views,* a collection of essays by Steven Weinberg, gave Dyson one more chance (probably not the last) to spar with his longtime friend. The two have repeatedly bumped up against each other over the years. Dyson has made repeated reference to Weinberg's famous dictum, "The more the universe seems comprehensible, the more it also seems pointless." So it is ironic that Dyson should refer to Weinberg, an outspoken atheist, as a man of faith. According to Dyson, Weinberg's "faith" is for the existence of a Final Theory, a comprehensive mathematical formalism that will account for physical phenomena in the universe, and a belief that humans can uncover this theory through thinking and experimenting.

"I think he overrates the capacity of the human mind to comprehend the totality of nature," Dyson said. "I find the idea of a Final Theory repugnant because it diminishes both the richness of nature and the richness of human destiny. I prefer to live in a universe full of inexhaustible mysteries and to belong to a species destined for inexhaustible intellectual growth."[28]

DELPHIC ORACLE

Freeman Dyson loves to speak at colleges, where he is often accorded reverence approaching that reserved for the Dalai Lama. Even if you disagree with his view on climate change or string theory or religion or ESP, you expect him to say something interesting. You don't want to miss hearing the Delphic Oracle. So if a poster goes up announcing a campus appearance of Freeman Dyson, then buy tickets quickly.

In December 2009 Dyson was at the University of Portland to talk about the relation of science and society, a broad area of concern that includes some of his favorite topics. Two days later he was scheduled to talk at the physics department of the University of Oregon. He went to dinner with some of his hosts but was too ill to eat. After some vomiting he took a nap on a couch at the university. A huge crowd had filled the lecture hall, but the organizers were prepared to call off the event. Dyson woke up and claimed he was ready to proceed.

And proceed he did in the form of an extensive question-and-answer dialogue. He touched upon his days at General Atomic, a company he claimed was to the 1950s what Google is now—an exciting place to work since fresh ideas could be turned into action. Asked about string theory, Dyson said he respected it but figured that we didn't need 10,000 string theorists. About 1,000 would be enough. Bioengineering of flowers and lizards? Yes. Of humans? No, not yet. We need to go slow. Was he religious? Not particularly, although he did relish mystery in the universe. Unanswered questions kept the human race on the move.

Had Dyson's illness in Oregon been a passing virus? For the previous two weeks he'd been staying at the home of his daughter Rebecca, the radiologist, in northern California. He'd been listless the whole time, unlike his usual self. Right after the Oregon event he visited his other physician daughter, Emily, the cardiologist, in San Diego. There they finally figured out what was wrong. No one had thought to measure his pulse. It was ticking along at only 30 beats per minute. Freeman received a pacemaker, felt much better immediately, and returned safely to his home in Princeton.[29]

It wasn't yet time for Dyson to die. But occasionally he thinks about mortality. He thinks back to that startling Tolystoyan moment decades before when he was mugged near the National Academy, when he was left bleeding underneath a bush, when his most vivid impression was not the pain of the injury to his skull but the joy of seeing and appreciating the greenness of the leaves all about and the blueness of the sky. "Perhaps, when death comes," Dyson said when he recalled the event, "he will once again come as a friend."[30]

It takes equanimity to say something like that. This sentiment appeared in an essay Dyson contributed to an anthology called *Living Philosophies*.[31] Dyson's essay was devoted, not surprisingly, to drawing out the widest hierarchy of perspective. First, he said, there is the individual, whose purview is measured in years. Next are families, which stretch out across decades; then tribes and nations over centuries; then culture, over a millennium; then the human species over tens and hundreds of millennia; and finally life on Earth over billions of years. No wonder any single person had divided loyalties, since he or she encountered life as part of all these inclusive realms.[32]

Dyson recalls several walks he took with his mother around Winchester in her final years (she died at the age of ninety-four). In the distance were the medieval buildings, the gardens, and the cathedral. She liked visiting a particular cemetery, but was mostly cheerful on these walks. Mother and son discussed Freeman's boyhood idea of Cosmic Unity. "She imagined that she was herself a piece of the world soul that had been given freedom to grow and develop independently as long as she was alive," said Dyson about his mother's attitude. "After death, she expected to merge back into the world soul, losing her personal identity but preserving her memories and her intelligence."[33]

Death is in our future. Every tombstone has a start date and a stop date. Amid his biology career in the 1980s, Dyson had declared that death was one of the more important innovations in history. Without death there wouldn't be room for the new creatures that keep coming along. "Life had to invent death to evolve."[34]

As Richard Feynman was dying of cancer, he told a friend—in an anecdote retold by Freeman Dyson—that the thought of death wasn't as bothersome as you'd think. "I've told most of the good stuff," Feynman said, "so I'm ready to go." Dyson feels the same way. If anything Dyson's greatest fear, on the subject of mortality, is related to the very biotech progress he has been promoting for many years. "One of the worst disasters would be if biologists find a cure for death," Dyson said. "I worry about this."[35]

THE DYSONS THEN

The death of death is not expected soon. Nor the death of the Dyson tribe. Here, for the record, is a succession of Dyson sons and fathers. Freeman Dyson (born 1923), a scientist, is son of George (1883–1964), a musician; who was a son of John (1859–1923), a blacksmith; son of

Jeremiah (1835–1900), a painter and wallpaper hanger; son of John (b. 1810), a butcher; son of Thomas (b. 1782), an innkeeper; son of George (b. 1755), who established the Stirk Bridge Inn near Halifax, which still stands. He was son of John (b. 1725), son of Henry (b. 1678), son of Henry (b. 1636), son of Simeon (b. 1603). Simeon was the first of four generations of Dysons to live at Goat House, still standing in Rishworth, near Halifax. Simeon was son of Abraham Dyson (b. 1563).

We're not yet done with our rearward odyssey through the Dysons, but the dates are less reliable hereafter. Abraham was son of Thomas (born circa 1540), son of Henry (c. 1519), son of Christopher (c. 1488), son of John (c. 1459). This lengthy scroll of generations was lovingly compiled by Freeman's cousin, Judith (Bracewell) Dyson, and comes mostly from parish records in and around Halifax in the north of England. The mortal remains of most of these Dysons repose in a stretch of ground some dozen miles across centered on the town of Elland in Yorkshire. The earliest Dyson, a woman named Dionysia, was born in the 1250s. She enters the documentary world because she was suspected of horse thievery.

In this book we are naturally interested in Freeman and the pivotal events in his life: meeting the women who became his wives, the births of his children, his not having died in the world war, his scholarship to study physics in America. But we could also say that equally important were the fact that Freeman's father, George, did not die in the earlier world war, or that George's scholarships to study music in London and then in Italy and Germany opened up a wider intellectual world, or that George's mother, Alice, had persevered in getting the boy proper music lessons, enabling his departure from Yorkshire down to the great metropolis to the south, or that George's blacksmith father, John, was a choirmaster and lover of music.

Notice that in the genealogy above it is all sons and fathers. That's because by tradition the family name is carried down by sons. Freeman has five daughters and one son. The son, George, has only a daughter himself, so it would seem that the Dyson name, at least the American branch, would peter out. But Freeman's daughter Rebecca, in agreement with her husband, Peter, decided that their children, including three sons, would retain the Dyson name. When told of this decision over the phone, Freeman said only "marvelous." The youngest of those grandsons, the youngest of all the Dysons, is named Jack Freeman Dyson. So the Dysons, and even the Freemans, will persist.

The Dyson lineage is short by geologic standards but long as ordinary family histories go. The detail is due to careful church records, supplemented by the organizational efforts of the Halifax Antiquarian Society. All this, Dyson notes, is just part of our growing ability to retain a record of our ancestors: their words through writing, their faces through photography, their gestures through movies, and their voices through recordings. Now we can even map the sequence of the genetic blueprint used to make the cells that constituted our bodies. What's next? The ability to clone a new individual from DNA information? The ability to reconstruct an individual's memories and thoughts—in effect to replay that person's entire experience?[36]

Dyson has done a pretty good job of preserving a record of his existence—through his scientific publications, his books, and his children and grandchildren. He has cast a wide net and found the universe to be anything but pointless. Meanwhile, he is living as long as he can in order to see what happens.

Acknowledgments

Freeman Dyson, the man who over the years has submitted to a hundred interviews, did not relish being interviewed for this book. "Maybe in fifty years," he said, "you'll be able to tell whether I did anything important." I couldn't wait that long. Instead I believed that substantive things could be said about Mr. Dyson right now. Asked whether he would mind if I proceeded with an independent book about him, he gave me his "blessing" (his word) for my project, "especially if it is honestly critical." I assured him that it would be.

Fortunately, many Dyson family members were forthcoming. Freeman Dyson's wife Imme, his sister Alice, his son George, his daughters Esther, Mia, and Rebecca, his daughter-in-law Ann Yow-Dyson, and his stepdaughter Katarina all kindly provided valuable information and insights. I appreciate their crucial help. Freeman Dyson's second cousin, Judith Bracewell, who has made quite a study of the Dyson family going back generations, supplied many interesting facts and pictures. Imme Dyson's cousin Joerg Deibert provided useful photographs. George Dyson was generous with family pictures.

I owe a special debt of gratitude to Freeman Dyson's first wife, Verena Huber-Dyson. Over the course of more than ninety e-mail messages (she did not wish to be visited and didn't want to speak on the phone) Dr. Huber-Dyson supplied a rich tapestry of events and impressions from her years with Mr. Dyson. Her remarks helped furnish a complex emotional component to the story of Freeman Dyson's life, which might otherwise have gotten lost amid the bustle of his professional activities. It's important to point out that Freeman declined to read any of the chapters of my book before publication, and so in the text he will not be seen as refuting or commenting upon Verena's remarks, many of which are critical.

I was fortunate in being able to interview dozens of Freeman Dyson's professional colleagues, some of whom are eminent scientists or writers in their own right. The interviews were carried out in a variety of modes—in person, over the phone, by e-mail, or by video/Internet. For supplying information or talking with me, and in many cases reading text from the chapters, I thank the following: Henry Abarbanel, Steven Aftergood, Finn Aserud, Richard Askey, Robert Austin, Kenneth Brower, Predrag Cvitanovic, Cees Dekker, Cecile Morette DeWitt, Sidney Drell, Harold Feiveson, Charles Ferguson, Richard Garwin, Gary Hudson, William Happer, Stephen Hsu, David Kaiser, Paul Koehler, Lawrence Krauss, Georg Kreisel, Joel Lebowitz, Andrew Lenard, Elliott Lieb, Avishai Margalit, Gregg Maryniak, Robert Moore, Richard Muller, Edward Neuenschwander, Theo Nieuwenhuizen, Joseph Pelton, Larry Potts, Martin Rees, Sam Schweber, Roy Schwitters, Martin Sherwin, Lee Silver, Vaclav Smil, Mosur Sundaresan, Scott Tremaine, Lee Valentine, Frank von Hippel, Steven Weinberg, Paul Weingartner, Frank Wilczek, Edward Witten, and Carl Woese.

Discussions with other experts and friends of mine were useful in preparing the book. For this I thank Steven Blau, Keay Davidson, Nancy Forbes, John Gillick, Chris Gorski, Paul Ricer, and Neal Singer.

I received cheerful help from archivists and public-information officials at several organizations. I am grateful to Christine Ferrara, Christine DeBella, and Erica Mosner at the Institute for Advanced Study; Mary Ann Meyer, Pamela Thompson, and Donald Lehr at the Templeton Foundation; Joseph Anderson and Scott Prouty at the Center for the History of Physics at the American Institute of Physics; Constance Chatfield-Taylor and Monica Morgan at the Arthur C. Clarke Foundation, Douglas Fouquet at General Dynamics, and Suzanne Foster and Madeleine Copin at Winchester College.

Two people played pivotal roles in producing this book, my literary agent John Thornton and my editor Marcia Markland at the Thomas Dunne Books division of St. Martin's Press. I also thank Marcia's assistant Kat Brzozowski. Other St. Martin's people who made valuable contributions were Michael Cantwell, Fred Chase, and Joan Higgins. The cover was designed by James Iacobelli.

NOTES

The most important source material for this book comes from Freeman Dyson's own books and from interviews I conducted with his family, friends, and colleagues. Two other books provide an expert, if somewhat technical, context for Dyson's quantum career: Silvan Schweber's *QED and the Men Who Made It* and David Kaiser's *Drawing Theories Apart*.

Dyson has been interviewed many times. The most valuable of these for the purpose of writing this book were Schweber's extensive conversations with Dyson, available on the Internet in video format, and an oral history audio interview of Dyson appearing on the website of the American Institute of Physics. Two other books provide valuable scenes from Dyson's life but are not themselves full biographies of him: George Dyson's *Project Orion* and Kenneth Brower's *The Starship and the Canoe*.

The notes that follow use a number of abbreviations to denote key works referenced in this book.

ABBREVIATIONS USED FOR DYSON AND HIS WORKS:

Disturbing: *Disturbing the Universe* (New York: Harper & Row, 1979).

Eros: *From Eros to Gaia* (London: Penguin, 1992).

FJD: Freeman J. Dyson

Glass: *A Many-Colored Glass: Reflections on the Place of Life in the Universe* (Charlottesville: University of Virginia Press, 2007).

Imagined: *Imagined Worlds* (Cambridge: Harvard University Press, 1997; paperback, 1998).

Infinite: *Infinite in All Directions* (New York: Harper & Row, 1998; paperback, 2004).

Origins: *Origins of Life* (Cambridge: Cambridge University Press, 1985; second edition, 1999).

Rebel: *The Scientist as Rebel* (New York: New York Review Books, 2006).

Selected: *Selected Papers and Commentary* (Providence: American Mathematical Society, 1996).

Sun: *The Sun, the Genome, and the Internet: Tools of Scientific Revolution* (New York: Oxford University Press, 1999; paperback, 2000).

W&H: *Weapons and Hope* (New York: Harper & Row, 1984).

OTHER ABBREVIATIONS:

AIP: American Institute of Physics Oral History, FJD interviewed by Finn Aserud, 17 December 1986, transcript at www.aip.org/history/ohilist/4585.html.

IAS: Institute for Advanced Study

IJ: Imme Jung

Kaiser: David Kaiser, *Drawing Theories Apart: The Dispersion of Feynman Diagrams in Postwar Physics* (Chicago: University of Chicago Press, 2005).

NYRB: *The New York Review of Books*

NYT: *The New York Times*

Orion: George Dyson, *Project Orion: The True Story of the Atomic Spaceship* (New York: Henry Holt, 2002).

PFS: Phillip F. Schewe

PT: *Physics Today* magazine

QED: Silvan S. Schweber, *QED and the Men Who Made It: Dyson, Feynman, Schwinger, and Tomonaga* (Princeton: Princeton University Press, 1994).

SA: *Scientific American*

Starship: Kenneth Brower, *The Starship and the Canoe* (New York: Holt, Rinehart & Winston, 1978; paperback edition, Perennial Library, 1983).

VHD: PFS interview with Verena Huber-Dyson

WEB: Silvan S. Schweber online interviews of FJD, "Web of Stories," 157 segments, http://www.webofstories.com/play/4309.

1. KILLING TIME

1. *W&H*, p. 109.
2. Ibid., p. 17.
3. Ibid., p. 112.
4. *Sun*, p. 54.
5. *QED*, p. 476; also FJD in *Curious Minds: How a Child Becomes a Scientist*, John Brockman, ed. (New York: Pantheon, 2004), p. 63.
6. WEB, 7.
7. Ibid., 15.
8. *QED*, p. 477.
9. *Disturbing*, p. 34.
10. FJD in *Nature's Imagination*, John Cornwell, ed. (Oxford: Oxford University Press, 1995), p. 4.
11. WEB, 13.
12. PFS interview with Esther Dyson.
13. WEB, 17.
14. *Disturbing*, p. 16.
15. WEB, 19.
16. *Selected*, p. 4.
17. PFS interview with Madeleine Copin, mathematics teacher at Winchester College.
18. "Chamber Annals," Winchester College, 1938–1940.
19. "The Wykemhamist," Winchester College, 1938–1941.
20. PFS interview with Suzanne Foster, archivist at Winchester College; the number she supplied for Winchester College war dead is 500, not the 600 cited by Freeman Dyson (*W&H*, p. 110).
21. *Disturbing*, p. 17.
22. WEB, 22.
23. FJD, Foreword to Clement Durrell, *Readable Relativity* (New York: Harper & Row, 1971; originally published, 1926), p. v.
24. G. H. Hardy, *A Mathematician's Apology* (Cambridge: Cambridge University Press, 1969; originally published, 1940), p. 185.
25. WEB, 24.
26. *Selected*, p. 7.
27. Graham Farmelo, *The Strangest Man: The Hidden Life of Paul Dirac, Mystic of the Atom* (New York: Basic, 2009), p. 320.
28. WEB, 35
29. Ibid., 29
30. Ibid., 30.
31. *W&H*, p. 100.
32. Ibid., p. 98.
33. FJD in *Technology Review*, November/December 2006.
34. *Disturbing*, p. 23.
35. FJD, *Technology Review*.
36. *W&H*, p. 119.
37. FJD, *Technology Review*.
38. WEB, 37.
39. *QED*, p. 489.
40. FJD, *Technology Review*.
41. *W&H*, p. 117.
42. Ibid., p. 120.

43. Ibid., p. 61.
44. Ibid., p. 120.
45. FJD interviewed by Wim Kayzer, *Glorious Accident,* PBS, aired 1994.

2. LIFE IS A BLUR

1. George Dyson, *Fiddling While Rome Burns: A Musician's Apology* (London: Oxford University Press, 1954), p. 3.
2. *Winchester College:* A Register for the Years 1930 to 1975, C. F. Badcock and J. R. La T. Carrie, ed. (Winchester College, 1992).
3. George Dyson, *Fiddling While Rome Burns,* p. 7.
4. *Selected,* p. 9.
5. Ibid.
6. *Selected,* p. 9.
7. David Deutsch, *The Beginning of Infinity: Explanations That Transform the World* (New York: Viking, 2011), p. 291.
8. *Selected,* p. 10.
9. WEB, 47.
10. FJD, talk at the University of Portland, December 3, 2009.
11. *Selected,* p. 11.
12. *QED,* p. 493.
13. Ibid., p. 492.
14. Letter from Rudolf Peierls to Hans Bethe, *The Bethe-Peierls Correspondence,* Sabine Lee, ed. (Singapore: World Scientific, 2007), p. 312.
15. *Disturbing,* p. 61.
16. VHD.

3. ECUMENICAL COUNCILS

1. WEB, 54.
2. Ibid., 65.
3. *QED,* p. 495.
4. WEB, 58.
5. Kaiser, p. 68.
6. AIP.
7. WEB, 49.
8. Ibid., 50.
9. T. S. Eliot, *Selected Prose of T. S. Eliot,* edited with an introduction by Frank Kermode (New York: Harcourt Brace Jovanovich; Farrar, Straus & Giroux, 1975), p. 39.
10. *Disturbing,* p. 48.
11. *QED,* p. 495.
12. *Selected,* p. 12.
13. WEB, 88.
14. Kaiser, p. 71.
15. K. A. Milton, "Julian Schwinger," June 2006, http://www.nhn.ou.edu/~milton/bio.pdf, p. 8; Hans Bethe interviewed by Silvan Schweber, "Web of Stories," http://www.webofstories.com/play/4571.
16. Richard Feynman, *PT,* June 1948.
17. WEB, 57.
18. *Rebel,* p. 315.
19. WEB, 58; *Disturbing,* p. 55.
20. *Disturbing,* p. 56.

21. Ibid., p. 54.
22. *PT,* February 1989; *Eros,* p. 322.
23. James Gleick, *Genius: The Life and Science of Richard Feynman* (New York: Pantheon, 1992), p. 264.
24. Ibid., p. 263.
25. *Disturbing,* p. 62.
26. Richard P. Feynman, *What Do You Care What Other People Think?* (New York: Norton, 1988), p. 65.
27. VHD.
28. *QED,* p. 503.
29. *Disturbing,* p. 65.
30. WEB, 74.
31. *QED,* p. 503.
32. Ibid., p. 504.
33. WEB, 68.
34. *QED,* p. 500.

4. The Secret Signature of Things

1. *Disturbing,* p. 66.
2. WEB, 75.
3. *Disturbing,* p. 67.
4. *QED,* p. 571.
5. James Joyce, *A Portrait of the Artist as a Young Man* (New York: Viking, 1964, Viking Critical Edition; originally published, 1916), p. 215.
6. *QED,* p. 571.
7. *Joyce, A Portrait of the Artist as a Young Man,* p. 212.
8. FJD letter to his parents, September 14, 1948, reported in Kaiser, p. 74.
9. Kaiser, p. 95.
10. WEB, 84.
11. FJD letter to his parents, September 30, 1948, reported in Kaiser, p. 93.
12. Kaiser, p. 74; *QED,* p. 505.
13. Kaiser, p. 77.
14. Ibid.
15. Jagdish Mehra, *The Beat of a Different Drum: The Life and Science of Richard Feynman* (Oxford: Oxford University Press, 1994), p. 265.
16. *QED,* p. 449.
17. WEB, 68.
18. *QED,* p. 522.
19. Kaiser, p. 94.
20. *QED,* p. 552; *Disturbing,* p. 74.
21. *QED,* p. 550; Kaiser, p. 79.
22. Kaiser, p. 81.
23. Gleick, *Genius,* p. 272.
24. Abraham Pais, *J. Robert Oppenheimer: A Life* (Oxford: Oxford University Press, 2006), p. 117.
25. FJD, obituary of Edward Teller, National Academy of Sciences, 2007.
26. *QED,* p. 527.
27. Kaiser, p. 79.
28. AIP.
29. *QED,* p. 526.

30. *The Bethe-Peierls Correspondence*, p. 288.
31. WEB, 80.
32. VHD.
33. *QED*, pp. 487–88.
34. Ibid., p. 503.
35. *Disturbing*, p. 75.
36. VHD.
37. PFS interview with Cécile Morette.

5. RECESSIONAL
1. *The Bethe-Peierls Correspondence*, p. 347.
2. *QED*, p. 556.
3. Kaiser, p. 97.
4. Ibid., p. 111.
5. Ibid., p. 139.
6. Ibid., p. 158.
7. *QED*, p. 554.
8. Ibid., p. 556.
9. Rudolf Peierls, *Bird of Passage: Recollections of a Physicist* (Princeton: Princeton University Press, 1989), p. 292.
10. WEB, 90.
11. Ibid., 88.
12. VHD.
13. Ibid.
14. Ibid.
15. Ibid.
16. Wedding announcement card, IAS archive.
17. VHD.
18. Ibid.
19. Peierls, *Bird of Passage*, p. 226.
20. *Selected*, p 15.
21. *QED*, p. 566.
22. *Selected*, p. 15.
23. *QED*, p. 567.
24. WEB, 92.
25. *QED*, p. 567.
26. *PT*, August 2006.
27. VHD.
28. PFS interview with Steven Weinberg.
29. Kaiser, p. 82.
30. Actually, many years later the quantum notes were assembled into book form and published: FJD, *Advanced Quantum Mechanics*, transcribed by David Derbes (Singapore: World Scientific, 2007).
31. PFS interview with Mosur K. Sundaresan.
32. FJD in *PT*, September 1952.
33. Jacob Bronowski, *The Visionary Eye: Essays in the Arts, Literature, and Science* (Cambridge: MIT Press, 1979), p. 23.
34. FJD in *SA*, April 1953, September 1954, September 1958, September 1964.
35. FJD in *SA*, September 1964.
36. FJD in *Nature*, 22 January 2004.

37. WEB, 99.

38. Mehra, *The Beat of a Different Drum*, p. 578.

39. Letter from J. Robert Oppenheimer to FJD, December 8, 1952, IAS archives, Oppenheimer papers.

40. WEB, 99.

41. *Selected,* p. 19.

42. FJD in *PT,* September 1967.

6. NUCLEAR OPERA

1. George B. Dyson, *Darwin Among the Machines: The Evolution of Global Intelligence* (New York: Perseus, 1997), p. 111.

2. Richard A. Muller, *Physics and Technology for Future Presidents: An Introduction to the Essential Physics Every World Leader Needs to Know* (Princeton: Princeton University Press, 2010), p. 152.

3. FJD in *Science,* 20 August 1976.

4. Ed Regis, *Who Got Einstein's Office? Eccentricity and Genius at the Institute for Advanced Study* (Reading, MA: Addison-Wesley, 1987), p. 139.

5. *Disturbing,* p. 91.

6. Ibid., p. 90.

7. Kai Bird and Martin J. Sherwin, *American Prometheus: The Triumph and Tragedy of J. Robert Oppenheimer* (New York: Knopf, 2005), p. 534.

8. WEB, 97.

9. Bird and Sherwin, *American Prometheus,* p. 548.

10. Regis, *Who Got Einstein's Office?,* p. 150.

11. Ibid., p. 191.

12. Lee Smolin, *The Trouble with Physics: The Rise of String Theory, the Fall of a Science, and What Comes Next* (Boston: Houghton Mifflin, 2007), p. 49.

13. "Remembering Gödel," by Paul Benacerraf, IAS, http://www.ias.edu/people/godel/remembering.

14. The story of von Neumann's computer is told in George B. Dyson, *Turing's Cathedral: The Origins of the Digital Universe* (New York: Pantheon, 2012); additional remarks thereon at a public interview of George Dyson and Freeman Dyson conducted at the 92nd Street Y, New York City, March 15, 2012.

15. *Selected,* p. 21.

16. Ibid., p. 22.

17. FJD profile in *SA,* August 1993.

18. *PT,* June 2002.

19. FJD in *SA,* September 1954.

20. FJD in *SA,* September 1958.

21. VHD.

22. Ibid.

23. Ibid.

24. *Disturbing,* p. 92.

25. Anita Burdman Feferman and Solomon Feferman, *Alfred Tarski: Life and Logic* (Cambridge: Cambridge University Press, 2004), p. 225.

26. VHD.

27. Ibid.

28. Ibid.

29. *QED,* p. 459.

30. Pais, *J. Robert Oppenheimer,* p. 103.

31. VHD.
32. Ibid.
33. PFS interview with Katarina Halm.
34. Ibid.
35. VHD.

7. INTRINSICALLY SAFE

   1. VHD.
   2. Ibid.
   3. Ibid.
   4. *Orion*, p. 67.
   5. John McPhee, *The Curve of Binding Energy* (New York: Farrar, Straus & Giroux, 1973; paperback, 1980), p. 79.
   6. *Disturbing*, p. 96.
   7. WEB, 114.
   8. *Disturbing*, p. 102.
   9. *Nuclear News,* November 2003.
  10. *Disturbing*, p. 42.
  11. Ibid., p. 46.
  12. *Orion*, p. 44.
  13. *Disturbing*, p. 103.
  14. *Infinite*, p. 145.
  15. Ibid., p. 146.
  16. *Imagined*, p. 34.
  17. *Disturbing*, p. 104.
  18. *Orion,* p. 112.
  19. VHD.
  20. IAS archive, office of the director, box 6.
  21. Francis Crick, *What Mad Pursuit: A Personal View of Scientific Discovery* (New York: Basic, 1988), p. xi.
  22. VHD.
  23. Verena Huber-Dyson, in *Kreisliana: About and Around Georg Kreisel*, Piergiorgio Odifreddi, ed. (Wellesley, MA: A. K. Peters, 1996), p. 57. When the editor of this Kreisel celebratory book showed Verena Huber-Dyson's remark to Freeman Dyson, he responded with a short note, which he allowed to be included in the volume, as if it were any other contribution to the collection of Kreisel accolades. The one assertion of Verena's that Freeman chose to rebut, the lone objection he cared to make against his former wife's charges, was the one about the mathematics competition at Cambridge. There was no rivalry, Freeman Dyson claimed. He and Kreisel had different interests and had been mentored by different famous mathematicians. There needn't have been any vendetta on that score.
  24. VHD.
  25. Verena Huber-Dyson in *Kreisliana*, p. 59.
  26. VHD.
  27. Ibid.
  28. PFS interview with IJ.
  29. VHD.
  30. Feferman and Feferman, *Alfred Tarski*, p. 226.
  31. VHD.
  32. *Selected*, p. 24.

8. SPACE TRAVELER'S MANIFESTO

1. *Eros,* p. 3.
2. WEB, 115.
3. *Orion,* p. 35.
4. *Selected,* p. 26.
5. FJD in *Perspectives in Modern Physics: Essays in Honor of Hans A Bethe,* Robert Marshak, ed. (New York: Interscience, 1966), p. 641.
6. VHD.
7. *Starship,* p. 56.
8. McPhee, *The Curve of Binding Energy,* p. 174.
9. *Starship,* p. 62.
10. Ibid., p. 65.
11. FJD letter to J. Robert Oppenheimer, 4 July 1958, IAS archives, office of the director, box 6.
12. *Starship,* p. 221.
13. VHD.
14. Ibid.
15. FJD letter to J. Robert Oppenheimer, 7 September 1958, IAS archives, office of the director, box 6.
16. VHD.
17. Ibid.
18. FJD letter to J. Robert Oppenheimer, 23 October 1958, IAS archives, office of the director, box 6.
19. PFS Interview with IJ.
20. VHD.
21. Ibid.
22. Ibid.
23. FJD letter to Oppenheimer, 23 October 1958, IAS archives, office of the director, box 6.
24. VHD.
25. FJD letter to J. Robert Oppenheimer, 7 November 1958, Library of Congress, Oppenheimer papers.
26. Ibid.
27. VHD.
28. Feferman and Feferman, *Alfred Tarski,* p. 228.
29. FJD letter to J. Robert Oppenheimer, 16 November 1958, Library of Congress, Oppenheimer papers.
30. *Disturbing,* p. 112.
31. *Orion,* p. 87.
32. *Disturbing,* p. 111.
33. *Orion,* p. 105.
34. Ibid., p. 230.
35. *Disturbing,* p. 115.
36. Ibid., p. 128.
37. Ibid., p. 114.
38. Ibid., p. 128.

9. CIVILIZED BEHAVIOR

1. Olaf Stapledon, *Last and First Men and Star Maker: 2 Science Fiction Novels* (New York: Dover, paperback 1968; *Last and First Men,* originally published, 1931, *Star Maker* originally published 1937), p. 118.

2. Leslie Fiedler, *Olaf Stapledon: A Man Divided* (Oxford: Oxford University Press, 1983), p. viii.

3. Patrick A. McCarthy, *Olaf Stapledon* (Boston: Twayne, 1982), p. 141.

4. *Nature*, 19 September 1959.

5. WEB, 137.

6. *Science*, 3 June 1960.

7. Marshak, ed., *Perspectives in Modern Physics*, p. 50.

8. Stapledon, *Last and First Men and Star Maker*, p. 365.

9. *Disturbing*, p. 213.

10. FJD letter to J. Robert Oppenheimer, 9 May 1960, Library of Congress, Oppenheimer papers.

11. *Disturbing*, p. 209.

12. Kenneth Clark, *Civilisation* (New York: Harper & Row, 1969), p. 1.

13. Ibid., p. 4.

14. *Disturbing*, p. 212.

15. Ibid., p. 210.

16. Marshak, ed., *Perspectives in Modern Physics*, p. 652.

17. *Star Trek: The Next Generation*, season 6, episode 4, aired 12 October 1992.

18. *Selected*, p. 27.

19. *Project Cyclops: A Design Study for Detecting Extraterrestrial Intelligent Life*, Stanford/NASA/Ames Research Center summer faculty fellowship program in engineering design, 1971, Bernard M. Oliver and John Billingham, codirectors, p. 178.

20. *Disturbing*, p. 192.

21. Carl Sagan, *Astrophysical Journal*, vol. 144, p. 1216 (1966).

22. *W&H*, p. 66.

23. *Orion*, p. 221.

24. *Science*, 9 July 1965.

25. Ibid.

26. McPhee, *The Curve of Binding Energy*, p. 173.

27. *Disturbing*, p. 188.

28. Ibid., p. 189.

10. NUCLEAR MANIFESTO

1. Glenn T. Seaborg, *Kennedy, Khrushchev, and the Test Ban* (Berkeley: University of California Press, 1981), p. 151.

2. *W&H*, p. 184.

3. *Disturbing*, p. 197.

4. Ibid., p. 135.

5. Ibid., p. 132.

6. Herman Kahn, *On Thermonuclear War: Three Lectures and Several Suggestions* (Princeton: Princeton University Press, 1960), p. 20.

7. Ibid., p. 597.

8. Ibid., p. 145.

9. FJD in *PT*, November 1962; reprinted in *Eros*, p. 203.

10. *W&H*, p. 34.

11. Seaborg, *Kennedy, Khrushchev, and the Test Ban*, p. 175.

12. *Disturbing*, p. 6.

13. Ibid., p. 131.

14. FJD in *Bulletin of the Atomic Scientists*, September 1961.

15. Ibid., March 1962.

16. *Science*, 23 March 1962.
17. Seaborg, *Kennedy, Khrushchev, and the Test Ban*, p. 205.
18. *Disturbing*, p. 139.
19. Seaborg, *Kennedy, Khrushchev, and the Test Ban*, p. 197.
20. *Disturbing*, p. 141.
21. *New York Times*, 10 August 1963.
22. *Bulletin of the Atomic Scientists*, September 1963.

11. ON THE OREGON TRAIL
 1. Dyson and the others present on that occasion have over the years provided accounts of the event without naming the general: in Ann Finkbeiner's *The Jasons: The Secret History of Science's Postwar Elite* (New York: Viking, 2006), p. 94; in AIP oral history of FJD; in Dyson's book *Disturbing the Universe*, p. 149; and in the report by the Nautilus Institute, www.nautilus.org/archives/VietnamFOIA/press .html. Dyson specifically refers to the general as Maxwell Taylor in WEB, 128.
 2. Finkbeiner, *The Jasons*, p. xii.
 3. AIP.
 4. *Disturbing*, p. 50.
 5. Report obtained by the Nautilus Institute through the Freedom of Information Act, 4 December 2002; see also *Bulletin of the Atomic Scientists*, May/June 2003.
 6. Finkbeiner, *The Jasons*, p. 92.
 7. Ibid., p. 103.
 8. PFS interview with Steven Weinberg.
 9. FJD in *PT,* April 1973.
10. *Disturbing*, p. 155.
11. Horace W. Babcock, *Science*, 20 July 1990.
12. PFS interview with Richard Muller.
13. FJD in *Journal of the Optical Society of America*, May 1975.
14. WEB, 127.
15. Finkbeiner, *The Jasons*, p 158.
16. *Selected*, p. 42.
17. Intergovernmental Panel on Climate Change, Fourth Assessment Report: Climate Change 2007.
18. *Eros*, 239.
19. Ibid., p. 136.
20. FJD in *Energy*, vol. 2, p. 287 (1977).
21. *Selected*, p. 44.
22. PFS interview with Henry Abarbanel.

12. SUCCESS IN LIFE
 1. FJD in *Science*, 29 October 1965; reprinted in *Eros*, p. 113.
 2. Chen Ning Yang, *Select Papers, 1945–1980* (San Francisco: W. H. Freeman, 1983), p. 65.
 3. PFS interview with Frank Wilczek.
 4. Murray Gell-Mann interview on "Web of Stories," http://www.webofstories.com /people/murray.gell-mann;jsessionid=730D114463047B5AE1D0EBEFF9E2F9C9.
 5. *Eros*, p. 339.
 6. PFS interview with Mia Dyson.
 7. VHD.
 8. PFS interview with George Dyson.

9. PFS interview with IJ.
10. PFS interview with George Dyson.
11. PFS interview with Rebecca Dyson.
12. PFS interview with IJ.
13. PFS interview with Mia Dyson.
14. VHD.
15. WEB, 31.
16. PFS interview with Esther Dyson.
17. Pais, *J. Robert Oppenheimer,* p. 296.
18. *Rebel,* p. 241.
19. PFS interview with Steven Weinberg.
20. John Aristotle Phillips and David Michaelis, *Mushroom: The Story of the A-Bomb Kid* (New York: Morrow, 1978), p. 87.
21. *Disturbing,* p. 164.
22. Ibid.
23. *Selected,* p. 30.
24. Ibid., p. 28.
25. WEB, 104; *Selected,* p. 31.
26. *Selected,* p. 38.
27. PFS interview with Andrew Leonard.
28. *Selected,* p. 32.
29. Ibid., p. 35.
30. Ibid., p. 34.
31. *Eros,* p. 118.
32. Ibid., p. 129.
33. WEB, 134.
34. *Selected,* p. 38.
35. Ibid.
36. PFS interview with FJD.

13. Science and Sublime

1. *Disturbing,* p. 240.
2. *Starship,* p. 247.
3. Ibid., p. 248.
4. Ibid., p. 255.
5. *Disturbing,* p. 243.
6. Ibid., p. vii.
7. *Selected,* p. 43.
8. *Eros,* p. vii.
9. *Disturbing,* p. 5
10. *New Republic,* 18 August 1979.
11. *Science,* 9 November 1979.
12. Steven Weinberg, *The First Three Minutes: A Modern View of the Origin of the Universe* (New York: Basic, 1977), p. 154.
13. *Disturbing,* p. 251.
14. Ibid., p. 250.
15. Ibid., p. 258.
16. George B. Dyson, *Baidarka* (Edmonds, WA: Northwest Publishing Company, 1986).
17. *Disturbing,* p. 257.
18. Ibid., p. 258.

19. Ibid., p. 261.
20. WEB, 152.
21. PFS interview with Rebecca Dyson.
22. PFS interview with Richard Askey.
23. *Infinite*, p. 35.
24. Ibid.
25. *Eros*, p. 173.
26. Ibid., p. 335.
27. Ibid., p. 299.
28. *Infinite*, p. 243.
29. FJD, Foreword to *The Ultimate Quotable Einstein*, Alice Calaparice, ed. (Princeton: Princeton University Press, 2011), p. xv.
30. *Infinite*, p. 230.
31. Ibid., p. 3.
32. Ibid., p. 125.
33. Ibid., p. 180.
34. FJD in *NYT*, 5 April 1987.
35. FJD in *PT*, February 1988.
36. *Eros*, p. 278
37. Ibid., p. 320.
38. FJD in *NYRB*, 17 August 1989.
39. *Selected*, p. 48.
40. *Eros*, p. 8.
41. Ibid., p. 309.
42. Ibid., p. 188.

14. NUCLEAR SLAVERY
1. *Eros*, p. 338.
2. *W&H*, title page.
3. Frank von Hippel, *Physics Today*, November 1984; charts showing buildup of stockpiles at *NYT*, 8 April 2010.
4. *W&H*, p. 201.
5. *W&H*, p. 223.
6. Ibid., p. 224.
7. Ibid., p. 227.
8. Ibid., p. 230.
9. Ibid., p. 231.
10. Ibid., p. 245.
11. Ibid., p. 181.
12. Ibid., p. 187.
13. Ibid., p. 300.
14. Garry Wills, *Bomb Power: The Modern Presidency and the National Security State* (New York: Penguin, 2010), p. 47.
15. *W&H*, p. 273.
16. Ibid., p. 275.
17. Ibid., p. 290.
18. Ibid., p. 297.
19. Ralph Waldo Emerson, *Selections from Ralph Waldo Emerson: An Organic Anthology*, Stephen E. Whicher, ed. (Boston: Houghton Mifflin, 1960), p. 355.
20. *W&H*, p. viii.

21. *PT,* November 1984.
22. *W&H,* p. 41.
23. FJD, Edward Teller obituary, National Academy of Sciences, 2007.
24. *Eros,* p. 76.
25. Ibid., p. 74.
26. *Rebel,* p. 127.
27. *Eros,* p. 72.
28. *W&H,* p. 308.
29. *Eros,* p. 81.
30. Ibid., p. 83.
31. *Infinite,* p. 249.
32. David E. Hoffman, *The Dead Hand: The Untold Story of the Cold War Arms Race and Its Deadly Legacy* (New York: Doubleday, 2009), p. 23.
33. PFS interview with Harold Feiveson; estimates of possible fatalities under SIOP discussed by David Alan Rosenberg in *Race for the Superbomb,* aired January 1999 by the PBS program *The American Experience,* http://www.pbs.org/wgbh/amex/bomb/filmmore/reference/interview/rosenberg02.html.
34. Hoffman, *The Dead Hand,* p. 16.
35. *Infinite,* p. 250.
36. *Eros,* p. 87.
37. *Rebel,* p. 129.
38. *Infinite,* p. 243.
39. *PT,* November 1994.
40. PFS interview with Charles Ferguson.
41. PFS interview with Robert Moore.
42. *Eros,* p. 87.

15. THE ARC OF LIFE

1. *Glass,* p. 58.
2. *Origins,* p. 38.
3. Ibid., p. 65.
4. *Infinite,* p. 96.
5. *Selected,* p. 46.
6. PFS interview with Carl Woese.
7. *Origins,* p. 89.
8. *Infinite,* p. xi.
9. *Starship,* p. 158.
10. *Sun,* p. 81.
11. *Eros,* p. 64.
12. *Infinite,* p. 196.
13. FJD in *Science,* 1 October 1999.
14. *Glass,* p. 117; *Infinite,* p. 165.
15. *Glass,* p. 117.
16. Ibid., p. 106.
17. *Rebel,* p. 296.
18. Ibid., p. 298.
19. *Glass,* p. 173.
20. *Sun,* p. 102.
21. Ibid., p. 103.
22. *Infinite,* p. 118.

23. Ibid., p. 99.

24. FJD in *Review of Modern Physics*, 3 July 1979, p. 453.

25. Ibid., p. 454.

26. *Infinite*, p. 99.

27. *Selected*, p. 45.

28. FJD in *Review of Modern Physics*, p. 454.

29. Ibid., p. 455.

30. Ibid., p. 456.

31. Lawrence M. Krauss and Glenn D. Starkman, *SA*, November 1999.

32. *NYT*, 1 January 2002.

33. Lawrence M. Krauss, *Atom: An Odyssey from the Big Bang to Life on Earth . . . and Beyond* (Boston: Little, Brown, 2001), p. 279.

34. *Glass*, p. 93.

35. *Infinite*, p. 9.

16. GOD AND MAN AT PRINCETON

1. Printed program and audiotapes of "Around the Dyson Sphere," IAS archives.

2. PFS interview with Frank Wilczek.

3. PFS interview with IJ.

4. PFS interviews with Esther Dyson and IJ.

5. PFS interview with Rebecca Dyson.

6. *Infinite*, p. xi.

7. Ibid., p. xii.

8. Ibid., p. 294.

9. Richard Dawkins, *The God Delusion* (Boston: Houghton Mifflin, 2006), p. 100.

10. *Infinite*, p. 255.

11. Ibid., p. 295.

12. *Disturbing*, p. 249.

13. PFS interview with Lawrence Krauss.

14. *Disturbing*, p. 246.

15. *Infinite*, p. 100.

16. Ibid., p. 116.

17. Ibid., p. 117.

18. Carl Sagan, *The Varieties of Scientific Experience: A Personal View of the Search for God*, Ann Druyan, ed. (New York: Penguin, 2006), p. 30.

19. *Infinite*, p. 296.

20. *Glass*, p. 132.

21. Henry James, *The Varieties of Religious Experience* (New York: Penguin, 1982; originally published, 1902), p. 53.

22. Sagan, *The Varieties of Scientific Experience*, p. 218.

23. Daniel Dennett, *Breaking the Spell: Religion as a Natural Phenomenon* (New York: Viking, 2006), p. 249.

24. *Rebel*, p. 350.

25. Ralph Waldo Emerson, *Selections from Ralph Waldo Emerson*, Stephen E. Whicher, ed. (Boston: Houghton Mifflin, paperback edition, Riverside, 1960), p. 193.

26. FJD in Cornwell, ed., *Nature's Imagination*, p. 8.

27. Peter Atkins in ibid., p. 123.

28. FJD in ibid., p. 10.

29. Peter Atkins in ibid., p. 125.

30. *Rebel*, p. 330.

31. *Glass,* p. 134.
32. *Imagined,* p. 9.
33. *Glass,* p. 139.
34. *Rebel,* p. 336.
35. *Infinite,* p. 119.
36. Ibid.
37. Steven Weinberg, *Lake Views: This World and the Universe* (Cambridge: Harvard University Press, 2009), p. 21.
38. Jacob Bronowski, *Science and Human Values* (New York: Harper & Row, 1956), pp. 52–64.
39. *Sun,* p. 74.
40. FJD *Ad Portas* speech as recorded in "The Wykehamist," Winchester College, June 1995.
41. FJD acceptance speech for Templeton Prize, May 2000, http://www.templetonprize .org.
42. *Physics World* magazine, June 2000.
43. Dawkins part of discussion about the Templeton Prize, discussion forum at the Edge Foundation, 13 April 2006, http://www.edge.org/discourse/templeton_index .html.
44. Dawkins, *The God Delusion,* p. 18.
45. *Infinite,* p. 118.
46. Emerson, *Selections,* p. 20.

17. SPLINTERING THE SPECIES

1. WEB, 22.
2. PFS interview with Lawrence Krauss.
3. Dennett, *Breaking the Spell,* p. 262.
4. FJD in *NYRB,* 24 March 2004, reprinted in *Rebel,* p. 330.
5. *Rebel,* p. 331.
6. Ibid.
7. FJD in *This Will Change Everything: Ideas That Will Shape the Future,* John Brockman, ed. (New York: Harper Perennial, 2010), p. 146.
8. *Rebel,* p. 332.
9. FJD Foreword to Elizabeth Lloyd Mayer, *Extraordinary Knowing: Science, Skepticism, and the Inexplicable Powers of the Human Mind* (New York: Bantam, 2007).
10. FJD in *NYRB,* 25 September 2008.
11. FJD interviewed by *Environment 360,* Yale University, 4 June 2009.
12. FJD in *NYRB,* 10 November 2011.
13. *Selected,* p. 44; *Eros,* p. 135.
14. FJD in *Energy,* vol. 2, p. 287 (1977).
15. *Eros,* p. 238.
16. *Rebel,* p. 59.
17. Ibid., p. 65.
18. Arnold Bloom et al., *Science,* 14 May 2010.
19. *Rebel,* p. 65.
20. *Glass,* p. 8.
21. *Rebel,* p. 182.
22. FJD in *NYRB,* 19 July 2007; *Glass,* p. 9.
23. FJD in *NYRB,* 19 July 2007.
24. *Disturbing,* p. 179; *Glass,* p. 27.

25. WEB, 133.
26. *Disturbing*, p. 169.
27. Ibid., p. 170.
28. *Glass*, p. 29.
29. Ibid., p. 32.
30. FJD in *NYRB*, 19 July 2007.
31. Lee Silver, *Challenging Nature: The Clash of Science and Spirituality at the New Frontiers of Life* (New York: HarperCollins, 2006), p. 225.
32. Ibid., p. 267.
33. PFS interview with Lee Silver.
34. PFS interview with Laurence Potts.
35. PFS interview with Roy Schwitters.
36. *Sun,* p. 108.
37. Ibid., p. 111.
38. FJD interviewed by Salon.com, 27 September 2007.
39. PFS interview with Lee Silver.
40. FJD at "Life: What a Concept," transcript of a discussion organized by Edge Foundation, August 2007, www.edge.org
41. *Sun*, p. 112; *Infinite*, p. 287.
42. *Sun*, p. 113.
43. *Imagined*, p. 99.
44. *Rebel*, p. 288.
45. *Eros*, p. 342.
46. *Disturbing*, p. 192.
47. FJD interview in *Wired*, February 1998.
48. *Disturbing*, p. 233.
49. *Infinite*, p. 128.
50. *Sun*, p. 47.
51. Ibid., p. 99.
52. *Infinite*, p. 134.
53. *Glass*, p. 125.

18. Long-Term Thinking

1. Reiner Stach, *Kafka: The Decisive Years,* translated by Shelley Frisch (New York: Harcourt, 2005; originally published, 2002), p. 3.
2. Flickr, http://www.flickr.com/photos/edyson/2204173674/sizes/o/.
3. *Disturbing*, p. 192.
4. Ibid., p. 193.
5. Cornwell, *Nature's Imagination*, p. 2.
6. Seminar at Long Now Foundation, 5 October 2005; video on YouTube.
7. PFS interviews with IJ and Esther Dyson.
8. *Infinite*, p. 45.
9. *The Making of Kubrick's 2001*, Jerome Agel, ed. (New York: Signet, 1970), p. 142.
10. PFS interview with Cees Dekker.
11. *NYT,* 30 May 2010.
12. FJD quoted in news summary of Craig Venter's chemically synthesized genome, Edge Foundation website, 20 May 2010.
13. FJD in *Is Science Nearing Its Limits?*, George Steiner, ed. (Manchester, UK: Carcanet, 2008), p. 155.
14. FJD in *NYRB*, 10 March 2011.

15. PFS interview with IJ.
16. FJD in *NYRB,* 23 October 2008.
17. PFS interview with Esther Dyson.
18. PFS interview with IJ.
19. PFS interview with Esther Dyson.
20. FJD, John S. Lewis, and Lee Valentine, Open Letter to Congress, 10 September 2010, Space Studies Institute.
21. FJD remarks at Arthur C. Clarke Foundation awards banquet, 5 April 2011.
22. PFS interview with Roy Schwitters.
23. FJD biographical sketch of John Wheeler, Proceedings of the American Philosophical Society, 1 March 2010.
24. FJD in *NYRB,* 13 August 2009.
25. Ibid., 10 March 2011.
26. Ibid., 10 November 2011.
27. Ibid., 22 December 2011.
28. Ibid., 10 June 2010.
29. PFS interview with Rebecca Dyson.
30. *Eros,* p. 339.
31. FJD in *Living Philosophies,* Clifton Fadiman, ed. (New York: Doubleday, 1990).
32. Essay by FJD from *Living Philosophies*, reprinted in *Eros,* p. 341.
33. *Disturbing,* p. 252.
34. *Origins,* p. 67.
35. FJD interviewed by Marty Nemko, 15 May 2011, www.spokenword.org/program /1512702.
36. *Infinite,* p. 289.

INDEX